Communications
in Computer and Information Science   2014

Rationale

The CCIS series is devoted to the publication of proceedings of computer science conferences. Its aim is to efficiently disseminate original research results in informatics in printed and electronic form. While the focus is on publication of peer-reviewed full papers presenting mature work, inclusion of reviewed short papers reporting on work in progress is welcome, too. Besides globally relevant meetings with internationally representative program committees guaranteeing a strict peer-reviewing and paper selection process, conferences run by societies or of high regional or national relevance are also considered for publication.

Topics

The topical scope of CCIS spans the entire spectrum of informatics ranging from foundational topics in the theory of computing to information and communications science and technology and a broad variety of interdisciplinary application fields.

Information for Volume Editors and Authors

Publication in CCIS is free of charge. No royalties are paid, however, we offer registered conference participants temporary free access to the online version of the conference proceedings on SpringerLink (http://link.springer.com) by means of an http referrer from the conference website and/or a number of complimentary printed copies, as specified in the official acceptance email of the event.

CCIS proceedings can be published in time for distribution at conferences or as post-proceedings, and delivered in the form of printed books and/or electronically as USBs and/or e-content licenses for accessing proceedings at SpringerLink. Furthermore, CCIS proceedings are included in the CCIS electronic book series hosted in the SpringerLink digital library at http://link.springer.com/bookseries/7899. Conferences publishing in CCIS are allowed to use Online Conference Service (OCS) for managing the whole proceedings lifecycle (from submission and reviewing to preparing for publication) free of charge.

Publication process

The language of publication is exclusively English. Authors publishing in CCIS have to sign the Springer CCIS copyright transfer form, however, they are free to use their material published in CCIS for substantially changed, more elaborate subsequent publications elsewhere. For the preparation of the camera-ready papers/files, authors have to strictly adhere to the Springer CCIS Authors' Instructions and are strongly encouraged to use the CCIS LaTeX style files or templates.

Abstracting/Indexing

CCIS is abstracted/indexed in DBLP, Google Scholar, EI-Compendex, Mathematical Reviews, SCImago, Scopus. CCIS volumes are also submitted for the inclusion in ISI Proceedings.

How to start

To start the evaluation of your proposal for inclusion in the CCIS series, please send an e-mail to ccis@springer.com.

De-Shuang Huang · Prashan Premaratne ·
Changan Yuan

Editors

Applied Intelligence

First International Conference, ICAI 2023
Nanning, China, December 8–12, 2023
Proceedings, Part I

 Springer

Editors
De-Shuang Huang
Eastern Institute of Technology
Zhejiang, China

Prashan Premaratne
University of Wollongong
North Wollongong, NSW, Australia

Changan Yuan
Guangxi Academy of Sciences
Guangxi, China

ISSN 1865-0929   ISSN 1865-0937 (electronic)
Communications in Computer and Information Science
ISBN 978-981-97-0902-1   ISBN 978-981-97-0903-8 (eBook)
https://doi.org/10.1007/978-981-97-0903-8

This Springer imprint is published by the registered company Springer Nature Singapore Pte Ltd.
The registered company address is: 152 Beach Road, #21-01/04 Gateway East, Singapore 189721, Singapore

Paper in this product is recyclable.

Preface

The first International Conference on Applied Intelligence (ICAI 2023) was held during December 8–12, 2023, in Nanning, Guangxi, China. The conference was started to provide an annual forum dedicated to emerging and challenging topics in artificial intelligence, machine learning, pattern recognition, bioinformatics, and computational biology. It aimed to bring together researchers and practitioners from both academia and industry to share ideas, problems, and solutions related to the multifaceted aspects of Applied Intelligence.

This year, the conference concentrated mainly on the theories and methodologies as well as the emerging applications of Applied Intelligence. Its aim was to unify the picture of contemporary Applied Intelligence techniques as an integral concept that highlights the trends in advanced computational intelligence and bridges theoretical research with applications. Therefore, the theme for this conference was "Advanced Applied Intelligence Technology and Applications". Papers that focused on this theme were solicited, addressing theories, methodologies, and applications in science and technology.

ICAI 2023 received 228 submissions from 10 countries and regions. All papers went through a rigorous peer-review procedure and each paper received at least three review reports. Based on the review reports, the Program Committee finally selected 64 high-quality papers for presentation at ICAI 2023, and inclusion in the proceedings published by Springer: two volumes of Communications in Computer and Information Science (CCIS).

The organizers of ICAI 2023, including Eastern Institute of Technology and Guangxi Academy of Sciences, China, made an enormous effort to ensure the success of the conference. We hereby would like to thank the members of the Program Committee and the referees for their collective effort in reviewing the papers. In particular, we would like to thank all the authors for contributing their papers. Without the high-quality submissions from the authors, the success of the conference would not have been possible. Finally, we are especially grateful to the International Neural Network Society and the National Science Foundation of China for their sponsorship.

December 2023

Changan Yuan
De-Shuang Huang
Prashan Premaratne

Organization

General Chair

Changan Yuan   Guangxi Academy of Sciences, China

Steering Committee Chair

De-Shuang Huang   Eastern Institute of Technology, China

Program Committee Co-chairs

De-Shuang Huang   Eastern Institute of Technology, China
Kang-Hyun Jo   University of Ulsan, South Korea
Prashan Premaratne   University of Wollongong, Australia
Abir Hussain   Liverpool John Moores University, UK

Organizing Committee Co-chairs

Yingzhou Bi   Nanning Normal University, China
Jianbo Lu   Nanning Normal University, China

Organizing Committee Members

Xu Guilin   Nanning Normal University, China
Yuzhong Peng   Nanning Normal University, China
Xiao Qin   Nanning Normal University, China
Chao Wang   Guangxi Academy of Sciences, China
Wanxian He   Guangxi Academy of Sciences, China

Award Committee Chair

Michal Choras   Bydgoszcz University of Science and Technology,
                                       Poland

Tutorial Co-chairs

Jair Cervantes Canales   Autonomous University of Mexico State, Mexico
Yu-Dong Zhang   University of Leicester, UK

Special Issue Chair

Chandratilak De Silva Liyanage   University Brunei Darussalam, Brunei

Publication Chair

Damith Mohotti   University of New South Wales, Australia

Special Session Chair

Arturo Yee Rendon   Autonomous University of Sinaloa, Mexico

Workshop Chair

Josué Espejel Cabrera   Autonomous University of Mexico State, Mexico

International Liaison Chair

Prashan Premaratne   University of Wollongong, Australia

Publicity Co-chairs

Chun-Hou Zheng   Anhui University, China
Jair Cervantes Canales   Autonomous University of Mexico State, Mexico

Program Committee Members

Jing Chen	Suzhou University of Science and Technology, China
Chenxi Huang	Xiamen University, China
Wenzheng Bao	Xuzhou University of Technology, China
Lin Yuan	Qilu University of Technology (Shandong Academy of Sciences), China
Vasu Alagar	Concordia University, Canada
Prashan Premaratne	University of Wollongong, Australia
Chin-Chih Chang	Chung Hua University, Taiwan
Michal Choras	Bydgoszcz University of Science and Technology, Poland
Haijun Gong	Saint Louis University, USA
Daowen Qiu	Sun Yat-sen University, China
Rui Li	Montclair State University, USA
Boudhayan Bhattacharya	Brainware University, India
Jing Hu	Wuhan University of Science and Technology, China
Bo Li	Wuhan University of Science and Technology, China
Weitian Wang	Montclair State University, USA
Dingjiang Huang	East China Normal University, China
Laurent Heutte	Université de Rouen Normandie, France
Chengcai Fu	Shandong Jiaotong University, China
Fengying Ma	Qilu University of Technology, China
Wei Chen	China University of Mining and Technology, China
Song Deng	Nanjing University of Posts and Telecommunications, China
Yiran Huang	Guangxi University, China
Wei Lan	Guangxi University, China
Yuzhong Peng	Nanning Normal University, China
Qing Tian	Nanjing University of Information Sciences and Technology, China

Reviewers

Alaa Alsaig
Ammar Alsaig
Bo Li
Chin-Chih Chang
Chonglin Gu
Chunyan Liu
Dandan Zhu
Faquan Chen
Federica Uccello
Fuchun Liu
Gong Daoqing
Guokai Zhang
Hongguo Cai
Hongxuan Hua
Huan Ning
Hung-Chi Su
Jing Hu
Jingkai Yang
Jixin Sun
Jordan Murphy
Jun Li
Kaushik Chanda
Lei Wang
Liangyu Zhou
Ligang Xiao
Lihua Jiang
Lin Li
Lingyun Yu
Marek Pawlicki
Michael Yang
Minda Yao
Minglong Cheng
Nuo Yu
Odbal H.

Prashan Premaratne
Qing Ye
Qinhu Zhang
Rafal Kozik
Rongcan Chen
Rui Li
Ruizhi Fan
Shengzu Huang
Shijia Liao
Shuting Jin
Subhadip Nandi
Tong Si
Wang Zhi
Wei Lan
Wei Deng
Wrong Chang
Xiaoli Lin
Xiaoming Liu
Yang Liu
Yao-Hong Tsai
Yaqi Chen
Yi Zhao
Ying Sheng
Yongyong Chen
Yunzhe Qian
Yuquan Tong
Zhang Liang
Zhen Shen
Zhihong Zhang
Zhujun Zhang
Ziheng Duan
Zishan Xu
Ziyuan Dong
Zhongpeng Cai

Contents – Part I

Computer Vision

Deep Learning

Contents – Part II

Machine Learning

Natural Language Processing and Computational Linguistics

Biomedical Data Modeling and Mining

Investigation and Analysis of Corneal Morphology in Young Divers

Chenyang Mao[1], Xin Wang[2], Heng Li[1(✉)], Haojin Li[1], Dan Zhou[3], Jianwen Chen[4], Honglun Dong[2], Yan Hu[1], and Jiang Liu[1,3(✉)]

[1] Research Institute of Trustworthy Autonomous Systems and Department of Computer Science and Engineering, Southern University of Science and Technology, Shenzhen 518055, China
{lih3,liuj}@sustech.edu.cn
[2] Sport Center, Southern University of Science and Technology, Shenzhen 518055, China
[3] School of Ophthalmology and Optometry, Wenzhou Medical University, Wenzhou 325027, China
[4] Department of Orthopedics Medicine, Southern University of Science and Technology Hospital, Shenzhen, Guangdong, China

Abstract. To investigate the corneal morphology of adolescent diving athletes and analyze the related influencing factors. Corneal topographic maps were taken of 42 young athletes (19 males and 23 females, aged 9–17 years) from the diving team of Shenzhen Sports School, and then three morphological data of corneal curvature, astigmatism, and thickness were measured based on the topographic maps. A study was conducted to analyze the influence of diving on corneal morphology by comparing with the reference data of children of the same age in the literature, and statistically analyzing the relationship between different genders, ages, exercise levels, training time, and corneal morphology. The radius of the corneal curvature of athletes was significantly smaller than that of children of the same age (P < 0.01). There were statistical differences in the corneal curvatures of athletes in different age groups and training time groups (P < 0.05), and there were also differences in corneal thickness in different training time groups (P < 0.05). There were no statistically significant differences in corneal morphology among gender and exercise level groups. Diving can affect the corneal morphology of adolescent athletes, and the radius of corneal curvature is significantly lower than that of children of the same age. Corneal curvature is related to athletes' age and training time, and corneal thickness is affected by training time. Attention should be paid to the changes in the corneal morphology of diving athletes.

Keywords: Diving · Young athletes · Corneal topography · Corneal morphology

1 Introduction

China has demonstrated significant prowess in the sport of diving, having attained remarkable success in international competitions. With the development of China's diving industry, a comprehensive system for nurturing and cultivating diving talents has

---

C. Mao and X. Wang—These authors contributed equally to this work.

D.-S. Huang et al. (Eds.): ICAI 2023, CCIS 2014, pp. 3–12, 2024.
https://doi.org/10.1007/978-981-97-0903-8_1

been established, achieving outstanding results on skills training and health security of divers [1, 2]. Given the prolonged exposure to diving activities, divers experience repeated compression and shaking of the eyeballs, which will cause visual impairments [3, 4]. Therefore, eye health is an important factor to preserve the technical proficiency and overall quality of life of divers, and has been a wide concern [5].

However, as retinopathy is the main cause of visual impairments of divers, the eye examination and related research of athletes at present mainly focus on the retina, vitreous, and other posterior ocular tissues [6, 7]. While some studies have identified a considerable number of athletes with eye injuries experiencing eyeball protrusion [8], this issue has not received much attention, and there is a lack of investigation and research regarding the cornea and other anterior segment tissues of divers. In recent years, with the increasing emphasis placed by the government on the ocular health of children and adolescents [9–11], the health of anterior segment tissues such as the cornea has become an urgent research field to protect and improve the eyesight of young divers.

Through the collection of corneal topographies from a sample of 42 young athletes belonging to the diving team of Shenzhen Sports School, we investigated the corneal morphology related to diving. Our findings revealed a significant decrease in the corneal curvature radius among athletes compared to children of the same age, thereby increasing the risk of diseases such as refractive error and keratoconus. Notably, corneal curvature was found to be influenced by both the athletes' age and their time of training, with the latter also impacting corneal thickness. These corneal abnormalities have a potential impact on the training routines and daily lives of athletes and increase the risk of other eye injuries, which should be paid attention to and monitored.

Table 1. Number of Diving Athletes at Each Sport Level and Training Events.

Sport level	Male	Female	Training Events
Group A	5	3	1-m springboard, 3-m springboard, 10-m platform, 3-m synchronized springboard, 10-m synchronized platform
Group B	8	10	1-m springboard, 3-m springboard, 10-m platform, 3-m synchronized springboard, 10-m synchronized platform, Team event, Individual all-around, Mixed synchronized platform, Mixed synchronized 3-m springboard
Group C	6	10	1-m springboard, 3-m springboard, 10-m platform, 3-m synchronized springboard, Team event, Individual all-around

2   Methods

2.1   Study Participants

The diving team of Shenzhen Sports School consists of 46 young athletes. After excluding those who have not participated in diving training within the past 3 months, there are 42 remaining individuals, including 19 males and 23 females, aged between 9 and

17 years, with an average age of 12.6 years. The athletes' sport levels were categorized into Group A, Group B, and Group C, with corresponding training events outlined in Table 1. The training time varied from 2 to 12 years, with an average time of 5.1 years.

As shown in Tables 2 and 3, considering the number of individuals in each age group and training time, the athletes were divided into three groups based on age: 9–11 years, 12–14 years, and 15–17 years. According to the training time, they were divided into 4 groups: 2–3 years, 4–5 years, 6–7 years, and more than 8 years.

Table 2. Number of Diving Athletes According To Age (Years).

Gender	9y	10y	11y	12y	13y	14y	15y	16y	17y
Male	1	1	4	4	3	1	1	3	1
Female	1	2	6	3	6	2	0	3	0

Table 3. Number of Diving Athletes According To Training Time (Years).

Gender	2y	3y	4y	5y	6y	7y	8y	9y	10y	11y	12y
Male	1	5	3	2	2	2	1	1	1	0	1
Female	0	8	5	3	4	0	0	2	1	0	0

2.2 Experimental Design

The TOMEY TMS-5 was used to collect corneal topographies of both eyes of the athletes. Average keratometry (AvgK) was measured as a corneal curvature index, cylinder (CYL) was measured as a corneal astigmatism index, and corneal apex thickness (ApeX) was measured as a corneal thickness index. In addition, to facilitate the comparison with the corneal curvature data of school-age children collected by the Public Health Ophthalmology Branch of the Chinese Preventive Medicine Association [9], the curved refractive index formula was used to further convert the average corneal refractive power d into corneal curvature radius r as the corneal curvature index for comparison:

$$r = \frac{n - n'}{d} \tag{1}$$

In this equation, where n denotes the corneal refractive index, usually taking the value of 1.3375, and n' denotes the refractive index of air, taking the value of 1, then r = 0.3375/d.

2.3 Statistical Analysis

One-way analysis of variance was used to compare the differences in basic information between groups, and the results were expressed as the mean $\pm$ standard deviation ($\bar{x} \pm SD$). A hypothesis test was used to compare the experimental data between the two groups, $P < 0.05$ indicates the statistical significance of the difference.

3 Results

3.1 Comparison of Corneal Morphology Between Divers and Age-Matched Children

The Public Health Ophthalmology Branch of the Chinese Preventive Medicine Association conducted a statistical analysis of corneal curvature among Chinese school-age children aged 6–15 years and provided detailed data [9]. We compared the corneal curvature data of divers with those of age-matched children. As shown in Fig. 1, the curve plots the individual percentile data of corneal curvature from 9–15 years of age for ordinary school-age children of the same age as divers and marks the distribution of corneal curvature of athletes of the same age.

Compared with ordinary school-age children, the corneal radius of divers is generally lower. The corneal radius of most divers is smaller than the median (P_{50} curve) of children of the same age, and the overall distribution of the two in 9–15 years old is significantly different ($P < 0.01$). Furthermore, statistical analysis was carried out for each age. Except for 10, 13, and 15 years old, there were statistical differences in corneal radius between athletes of other ages and children of the same age ($P < 0.05$). Therefore, it is believed that diving has some influence on corneal curvature.

According to the survey of Peking University Shenzhen Hospital [12], the average corneal thickness of age-matched children aged 6 to 18 years was 546.58 ± 33.47 μm. The average corneal thickness of athletes collected by us was 549.60 ± 28.34 μm, which was very close to that of athletes. However, due to the large age span of data collection and the lack of more detailed data, it is difficult to judge the effect of diving on corneal thickness.

Because the definition of astigmatism data measured by corneal topography instrument is different from that of the optometric test, the astigmatism data measured in this project and the children's astigmatism data statistically analyzed in the literature are not comparable and will not be discussed.

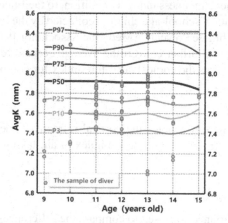

Fig. 1. Comparison of Corneal Curvature between Divers and Same-Age Children, P_{th} Represents the Value at the *th* Percentile.

3.2 Relationship Between Gender and Corneal Morphology

The statistical results of corneal curvature, astigmatism, and thickness of athletes according to gender are shown in Table 4, corresponding to the box plot of Fig. 2.

According to statistical analysis, there is no statistical difference in the distribution of corneal morphology data between male and female athletes ($P > 0.05$), so the changes in corneal morphology of divers are not related to gender.

Table 4. Corneal Morphological Data according to Gender.

Ocular Classification	AvgK (mm)	CYL (D)	ApeX (μm)
Male	7.76 ± 0.22	1.08 ± 0.56	550.68 ± 28.42
Female	7.69 ± 0.31	1.09 ± 0.57	548.70 ± 28.55

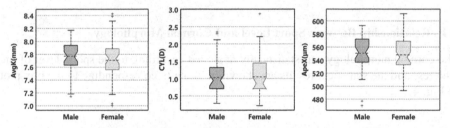

Fig. 2. Box Plot of Corneal Morphology Data according to Gender.

3.3 Relationship Between Age and Corneal Morphology

The athletes were divided into three groups according to the age of 9–11 years, 12–14 years, and 15–17 years, respectively. The statistical results are shown in Table 5, corresponding to the box diagram of Fig. 3.

Table 5. Corneal Morphological Data according to Age.

Ocular Classification	AvgK (mm)	CYL (D)	ApeX (μm)
9–11 years old	7.69 ± 0.26	1.14 ± 0.52	551.37 ± 24.01
12–14 years old	7.70 ± 0.30	1.07 ± 0.65	545.55 ± 32.44
15–17 years old	7.84 ± 0.20	1.01 ± 0.39	555.88 ± 25.39

By comparing the data of each group, the average radius of corneal curvature of athletes in the 15–17 years old group is larger than that of the other two age groups, and there is a statistically significant difference between the athletes in the 9–11 years old

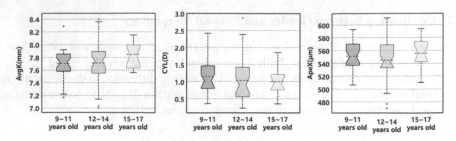

Fig. 3. Box Plot of Corneal Morphology Data according to Age.

group (P = 0.046). However, this phenomenon is not consistent with the data of ordinary children and adolescents. Relevant studies [11–13] show that the corneal curvature of age-matched children and adolescents shows little change with age, and there is no statistically significant difference among different age groups. The reason for this may be related to diving.

3.4 Relationship Between Sport Level and Corneal Morphology

The corneal morphology was statistically analyzed according to the sports level of the athletes, and the statistical results are shown in Table 6, corresponding to the box plot of Fig. 4.

Table 6. Corneal Morphological Data according to Sport Level.

Ocular Classification	AvgK (mm)	CYL (D)	ApeX (μm)
Group A	7.84 ± 0.20	1.01 ± 0.39	555.88 ± 25.39
Group B	7.70 ± 0.30	1.08 ± 0.66	544.76 ± 31.30
Group C	7.69 ± 0.26	1.13 ± 0.50	552.37 ± 25.59

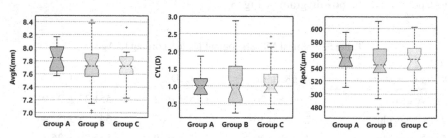

Fig. 4. Box Plot of Corneal Morphology Data according to Sport Level.

There was a great coincidence between the sports level and the age distribution of athletes, 8 athletes in Group A were 15–17 years old, 18 athletes in Group B were 12–14 years old, and 15 athletes in Group C were 9–11 years old except for one person who is 12 years old. However, there was no statistical difference between the data of each movement level (P > 0.05), so it is believed that the corneal morphology of athletes is not directly related to the movement level.

3.5 Relationship Between Training Time and Corneal Morphology

According to the training time of 2–3 years, 4–5 years, 6–7 years, and ≥8 years, the athletes were divided into four groups. The statistical results are shown in Table 7, corresponding to the box chart of Fig. 5.

Table 7. Corneal Morphological Data according to Training Time.

Ocular Classification	AvgK (mm)	CYL (D)	ApeX (μm)
2–3 years	7.66 ± 0.27	1.21 ± 0.63	556.54 ± 35.40
4–5 years	7.81 ± 0.23	1.10 ± 0.54	538.81 ± 22.50
6–7 years	7.60 ± 0.33	1.01 ± 0.64	551.31 ± 17.05
≥8 years	7.83 ± 0.19	0.87 ± 0.23	553.79 ± 29.27

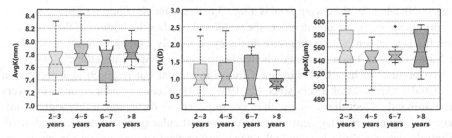

Fig. 5. Box Plot of Corneal Morphology Data according to Training Time.

There were significant differences in corneal curvature between groups with different training time, and the P values between groups are shown in Fig. 6. The corneal radius of athletes in the 2–3 years and 6–7 years groups was smaller than that in the 4–5 years and ≥8 years groups, and the difference was statistically significant (P < 0.05). In addition, the corneal thickness of the 4–5 years group was lower than that of the other training time groups, and the difference was statistically significant compared with the 2–3 years group (P = 0.031). This reflects that the corneal morphology of divers is closely related to the training time, and the same phenomenon has also been found in the research on retinal injury in athletes [8].

4 Discussion

The eye is an organ that is partially exposed to the external environment, possessing delicate tissue structures and being susceptible to injuries from external forces. In diving, athletes jump from the high platform and fall into the water head down. The reaction

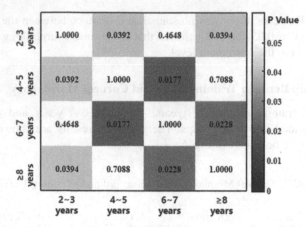

Fig. 6. Plot of Inter-group Values of Corneal Curvature according to Training Time.

force of the water surface will exert impact, perturbation, and pressure on the eyeball. For example, in 10-m platform diving, the athlete reaches a speed of approximately 14 m per second before entering the water. Upon entry, the athlete experiences an impact force of up to 4000 Newtons (approximately 400 kg), posing a significant risk of ocular injuries. In addition, the diving pool is about 5 m deep, and the bottom pressure is about 1.5 atmospheres. If the athlete enters the water and reaches the bottom of the water and then floats to the surface, the pressure on the eye is rapidly increased from 1 atmosphere to 1.5 and back to 1, and the rapid change in pressure will also cause the eye injury.

To protect the health of athletes, China has carried out research and prevention of visual impairment of divers since the 1980s [14]. Because ocular injuries in divers predominantly affect the retina, with direct implications for vision, a thorough examination of the posterior segment of the eye is of particular importance. This is done to promptly detect early lesions and take necessary preventive measures when necessary. With the development of the economy and technology, the protection of athletes' vision has become more than just "seeing". Considering that the cornea is the area where the eye directly contacts the water surface in diving, this study investigated the morphological condition of the cornea of diving athletes. By collecting the corneal topography of adolescent divers, we aimed to study the influence of diving on corneal morphology.

By comparing the corneal morphology data of divers with age-matched children, it is found that athletes have a significantly lower corneal curvature radius. It is inferred that long-term diving, water surface impact, and pressure change have certain effects on corneal morphology, which will increase the risk of refractive error, keratoconus, and other diseases. By comparing the data of athletes with different gender, ages, sports level, and training time, it was found that there was no statistical difference in corneal morphology data between groups with different gender and sports level, while there were statistical differences in corneal curvature between groups with different age and training time, and there were also statistical differences in corneal thickness between groups with different training time. Therefore, gender and sports level are not the main factors affecting the corneal morphology of athletes, while age and training time have a great relationship with it. On the other hand, the training and selection of divers mostly start from young children [1], and there is a correlation between the age of athletes and the training time, so whether the age has a greater impact on the corneal morphology or the training time still needs to be further studied.

In addition, according to the investigation, the corneal morphological changes of athletes are not monotonically increasing or decreasing with age or training time. Therefore, it is judged that there are still other influencing factors that were not counted in this investigation. Given the limited motor ability and self-protection awareness of young children, it is speculated that at the beginning of training, the standardization of athletes' technical movements and the protection of vision may be one of the factors that interfere with corneal morphology. As the athlete grows, the influence of the above two factors gradually decreases, leading to corresponding changes in the data.

In related studies, axial length and intraocular pressure are considered to have an impact on the overall shape and health of the eyeball, not only causing retinopathy, but also affecting corneal curvature. In the follow-up work, axial length and intraocular pressure measurements will be further combined to deepen the research work.

5   Conclusion

The examination of the posterior segment of the eye retina of divers has been widely concerned, and effective protective measures have been taken, but the cornea and other anterior segment tissues have not been concerned, and there is a lack of relevant research. In this study, the corneal morphology data of 42 adolescent athletes in the diving team of Shenzhen Sports School were collected. It was found that the corneal radius of adolescent athletes was significantly lower than that of ordinary children of the same age, and was related to the age and training time of the athletes. It was verified from the side that diving has a certain influence on the corneal morphology and increases the risk of refractive error, keratoconus, and other diseases, which should be paid attention to. However, the effect of diving on corneal morphology needs to be further studied with larger samples and data.

Acknowledgement. This work was supported in part by National Natural Science Foundation of China (82102189), Guangdong Provincial Department of Education (2020ZDZX3043), Guangdong Basic and Applied Basic Research Foundation (2022A1515010487), and Shenzhen Natural Science Fund (JCYJ20210324103800001, JCYJ202205301126090 22).

References

1. Li, Z.: Discussion on training and selection of junior diving athletes at basic level (in Chinese). Contemp. Sports Technol. **9**(30), 179–180 (2019)
2. Huang, J.: The way of training the action consciousness of the young diver (in Chinese). Contemp. Sports Technol. **10**(02), 50–51 (2020)
3. Li, F.: Retinal injury in divers: report of 26 cases (in Chinese). Chin. J. Sports Med. (06), 746+745 (2007)

4. Zhang, X., Xu, L., Lei, M., et al.: Investigation and analysis of retinal and vitreous changes in elite divers (in Chinese). Chin. J. Sports Med. **28**(05), 549–550 (2009)
5. Wang, Y.: Etiology and prevention of retinal detachment in divers (in Chinese). Chin. J. Sports Med. **01**, 87–88 (2000)
6. Zhou, D., Wei, W., Tian, B., et al.: Observation and management of retinal changes related to diving in professional divers. Chin. Med. J. **127**(04), 729–733 (2014)
7. Zhou, D., Wei, W., Yang, L., et al.: Comparison of Optomap scanning laser ophthalmoscope and indirect ophthalmoscopy for detecting retinal lesions of professional diving athletes. Beijing Med. J. **40**(09), 865–869 (2018)
8. Wu, H.: Causes and basic mechanism of retina injury in divers (in Chinese). Swimming **01**, 18–20 (1999)
9. Public Health Ophthalmology Branch of Chinese Preventive Medicine Association: Chinese expert consensus on the reference interval of ocular hyperopia reserve, axial length, corneal curvature and genetic factors in school-age children (2022). Chin. J. Ophthalmol. **58**(02), 96–102 (2022)
10. Wu, S., Chen, G., Xiao, Y.: Clinical studies on the changes of intraocular pressure and keratometry before and after pupil dilation in children and teenagers. J. Kunming Med. Univ. **43**(01), 102–106 (2022)
11. Gao, L., Li, X., Li, T.: Relationship between age, axial length, corneal surface morphology and refractive error in children with aged 5 to 14years. Health Med. Res. Pract. **19**(01), 26–29 (2022)
12. Qiao, F., Liu, C., Wu, Y., et al.: Corneal thickness and its correlated factors in schoolchildren aged 6 to 18 years. J. Clin. Ophthalmol. **20**(05), 433–435 (2012)
13. Li, J., Wang, J.: Axial length and corneal curvature and their associations in 4 to 16-year-old children. Ophthalmol. CHN **26**(05), 307–312 (2017)
14. Li, F.: Etiological analysis and prevention of retinal and vitreous lesions in divers (in Chinese). Chin. J. Sports Med. (04), 244–246 (1988)

EEG Channels Selection Based on BiLSTM and NSGAII

Shun Wang[✉] and Liangzhi Gan

School of Electrical Engineering and Automation, Jiangsu Normal University,
Xuzhou 221116, China
2801700786@qq.com

Abstract. Emotion recognition work for EEG signals has become one of the most important measures for researchers to explore human-computer interaction work. However, the traditional emotion recognition approach utilizes all EEG channels which may lead to increased computational degree as well as un-wanted interfering information affecting the accuracy. And it is not suitable for all emotion recognition work. In this paper, we propose an EEG selection framework based on bidirectional long short-term memory network (BiLSTM) and non-dominated sorting genetic algorithm-II (NSGAII) to select the optimal set of EEG channels for emotion recognition. The EEG data is first identified using BiLSTM, followed by optimization of the results using NSGAII, and continuous iteration to arrive at the optimal channel set. The experiments were conducted using the publicly available dataset DEAP, and the experimental results show that the method reduces the number of channels and maintains a high emotion recognition accuracy.

Keywords: Emotion Recognition · Channel Selection · BiLSTM · NSGAII

1 Introduction

With the deepening research in the field of electroencephalogram (EEG), a series of studies have been developed, such as emotion recognition [1], fatigue monitoring, and attention detection [2]. Without exception, these studies require the processing of EEG signals. In extensive experimental research, it has been found that different brain detection positions, namely electrode positions, represent different functions. Emotion is one of the most representative signs of human beings, and it can effectively reflect a person's mental state, which has an important impact on our lives. Researchers use various methods, such as facial expressions and voice, to identify emotional states. However, people can easily use these external physiological responses to conceal their true emotions. EEG is the autonomous activity of the nervous system. Its objectivity makes it difficult for people to consciously control their emotional expressions. This physiological response can more truthfully and objectively reflect a person's emotional state, thus the EEG signals are increasingly valued in recognition research.

EEG signals are generally multi-channel signals [3]. Currently, common EEG channel selection [4]strategies can be divided into two types: whole-brain channels and local channels. The whole-brain channel strategy uses EEG signals from all available channels for analysis, which has the advantage of obtaining more comprehensive EEG information. However, it also brings higher computational complexity and possible signal interference. The local channel strategy selects a subset of channels for analysis to reduce computational pressure and signal interference, but it may lose some EEG information. In addition, there are also channel selection methods based on feature selection, which optimize the performance of brain-computer interface systems by selecting channels higher information content.

In this paper, we extract the preprocessed EEG data using bi-directional long short-term memory networks [5], and optimized the classification accuracy and the number of channels to select the best channel set using NSGAII [6].

2 Related Work

This section describes in detail the dataset DEAP used for the model as well as the associated algorithms BiLSTM and NSGAII.

2.1 EEG Dataset

The DEAP dataset is an EEG emotion dataset containing multi-channel physiological signals, facial expressions, and emotional self-assessment labels of human body, which is jointly designed by Koelstra et al. The DEAP dataset includes the EEG signals recorded by 32 subjects while watching the video. For each emotion-evoking experiment, 40 channels of physiological signals were captured, with physiological signals occupying 8 channels and EEG signals occupying 32 channels of the recording.

2.2 Bi-directional Long Short-Term Memory

During the analysis of electroencephalogram (EEG) signal features, Recurrent Neural Network (RNN) is more suitable for handling tasks related to time series. Among them, Long Short-Term Memory (LSTM) has been proven to possess the ability to capture temporal information in the field of emotion recognition.

The principle of LSTM and ordinary recurrent neural networks are roughly the same, both repeatedly use a module to achieve the effect of recurrence. The internal structure of ordinary recurrent neural networks is relatively simple, using the input from the input layer and the output from the previous layer to generate an output through the operation of an activation function. LSTM is based on ordinary recurrent neural networks and adds multiple operations and states. In addition to the input from the input layer, each LSTM unit also receives two inputs from the previous time step, one is the output from the previous time step and the other is the state from the previous time step. After multiple calculations, LSTM produces an output and the current cell's state. LSTM is implemented through three "gates": input gate, forget gate, and output gate. These three gates can be used to define and explain the internal structure and implementation principle of LSTM.

The input gates are as follows:

$$i_t = \sigma(W_i[h_{t-1}, x_t] + b_i) \tag{1}$$

i_t is the input gate of the LSTM cell at the moment t, σ is the sigmoid function, W_t and b_i are the weight matrix and the bias term respectively, h_{t-1} is the output of the LSTM cell at the previous moment, and x_t is the input at the moment t.

The Oblivion Gate is as follows:

$$f_t = \sigma(W_i[h_{t-1}, x_t] + b_f). \tag{2}$$

The Oblivion Gate f_t, which represents at the t moment, has the same parameters as those in the Input Gate, which represent the same significance, only the specific values are different.

$$z = tanh(W_z[h_{t-1}, x_t] + b_z) \tag{3}$$

$$c_t = f \cdot c_{t-1} + i_t \cdot z \tag{4}$$

z is a new candidate vector that participates in the computation of the new state and, together with the state of the previous moment, influences the update of the state of the current moment. c_t represents the current state. The forgetting gate is multiplied with the previous state, and the value of the forgetting gate is a value between 0 and 1.

The input gate is as follows:

$$o_t = \sigma(W_o[h_{t-1}, x_t] + b_o) \tag{5}$$

$$h_t = o_t \cdot tanhc_t \tag{6}$$

The final output of the LSTM cell, which depends on the output gate and the current state of the cell, is mainly controlled by the output gate.

As in Fig. 1, the bidirectional LSTM is composed of two layers of LSTMs, the first LSTM loops forward and each LSTM cell memorizes the information from the previous cell, and the second LSTM loops backward and passes the information from the last to the front. In the figure, for each moment, the input is provided to both LSTM units, and the output also contains both units, which are jointly determined by these two units. In the figure x_1 are the electrode input features of different channels of the EEG signal are fed into the forward LSTM and reverse LSTM networks respectively, the forward features $\overleftarrow{h}_1$ and reverse features $\overrightarrow{h}_1$ are extracted through the network, and the resulting bi-directional features are spliced to obtain the feature set y_1, which is used for feature recognition.

In this paper, the network structure of BiLSTM is employed, as illustrated in Fig. 4. The signal sample features are inputted, along with the enhanced DE features mentioned earlier, and subsequently processed by the LSTM network layer. This processing entails segregating the features into the forward feature index1 and the backward feature index2, enabling bidirectional LSTM feature analysis. Moreover, for the purpose of improved fusion of differential features, two BiLSTM modules are employed to simultaneously capture the characteristics of both the forward index1 and the reverse index2 of the extracted DE features. This approach effectively preserves the temporal characteristics of the EEG signal, resulting in more comprehensive feature information in the output values at this instance, when compared to the traditional unidirectional LSTM network.

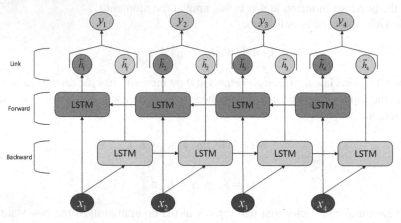

Fig. 1. Basic Structure of BiLSTM

The BiLSTM model constructed within this paper combines the aforementioned mechanisms. Similar to the previous experimental setups, individual experiments are conducted on different channels. The time-frequency data of single-channel EEG signals are utilized as inputs for the model. Each moment of the time-frequency data is represented by a spectrogram, encompassing crucial frequency information. Subsequently, the spectrogram features of each moment are fed into the units of different moments within the BiLSTM. The outputs from each moment of the BiLSTM are then concatenated together. Utilizing the attention mechanism, the attention weights for different moments are calculated, culminating in a weighted average that serves as the output of the entire BiLSTM. This output represents the extracted features of the BiLSTM, effectively synthesizing the temporal information of the EEG signal sequence. Following this, the extracted features are propagated through a fully connected neural network, ultimately yielding the probability of final emotion classification through the Softmax layer.

2.3 Non-dominated Sorting Genetic Algorithm-II

In this paper, genetic algorithm is used as the optimizer to solve the channel selection problem of EEG. The channel electrodes are selected by setting the first-off fitness function, but the local optimization occurs in the process of feature calculation, and the global optimal solution set cannot be obtained. On this basis, Non-dominated Sorting Genetic Algorithm-II (NSGAII) is introduced to find the optimal solution set.

In this paper, the improved NSGAII is used to generate a new population size of greater than or equal to N after combining the generated child and parent populations in the computational iterations, in which the duplicate individuals are deleted, and the size of the new individual-selectable population generated by the unimproved NSGA-II is less, which does not contain the duplicate individuals, and the subsequent use of the elite strategy for the selection of the electrode set of the EEG signal In the subsequent selection of the EEG electrode set using the elite strategy, after multiple iterations of selecting N populations, redundant duplicate individuals can be effectively deleted, and the selection of the spatial electrode set that is conducive to emotion recognition is better able to achieve the global optimum. The flowchart of the elite strategy is shown in Fig. 2.

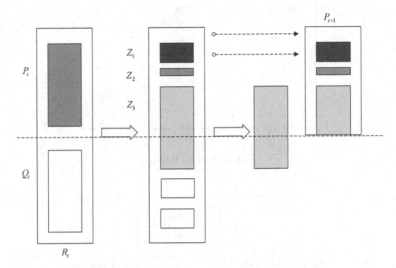

Fig. 2. Process of Improving Elite Strategy

Pareto dominance relation: In optimizing the selection of the minimum sample set for multi-objective is that any n objective has $f_i(x)$, $i = 1, 2, \ldots, n$, the decision variables X_a and X_b are defined respectively, and at the same time satisfy the following conditions, then X_a is said to dominate X_b.

$$X_a < X_b \iff \begin{cases} (\forall_i \in \{1, 2, 3, \ldots, n\} : f_i(X_a) \leq f_i(X_b)) \\ (\exists_i \in \{1, 2, 3, \ldots, n\} : f_i(X_a) < f_i(X_b)) \end{cases} \tag{7}$$

Fast non-dominated sorting is a multi-objective optimization algorithm based on Pareto optimal solution. Pareto solution is also called non-dominated solution: when there are multiple task objectives, because of the contradiction or incomparable between the objectives, one indicator is the best for one indicator and the worst for the other. When an objective function is improved, another objective function will be weakened to some extent, which is called Pareto solution, that is, the set of optimal solutions of a group of objective functions is called Pareto optimal set. The basic structure of Pareto is shown in Fig. 3.The surface formed by the optimal set in two-dimensional space is called Pareto frontier, which is the most suitable channel set for emotion recognition.

For the multi-objective optimization of EEG signal spatial lead electrodes in this paper, the selection conditions are the number of channels used simultaneously must be as small as possible and Emotion recognition accuracy must be as high as possible.

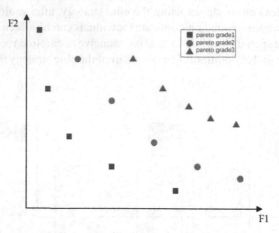

Fig. 3. Pareto Grade

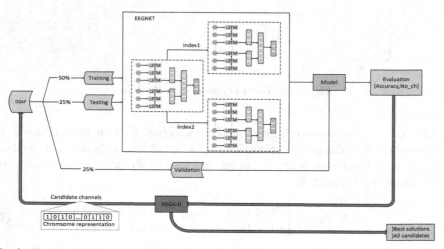

Fig. 4. Flowchart of the optimization process for EEG channel selection using a chromosome representation for NSGA-II.

3   Experiment Setting and Results

We use multi-objective optimization with the improved NSGAII algorithm to select the most suitable set of channel electrodes for emotion recognition. We analyze 32 EEG signals from the DEAP dataset and consider the spatial electrodes. By considering the different features in the EEG signals from different brain regions, we identify the optimal Pareto feature set using the multi-objective optimization algorithm. In our experiment, we divide the EEG signal segments into 2-s intervals to categorize low arousal and high arousal, and create a model for each subject.

The problem to be optimized is defined by two unconstrained objectives based on the structure of NSGAII as shown in the flowchart of Fig. 4; (1) reduce or select the number of EEG channels that are required and most relevant for the classification of high arousal/valence versus low arousal/valence; and (2) improve or at least maintain the eegnet-based classification accuracy. NSGA-II uses a fitness function to evaluate the solution domain of the two-objective optimization problem, which is defined in this example as [Accuracy, No_ch], where Acc is the eegnet-based classification accuracy obtained from Fig. 4.

The optimization process of the NSGAII algorithm starts with the creation of possible candidates or chromosomes in the population, which represents the iteration of NSGA-II. It obtains the corresponding raw EEG data for the channels represented as 1 in each chromosome, and then we use 50% of the data to create the EEGNet model, 25% for testing, and 25% for validating the created model. The accuracy obtained and the number of EEG channels used ([Accuracy, No_ch]) were returned to NSGAII to evaluate each chromosome in the current population.

In the experiments, the process was repeated several times to determine if using a different subset of channels would increase the accuracy. To this end, we designed and implemented an optimization process for NSGAII. Briefly, NSGAII uses a binary chromosome representation of 32 genes, one gene per EEG channel, with two possible values for each gene; 1 if the channel is used and 0 otherwise. The chromosome population generated by the optimization algorithm is evaluated based on the highest accuracy and the chromosome population with the highest accuracy is reused to generate a new population. In this way, the set of spatial lead electrodes that is most optimal for emotion recognition is found.

The process was repeated to produce a population of 10 chromosomes, which was experimentally determined. The termination criterion for the optimization process is defined by the target space tolerance, defined as 0.001, which is calculated every 10 generations. If optimization is not achieved, the process stops after a maximum of 100 generations, which is also experimentally determined.

Figure 5 and Fig. 6 show, respectively, the optimization process for low arousal/high valence classification of subject 1 after the channel selection process of NSGAII. In Fig. 5, each candidate (blue dot) represents the combination of channels used to acquire the sub dataset and it is used as an input to the network model. The optimal point (red point) appearing on the Pareto front indicates the maximum accuracy that can be achieved for that number of channels.

In order to verify the superiority of the selected channel set for the validation experiment, the NSGA-II optimization algorithm was used to select a 12-channel set feature combined with the BiLSTM neural network model mentioned in the previous chapter for emotion accuracy recognition. At the same time, the full channel data, including 32 channels and the common 18-channel EEG data, were input into the BiLSTM neural network model for data comparison and result analysis.

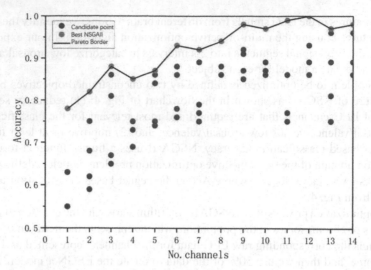

Fig. 5. EEG Channel Selection Results of Subject 1 (Arousal)

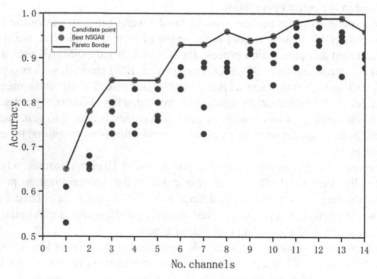

Fig. 6. EEG Channel Selection Results of Subject 1 (Valence)

The training time and accuracy comparison are shown in Table 1 and Table 2, respectively. The NSGA-II optimized channel set achieved the shortest training time and highest accuracy, reaching 93.86%. Compared to using all 32 channels, there was a significant improvement in electrode feature selection and the model training speed was greatly optimized.

Table 1. Comparison of model training time of different channel selection methods for single subject

Channel Selection	model	Training time (s)
full channel	BiLSTM	4823
Common 18 channels	BiLSTM	2086
NSGA-II optimized channel set	BiLSTM	1403

Table 2. Comparison of Classification Accuracy of Different Channels (Arousal)

hallmark	model	Channel Selection	Accuracy
Improvement of DE	BiLSTM	full channel	93.86
Improvement of DE	BiLSTM	Common 18 channels	96.01
Improvement of DE	BiLSTM	NSGAII optimized channel set	97.53

4 Conclusion

The content of this article mainly focuses on the selection of spatial electrodes for electroencephalogram (EEG) signals. Firstly, the important significance of spatial electrode selection for emotion recognition is introduced. Then, a multi-objective genetic algorithm is introduced to optimize the spatial electrodes. Considering the complex distribution of spatial electrodes, large number and diverse types of EEG signals, and non-unique features, the NSGA-II algorithm is improved by introducing an improved elitist strategy to effectively eliminate redundant sets between electrode collections. Combined with the DEAP dataset, it is found that higher classification accuracy can be achieved when using 8–12 spatial electrodes. Combined with the RNN-BiLSTM network algorithm for classification verification, it can effectively accelerate model training speed and emotion recognition accuracy. EEG channel optimization is an important research area, which is of great significance for improving the quality and application value of EEG signals. However, there are still some shortcomings in current research, such as limitations in using only the DEAP dataset and channel selection methods. Future research can explore the combination of multimodal data, introduction of other machine learning methods, and establishment of a standard evaluation system to promote the development of EEG channel optimization and provide a more reliable foundation for EEG signal research.

References

1. Anubhav, D.N., Singh, M., Sethia, D., Kalra, D., Indu, S.: An efficient approach to EEG-based emotion recognition using LSTM network. In: 2020 16th IEEE International Colloquium on Signal Processing & Its Applications (CSPA), Langkawi, Malaysia, pp. 88–92 (2020). https://doi.org/10.1109/CSPA48992.2020.9068691

2. Liu, Y., Lan, Z., Khoo, H.H.G., Li, K.H.H., Sourina, O., Mueller-Wittig, W.: EEG-based evaluation of mental fatigue using machine learning algorithms. In: 2018 International Conference on Cyberworlds (CW), Singapore, pp. 276–279 (2018). https://doi.org/10.1109/CW.2018.00056

3. Wang, Z., Song, H., Hu, S., Liu, G.: Channel selection method based on CNNSE for EEG emotion recognition. In: 2019 IEEE 14th International Conference on Intelligent Systems and Knowledge Engineering (ISKE), Dalian, China, pp. 654–658 (2019). https://doi.org/10.1109/ISKE47853.2019.9170317

4. Dai, C.P., Becker, D., Stefanie, I.: Shapelet-transformed multi-channel EEG channel selection. ACM Trans. Intell. Syst. Technol. **11**(5). https://doi.org/10.1145/3397850

5. Hochreiter, S., Schmidhuber, J.: Long short-term memory. Neural Comput. **9**(8), 1735–1780 (1997)

6. Deb, K., Agrawal, S., Pratap, A., Meyarivan, T.: A Fast Elitist non-dominated sorting genetic algorithm for multi-objective optimization: NSGA-II. In: Schoenauer, M. (ed.) PPSN 2000. LNCS, vol. 1917, pp. 849–858. Springer, Heidelberg (2000). https://doi.org/10.1007/3-540-45356-3_83

7. Huang, D., Zhang, S., Zhang, Y.: EEG-based emotion recognition using empirical wavelet transform. In: 2017 4th International Conference on Systems and Informatics (ICSAI), Hangzhou, China, pp. 1444–1449 (2017). https://doi.org/10.1109/ICSAI.2017.8248513

8. Moctezuma, L.A., Abe, T., Molinas, M.: Two-dimensional CNN-based distinction of human emotions from EEG channels selected by multi-objective evolutionary algorithm. Sci. Rep. **12**, 3523 (2022). https://doi.org/10.1038/s41598-022-07517-5

9. Kumar, R., Kaushik, S.C., Arora, R.: Multi-objective thermodynamic optimisation of solar parabolic dish Stirling heat engine using NSGA-II and decision making. Int. J. Renewable Energy Technol. **8**(1), 64 (2017)

10. Mert, A., Akan, A.: Emotion recognition from EEG signals by using multivariate empirical-mode decomposition. Pattern Anal. Appl. **21**(1), 81–89 (2016)

11. Soleymani, M., Asghari-Esfeden, S., Fu, Y., Pantic, M.: "Analysis of EEG signals and facial expressions for continuous emotion detection. IEEE Trans. Affect. Comput. **7**(1), 17–28 (2016). https://doi.org/10.1109/TAFFC.2015.2436926

12. Garrett, D., Peterson, D.A., Anderson, C.W., Thaut, M.H.: Comparison of linear, nonlinear, and feature selection methods for EEG signal classification. IEEE Trans. Neural Syst. Rehabil. Eng. **11**(2), 141–144 (2003). https://doi.org/10.1109/TNSRE.2003.814441

Self-Guided Local Prototype Network for Few-Shot Medical Image Segmentation

Pengrui Teng[1(✉)], Yuhu Cheng[1], Xuesong Wang[1], Yi-Jie Pan[2], and Changan Yuan[3]

[1] China University of Mining and Technology, Xuzhou, China
tpr9714@163.com
[2] Eastern Institute of Technology, Tongxin Road No. 568, Ningbo 315201, Zhejiang, China
[3] Guangxi Academy of Science, Nanning 530025, China

Abstract. Recently, few-shot medical image segmentation approaches have been extensively explored to tackle the challenge of scarce labeled data in medical images. The majority of existing methods employ prototype-based techniques and have achieved promising results. However, conventional prototype extraction approaches inherently lead to loss of spatial information, thus degrading model performance, an issue further aggravated in medical images with large background regions. In this work, we propose a self-guided local prototype generation module (SLP), which progressively splits support masks into sub-mask, thereby producing a set of local prototype that preserve richer support image information. Moreover, in order to take full advantage of the information contained within the prototype sets during the iterative process, we generate a prior mask from this information and provide coarse spatial location about the target for the model through a simple prior-guided attention module (PGA). Experiments on three different datasets validate that our proposed approach outperforms existing methods.

Keywords: Few-shot learning · Medical image segmentation · Prototype-based

1 Introduction

As an important component of medical image analysis, semantic segmentation of medical images plays a crucial role in various clinical applications such as lesion diagnosis, disease assessment, and surgical planning [1, 2]. With the development of deep learning techniques, fully supervised models [3–5] trained on datasets with abundant annotations have achieved superior performance on various medical image segmentation tasks. However, constructing well-annotated datasets for training such fully supervised models is extremely expensive in the medical image domain, because the annotation of medical images typically requires professionals with expertise. Furthermore, these fully supervised models tend to be customized to particular tasks. When confronted with a novel target, re-training a model becomes necessary, which further intensifies the conflict between data requirements and annotation challenges.

Few-shot learning provides an effective solution to address the aforementioned challenges. It can train a model that only needs few samples to grasp the knowledge of new classes. Owing to this formidable capability, few-shot medical image segmentation has been extensively researched in recent years [6–8]. Among them, prototype-based approaches [9] are a common method. These methods typically represent semantic classes as prototype vectors extracted by masked average pooling, and perform segmentation by computing distances between query features and prototypes. However, such an approach inherently leads to the loss of spatial information [10]. The severely imbalanced foreground and background classes in medical images, where the background frequently contains diverse organs and tissues, further exacerbate the issues induced by masked average pooling. Several recent few-shot medical image studies have strived to alleviate this problem from different perspectives, including extracting local prototypes with local patches [7], representing only foreground prototypes coupled with anomaly detection [8], and regarding prototypes merely as extra priors [11].

However, these methods cannot fully represent the information of the support image. In this work, we propose a self-supported local prototype generation module. It iteratively splits the support mask into a set of sub-masks, thereby extracting a collection of local prototypes that can preserve more information of the support image. Furthermore, in order to fully utilize the information carried by the prototypes during the iterative process, we generate a prior mask using them and enhance the query features through a simple prior-guided attention module.

The contributions of this work are summarized as follows:

- We propose a self-guided local prototype generation module, which is capable of preserving more information regarding the support class and thus better guide the model for segmentation.
- We propose a simple prior-guided attention module to provide coarse localization cues of the target for the model.
- We validate the efficacy of the proposed method on three datasets with multiple semantic classes and imaging modalities.

2   Related Work

2.1   Few-Shot Learning

Few-shot learning, as a promising paradigm for enhancing model generalization, has been extensively researched in recent years. Existing methods can be categorized into: metric learning based methods [9, 12], optimization based methods [13–15], and data augmentation based methods [16–18]. Specifically, metric learning based approaches classify targets based on distances between the target samples and class representations. Optimization based methods learn a good initialization so models can quickly adapt to new tasks through just a few gradient updates. Data augmentation based methods train models by generating more training data. In this paper, we propose a metric learning based approach.

2.2   Few-Shot Semantic Segmentation for Medical Image

Due to the expensive annotation of medical data, data-efficient few-shot learning has attracted the attention of researchers in the field of medical image semantic segmentation. SENet [6] proposed the first dual-branch architecture for few-shot medical image segmentation, and promoted the interaction between the conditioner branch and the segmentor branch through excitation and squeeze modules. GCN-DE [20] introduced a global correlation module that can effectively capture the foreground relevance between support and query image pairs. MprNet[21] applied a fusion module based on cosine similarity to aid information exchange between the two branches. AAS-DCL [22] enhances the ability of the model to discriminate features through dual contrastive learning.

On the other hand, metric learning based few-shot medical image segmentation methods have also made significant progress. ALPnet [7] developed a self-supervised approach for few-shot medical image segmentation and achieved satisfactory results. ADNet [8] proposed a network based on anomaly detection in order to avoid modeling the background regions of medical images. Q-Net [23] improves ADNet [8] by utilizing dual-path feature extraction. RPNet [24] captured local relational features between foreground and background regions through a context encoder and iteratively refined the segmentation mask. RAP [11] introduced a spatial branch to provide spatial information of the target. Within the framework of this metric learning, we propose SLPNet. Unlike these existing methods, SLPNet utilizes the support mask to generate local prototypes in a self-guided way.

3 Methods

3.1 Problem Definition

The goal of few-shot semantic segmentation is to train a model with strong generalization capability, enabling it to produce accurate segmentations for new classes given only a few annotated examples. Typically, the model is trained on dataset D_{tr} containing training classes (e.g., $c_{tr} = \{liver, left\ kidney, right\ kidney\}$ and evaluated on test set D_{te} with novel classes c_{te} (e.g., $c_{te} = \{spleen\}$), where $c_{tr} \cap c_{te} = \varnothing$. Both D_{tr} and D_{te} consist of multiple episodes, each with a support set $S = \{(I^s, M^s)\}_{K=1}^{k}$ and query set $Q = \{I^q, M^q\}$, where (I^*, M^*) denotes an image and corresponding binary mask pair, and K is the number of support samples. In the training phase, the model randomly samples a support set S and a query set Q from dataset D_{tr}. It takes S and query image I^q as input and predicts the binary mask $\tilde{M}^q$ for I^q. Once training is finished, the model is evaluated on episodes from test set D_{te} using fixed parameters, with no further optimization.

3.2 Self-guided Local Prototype Generation Module

In contrast to previous work [7] which directly generates local prototype representations of classes through local patches, the SLP utilizes masks of support images to evaluate the information encapsulated in the prototypes. In SLP, the masks of support images are split into a set of sub-mask that comprehensively represent the information of the supporting images. These sub-masks are then used to generate local prototypes.

Specifically, we first put the foreground and background masks of the support image into two sets M_{fg} and M_{bg}, respectively. Then these mask sets along with the support features F^s are input into the self-guided local prototype generation module, and the prototypes are computed:

$$p_{fg} = \frac{\sum_{x,y} F^s_{(x,y)} 1[M^{fg,i}_{(x,y)} = 1]}{\sum_{x,y} 1[M^{fg,i}_{(x,y)} = 1]} \tag{1}$$

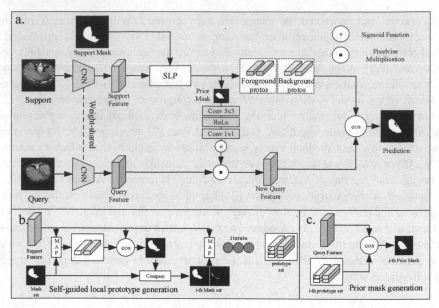

Fig. 1. (a) The overall workflow of the proposed network is as follows: The input support image and query image are fed into a feature extractor with shared parameters to produce support features F^s and query features F^q, respectively. The proposed self-guided local prototype generation module accepts the support features, query features, and support labels as inputs, and yields a set of local prototypes along with a prior mask M_{pri} for the query image. Subsequently, the prior mask of the query image is to enhance the query features through a simple attention network. Finally, the enhanced query features and the prototype set are exploited by a similarity-based classifier to execute segmentation. (b) Illustration of the generation process of self-guided local prototypes. (c) Illustration of the generation process of the i-th prior mask.

$$p_{bg} = \frac{\sum_{x,y} F^s_{(x,y)} 1[M^{bg,i}_{(x,y)} = 1]}{\sum_{x,y} 1[M^{bg,i}_{(x,y)} = 1]} \qquad (2)$$

Where $M^{*,i}$ is the i-th sub-mask in the mask set, and (x, y) is the spatial location index. After each element in the mask sets is computed, we can obtain a local prototype set, which is used to guide the segmentation of the support image and generate its predicted mask $\tilde{M}$. The prediction mask $\tilde{M}$ is compared with each element in the mask set, splitting each sub-mask into a correctly predicted part M_{TP} and a missing information part M_{FN}, and accordingly updating the mask set. The mask sets are iteratively updated until no information is lost when partitioning, and the final local prototype set is output.

3.3 Prior-Guided Attention Module

Although the prototype sets during the iterative process cannot comprehensively represent class information, they can provide the model with a rough localization of the target. To make full use of this information, we propose a prior-guided attention module

(PGA). The PGA generates a prior mask M_{pri} for the query image using the prototype sets during the iteration, and enhances the query feature through a lightweight attention network.

As shown in Fig. 1(c), we use the local prototype set from the i-th iteration to obtain the predicted mask M_{pri}^i for the query image. After obtaining the predicted mask of the query image over the whole iteration process, we sum them up to get the prior mask M_{pri}. And we normalize it using the Eq. (3), where ϵ is set to $1e-7$ in the experiments.

$$M_{pri} = \frac{M_{pri} - \min(M_{pri})}{\max(M_{pri}) - \min(M_{pri}) + \epsilon} \tag{3}$$

Then, the prior mask is utilized to obtain the attention vector using Eq. (4).

$$V_\alpha = \sigma(C_N(M_{pri})) \tag{4}$$

Here C_N and σ denote the convolution and activation functions, respectively. Finally, the query feature with spatial prior enhancement is generated using Eq. (5).

$$F_n^q = F^q \odot V_a \tag{5}$$

3.4 Similarity-Based Segmentation

After obtaining the prototype set P and enhanced query feature F_n^q, we adopt a similarity-based approach for segmentation. We compute the similarity map S_j between the query image and the j-th prototype p_j in the prototype set using Eq. (6).

$$S_j^{x,y} = -\alpha \frac{F_{n,(x,y)}^q \cdot p_j}{||F_{n,(x,y)}^q|| ||p_j||} \tag{6}$$

where α denotes a temperature parameter, which is set to 20 following previous work [21]. After computing similarities with all elements in the prototype set, we concatenate these similarity maps and apply a softmax function to obtain the final prediction. $\tilde{Y}^q$:

$$\tilde{Y}^q = softmax(S_j^{x,y} \cdot softmax(S_j^{x,y})) \tag{7}$$

3.5 Training Strategy

The SLPNet is trained in an end-to-end manner, where a support set and a query set containing annotations of the same class are randomly sampled during each iteration. The support set and query image are fed into the network to predict segmentation mask $\tilde{Y}^q$ for the query image. We supervise the network using a cross-entropy loss between the predicted segmentation mask $\tilde{Y}^q$ and the ground truth mask Y^q. For each episode, we have:

$$L_{ce} = -\frac{1}{N}\sum_{x,y} Y^q(x, y) log(\tilde{Y}^q(x, y)) \tag{8}$$

Additionally, following previous works [7, 8, 19], we adopt prototype alignment regularization. It segments the support image using the query image, where the ground truth of the query image is replaced by the predicted mask $\tilde{Y}^q$. The prototype alignment is formulated as:

$$L_{re} = -\frac{1}{N}\sum_{x,y} Y^s(x, y)log(\tilde{Y}^s(x, y)) \tag{9}$$

The overall loss function L per iteration is defined as:

$$L = L_{ce} + \lambda L_{re} \tag{10}$$

where λ is the temperature parameter, set to 1 in experiments. After training, the network can directly segment new classes without fine-tuning.

4 Experiments

4.1 Datasets

To fully assess the performance and generalization capability of the proposed method, we conducted experiments on three public datasets with different modalities and semantic classes. They are abdominal MRI dataset [26], abdominal CT dataset [27] and cardiac MRI dataset [28], respectively.

(1) **Abdominal MRI** dataset is from the challenge of ISBI 2019. It contains 20 3D scans and 4 labels, each scan with an average of 36 slices.
(2) **Abdominal CT** dataset is from the Challenge of MICCAI 2015 Multi-Atlas Abdomen Labeling. The dataset contains 13 different labels, and the entire dataset includes 3D CT scans from 30 different patients.
(3) **Cardiac MRI** (bSFP-fold) dataset is from the Challenge of MICCAI 2019 Multi-Sequence Cardiac MRI Segmentation, which contains 35 3D cardiac MRI scans.

For the two abdominal datasets, we selected the same labels (e.g., liver, right kidney (RK), left kidney (LK), and spleen) for experiments to evaluate performance across semantically identical classes with modality differences. For the cardiac dataset, we conducted experiments using left ventricular myocardium (LV-MYO), left ventricular blood pool (LV-BP), and right ventricle (RV). For fair comparison, all datasets were divided into 5 parts for 5-fold cross-validation, with the validation set in each fold further partitioned into disjoint support image and query image sets. We utilized 2D model frameworks, with all 3D scans preprocessed into 2D slices and resized to 256 × 256 pixels following common practice.

4.2 Experimental Setup and Evaluation Metrics

To better compare with state-of-the-art methods, we adopted the experimental setup established in [7]. Specifically, we removed all slices containing target classes to ensure all semantic classes were unseen in the test set. Furthermore, we utilized the Dice score as the evaluation metric to measure model performance. It ranges from 0 to 100, with higher

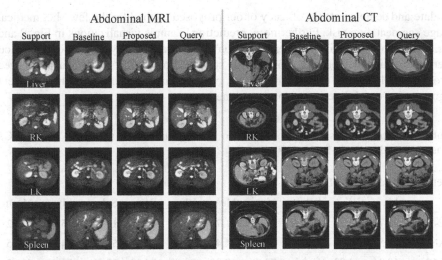

Fig. 2. Qualitative comparisons on abdominal MRI and CT dataset.

scores indicating greater overlap between predicted and ground truth segmentation mask and thus superior model performance. The Dice score is calculated as:

$$Dice(A, B) = 2 * \frac{|A \cap B|}{|A| + |B|} * 100\% \tag{11}$$

where A and B denote the predicted and ground-truth segmentation mask, respectively.

4.3 Implementation Details

The model utilizes a Resnet-101 network [25] pretrained on MS-COCO as the backbone, which maps the $3 \times 256 \times 256$ input image into a $256 \times 32 \times 32$ feature map. Following [8, 34], the experiment adopts a 1-way 1-shot training strategy and utilizes pseudo-labels of superpixels to train the network. We optimize the network using an SGD optimizer with an initial learning rate of $1e-3$ and utilize a multi-step learning rate scheduler to dynamically adjust the learning rate every 1000 iterations. The network was trained on a NVIDIA GeForce RTX3090 GPU for a total of 100k iterations.

4.4 Results and Analysis

We conduct experiments on three different datasets to compare our method against existing few-shot medical image segmentation approaches. The experimental results across the methods on the abdominal and cardiac datasets are presented in Table 1 and Table 2, respectively. As shown in Table 1, on the abdominal dataset our method improves performance on multiple organs except for the liver, and increases the average Dice score by 1.10% and 0.98%. Regarding the experiments on the cardiac dataset (Table 2), our method achieves comparable performance to the leading approach, in terms of both the single organ and average Dice scores. Taken together, these experiments thoroughly validate and demonstrate the efficacy of our proposed method for the few-shot medical image segmentation task. Furthermore, prediction example visualizations in Fig. 2 and Fig. 3 illustrate substantially higher prediction accuracy attained by our proposed method over the baseline methods. The consistently strong segmentation performance achieved across multiple organs, except for the liver, provides further evidence of the proficient segmentation capabilities of our proposed method.

Table 1. Comparison of segmentation results by existing methods on abdominal MRI and CT datasets. Bold denotes the best results.

Method	Abdominal-CT					Abdominal-MRI				
	LK	RK	Spleen	Liver	Mean	LK	RK	Spleen	Liver	Mean
SE-Net	32.70	23.60	32.53	38.20	31.76	63.85	64.56	11.78	55.08	48.82
PANet	37.58	34.69	43.73	61.71	44.42	47.71	47.95	58.73	64.99	54.85
ALPNet	63.34	54.82	60.25	73.65	63.02	73.63	78.39	67.02	73.05	73.02
ADNet	63.84	56.98	61.84	73.95	64.15	71.89	76.02	65.84	76.03	72.70
Q-Net	63.26	58.37	63.36	**74.36**	64.83	74.05	77.52	67.43	**78.71**	74.43
Ours	**67.13**	**59.18**	**65.21**	71.71	**65.81**	**78.40**	**80.32**	**70.82**	72.57	**75.53**

4.5 Ablation Analysis

Ablation experiments were conducted on the abdominal MRI dataset to validate the efficacy of each proposed component in our method and the experiments results are presented in Table 3. As exhibited, integrating the proposed SLP module into the baseline model leads to consistent performance improvements across all organs, with the average Dice score increased by 18.26%.

Table 2. Comparison of segmentation results by existing methods on cardiac MRI dataset. Bold denotes the best results.

Method	Cardiac MRI			
	LV-BP	LV-MYO	RV	Mean
SE-Net	58.04	25.18	12.86	32.03
PANet	70.42	46.79	69.52	62.25
ALPNet	83.99	66.74	79.96	76.90
ADNet	88.36	65.47	78.35	77.39
Q-Net	**89.63**	**66.87**	79.25	**78.58**
Ours	87.96	65.46	**82.11**	78.51

Table 3. Ablation study results on abdominal MRI dataset.

	LK	RK	Spleen	Liver	Mean
Baseline	47.71	47.95	58.73	64.99	54.85
Baseline + SLP	74.38	76.86	66.9	74.28	73.11
Baseline + SLP + PGA	78.40	80.32	70.82	72.57	75.53

This can be attributed to the prototype set generated by SLP providing richer semantic class information compared to the global average prototypes obtained through global average pooling.

Furthermore, the addition of the proposed PGA component enables the model to achieve optimal segmentation performance, thus demonstrating the beneficial prior information provided by incorporating PGA. Taken together, these ablation studies validate the efficacy of each key component proposed in our method for few-shot medical image segmentation.

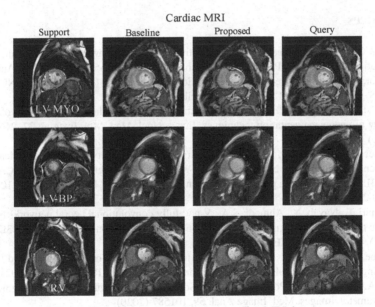

Fig. 3. Qualitative comparisons on cardiac MRI dataset.

5 Conclusion

In this paper, we propose SLPNet for few-shot medical image segmentation. It is a prototype-based approach that introduces two new modules - a self-guided local prototype generation module and a prior-guided attention module. The first module produces a set of local prototypes that capture more comprehensive information from the support image to better guide the segmentation of the query image. The latter provides the model with coarse spatial localization cues of the segmentation target. We evaluate SLPNet on multi-modality datasets across various organs. These experimental results validate the effectiveness of SLPNet.

Acknowledgement. This work was supported in part by STI 2030—Major Projects, under Grant 2021ZD0200403, and partly supported by grants from the National Science Foundation of China, Nos. 62333018, 62372255, U22A2039, 62073231, and 62372318, and supported by the Key Project of Science and Technology of Guangxi (Grant no. 2021AB20147), Guangxi Natural Science Foundation (Grant nos. 2022JJD170019 & 2021JJA170204 & 2021JJA170199) and Guangxi Science and Technology Base and Talents Special Project (Grant nos. 2021AC19354 & 2021AC19394) and by Guangxi Key Lab of Human-machine Interaction and Intelligent Decision, Guangxi Academy Sciences, and supported by Key Research and Development (Digital Twin) Program of Ningbo City under Grant No. 2023Z219, 2023Z226, and supported by the China Postdoctoral Science Foundation under Grant No. 2023M733400 (Corresponding author: De-Shuang Huang.)

References

1. Wang, G., et al.: DeepiGeoS: a deep interactive geodesic framework for medical image segmentation. IEEE Trans. Pattern Anal. Mach. Intell. **41**(7), 1559–1572 (2018). Author, F., Author, S.: Title of a proceedings paper. In: Editor, F., Editor, S. (eds.) CONFERENCE 2016, LNCS, vol. 9999, pp. 1–13. Springer, Heidelberg (2016)
2. Zaidi, H., El Naqa, I.: PET-guided delineation of radiation therapy treatment volumes: a survey of image segmentation techniques. Eur. J. Nucl. Med. Mol. Imaging **37**, 2165–2187 (2010)
3. Ronneberger, O., Fischer, P., Brox, T.: U-net: convolutional networks for biomedical image segmentation. In: Navab, N., Hornegger, J., Wells, W.M., Frangi, A.F. (eds.) MICCAI 2015, Part III. LNCS, vol. 9351, pp. 234–241. Springer, Cham (2015). https://doi.org/10.1007/978-3-319-24574-4_28
4. Milletari, F., Navab, N., Ahmadi, S.A.: V-net: fully convolutional neural networks for volumetric medical image segmentation. In: 2016 Fourth International Conference on 3D Vision (3DV), pp. 565–571. IEEE (2016)
5. Isensee, F., Jaeger, P.F., Kohl, S.A.A., et al.: NnU-Net: a self-configuring method for deep learning-based biomedical image segmentation. Nat. Methods **18**(2), 203–211 (2021)
6. Roy, A.G., Siddiqui, S., Pölsterl, S., et al.: 'Squeeze & excite' guided few-shot segmentation of volumetric images. Med. Image Anal. **59**, 101587 (2020)
7. Ouyang, C., Biffi, C., Chen, C., et al.: Self-supervision with superpixels: training few-shot medical image segmentation without annotation. In: Vedaldi, A., Bischof, H., Brox, T., Frahm, J.M. (eds.) Computer Vision–ECCV 2020, Part XXIX, pp. 762–780. Springer, Cham (2020). https://doi.org/10.1007/978-3-030-58526-6_45
8. Hansen, S., Gautam, S., Jenssen, R., et al.: Anomaly detection-inspired few-shot medical image segmentation through self-supervision with supervoxels. Med. Image Anal. **78**, 102385 (2022)
9. Snell, J., Swersky, K., Zemel, R.: Prototypical networks for few-shot learning. In: Advances in Neural Information Processing Systems, vol. 30 (2017)

10. Iqbal, E., Safarov, S., Bang, S.: MSANet: multi-similarity and attention guidance for boosting few-shot segmentation. arXiv preprint arXiv:2206.09667 (2022)
11. Feng, Y., Wang, Y., Li, H., et al.: Learning what and where to segment: a new perspective on medical image few-shot segmentation. Med. Image Anal. **87**, 102834 (2023)
12. Sung, F., Yang, Y., Zhang, L., et al.: Learning to compare: relation network for few-shot learning. In: Proceedings of the IEEE Conference on Computer Vision and Pattern Recognition, pp. 1199–1208 (2018)
13. Finn, C., Abbeel, P., Levine, S.: Model-agnostic meta-learning for fast adaptation of deep networks. In: International Conference on Machine Learning, PMLR, pp. 1126–1135 (2017)
14. Jamal, M.A., Qi, G.J.: Task agnostic meta-learning for few-shot learning. In: Proceedings of the IEEE/CVF Conference on Computer Vision and Pattern Recognition, pp. 11719–11727 (2019)
15. Ravi, S., Larochelle, H.: Optimization as a model for few-shot learning. In: International Conference on Learning Representations (2016)
16. Chen, Z., Fu, Y., Wang, Y.X., et al.: Image deformation meta-networks for one-shot learning. In: Proceedings of the IEEE/CVF Conference on Computer Vision and Pattern Recognition, pp. 8680–8689 (2019)
17. Chen, Z., Fu, Y., Chen, K., et al.: Image block augmentation for one-shot learning. In: Proceedings of the AAAI Conference on Artificial Intelligence, vol. 33, no. 01, pp. 3379–3386 (2019)
18. Zhao, A., Balakrishnan, G., Durand, F., et al.: Data augmentation using learned transformations for one-shot medical image segmentation. In: Proceedings of the IEEE/CVF Conference on Computer Vision and Pattern Recognition, pp. 8543–8553 (2019)
19. Wang, K., Liew, J.H., Zou, Y., et al.: PANet: few-shot image semantic segmentation with prototype alignment. In: Proceedings of the IEEE/CVF International Conference on Computer Vision, pp. 9197–9206 (2019)
20. Sun, L., Li, C., Ding, X., et al.: Few-shot medical image segmentation using a global correlation network with discriminative embedding. Comput. Biol. Med. **140**, 105067 (2022)
21. Feng, R., Zheng, X., Gao, T., et al.: Interactive few-shot learning: limited supervision, better medical image segmentation. IEEE Trans. Med. Imaging **40**(10), 2575–2588 (2021)
22. Wu, H., Xiao, F., Liang, C.: Dual contrastive learning with anatomical auxiliary supervision for few-shot medical image segmentation. In: Avidan, S., Brostow, G., Cissé, M., Farinella, G.M., Hassner, T. (eds.) ECCV 2022. LNCS, vol. 13680, pp. 417–434. Springer, Cham (2022). https://doi.org/10.1007/978-3-031-20044-1_24
23. Shen, Q., Li, Y., Jin, J., et al.: Q-net: query-informed few-shot medical image segmentation. arXiv preprint arXiv:2208.11451 (2022)
24. Tang, H., Liu, X., Sun, S., et al.: Recurrent mask refinement for few-shot medical image segmentation. In: Proceedings of the IEEE/CVF International Conference on Computer Vision, pp. 3918–3928 (2021)
25. He, K., Zhang, X., Ren, S., et al.: Deep residual learning for image recognition. In: Proceedings of the IEEE Conference on Computer Vision and Pattern Recognition, pp. 770–778 (2016)
26. Kavur, A.E., Gezer, N.S., Barış, M., Aslan, S., Conze, P.-H., et al.: CHAOS challenge - combined (CT-MR) healthy abdominal organ segmentation. Med. Image Anal. **69**, 101950 (2021)
27. Bennett, L., Xu, Z., Eugenio, I.J., Martin, S., Robin, L.T., Arno, K.: MICCAI multi-atlas labeling beyond the cranial vault–workshop and challenge (2015)
28. Zhuang, X.: Multivariate mixture model for cardiac segmentation from multi-sequence MRI. In: Ourselin, S., Joskowicz, L., Sabuncu, M.R., Unal, G., Wells, W. (eds.) MICCAI 2016. LNCS, vol. 9901, pp. 581–588. Springer, Cham (2016). https://doi.org/10.1007/978-3-319-46723-8_67

Staphylococcus Aureus Function Proteins Classification with Time Series Forest

Qi Wang, Luying He, Mingzhi Song$^{(\boxtimes)}$, and Wenzheng Bao$^{(\boxtimes)}$

School of Information and Engineering, Xuzhou University of Technology, Xuzhou 221018, China
wwwsongmz@163.com, baowz55555@126.com

Abstract. Oral microbial communities play different roles in systemic human physiology. The oral microbial community is a dynamic system, and its composition and structure will be affected by many factors. In this work, we proposed a method to classify the active function site of a kind of oral microorganism, which is Staphylococcus aureus. We employed the time series forest method to classify the active function of Staphylococcus aureus. In order to test the performances of this algorithm, we utilized several typical features in this work.

Keywords: Staphylococcus aureus · time series forest · classification · oral microorganism

1 Introduction

The human oral cavity is a natural gathering place of microbial ecology. The oral cavity presents a series of substrates, such as teeth, tongue, cheeks, and gums, whose chemical properties, morphology, and stability provide different habitats for microbial communities [1]. Each habitat in the mouth supports a complex and unique community. This uniqueness provides an opportunity to use the oral microbiome to understand the microbial community. The oral cavity is one of the human body's most complex and abundant microbial communities. There are thousands of microorganisms in the mouth. Bacteria are the most common type of oral microorganisms. They form communities and ecosystems and maintain a symbiotic relationship with the human body for a long time. Most oral bacteria are non-pathogenic symbionts, which help maintain oral health and maintain oral ecological balance. However, some bacterial strains are pathogenic bacteria, which cause oral diseases, such as bad breath [2], dental caries and periodontal disease. Oral microbial community not only affects oral health and disease, but also affects the health and infection of the whole body [3], including adverse pregnancy [4], and leukemia [5].

Moreover, oral microbial communities play different roles in systemic human physiology. The oral microbial community is a dynamic system, and its composition and structure will be affected by many factors [6]. Daily oral hygiene habits, eating habits, antibiotic use, and oral diseases will have different degrees of impact on the microbial

D.-S. Huang et al. (Eds.): ICAI 2023, CCIS 2014, pp. 34–41, 2024.
https://doi.org/10.1007/978-981-97-0903-8_4

community. It is worth noting that the normal microbial community has specific stability and resilience, can resist external interference, and maintain a relatively stable state. Understanding the ecological characteristics of oral microorganisms is very important for maintaining oral health. By studying the composition and function of microbial communities, we can develop prevention and treatment strategies for oral diseases. In addition, the study of oral microbial ecology also provides new ideas and possibilities for individualized medical treatment and oral microbial regulation. Personalized oral medicine can be achieved through an in-depth understanding of the characteristics and changes of individual oral microorganisms. Oral microorganisms can be used as unique biomarkers for early diagnosis of oral diseases, predicting the risk of disease progression and guiding the formulation of individualized treatment.

The human oral microbiome database (HOMD) is the first database systematically describing human-related microbiomes established by Dewhirst et al. in 2010. Currently, the database includes 687 species of oral microorganisms, of which 461 have been annotated, and their protein sequences are obtained by 16S RNA sequencing. This database is a typical sequence database for oral macroproteome research. In recent years, with the development of macroproteomics, some research achievements have been made in protein data analysis, and researchers have developed many bioinformatics analysis tools. However, these tools are suitable for different application scenarios. Graph2pep/graph2pro and compile focus on customizing the protein database to obtain the best protein identification. Proteostorm is an efficient database search framework for large-scale proteomics research. It can identify peptide spectrum match (PSM) with high reliability and achieve acceleration of two to three orders of magnitude higher than popular tools. Unipept, prophane, Megan CE, and pipasic realized taxonomic analysis, functional data evaluation, and protein grouping, respectively. In addition, several research teams have assembled comprehensive software workflow for proteomic analysis, such as Galaxy-p, meta Pro IQ, meta proteome analyzer (MPA), and other workflows.

In this work, we proposed a method to classify the active function site of a kind of oral microorganism, which is Staphylococcus aureus. We employed the time series forest method to classify the active function of Staphylococcus aureus. In order to test the performances of this algorithm, we utilized several typical features in this work..

2   Methods and Materials

2.1   Data

The benchmark dataset for this experiment is obtained from protein specific websites through crawling to obtain the corresponding organelle sequences and characteristic sites https://www.uniprot.org. This dataset contains the biological sequences of one oral microorganism, with a specific sample size of 1063 Staphylococcus aureus. Then, active site data were extracted, and feature extraction was performed. By selecting appropriate feature extraction methods, the corresponding indicators can be more accurately represented, providing a reliable data foundation for subsequent classification accuracy. In previous studies, it was found that feature extraction mainly focused on the functional sites of microbial sequence sites, taking into account the auto-correlation of the sequence directed by this site, including extraction methods.

In order to preserve as much information as possible, we use the entire oral microbial protein sequence as feature extraction data. We used several feature extraction methods. The protein sequences can be transfer as a numeric vector. Meanwhile, we put the label in the end of each vector. In this classification model, the function protein can be defined as the positive sample and the non-function protein can be defined as the negative ones.

In this work, we employed several features including Auto covariance (AC), Cross covariance (CC), Auto-cross covariance (ACC), Physicochemical distance transformation (PDT), Parallel correlation pseudo amino acid composition (PC-PseAAC), Series correlation pseudo amino acid composition (SC-PseAAC), General parallel correlation pseudo amino acid composition (PC-PseAAC-General), and General series correlation pseudo amino acid composition (SC-PseAAC-General). In this section, we introduce the PC-PseAAC features.

2.2 PC PseAAC

When it comes to the feature of PC PseAAC, this feature is a method that combines continuous local sequence order information and global sequence order information to convert protein sequences.

2.3 Classification Model

Time series forest (TSF) is a machine learning model for time series classification, which belongs to a kind of ensemble learning method. It is based on the idea of integrated learning of random forest, uses multiple decision trees to build a classification model, and has a special design for time series data [9].

Time series tree is the key component of constructing time series forest. It is responsible for deciding how to segment the nodes in the tree to achieve the best segmentation method. Each node in the time series tree considers some candidate splits (called s) to meet specific segmentation conditions, which can be used to help determine the optimal segmentation method. This process aims to ensure that the segmentation of each tree node is based on effective segmentation criteria, so as to obtain accurate and reliable results in the time series forest, shown in Eq. (1).

$$f_k(t_1, t_2) \leq \tau \tag{1}$$

Instances that meet this condition will be sent to the left child node. Others are sent to the right child node.

Considering the particularity of time series data, we use a different strategy to select the segmentation point of nodes in the process of building time series tree [10]. Compared with directly selecting a single best segmentation point, we first consider the weight of time steps, and select a series of possible segmentation points on the node. Then, we calculate the prediction accuracy of each candidate segmentation point. Finally, the best performing segmentation point is selected from these candidate segmentation points as the final segmentation point of the node. This method aims to better adapt to the characteristics of time series data and improve the performance and accuracy of time series tree.

For the candidate threshold of a specific type of feature f_k, $[\min_{n-1}^{N}(f_k^n(t_1, t_2)), \max_{n=1}^{N}(f_k^n(t_1, t_2))]$ is divided into equal width intervals. The number of candidate thresholds is fixed. Then select the best threshold from these candidate thresholds to avoid sorting, and only K tests are required f_k.

In addition, a splitting criterion is needed to define the optimal splitting $S^*: f_*(t_1^*, t_2^*) \leq \tau^*$. We use the combination of entropy gain and distance measure as the splitting criterion [12]. Entropy gain is a common segmentation criterion in tree model. Represents the proportion of instances corresponding to class $\{1, 2, \ldots, c\}$ on a tree node, which are respectively represented as $\{\gamma_1, \gamma_2, \ldots, \gamma_C\}$. The entropy at this node is defined in Eq. (2)

$$Entropy = -\sum_{c=1}^{C} \gamma_C \log \gamma_C \tag{2}$$

Entropy gain is used to determine the effectiveness of a partition. It represents the difference between the weighted sum of the entropy of the child node and the entropy of the parent node. Here, the weight of a child node refers to the proportion of instances assigned to the child node. In addition, we should also consider the additional metric of margin, which calculates the distance between the candidate threshold and its nearest eigenvalue $f_k(t_1, t_2) \leq \tau$. Margin is calculated in Eq. (3)

$$M \arg in = \min_{n-1,2,\ldots,N} \left| f_k^n(t_1, t_2) - \tau \right| \tag{3}$$

Where $f_k^n(t_1, t_2)$, is the value of $f_k(t_1, t_2)$ of the nth instance on the node. A new splitting criterion E is the entrance (entropy and distance) gain, and the formula is in Eq. (4).

$$E = \Delta \, Entropy + \alpha \cdot M \arg in \tag{4}$$

If α is small enough, its role in the model is to break the connection that may be generated only from the entropy gain. Or you can store the values of Δ Entropy and margin. When another partition has the same entropy, use margin to break the connection. Obviously, we use the segmentation with the maximum E to segment nodes. In addition, margin and E are sensitive to the scale of features. For different types of features with different scales, we adopt the following strategy. In order to select the best segmentation for different feature types, we will give priority to the segmentation method with maximum entropy. However, if the best segmentation of different feature types has the same maximum entropy, we will randomly select one of them as the best segmentation. This strategy aims to ensure a fair and orderly comparison among multiple feature types, while handling the case of equal maximum entropy to avoid arbitrary selection.

This modified decision tree construction method can better consider the temporal characteristics of time series data, make the decision tree better adapt to the changes and trends of time series data, and improve the classification performance.

2.4 Performances

In the classification of function protein of Staphylococcus aureus, it is an essential step to select appropriate evaluation indexes to evaluate the performance of the model. The non-function protein can be defined as the negative sample and the function protein can be defined as the positive ones in this work. In this experiment, accuracy (ACC), Recall, specificity (SP), and MCC score are utilized in this work. The calculation methods are shown in Eq. (5)–(8).

$$Sp = \frac{TN}{TN + FP} \tag{5}$$

$$Recall = \frac{TP}{TP + FN} \tag{6}$$

$$Acc = \frac{TP + TN}{TP + TN + FP + FN} \tag{7}$$

$$MCC = \frac{TP \times TN - FP \times FN}{\sqrt{(TP + FP) \times (TP + FN) \times (TN + FP) \times (TN + FP)}} \tag{8}$$

Where, P and N represent the scale of positive and negative samples, respectively. T and F represent sets of true and false predicted results, respectively.

3 Results

As the demonstration in Table 1, the values of Sp, Acc, Rcall and MCC, for the AC feature were 43.85%, 47.71%, 43.82%, and 0.3352, respectively, while the values of these indices for the ACC were 48.55%, 48.41%, 48.53% and 0.3616, respectively.

Tabel 1. The performances of different methods

method	SP	Acc	Recall	MCC
AC	43.85%	47.71%	43.82%	0.3352
ACC	48.55%	48.41%	48.53%	0.3616
ACC-PSSM	68.05%	59.66%	68.04%	0.5446
AC-PSSM	68.05%	59.66%	68.04%	0.5446
CC	48.85%	44.50%	48.86%	0.3338
CC-PSSM	68.05%	59.66%	68.04%	0.5446
DP	63.05%	62.31%	63.04%	0.5355
DR	59.40%	66.23%	59.36%	0.5424
DT	68.05%	59.66%	68.04%	0.5446
PC-PseAAC	68.05%	59.66%	68.04%	0.5446
PC-PseAAC-General	68.05%	59.66%	68.04%	0.5446
PDT-Profile	68.05%	59.66%	68.04%	0.5446
SC-PseAAC	60.30%	59.36%	60.27%	0.5018
SC-PseAAC-General	60.30%	59.36%	60.27%	0.5018
TOP-N-GRAM	68.05%	59.66%	68.04%	0.5446

The values of Sp, Acc, Rcall and MCC for the ACC-PSSM were 68.05%, 59.66%, 68.04% and 0.5446, respectively, while the values of these indices for the AC-PSSM were 68.05%, 59.66%, 68.04%, and 0.5446, respectively. The values of Sp, Acc, Rcall and MCC, for the CC feature were 48.85%, 44.50%, 48.86%, and 0.3338, respectively, while the values of these indices for the CC-PSSM were 68.05%, 59.66%, 68.04%, and 0.5446, respectively. The values of Sp, Acc, Rcall and MCC for the DP were 63.05%, 62.31%, 63.04%, and 0.5355, respectively, while the values of these indices for the DR were 59.40%, 66.23%, 59.36%, and 0.5424, respectively. The values of Sp, Acc, Rcall and MCC, for the DT feature were 68.05%, 59.66%, 68.04%, and 0.5446, respectively, while the values of these indices for the PC-PseAAC, PC-PseAAC-General, TOP-N-GRAM, and PDT-Profile were 68.05%, 59.66%, 68.04%, and 0.5446, respectively. The values of Sp, Acc, Rcall and MCC for the SC-PseAAC, and SC-PseAAC-General were 60.30%, 59.36%, 60.27%, and 0.5018, respectively.

4 Conclusions

In this work, we proposed a method to classify the active function site of a kind of oral microorganism, which is Staphylococcus aureus. We employed the time series forest method to classify the active function of Staphylococcus aureus. In order to test the performances of this algorithm, we utilized several typical features in this work.

Some issues should be considers in the future work. First of all, some useful features should be used in such classification issue. The effective features may improve the performances of classification model. Secondly, some high effective classification algorithms should be utilized in such classification issue. With the development of artificial intelligence, several methods, including deep learning, transfer learning and other related ones, have been proposed.

Acknowledgments. This work was supported by the National Natural Science Foundation of China (Grant No. 61902337), Xuzhou Science and Technology Plan Project (KC21047), Jiangsu Provincial Natural Science Foundation (No. SBK2019040953), Natural Science Fund for Colleges and Universities in Jiangsu Province (No. 19KJB520016) and Young Talents of Science and Technology in Jiangsu and ghfund 202302026465.

References

1. Yang, W., et al.: A brief survey of machine learning methods in protein sub-Golgi localization. Curr. Bioinform. **14**(3), 234–240 (2019)
2. Su, R., Yang, H., Wei, L., Chen, S., Zou, Q.: A multi-label learning model for predicting drug-induced pathology in multi-organ based on toxicogenomics data. PLoS Comput. Biol. **18**(9), e1010402 (2022)
3. Wang, C., Zou, Q.: Prediction of protein solubility based on sequence physicochemical patterns and distributed representation information with DeepSoluE. BMC Biol. **21**(1), 1–11 (2023)
4. Gonatas, N.K., Gonatas, J.O., Stieber, A.: The involvement of the Golgiapparatus in the pathogenesis of amyotrophic lateral sclerosis, Alzheimer's disease, and ricin intoxication. Histochem. Cell Biol. **109**(5–6), 591–600 (1998)

5. Elsberry, D.D., Rise, M.T.: Techniques for treating neuro degenerative disorders by infusion of nerve growth factors into the brain, U.S. Patents US6042579A, 5 August 1998
6. Yuan, L., Guo, F., Wang, L., Zou, Q.: Prediction of tumor metastasis from sequencing data in the era of genome sequencing. Brief. Funct. Genomics 18(6), 412–418 (2019)
7. Hummer, B.H., Maslar, D., Gutierrez, M.S., de Leeuw, N.F., Asensio, C.S.: Differential sorting behavior for soluble and transmembrane cargoes at the trans-Golgi network in endocrine cells. Mol. Biol. Cell, mbc-E19 (2020)
8. Zeng, X., Liu, L., Lü, L., Zou, Q.: Prediction of potential disease-associated microRNAs using structural perturbation method. Bioinformatics 34(14), 2425–2432 (2018)
9. Villeneuve, J., Duran, J., Scarpa, M., Bassaganyas, L., Van Galen, J., Malhotra, V.: Golgi enzymes do not cycle through the endoplasmic reticulum during protein secretion or mitosis. Mol. Biol. Cell 28(1), 141–151 (2017)
10. Hou, Y., Dai, J., He, J., Niemi, A.J., Peng, X., Ilieva, N.: Intrinsic protein geometry with application to non-proline cis peptide planes. J. Math. Chem. 57(1), 263–279 (2019)
11. Wei, L., Xing, P., Tang, J., Zou, Q.: PhosPred-RF: a novel sequence-based predictor for phosphorylation sites using sequential information only. IEEE Trans. Nano Biosci. 16(4), 240–247 (2017)
12. van Dijk, A.D.J., et al.: Predicting sub-Golgi localization of type II membrane proteins. Bioinformatics 24(16), 1779–1786 (2008)
13. Ding, H., et al.: Identify Golgi protein types with modified mahalanobis discriminant algorithm and pseudo amino acid composition. Protein Pept. Lett. 18(1), 58–63 (2011)
14. Ding, H., et al.: Prediction of Golgi-resident protein types by using feature selection technique. Chem. Intell. Lab. Syst. 124, 9–13 (2013)
15. Jiao, Y.-S., Du, P.-F.: Predicting Golgi-resident protein types using pseudo amino acid compositions: approaches with positional specific physicochemical properties. J. Theor. Biol. 391, 35–42 (2016)
16. Jiao, Y.-S., Pu-Feng, D.: Prediction of Golgi-resident protein types using general form of Chou's pseudo-amino acid compositions: approaches with minimal redundancy maximal relevance feature selection. J. Theor. Biol. 402, 38–44 (2016)
17. Lv, Z., et al.: A random forest sub-Golgi protein classifier optimized via dipeptide and amino acid composition features. Front. Bioeng. Biotechnol. 7, 215 (2019)
18. Wei, L., Zhou, C., Su, R., Zou, Q.: PEPred-Suite: improved and robust prediction of therapeutic peptides using adaptive feature representation learning. Bioinformatics 35(21), 4272–4280 (2019)
19. Chawla, N.V., Bowyer, K.W., Hall, L.O., Kegelmeyer, W.P.: SMOTE: synthetic minority over-sampling technique. J. Artif. Intell. Res. 16(1), 321–357 (2002)
20. Blagus, R., Lusa, L.: 'SMOTE for high-dimensional class-imbalanced data.' BMC Bioinf. 14(1), 106 (2013)
21. Díez-Pastor, J.F., Rodríguez, J.J., García-Osorio, C., Kuncheva, L.I.: Random balance: ensembles of variable priors classifiers for imbalanced data. Knowl.-Based Syst. 85, 96–111 (2015)
22. Ma, L., Fan, S.: CURE-SMOTE algorithm and hybrid algorithm for feature selection and parameter optimization based on random forests. BMC Bioinf. 18(1), 169 (2017)
23. Cateni, S., Colla, V., Vannucci, M.: A method for resampling imbalanced datasets in binary classification tasks for real-world problems. Neurocomputing 135, 32–41 (2014)
24. Sáez, J.A., Luengo, J., Stefanowski, J., Herrera, F.: SMOTE–IPF: addressing the noisy and borderline examples problem in imbalanced classification by a re-sampling method with filtering. Inf. Sci. 291, 184–203 (2015)
25. Nath, A., Subbiah, K.: Unsupervised learning assisted robust prediction of bioluminescent proteins. Comput. Biol. Med. 68, 27–36 (2016)

26. Wang, X.Y., Yu, B., Ma, A.J., Chen, C., Liu, B.Q., Ma, Q.: Protein– protein interaction sites prediction by ensemble random forests with synthetic minority oversampling technique. Bioinformatics **35**(14), 2395–2402 (2019)
27. Pedregosa, F., et al.: Scikit-learn: machine learning in Python. J. Mach. Learn. Res. **12**, 2825–2830 (2011)
28. Zeng, X., Lin, W., Guo, M., Zou, Q.: A comprehensive overview and evaluation of circular RNA detection tools. PLoS Comput. Biol. **13**(6) (2017). Art. no. e1005420
29. Wei, L., Xing, P., Su, R., Shi, G., Ma, Z.S., Zou, Q.: CPPred–RF: a sequence-based predictor for identifying cell–penetrating peptides and their uptake efficiency. J. Proteome Res. **16**(5), 2044–2053 (2017)
30. Wei, L., Xing, P., Zeng, J., Chen, J., Su, R., Guo, F.: Improved prediction of protein–protein interactions using novel negative samples, features, and an ensemble classifier. Artif. Intell. Med. **83**, 67–74 (2017)
31. Hu, Y., Zhao, T., Zhang, N., Zang, T., Zhang, J., Cheng, L.: Identifying diseases-related metabolites using random walk. BMC Bioinf. **19**(S5), 116 (2018)
32. Zhang, M., et al.: MULTiPly: a novel multi-layer predictor for discovering general and specific types of promoters. Bioinformatics **35**(17), 2957–2965 (2019)
33. Song, T., Rodriguez-Paton, A., Zheng, P., Zeng, X.: Spiking neural P systems with colored spikes. IEEE Trans. Cogn. Devel. Syst. **10**(4), 1106–1115 (2018)
34. Lin, X., Quan, Z., Wang, Z.-J., Huang, H., Zeng, X.: A novel molecular representation with BiGRU neural networks for learning atom. Brief. Bioinf. (2019). Art. no. bbz125
35. Zhou, Z.H., Feng, J.: Deep forest. Natl. Sci. Rev. **6**(1), 74–86 (2019)
36. Lee, S.C., Kwon, Y.S., Son, K.H., et al.: Antioxidative constituents from Paeonia lactiflora. Arch. Pharmacal. Res. **28**, 775–783 (2005)

Bradyrhizobium Elkanii's Genes Classification with SVM

Luying He[1], Qi Wang[1], Wenzheng Bao[1], Zhuo Wang[1(✉)], and Xiangwen Ji[2(✉)]

[1] School of Information and Engineering, Xuzhou University of Technology, Xuzhou 221018, China
77837292@qq.com
[2] London Metropolitan University, London, England
2728782894@qq.com

Abstract. The oral cavity is one of the five major human parts that the human microbiome. Microorganisms are a group of tiny, invisible organisms, which must be magnified thousands or even tens of thousands of times to be observed. Bradyrhizobium elkanii's is one of the most significant oral microorganisms. In this work, we focus on the classification of Bradyrhizobium elkanii's coding genes and non-coding ones. We selected the whole genome information from the web resource. And then, we extracted the coding genes and the non-coding genes. We employed the enhanced nucleic acid composition as the features and we utilized the linear SVM as the classification model.

Keywords: Bradyrhizobium elkanii · Support Vector Machine · Classification · Coding Genes

1 Introduction

Microorganisms are a group of tiny, invisible organisms, which must be magnified thousands or even tens of thousands of times to be observed. Among the many characteristics of microorganisms, the most amazing is that they have extremely diverse physiological functions and can survive in various environments. Generally, microorganisms are divided into fungi, actinomycetes, bacteria, spirochetes, Rickettsia, chlamydia, mycoplasma and viruses. However, with the continuous discovery of new microorganisms, the species are still increasing. The types of viruses (such as influenza virus and hepatitis virus) account for 75% of all kinds of pathogens causing human infectious diseases. Actinomycetes are the main source of antibiotics and microbial drugs. Serious human and animal diseases caused by bacteria still occupy a very important position. According to the prediction of the World Health Organization, without effective prevention and control measures, 30million people will die of tuberculosis and 300million people will be infected by tuberculosis in the world within 10 years.

The oral cavity is one of the five major human parts (gut, oral cavity, skin, nasal cavity and genitourinary tract) that the human microbiome program focuses on. The human oral microbial community is composed of morethan 700 species of bacteria,

D.-S. Huang et al. (Eds.): ICAI 2023, CCIS 2014, pp. 42–48, 2024.
https://doi.org/10.1007/978-981-97-0903-8_5

fungi, viruses and other microorganisms. The ecological imbalance of oral microorganisms can not only induce a variety of oral diseases (such as caries, pulp periapical disease, periodontal disease, etc.), but also is closely related to systemic diseases such as tumors, diabetes, rheumatoid arthritis, cardiovascular disease, premature birth, and has a great impact on human health. With the development of high-throughput technology, the use of multi omics data technology to study the composition of oral microbial community has become popular. In particular, genomic technology, periodontitis and the composition of oral microorganisms in healthy people have been widely reported, and some disease-related microorganisms have been found. With the development of mass spectrometry technology, oral genome research has become a new field. People have used this technology to study the correlation between bacterial composition and the incidence of dental caries, and found oral microorganisms used to distinguish periodontitis, dental caries and normal people.

The research platform of bioinformatics is generally composed of computer network, database and application analysis software. The use technology of various databases and related software is the core of bioinformatics. Among them, gene bank nucleic acid sequence database, Swiss prot protein sequence database and biomacromolecule spatial structure database are the three core databases of molecular biology; Blast and FASTA sequence alignment software are common information retrieval tools. Bioinformatics is widely used in various fields of life science research. Its major theories and technical methods are also being or gradually applied in many fields of biomedical research, mainly including: key gene identification of major diseases, epidemiological research, drug design, etc. In the field of Stomatology, bioinformatics is effectively applied in the research of genomics and proteomics, which is helpful to identify and describe the influencing factors and therapeutic targets of diseases related to stomatology at the molecular level. The technologies used in the research mainly include database retrieval, data software analysis, differential proteomics technology, DNA chip, etc. Its main application research fields include the growth and development of teeth, oral tumor and disease research, oral microorganism and saliva analysis research, etc.

In this work, we focus on the classification of Bradyrhizobium elkanii's coding genes and non-coding ones. We selected the whole genome information from the web resource. And then, we extracted the coding genes and the non-coding genes. We employed the enhanced nucleic acid composition as the features and we utilized the linear SVM as the classification model.

2   Methods and Materials

2.1   Data

In this work, the whole genome information of Bradyrhizobium elkanii's collected from the NCBI, which is a famous biology data in the world. With the data procession, we can easily find that there are 9728 coding genes sequences and 8252 non-coding gene ones in the Bradyrhizobium elkanii's whole genome sequences. And then, we selected the 20 length nucleic acid segment in the head section and 20 length nucleic acid segment in the end section for both the coding sequences and the non-coding sequences. Therefore, we constructed a 40 length nucleic acid segment for each sample.

2.2 Support Vector Machine

SVM was proposed in 1964, and developed rapidly after the 1990s. A series of improved and extended algorithms have been derived, which have been applied in pattern recognition problems such as portrait recognition and text classification. Support vector machine (SVM) is a class of generalized linear classifiers that classify data in a supervised learning way. Its decision boundary is the maximum margin hyperplane for the learning samples. SVM uses hinge loss function to calculate empirical risk and adds regularization term to the solution system to optimize structural risk. It is a sparse and robust classifier. SVM is one of the common kernel learning methods, which can carry out nonlinear classification through kernel method. SVM is a classifier developed from the generalized portrait algorithm in pattern recognition. Its early work came from the research published by Vladimir n. Vapnik and Alexander y. Lerner in 1963. In 1964, Vapnik and Alexey y y. chervonenkis further discussed the generalized portrait algorithm and established a hard margin linear SVM. Since then, in the 1970s and 1980s, with the theoretical research on the maximum margin decision boundary in pattern recognition, the emergence of planning problem solving technology based on slack variable, and the proposal of VC dimension, SVM has been gradually theorized and become a part of statistical learning theory. In 1992, Bernhard E. Boser, Isabelle M. Guyon and Vapnik obtained nonlinear SVM through kernel method. In 1995, Corinna Cortes and Vapnik proposed soft margin nonlinear SVM and applied it to handwritten character recognition. This research has been paid attention to and cited since its publication, providing a reference for the application of SVM in various fields.

For the linear SVM, this is a typical type in the field of SVM and its function shown in Fig. 1.

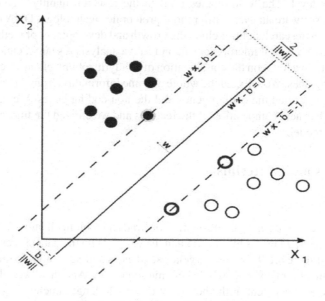

Fig. 1. The function of linear SVM

Form Fig. 1, all the sample should be followed in Eq. (1).

$$\omega * x + b = 0 \tag{1}$$

Such formulation also can be utilized in the high dimensional space. It can be defined as the hyperplane. The distance between each to the hyperplane can be defined in Eq. (2).

$$d = \frac{|\omega * x + b|}{\|\omega\|} \tag{2}$$

With the formulation (2), each sample can be classified as different types, shown in Eq. (3).

$$y_i(\omega * x_i + b) \geq 1 \tag{3}$$

Where, i means i-th sample in this classification issue.

2.3 Enhanced Nucleic Acid Composition (ENAC)

When it comes to the Enhanced nucleic acid composition, this feature has ability to demonstrate the frequency of each nucleotide acid occurring within a window length, which slides the head segment and the end segment of each sample.

2.4 Evaluation Metrics and Methods

In the classification of coding genes and non-coding genes of Bradyrhizobium elkanii, it is an essential step to select appropriate evaluation indexes to evaluate the performance of the model. The non-coding genes can be defined as the negative sample and the coding genes can be defined as the positive ones in this work. In this experiment, accuracy (ACC), precision, recall, and F1 score are utilized in this work. The calculation method is as follows in Eq. (4)–(7)

$$precision = \frac{TP}{TP + FP} \tag{4}$$

$$recall = \frac{TP}{TP + FN} \tag{5}$$

$$ACC = \frac{TP + TN}{TP + FN + TN + FP} \tag{6}$$

$$F1 - score = \frac{2 \times TP}{2 \times TP + FN + FP} \tag{7}$$

Where, P and N represent the scale of positive and negative samples, respectively. T and F represent sets of true and false predicted results, respectively.

3   Result and Discussions

In this section, we utilized the linear SVM model to classify coding genes and non-coding genes of Bradyrhizobium elkanii. There are 8252 non-coding gene sequences, which is the negative samples. At the same time, there are 9728 coding gene sequences, which is the positive samples. Therefore, it can be defined as a typical balance classification issue in the field of machine learning. In the first step, we employed the whole profile features to classify with the linear SVM. In order to compare with the performances, some typical machine learning methods, including logistic, KNN, tree construction classification model, have been utilized in this work.

Table 1. The performances of linear SVM and other methods

	Sn	Sp	Acc	F1
Tree	90.37%	94.65%	92.51%	0.9235
Tree Media	85.89%	94.95%	90.42%	0.8996
Tree Rough	82.20%	93.37%	87.78%	0.8706
KNN	71.25%	80.32%	75.79%	0.7464
KNN Media	73.38%	93.08%	83.23%	0.8140
KNN Rough	66.10%	98.91%	82.51%	0.7907
KNN Cosine	84.23%	73.90%	79.06%	0.8009
Logitic	87.90%	92.53%	90.22%	0.8999
Linear SVM	95.19%	98.32%	96.75%	0.9670

From the Table 1, we can find that the values of Sn, Sp, Acc, and F1 score, for the Tree construction classification method were 90.37%, 94.65%, 92.51%, and 0.9235, respectively. Meanwhile, the values of these indices for the Tree Media construction classification model were 85.89%, 94.95%, 90.42%, and 0.8996, respectively. For the Tree Rough construction classification method's performances were 82.2% in Sn, 93.37% in Sp, 87.78% in Acc, and 0.8706 in F1, respectively. The values of the four indices for the KNN were 71.25%, 80.32%, 75.79%, and 0.7464, respectively. The KNN Rough performances are 66.1% in Sn, 98.91% in Sp, and 82.51% in Acc, and 0.7907 in F1 score. The values of the four indices for the KNN Cosine were 84.235%, 73.9%, 79.06%, and 0.8009, respectively. The Logistic classification method's performances were 87.9% in Sn, 92.53% in Sp, 90.22% in Acc, and 0.8999 in F1, respectively. And the linear SVM's performances are 95.19% in Sn, 98.32% in Sp, 96.75% in Acc, and 0.967 in F1 score. The ROC curve of linear SVM show in Fig. 2

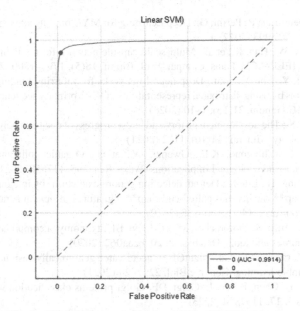

Fig. 2. The ROC curve of Linear SVM with ENAC feature

4 Conclusion

During this work, we classifies Bradyrhizobium elkanii's coding genes and non-coding ones. We selected the whole genome information from NCBI. And then, we extracted the coding genes and the non-coding genes. We employed the enhanced nucleic acid composition as the features and we utilized the linear SVM as the classification model. In the future work, some effective features should be utilized to deal with the classification of coding genes and non-coding genes.

Acknowledgments. This work was supported by the National Natural Science Foundation of China (Grant No. 61902337), Xuzhou Science and Technology Plan Project (KC21047), Jiangsu Provincial Natural Science Foundation (No. SBK2019040953), Natural Science Fund for Colleges and Universities in Jiangsu Province (No. 19KJB520016) and Young Talents of Science and Technology in Jiangsu and ghfund 202302026465.

References

1. Hutin, S., Blanc-Mathieu, R., Rieu, P., et al.: Identification of plant transcription factor DNA-binding sites using seq-DAP-seq. In: Kaufmann, K., Mueller-Roeber, B. (eds.) Plant Gene Regulatory Networks: Methods and Protocols, pp. 119–145. Springer, New York (2023). https://doi.org/10.1007/978-1-0716-3354-0_9
2. Li, M., Huang, S.S.C.: DNA affinity purification sequencing (DAP-Seq) for map** genome-wide transcription factor binding sites in plants. In: Accelerated Breeding of Cereal Crops, pp. 293–303 (2022)

3. Fioresi, R., Demurtas, P., Perini, G.: Deep Learning for MYC binding site recognition. Front. Bioinform. **2**, 1015993 (2022)
4. Zhang, Q., Yu, W., Han, K., et al.: Multi-scale capsule network for predicting DNA-protein binding sites. IEEE/ACM Trans. Comput. Biol. Bioinf. **18**(5), 1793–1800 (2020)
5. Deng, L., Liu, Y., Shi, Y., et al.: Deep neural networks for inferring binding sites of RNA-binding proteins by using distributed representations of RNA primary sequence and secondary structure. BMC Genom. **21**(13), 1–10 (2020)
6. Kang, Y., Liu, S.: The development history and latest progress of deep-sea polymetallic nodule mining technology. Minerals **11**(10), 1132 (2021)
7. Sanganyado, E., Chingono, K.E., Gwenzi, W., et al.: Organic pollutants in deep sea: occurrence, fate, and ecological implications. Water Res. **205**, 117658 (2021)
8. Wang, X., Zhang, H., Liu, X.: Defind: detecting genomic deletions by integrating read depth, gc content, map** quality and paired-end map** signatures of next generation sequencing data. Curr. Bioinform. **14**(2), 130–138 (2019)
9. Schoch, C.L., Ciufo, S., Domrachev, M., et al.: NCBI Taxonomy: a comprehensive update on curation, resources and tools. Database **2020**, baaa062 (2020)
10. Yan, J., Xu, Y., Cheng, Q., et al.: LightGBM: accelerated genomically designed crop breeding through ensemble learning. Genome Biol. **22**, 1–24 (2021)
11. Bao, W., Gu, Y., Chen, B., et al.: Golgi_DF: Golgi proteins classification with deep forest. Front. Neurosci. **17**, 1197824 (2023)
12. Hu, P., Peng, D., Sang, Y., et al.: Multi-view linear discriminant analysis network. IEEE Trans. Image Process. **28**(11), 5352–5365 (2019)
13. Singh, G., Kumar, B., Gaur, L., et al.: Comparison between multinomial and Bernoulli naïve Bayes for text classification. In: 2019 International Conference on Automation, Computational and Technology Management (ICACTM), pp. 593–596. IEEE (2019)
14. Charbuty, B., Abdulazeez, A.: Classification based on decision tree algorithm for machine learning. J. Appl. Sci. Technol. Trends **2**(01), 20–28 (2021)
15. Speiser, J.L., Miller, M.E., Tooze, J., et al.: A comparison of random forest variable selection methods for classification prediction modeling. Expert Syst. Appl. **134**, 93–101 (2019)
16. Desai, M., Shah, M.: An anatomization on breast cancer detection and diagnosis employing multi-layer perceptron neural network (MLP) and Convolutional neural network (CNN). Clin. eHealth **4**, 1–11 (2021)

Oral Lichen Planus Classification
with SEResNet

Xiaojing Hu[1], Baitong Chen[2,3], Xueyan Yang[4], Wenzheng Bao[4(✉)],
and Hongchuang Zhang[1,2,3(✉)]

[1] School of Stomatology, Xuzhou Medical University, Xuzhou 221004, China
591426198@qq.com
[2] The Affiliated Xuzhou Municipal Hospital of Xuzhou Medical University, Xuzhou 221006,
China
[3] Department of Stomatology, Xuzhou First People's Hospital, Xuzhou 221006, China
[4] School of Information and Engineering, Xuzhou University of Technology, Xuzhou 221018,
China
baowz55555@126.com

Abstract. Oral lichen planus, which is classified as a precancerous state by the
World Health Organization (WHO), is one of the most dangerous disease in the
filed of oral health. Such disease poses a serious threat to oral health. In this work,
we focus on classification the oral lichen planus photos between pro-treatment
and post-treatment. We selected 67 pro-treatment patients' photos and 41 post-
treatment patients' photos. And then, we employed SEResNet model to classify these photos. In order to compare the performances of this model, we also
employed other two classification models, including ResNet, and DenseNet, in
this work.

Keywords: Oral lichen Planus · Classification · Pro-treatment and
Post-treatment · SEResNet

1 Introduction

Oral lichen planus is a common chronic inflammatory disease of oral mucosa. The
prevalence rate of this disease ranges from 0.1% to 4%. Meanwhile, the malignant
transformation rate ranges from 0 to 5.3%. Therefore, oral lichen planus is classified
as a precancerous state by the World Health Organization (WHO). This disease can
occur in multiple locations of the oral mucosa simultaneously, most commonly in the
buccal mucosa. The typical manifestations of this disease are reticular, striate, atrophy,
erosion, and congestion. It is also worth noting that oral lichen planus is a common
chronic oral mucosal skin disease. It is generally not infectious. The pathogenesis of
the disease is not completely clear. Current studies show that the pathogenesis of the
disease is related to mental factors, such as fatigue, anxiety, tension, immune factors,
endocrine factors, infection factors, microcirculation disorders, trace element deficiency,
and some complex diseases, including diabetes, infection, hypertension, gastrointestinal

D.-S. Huang et al. (Eds.): ICAI 2023, CCIS 2014, pp. 49–56, 2024.
https://doi.org/10.1007/978-981-97-0903-8_6

dysfunction. At present, there is no radical cure for the disease. The treatment of this disease mainly uses adrenocortical hormone drugs and immunosuppressants to reduce inflammation and promote healing. Although the above treatment methods have achieved specific curative effects, there are adverse conditions that the disease is easy to repeat, and long-term hormone treatment has noticeable side effects.

Although many researchers focus on semi-supervised and unsupervised learning to relieve the pressure on data annotation, compared with the fully supervised method, it is still difficult to obtain robust feature representation due to the lack of annotation information. Finally, in view of the characteristics of small-scale medical data sets and insufficient data volume, technologies such as generating confrontation networks and transfer learning are used to solve the problem of the insufficient number of small samples. Different types of medical data sets are fully used to realize multimodal learning combined with patients' cases, to solve the problem of the unbalanced proportion of positive and negative samples in medical images, and to use multicenter data. The problem of putting forward methods with stronger robustness and more generalization ability is also worth studying and solving. Due to the structural characteristics of medical images and the often unbalanced categories of positive and negative samples, many researchers have improved the traditional cross-entropy loss function, such as using weighted cross entropy to enhance the sensitivity to samples with fewer categories or using the joint loss function to optimize the model from different angles and aspects to seek the optimal solution of the model. In addition, many researchers have adopted the method of deep supervision to construct the side output loss function at different decoding stages, which makes the final segmentation result more reliable and also can alleviate the problem of gradient disappearance caused by too deep network. In addition, although CNN, a typical feature extractor for deep learning, can better obtain local feature information, it has some shortcomings, such as the ability to obtain global context needs to be stronger. Therefore, using transformer modules to realize the construction of long-distance feature dependency and improve the segmentation effect of complex targets has also become a hot research direction. Considering the source of medical data, semi-supervised or unsupervised methods have become a powerful means to solve the problem of high cost and time-consuming in medical image annotation. In addition, reinforcement learning, meta-learning, and small sample learning methods for small data sets are also particularly suitable for the research of medical image segmentation. On the other hand, although the accuracy of some semantic segmentation methods based on deep learning is very high, the amount of parameters of the model is also a problem, which is significant in calculation and prone to overfitting, so the light weight of the model is also an urgent problem to be solved.

Medical image processing can be directly segmented by semantic segmentation method based on deep learning, or multi-stage method assisted by image classification. As the backbone network, the network model for deep learning mainly includes Alexnet, VGG, Googlenet, RESNET and Densenet. In these networks, convolution, pooling, full connection and other operations are basically included. Alexnet is the champion algorithm of the 2012 ILSVRC (Imagenet large scale visual recognition challenge). It is mainly composed of three convolution layers and three pooling layers. Finally, the dimension of the feature vector is adjusted through two full connection layers to output the probability value of each classification. Alexnet is characterized by only eight layers, which is a lightweight network structure with relatively simple structure. VGG was proposed by researchers at Oxford University, and this model won the championship of ILSVRC-2013. Compared with Alexnet, VGG has a greater depth. The network has 16 layers. The difference is that VGG does not have a full connection layer, but replaces the full connection layer with a full convolution layer. In addition, VGG reduces the size of convolution kernel, thus reducing the related parameters. Googlenet won the championship of ILSVRC-2014. Compared with VGG, Googlenet further deepens the depth of the network, which has 22 layers. In addition, the network also solves the problems of over fitting, gradient disappearance and gradient explosion caused by the increase of the depth of the network by introducing inception. The RESNET network proposed by hekaiming et al. In 2015 refers to the VGG19 network and has been modified on its basis. The residual unit is added through the short-circuit mechanism to solve the degradation problem in network training through residual learning, which has become a milestone in the field of computer vision and deep learning. RESNET makes it possible to train hundreds of layers of networks, and it can still show superior performance in this case. The basic idea of Densenet model is the same as RESNET, but it establishes the dense connection between all the front layers and the back layers, and its name comes from this. A major feature of Densenet is to realize feature reuse through the connection of features on the channel. In order to make the deep learning model lightweight and can be applied and deployed on mobile or embedded devices such as mobile phones, some lightweight models have been proposed in succession. As a representative of lightweight network, MobileNet has three versions, namely MobileNet V1, MobileNet V2 and MobileNet V3. This model was proposed by Google in 2017. Its design idea is to replace the conventional convolution in VGG network with deep separable convolution, reduce the amount of parameters, improve efficiency, and make the model lightweight. In 2018, Google released MobileNet V2 at the CVPR conference that year based on MobileNet V1 and the inverted residuals andlinear bots structure with linear bottlenecks. At the iccv2019 conference, Google released MobileNet V3. On the basis of V2, MobileNet V3 introduces the network architecture search algorithm net adapt, as well as improved methods such as squeeze and exception structure, h-swish activation and network tail optimization to form the next generation network model based on complementary search technology, and forms two versions of MobileNet v3 small and MobileNet tv3 large. On ICML2019, the paper published by the Google team proposed the compound scaling method and the network model EfficientNet, which greatly surpassed the previous network in terms of effect, parameter quantity and speed. In April 2021, the Google team proposed the optimized version EfficientNet v2 at the ICML2021 meeting. Compared with V1 version, the number of participants is smaller, but the training speed is faster.

In this work, we utilized the artificial intelligence method to classify the oral lichen planus patients' photos. In detailed, we firstly selected 67 pro-treatment patients' photos and 41 post-treatment patients' photos. And then, we employed SEResNet model to classify these photos. In order to compare the performances of this model, we also employed other two classification models, including ResNet, and DenseNet, in this work.

2 Methods and Materials

2.1 Data

In this work, the employed data, which selected from the Department of Stomatology of Xuzhou first people's Hospital, are the photos of oral lichen planus patients. Meanwhile, it was pointed that there are 67 photos of pro-treatment patients and 41 photos of post-treatment patients.

2.2 Classification Model

2.2.1 SEResNet Model (Using Attention Mechanism and Residual Network Fusion)

SEResNet is a deep convolutional neural network combining RESNET and senet attention mechanisms. Its core idea is to embed SEResNet model in the residual block of RESNET to enhance the network's attention to essential features. This model consists of two parts: squeeze and excite. The global average pooling layer is applied to the feature graph to compress the eigenvalue of each channel into a scalar. The result of this step is a scalar with the same number of channels as the input feature graph, and each scalar represents the global importance of the corresponding channel. The next step is to generate channel weights through a series of linear and nonlinear transformations, which are used to adjust the feature map of each channel in order to amplify important features and suppress unimportant features. Finally, the channel weights were normalized to 0 and 1 through the sigmoid function to obtain the attention weights. SEResNet is based on the basic architecture of RESNET, including the convolution layer, residual block, and pooling layer, which are used for feature extraction and depth modeling. The se attention module is embedded in each residual block of RESNET. The se attention module introduces the channel attention mechanism, uses the global average pooling layer to capture the global features, and then, through a series of linear transformations and activation functions, finally generates weights through the sigmoid function to dynamically adjust the weights of the feature map. The model can automatically learn the tasks' important features and strengthen their representation.

The model helps to enhance the network's perception of important features in oral images, enabling the model to distinguish pro-treatment and post-treatment images better while allowing the model to adaptively learn mission-critical features rather than relying on manually designed feature engineering.

2.2.2 General RESNET Model

RESNET (residual network) is a deep convolutional neural network architecture. The concept of residual learning is proposed to solve the problems of gradient disappearance and network degradation in deep neural networks. The residual block is the basic building block of RESNET, which contains one or more convolution layers and a shortcut connection. The core idea of the residual block is to learn the residual function rather than directly learning the underlying features. If the input is h(x) and the output of the residual block is f(x), then the final output is h(x) + f(x). This design allows the gradient to propagate directly through the jump connection, thus alleviating the gradient disappearance problem.

2.3 Evaluation Metrics and Methods

In the classification of pro-treatment and post-treatment patients' photos of oral lichen planus, it is an essential step to select appropriate evaluation indexes to evaluate the performance of the model. The post-treatment patients' photos can be defined as the negative sample and the pro-treatment patients' photos can be defined as the positive ones in this work. In this experiment, accuracy (ACC), precision, recall, and F1 score are utilized in this work. The calculation method is shown in Eq. (1) to (4).

$$precision = \frac{TP}{TP + FP} \tag{1}$$

$$recall = \frac{TP}{TP + FN} \tag{2}$$

$$ACC = \frac{TP + TN}{TP + FN + TN + FP} \tag{3}$$

$$F1 - score = \frac{2 \times TP}{2 \times TP + FN + FP} \tag{4}$$

where, P and N represent the scale of positive and negative samples, respectively. T and F represent sets of true and false predicted results, respectively.

3   Result

In this section, we utilized the SEResNet model to classify pro-treatment and post-treatment patients' photos of oral lichen planus. The detailed classification performances demonstrated in Table 1 and the performances of Seresne shown in Fig. 1.

Table 1. The performances of SEResNet model

Accuracy	Precision	Recall	F1 Score
62.5%	75%	27.27%	0.4

In order to compare the performance, we employed the ResNet and DenseNet to deal with this classification model. The detailed classification performances demonstrated in Table 2 and the performances of Seresne shown in Fig. 2 and Fig. 3.

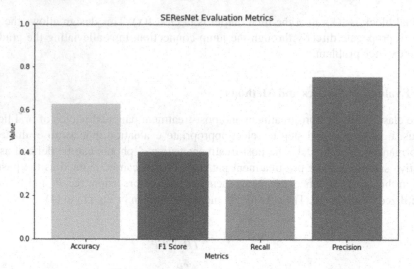

Fig. 1. The performances of SEResNet

Table 2. The performances of ResNet and DenseNet model

	Accuracy	Precision	Recall	F1 Score
ResNet	55%	44.44%	23.53%	0.307
DenseNet	56.25%	33.33%	16.67%	0.2222

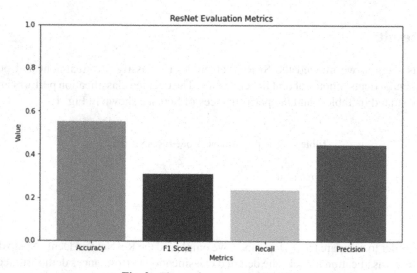

Fig. 2. The performances of ResNet

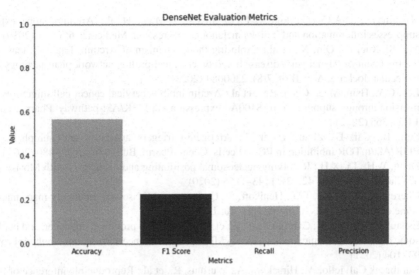

Fig. 3. The performances of DenseNet

4 Conclusion

In this work, we utilized the artificial intelligence method to classify the oral lichen planus patients' photos. In detailed, we firstly selected 67 pro-treatment patients' photos and 41 post-treatment patients' photos. And then, we employed SEResNet model to classify these photos. In order to compare the performances of this model, we also employed other two classification models, including ResNet, and DenseNet, in this work. However, there are some issues should be considered in the future work. Firstly, both the employed and the compared method can hardly get the ideal results in the classification issue. Some available and effective methods should be utilized in this work. Secondly, some effective features should be utilized in this work. Lastly, the scale of samples should be enriched.

Acknowledgments. This work was supported by the National Natural Science Foundation of China (Grant No. 61902337), Xuzhou Science and Technology Plan Project (KC21047), Jiangsu Provincial Natural Science Foundation (No. SBK2019040953), Natural Science Fund for Colleges and Universities in Jiangsu Province (No. 19KJB520016) and Young Talents of Science and Technology in Jiangsu and ghfund 202302026465 and Key Support Project for Elderly Oral Health Incubation in Jiangsu Province, and Qingmiao engineering by Xuzhou first People's Hospital.

References

1. Romualdo, G.R., Silva, E.A., Da Silva, T.C., et al.: Burdock (Arctium lappa L.) root attenuates preneoplastic lesion development in a diet and thioacetamide-induced model of steatohepatitis-associated hepatocarcinogenesis. Environ. Toxicol. **35**(4), 518–527 (2020)
2. Taleb Agha, M., Baharetha, H.M., Al-Mansoub, M.A., et al.: Proapoptotic and antiangiogenic activities of Arctium lappa L. on breast cancer cell lines. Scientifica **2020** (2020)

3. Nascimento, B.A.C., Gardinassi, L.G., Silveira, I.M.G., et al.: Arctium lappa extract suppresses inflammation and inhibits melanoma progression. Medicines **6**(3), 81 (2019)
4. Mu, S., Xue, D., Qin, X., et al.: Exploring the mechanism of Arctium Lappa L. leaves in the treatment of Alzheimer's disease based on chemical profile, network pharmacology and molecular docking. Adv. Biol. **7**(8), 2300084 (2023)
5. Lee, C.Y., Hsin, M.C., Chen, P.N., et al.: Arctiin inhibits cervical cancer cell migration and invasion through suppression of S100A4 expression via PI3K/Akt pathway. Pharmaceutics **14**(2), 365 (2022)
6. Sun, B., Cai, E., Zhao, Y., et al.: Arctigenin triggers apoptosis and autophagy via PI3K/Akt/mTOR inhibition in PC-3M cells. Chem. Pharm. Bull. **69**(5), 472–480 (2021)
7. Deng, W.H., Li, X.H.: Resolving nucleosomal positioning and occupancy with MNase-seq. Yi Chuan= Hereditas **42**(12), 1143–1155 (2020)
8. Chereji, R.V., Bryson, T.D., Henikoff, S.: Quantitative MNase-seq accurately maps nucleosome occupancy levels. Genome Biol. **20**, 1–18 (2019)
9. Esnault, C., Magat, T., García-Oliver, E., et al.: Analyses of promoter, enhancer, and nucleosome organization in mammalian cells by MNase-Seq. Enhancers Promoters Methods Protoc. 93–104 (2021)
10. Karabacak Calviello, A., Hirsekorn, A., Wurmus, R., et al.: Reproducible inference of transcription factor footprints in ATAC-seq and DNase-seq datasets using protocol-specific bias modeling. Genome Biol. **20**, 1–13 (2019)
11. Ma, S., Zhang, Y.: Profiling chromatin regulatory landscape: insights into the development of ChIP-seq and ATAC-seq. Mol. Biomed. **1**, 1–13 (2020)
12. Trieu, K., Bhat, S., Dai, Z., et al.: Biomarkers of dairy fat intake, incident cardiovascular disease, and all-cause mortality: a cohort study, systematic review, and meta-analysis. PLoS Med. **18**(9), e1003763 (2021)
13. Hutin, S., Blanc-Mathieu, R., Rieu, P., et al.: Identification of plant transcription factor DNA-binding sites using seq-DAP-seq. In: Kaufmann, K., Vandepoele, K. (eds.) Plant Gene Regulatory Networks: Methods and Protocols, pp. 119–145. Springer, New York (2023). https://doi.org/10.1007/978-1-0716-3354-0_9

Nucleotide Sequence Classification of Paeonia Lactiflora Based on Feature Representation Learning

Bolun Yang[1], Yi Cao[1(✉)], Ruizhi Han[1], and Wenzheng Bao[2(✉)]

[1] School of Information Science, University of Jinan, Jinan 250024, China
ise_caoy@ujn.edu.cn
[2] School of Information and Engineering, Xuzhou University of Technology, Xuzhou 221018, China
baowz55555@126.com

Abstract. For the treatment of recurrent oral ulcer, total glucosides of paeony is an ideal drug. Long term application of total glucosides of paeony has low side effects and better patient compliance. Nucleotide sequence is of great significance in the field of Botany. In order to further study the pharmacology of Radix Paeonia Alba, the classification and prediction of nucleotide sequence of Radix Paeonia Alba is an important challenge. In this paper, we design a deep learning model based on graph neural network framework. First, each nucleotide sequence is extracted by k-mer algorithm, and then the extracted features are composed and put into the graph convolution layer for information transmission. Finally, the low-dimensional vector that integrates the whole sequence information can help us classify nucleotide sequences well. The final results of the experiment were 96.00% in Acc, 0.9387 in F1 score, 95.57% in Sn, 96.21% in Sp, and 0.9094 in MCC.

Keywords: Paeonia lactiflora · nucleotide sequence · graph neural network · classification

1 Introduction

Recurrent aphthous stomatitis (RAS), also known as canker sores or oral sores, is a common oral mucosal disease, which usually manifests as small ulcers or sores in the oral mucosa. These ulcers may recur regularly, hence the name "recurrent". Long term infection will adversely affect the oral health and quality of life of patients. Researchers found that Radix Paeonia Alba is an ideal drug for the treatment of recurrent oral ulcer. Research showed that the application of total glucosides of Paeonia Alba can effectively prolong the interval of oral ulcer [1]. At the same time, compared with other drugs, the long-term application of total glucosides of Paeonia Alba has low side effects and better patient compliance. Paeonia lactiflora pall is derived from the peeled dry roots of Paeonia lactiflora pall, a Ranunculaceae plant. It contains monoterpenoids such as paeoniflorin, paeoniflorin, oxidized paeoniflorin, benzoyl paeoniflorin, and is collectively known as

D.-S. Huang et al. (Eds.): ICAI 2023, CCIS 2014, pp. 57–64, 2024.
https://doi.org/10.1007/978-981-97-0903-8_7

total glucosides of paeony (TGP) [2]. It is widely used as a commonly used traditional Chinese medicine. Professor Xu's team's systematic research on total glucosides of paeony found that it plays an important role in immune regulation, anti-inflammatory, analgesic, liver protection and other aspects. Nucleotide sequence is of great significance in the field of Botany. It is the basic unit to describe the genetic information of plants. Through the analysis of nucleotide sequence, we can determine the coding region, promoter, terminator and other important functional regions of genes, and then understand the function and expression regulation mechanism of genes. In order to further promote the research progress of total glucosides of paeony in Radix Paeonia Alba and provide more scientific basis for making full use of Radix Paeonia Alba, we decided to study the nucleotide sequence of Radix Paeonia Alba. The rapid progress of sequencing technology has produced a large number of biological sequences. DNA sequences are an important part of biological big data. Only a few DNA sequences have been verified by experiments. For DNA sequences with new sequencing or unknown functions, the reliable way to verify their functions is manual experiments. However, due to the large number of gene databases, it is not feasible to verify them all by experimental methods, Therefore, it is an efficient way to rapidly predict the potential function of genes with the help of machine learning and deep learning methods in the computer field.

In the past decades, more and more researchers have tried to use machine learning or deep learning methods to predict the functionality of DNA sequences. Du et al. present four different deep learning architectures for the purpose of chromosomal DNA sequence classification The results show that the architecture of convolutional neural networks combined with long short-term memory networks is superior to other methods with regards to the accuracy of chromosomal DNA prediction [3] Liu et al. proposed DeepTorrent for improved prediction of 4mC sites from DNA sequences. It combines four different feature encoding schemes to encode raw DNA sequences and employs multi-layer convolutional neural networks with an inception module integrated with bidirectional long short-term memory to effectively learn the higher-order feature representations [4]. Sarkar S used polynomial Naive Bayes classifier and logistic regression with k-mer coding to obtain good accuracy in the classification of DNA sequences, which were 93.16% and 93.13%, respectively [5]. Hemalatha Gunasekaran et al. employed CNN, CNN-LSTM, and CNN-Bidirectional LSTM architectures using Label and k-mer encoding for DNA sequence classification. And the CNN and CNN-Bidirectional LSTM with -mer encoding offers high accuracy with 93.16% and 93.13%, respectively, on testing data. [6] Quang D et al. proposed DanQ, a new hybrid convolutional and bidirectional long short-term memory recurrent neural network framework for predicting non-coding functions from sequences [7, 8]. As mentioned above, more and more research attempts have explored the potential of machine learning and deep learning in DNA sequence function prediction, and some progress has been made in improving the accuracy of prediction. However, the existing deep learning classifiers have not fully tapped the potential of feature representation learning. Some are shown in key sequence patterns that are crucial for gene regulation. This sometimes leads to poor interpretation ability of deep learning models, which has an important impact on our mining of potential functions in gene sequences.

With the continuous development of deep learning and neural network, many advanced technologies have emerged. The emergence of graph neural network can transfer information between input features well, and the integrated features will have more potential information in the context. For DNA sequences, some researchers usually use traditional feature extraction methods, such as k-mer to express the sequence as a matrix format required for deep learning, but the disadvantage is that it is easy to lose a lot of information between sequences, such as the correlation between k-mers. Therefore, we introduce graph neural network. For each DNA sequence, we can convert it into a graph. The point feature of the graph corresponds to the occurrence frequency of each k-mer, the edge of the graph corresponds to the correlation between each k-mer, and the feature is the frequency of two k-mers in the sequence within the distance of D. The following is the specific process of our work. Firstly, each DNA sequence is extracted as a feature vector by k-mer algorithm. Secondly, the sequence features are composed, and the input graph convolutional neural network is used for message transmission, so that the information of k-mer can be aggregated into other k-mers according to the information of the sequence. Lastly, each graph representing sequence features is transformed into a vector of low dimensional potential space, which is input into the full connection layer of neural network to classify and predict coding sequences and non-coding sequences (Fig. 1).

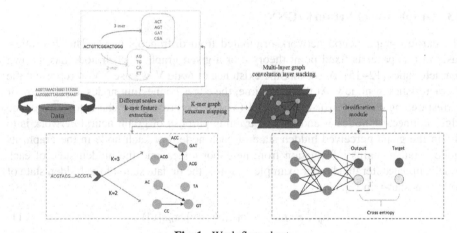

Fig. 1. Work flow chart

2   Methods and Materials

2.1   Data

The data used in this experiment were obtained from the gene library search in NCBI (National Center for Biotechnology Information) [9, 10]. The gene library is a searchable gene database that focuses on fully sequenced genomes and has an active research community to provide gene specific data. Gene information includes nomenclature, chromosomal localization, gene products and their attributes (e.g., protein interactions), relevant markers, phenotypes, interactions, citation links, sequences, mutation details, maps, expression reports, homologs, protein domain content, and external database links. Finally, we obtained a total of 92 DNA sequences of Paeonia lactiflora, including 58 protein coding sequences and 34 noncoding sequences.

2.2 k-mers Feature Extraction Method

For a given DNA sequence consisting of A, C, G and T and a positive integer k, the k-mers of the sequence are all sequence substrings of length k, so each DNA sequence has 4^k different k-mers [11, 12]. In the experiment, we used different scales of k = 2 and k = 3 for feature extraction. When k = 2, the examples of 2-mers are CG and AT, and when k = 3, the examples of 3-mers are ACT, CGA and TTG. When the value of k becomes larger and larger, the dimension of the eigenvector will also increase, and it can reflect the basic structure information in the sequence in more detail, providing reliable data for our subsequent series of operations such as classification and analysis of the sequence. However, too high value of k will lead to high latitude disasters and cause problems such as overfitting of our model. Therefore, it is an important problem to select the appropriate value of k in the experimental process.

2.3 Graph Neural Network (GNN)

The earliest graph neural network originated from dr.franco's paper. The theoretical basis in this paper is fixed point theory. For a given graph G, each node has its own characteristics [12–15]. Assuming the existence of node V, we use XV to represent the characteristics of node v. At the same time, the edges connecting nodes also have their corresponding characteristics. We use X (V, U) to represent the characteristics of the edges connecting nodes V and U. The training purpose of graph neural network is to obtain the graph perceived hidden state of each node. For each node in the graph, its hidden state contains information from neighbor nodes, and the hidden state of each node is updated iteratively. For example, at t + 1, the update state of the hidden state of node V is shown in Eq. (1)

$$h_v^{t+1} = f(x_v, x_c o[v], h_n^t e[v], x_n e[v]) \tag{1}$$

f in the formula is the state update function of the hidden state, also known as the local transition function. The feature of the edge adjacent $x_c o[v]$ to node v, $h_n^t e[v]$ refers to the hidden state of the neighbor node at time t. For deep learning, what we need to do is to fit this function f through neural network. In the process of network training, the hidden state of the neighbor node at the current time is continuously used as part of the input to generate the hidden state of the central node at the next time, until the change of the hidden state of each node is small, and the information flow of each graph tends to be stable. Now that each node has integrated the information of its neighbors, we use them to complete various downstream tasks. The downstream task of this paper is to determine whether the graph representing different gene sequences is coding genes.

2.4 Graph Convolutional Neural Network (GCN)

Graph convolution neural network gets rid of the method based on cycle and starts to move towards multi-layer graph neural network [16]. Similar to the well-known convolutional neural network, the concept of graph convolution is to superimpose a node and its neighbors according to different weights to achieve the purpose of information transmission. The transfer formula of GCN is shown in Eq. (2).

$$H^{(l+1)} = \sigma(\tilde{D}^{-\frac{1}{2}}\tilde{A}\tilde{D}^{-\frac{1}{2}}H^{(l)}W^{(l)}) \tag{2}$$

Where represents the weight matrix and represents the adjacency matrix with self-ring edges. Assuming that no self-ring edges are added to the adjacency matrix, the diagonal elements are all 0.

2.5 Construction of Graphs

For the sequences that have been feature extracted, we compose them. Given a sequence S, we construct a pattern graph G (S, k) of the sequence [17, 18]. Each vertex of the graph corresponds to the frequency of each k-mer in the sequence. For two vertices m and n, if and only if the distance between the k-mers corresponding to these two vertices in the sequence s is within a given range d, there will be edges. For example, if there is a sequence ACTGCA, the 3-mers of the sequence are ACT, CTG, TGC, GCA, which constitute the four vertices v_1, v_2, v_3, v_4. If d = 1 at this time, the graph has only one edge. The feature of the edge represents the frequency of two k-mers in the sequence when the adjacent distance is within d.

In this work, normalized counts were used for all frequency features. For example, the normalized count of k-mer refers to the number of occurrences of this k-mer in a sequence divided by the total number of occurrences of all k-mers.

2.6 Evaluation Metrics and Methods

Accuracy (Acc), sensitivity (Sn), specificity (Sp), Matthews correlation coefficient (MCC) and F1-score were used to evaluate the performance of the prediction system [19, 20]. The calculation method is shown in Eq. (3)–(7).

$$Sp = \frac{TN}{TN + FP} \tag{3}$$

$$Sn = \frac{TP}{TP + FN} \tag{4}$$

$$Acc = \frac{TP + TN}{TP + TN + FP + FN} \tag{5}$$

$$F1 = \frac{2 \times TP}{2 \times TP + FN + FP} \tag{6}$$

$$MCC = \frac{TP \times TN - FP \times FN}{\sqrt{(TP + FP) \times (TP + FN) \times (TN + FP) \times (TN + FP)}} \tag{7}$$

For a binary classification problem, the classification results are as follows: true class TP, false positive class FP, true negative class TN, false negative class FN. Among them, TP is a positive sample predicted as a positive class, FP is a negative sample predicted as a positive class, TN is a negative sample predicted as a negative class, and FN is a positive sample predicted as a negative class. SN and SP are the proportion of correct predictions in positive samples and negative samples. The f1 score reflects the robustness of the model. The higher the score, the more stable the model. Acc reflects the overall accuracy of the classifier. When the data set is unbalanced, Acc cannot really evaluate the quality of the classification results. In this case, we will choose MCC for evaluation. The horizontal axis of the ROC curve is generally the ratio of FPR, that is, the ratio of negative samples to positive samples, and the vertical axis is the ratio of FPR, that is, the ratio of positive samples to positive samples. AUC refers to the area under the ROC curve as an evaluation index. When AUC = 1, it is the ideal state of the model, but it is difficult to achieve in reality. When $0.5 < AUC < 1$, it shows that the model is useful. When AUC is closer to 1, the effect of the model is better.

3   Result and Discussions

After constructing the graph from the sequence, we convert these graphs into embedding through multi-layer GCN, connect the convolutional neural network to reduce the dimension first, and then we can input these features that integrate the information of vertices and edges into the neural network of the full connection layer for downstream analysis. In this work, we used to classify and predict the coding genes and non coding genes of Paeonia lactiflora. In the parameter selection, we used $k = 2$ and $k = 3$ to extract the features of gene sequences, respectively. The 2-mer and 3-mer were composed and input into GCN for classification, and the performance of the model was compared with that of the machine learning classifier used by Yang et al. When $k = 2$, the results are shown in Table 1.

Table 1. The performances in $k = 2$.

Model	Sn(%)	Sp(%)	Acc(%)	Mcc	F1	AUROC
2-mer-gcn	95.77	94.68	95.035	0.8824	0.9251	0.9534
Kmer-SVM	98.25	83.34	93.445	0.8702	0.9521	0.9333

From the table, we can see that in the case of $k = 2$, Sp compared with the machine learning model based on Kmer-SVM, the performance improved by 11.34%, MCC increased by 0.0122, and ACC also improved significantly, reaching 95.035% in the end, achieving a relatively ideal classification performance. When $k = 3$, the results are shown in Table 2.

In Table 2, we can see that in the case of $k = 3$, the performance of Sp, ACC, MCC and F1 is significantly improved compared with that of the machine learning model based on Kmer-SVM, and the ACC is 96.003%, which is increased compared with that of the

Table 2. The performances in k = 3.

Model	Sn(%)	Sp(%)	Acc(%)	Mcc	F1	AUROC
3-mer-gcn	95.573	96.205	96.003	0.9094	0.9387	0.9597
Kmer-SVM	98.25	83.34	93.445	0.8702	0.9521	0.9333
2-mer-gcn	95.77	94.68	95.035	0.8824	0.9251	0.9534

model with k = 2, while the AUROC increases less, only 0.0063. We believe that when k = 3, we can obtain more information than when k = 2, So in the later composition and embedding process, we extracted features that are more suitable for this model for training.

4 Conclusion

In this work, we convert the nucleotide sequence of Paeonia lactiflora Pall into a more interpretable sequence representation, each sequence can be constructed into a coding map based on k-mer feature extraction method. In order to compare these maps and classify and predict them, we used graph neural network to filter these maps into low-dimensional embedding, so that they can be applied to the framework of deep learning to do more downstream analysis. Based on this framework, we used two scales of feature extraction, k = 2 and k = 3, respectively. The experimental results show that the performance of the classification model based on machine learning is improved, and the effect is the best when k = 3, because we can get more information from the sequence.

Representational learning is not the first time that it has been applied to gene sequences, such as word2vec, a widely used natural language processing technology, which has made many contributions to coding the human genome and solving problems such as species recognition, methylation site prediction and so on. However, this method is based on the local context of sequence fragments for learning, and graph neural network provides the global information of the whole sequence. We believe that this more accurate model for functional analysis of gene sequences will provide more useful help for researchers.

Acknowledgments. This work was supported in part by Shandong Provincial Natural Science Foundation, China (ZR2021MF036), and in part by National Natural Science Foundation of China (31872415), the National Natural Science Foundation of China (Grant No. 61902337), Xuzhou Science and Technology Plan Project (KC21047), Jiangsu Provincial Natural Science Foundation (No. SBK2019040953), Natural Science Fund for Colleges and Universities in Jiangsu Province (No. 19KJB520016) and Young Talents of Science and Technology in Jiangsu and ghfund 202302026465.

References

1. He, D.Y., Dai, S.M.: Anti-inflammatory and immunomodulatory effects of Paeonia lactiflora Pall., a traditional Chinese herbal medicine. Front. Pharmacol. **2**, 10 (2011)

2. Lee, S.C., Kwon, Y.S., Son, K.H., et al.: Antioxidative constituents from Paeonia lactiflora. Arch. Pharmacal Res. **28**, 775–783 (2005)

3. Bowler, S., Papoutsoglou, G., Karanikas, A., et al.: A machine learning approach utilizing DNA methylation as an accurate classifier of COVID-19 disease severity. Sci. Rep. **12**(1), 17480 (2022)

4. Leitheiser, M., Capper, D., Seegerer, P., et al.: Machine learning models predict the primary sites of head and neck squamous cell carcinoma metastases based on DNA methylation. J. Pathol. **256**(4), 378–387 (2022)

5. Sarkar, S., Mridha, K., Ghosh, A., et al.: Machine learning in bioinformatics: new technique for DNA sequencing classification. In: Shaw, R.N., Das, S., Piuri, V., Bianchini, M. (eds.) Advanced Computing and Intelligent Technologies: Proceedings of ICACIT 2022. LNEE, vol. 914, pp. 335–355. Springer, Singapore (2022). https://doi.org/10.1007/978-981-19-2980-9_27

6. Mridha, K.: Early prediction of breast cancer by using artificial neural network and machine learning techniques. In: 2021 10th IEEE International Conference on Communication Systems and Network Technologies (CSNT), pp. 582–587. IEEE (2021)

7. Sun, T., Zhou, B., Lai, L., et al.: Sequence-based prediction of protein protein interaction using a deep-learning algorithm. BMC Bioinform. **18**, 277 (2017)

8. Tampuu, A., Bzhalava, Z., Dillner, J., et al.: ViraMiner: deep learning on raw DNA sequences for identifying viral genomes in human samples. PLoS ONE **14**(9), e0222271 (2019)

9. Quang, D., Xie, X.: DanQ: a hybrid convolutional and recurrent deep neural network for quantifying the function of DNA sequences. Nucl. Acids Res. **44**(11), e107–e107 (2016)

10. Mahmoud, M.A.B., Guo, P.: DNA sequence classification based on MLP with PILAE algorithm. Soft. Comput. **25**(5), 4003–4014 (2021)

11. Melsted, P., Pritchard, J.K.: Efficient counting of k-mers in DNA sequences using a bloom filter. BMC Bioinform. **12**(1), 1–7 (2011)

12. Déraspe, M., Raymond, F., Boisvert, S., et al.: Phenetic comparison of prokaryotic genomes using k-mers. Mol. Biol. Evol. **34**(10), 2716–2729 (2017)

13. Dao, F.Y., Lv, H., Su, W., et al.: iDHS-Deep: an integrated tool for predicting DNase I hypersensitive sites by deep neural network. Brief. Bioinform. **22**(5), bbab047 (2021)

14. Chen, W., Lin, H., Chou, K.C.: Pseudo nucleotide composition or PseKNC: an effective formulation for analyzing genomic sequences. Mol. BioSyst. **11**(10), 2620–2634 (2015)

15. Chen, W., Feng, P.M., Lin, H., et al.: IRSpot-PseDNC: identify recombination spots with pseudo dinucleotide composition. Nucl. Acids Res. **41**(6), e68–e68 (2013)

16. Hearst, M.A., Dumais, S.T., Osuna, E., et al.: Support vector machines. IEEE Intell. Syst. Appl. **13**(4), 18–28 (1998)

17. Ma, Y., Guo, G.: Support Vector Machines Applications. Springer, New York (2014). https://doi.org/10.1007/978-3-319-02300-7

18. Cherkassky, V., Ma, Y.: Practical selection of SVM parameters and noise estimation for SVM regression. Neural Netw. **17**(1), 113–126 (2004)

19. Huang, S., Cai, N., Pacheco, P.P., et al.: Applications of support vector machine (SVM) learning in cancer genomics. Cancer Genom. Proteom. **15**(1), 41–51 (2018)

20. Wei, L., Xing, P., Su, R., Shi, G., Ma, Z.S., Zou, Q.: CPPred-RF: a sequence-based predictor for identifying cell–penetrating peptides and their uptake efficiency. J. Proteome Res. **16**(5), 2044–2053 (2017)

Semantic Similarity Functions and Their Applications

Yang Liu[1], Alaa Alsaig[2(✉)], and Vasu Alagar[1]

[1] Concordia University, Montreal, Canada
vangalur.alagar@concordia.ca
[2] Jeddah University, Jeddah, Saudi Arabia
aalsaig@uj.edu.sa

Abstract. Similarity is a rich concept deeply rooted in human knowledge and perception. Interest in similarity and categorization of objects can be traced back to Plato. Although studied by philosophers, and mathematicians for a long time, there was no agreement on the "best way" to define it and measure it. Recently, the concept of similarity and methods to assess similarity between objects have assumed great importance in Data Mining (DM), Machine Learning (ML), and Bioinformatics (BI). The various proposed methods to measure semantic similarity do not use semantics and fully agree with human judgement. In this paper we construct semantic similarity functions that remedy this situation.

Keywords: Semantic similarity scoring functions · data mining · machine learning · healthcare informatics

1 Introduction

Similarity, and categorization of objects are deeply rooted in human knowledge and perception. Gini [1] traces the evolution of these concepts from early to modern times, and deals with the role of similarity in categorizing molecules. He explains that these early ideas lead to the *geometrical model* of similarity due to Carnap in which every object is represented as a point in an *n dimensional* metric space (X, δ). The well-understood Euclidean distance formula

$$\delta(a, b) = (a_1 - b_1)2 + \cdots + (a_n - b_n)2$$

is the most popular function used by a large number of researchers in geometric models to assess similarity between objects. Tversky [2] is the first to refuse geometric model, observing that they *violate* their three basic axioms on *reflexivity, symmetry*, and *tri- angle inequality*. He introduced a new model for objects, called the *contrast model*, in which an object is represented as a set of *features* of the object. In this model similarity of objects is calculated using functions defined on the set-theory operators *union, intersection, and*

D.-S. Huang et al. (Eds.): ICAI 2023, CCIS 2014, pp. 65–76, 2024.
https://doi.org/10.1007/978-981-97-0903-8_8

difference of feature sets. If A, B and C respectively denote the set of features of objects a, b, and c, Tversky's "generic similarity" function is

$$STV(a, b) = \frac{f(A \cap B)}{f(A \cap B) + \alpha f(A \backslash B) + \beta f(B \backslash A)} \tag{1}$$

where α, $\beta > 0$, $f(X) > 0$, if $X/ = \emptyset$, and $f(\emptyset) = 0$. It is easy to prove that if $\alpha /= \beta$ then $S_{TV}(a, b) /= S_{TV}(b, a)$, and if $\alpha = \beta$ then $S_{TV}(a, b) = S_{TV}(b, a)$. For The set-theoretic functions listed in Table 1 are all *bounded* and can be derived from S_{TVM} as special cases. Many applications in ML, such as Recommender Systems and Match Making Systems, use one of these functions, although they do not *include domain-specific semantics* of the objects. However, objects of interest in biomedical and patient-centric healthcare domain will include *concept terms* that have domain *semantics*. Many terms and concepts that describe objects, like diseases, emotional aspects, and drugs have domain-specific meanings and relatedness. Drugs are usually coded with their approved medical names and they are of type *categorical*. A raw comparison of any two attribute values will only result in "total dissimilarity" between drugs. As an example, *ACANY A = ONEXTON* if the medicine names are viewed as of "categorical type" and comparison is done viewing them as "strings". However, in the medical domain "ACANYA" is a "generic" of "ONEXTON". As such they should be considered as "equivalent". From a survey of literature on similarity functions and their applications, we observe that researchers in DM and ML mostly use the distance functions in their research. In biomedical and healthcare, researchers have used *distance- based* functions or *set-theoretic measures* without semantics or a combination of both types. Only recently [3] methods that use ontologies (for semantics) to compute similarity and incorporate them in ML and DM have been investigated. An Ontology in Healthcare domain is used to provide relatedness of concept terms. Two of the well- known Ontology in Healthcare domain are SNOMED CT [4] for clinical terminology, and IC-10 for the classification of diseases.

Concepts in an Ontology are related by *is-A* $(x\, y)$ relation. It means that "the concept x is *subsumed by* or *a specific class of* concept y". An ontology is a semantic digraph (sometimes it can be a tree) in which every node is a concept name and edge directed from node x to node y means $x\, y$. We consider only an Ontology that has a unique maximal element C_0, called the "root concept". The relation is a partial order relation. Some of the partial order relations in Fig. 1 are C_4, C_1, C_5, C_2, ad C_6, C_3. From any node x in the Ontology there is at least one directed path from x to C_0. Between any two nodes in an ontology there may not exist a path or there could be many paths. For example, in Fig. 1 there is no path from C_1 to C_2, and there are three path from C_5 to C_0. If there is a (directed) path from x to y we define the length of the path as the *number of nodes* along the path (including sx and y). The semantic distances proposed by several researchers [5–9] have failed to respect the directions in the ontology graph. These inaccuracies have been extensively explained in [10]. The methods discussed in this paper remedy these deficiencies. In addition to remedying this, we integrate user-level semantic knowledge in the construction of scoring functions used for similarity calculation [10, 11]. Hence, our approach is likely to fulfill both domain knowledge (partial orders) and human judgement requirements.

In Sect. 2 we present our results on semantic distance functions, illustrate their empirical evaluations with the case study ontology example. We also include a summary

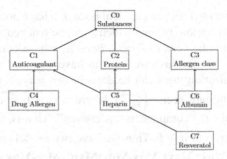

Fig. 1. Ontology - Rooted Digraph Example

on the performance of semantic distance function calculation on two large ontology examples chosen from the healthcare domain. In Sect. 3 we present a method that uses the results from Sect. 2 for assessing *drug-drug* similarity. In Section 4 we present a method that uses the results from Sect. 2 for identifying and retrieving *relevant* datasets that satisfy user-centric quality criteria. We conclude the paper in Sect. 5. We use the sample Ontology in Figure 1 as a reference point for discussion.

2   A Family of New Semantic Distance Functions

We introduce a new family of semantic similarity functions in this section. We recognize that every node x in an ontology has the following two properties: (1) from x the root node is "reachable" and (2) there is at least one "leaf node" from which x is reachable. The "reachable distance" from node x to root " measures the depth of node x " and the "reachable distance" from a leaf node to x measures the "height" of node x . The reachable distance itself can be measured either using "maximum path length" or "minimum path length". Because both height and depth are well-defined in an ontology digraph, we model every node x as a vector with two components $\langle depth(x), height(x) \rangle < depth(x)$, $height(x)>$. In fact, the depth and height can be measured using either "longest" or "shortest" path notions. Consequently, we end up with four different models, which we call **Max-Max (Mxx)**, **Max-Min (Mxn)**, **Min-Max(Mnx)**, and **Min-Min(Mnn)** . We emphasize that both *height(x)* and *depth(x)* have semantic interpretations based on subsumes (subsumed by). Below we use the generic names *Top(x)* and *Bot(x)* respectively for *depth(x)* and *height(x)*. For the sake of clarity we give below definitions and examples for **Mxx**. It is easy to define the other three models.

2.1   Semantic Measure for Mxx Model

We define *Top(x)* as the number of nodes in a longest chain from x to the *root* of the Ontology. That is, *Top(x)* is the maximum number of concepts that subsume x. This defines the depth for Mxx. We consider all chains starting at leaf nodes of the ontology and ending at x. Among all such chains, we pick a longest chain and let *Bot(x)* denote the number of nodes in that chain. So, *Bot(x)* is the maximum number of concept terms that inherit x and is the height of x in Mxx. From every node x in the Ontology the *root* concept can be reached. So, $Top(x) \geq 1$. Either x is a leaf node or it has a node inheriting it. Hence, there is a leaf node in the ontology from which x can be reached. Consequently, $Bot(x) \geq 1$. So, we model x by the vector $\langle Top(x), Bot(x) \rangle$, whose components are integers greater than or equal to 1. Because we want to have bounded values, we normalize the vector. The normalization itself can be done in two ways for a vector $\langle a, b \rangle$. The first normalization is the unit vector $\left(\frac{a}{r}, \frac{b}{r} \right)$, where $r = \sqrt{r} = a^2 + b^2$. The second normalization is to make the components "as convex". That is, the normalized vector of $\langle a, b \rangle$ is $\left(\frac{a}{s}, \frac{b}{s} \right)$, where $s = a + b$. Thus we have two models under each of the four different models **Max-Max (Mxx)**, **Max-Min (Mxn)**, **Min-Max (Mnx)**, and **Min-Min (Mnn)**, giving rise to eight models. We label them as **Mxx-u** (unit vector model under Max-Max) and **Mxx-c** (convex model under Max-Max). Similar labels are applied for the other models. Below we explain distance/similarity calculation for **Mxx-c**.

Semantic Distance Function for Mxx-c. The vector model for x is $\langle x_1, x_2 \rangle$, where

$$x_1 = \frac{Top(x)}{Top(x) + Bot(x)}, \quad x_1 = \frac{Bot(x)}{Top(x) + Bot(x)} \tag{2}$$

For two concepts x, and y, $x = y$ in the Ontology we first compute their vector models $x\langle x_1, x_2 \rangle$, and $y\langle y_1, y_2 \rangle$, and next we calculate the similarity as their inner product as defined in Eq. 3.

$$\underset{I}{\overset{f}{sim}} (x, y) = \begin{array}{ll} 1 & \text{if } x = y \\ x_1.y_1 + x_2.y_2 & \text{otherwise} \end{array} \tag{3}$$

Under **Mxx-c** model, the computed similarity measures for all pairs of concept terms in the ontology (Fig. 1) are shown in Table 1.

We notice that the computed values seem to agree with the level of semantic relatedness in the ontology. However, the similarity is "symmetric", although "relatedness" is only a *partial order*. In many applications where symmetry is required, we can use any one of the above eight distance functions. However, in applications where "dissimilarity" as reflected by "partial order" is required, we can use the Tversky's set-theoretic similarity function. We sum up our contributions on similarity for pairs of concept terms x, y in an ontology as follows:

Result 1

If $x = y$, $\sigma(x, y) = 1$.

If x and y are not related by partial order, then $\sigma(x, y)$ can be any one of the eight distance functions or the set theoretic Jaccard function $JS(A(x), A(y))$.

if $x \leq y$, either directly or transitively in the ontology, then

$$\sigma(x, y) = if\, x \leq y, \alpha = 0.45$$

$$\sigma(y, x) = if\, x \leq y, \alpha = 0.45$$

Table 1. Similarity Values for All Pairs of Concept Terms in the Ontology in Fig. 1

	C_0	C_1	C_2	C_3	C_4	C_5	C_6	C_7
C_0	1	$\frac{17}{30}$	$\frac{17}{30}$	$\frac{11}{18}$	$\frac{1}{3}$	$\frac{7}{18}$	$\frac{1}{2}$	$\frac{5}{18}$
C_1	$\frac{17}{30}$	1	$\frac{13}{25}$	$\frac{8}{15}$	$\frac{9}{20}$	$\frac{7}{15}$	$\frac{1}{2}$	$\frac{13}{30}$
C_2	$\frac{17}{30}$	$\frac{13}{25}$	1	$\frac{8}{15}$	$\frac{9}{20}$	$\frac{7}{15}$	$\frac{1}{2}$	$\frac{13}{30}$
C_3	$\frac{11}{18}$	$\frac{8}{15}$	$\frac{8}{15}$	1	$\frac{5}{12}$	$\frac{4}{9}$	$\frac{1}{2}$	$\frac{7}{19}$
C_4	$\frac{1}{3}$	$\frac{9}{20}$	$\frac{9}{20}$	$\frac{5}{12}$	1	$\frac{7}{12}$	$\frac{1}{2}$	$\frac{2}{3}$
C_5	$\frac{7}{18}$	$\frac{7}{15}$	$\frac{7}{15}$	$\frac{4}{9}$	$\frac{7}{12}$	1	$\frac{1}{2}$	$\frac{11}{18}$
C_6	$\frac{1}{2}$	$\frac{1}{2}$	$\frac{1}{2}$	$\frac{1}{2}$	$\frac{1}{2}$	$\frac{1}{2}$	1	$\frac{1}{2}$
C_7	$\frac{5}{18}$	$\frac{13}{30}$	$\frac{13}{30}$	$\frac{7}{18}$	$\frac{2}{3}$	$\frac{11}{8}$	$\frac{1}{2}$	1

Applying the above function rules to the Ontology in Fig. 1 we have the following result: The similarity of a concept term to itself is 1. The pairs of concepts (C_1, C_2), (C_1, C_3), (C_2, C_3), (C_1, C_6), (C_2, C_4), (C_2, C_6), (C_3, C_4), (C_4, C_5), (C_4, C_6), and (C_4, C_7) are not related by the partial order $\preceq$. Table 1 shows their symmetric values. For the rest of the pairs of concepts, the asymmetric function σ is used to calculate the similarity values with $\alpha = 0.4$. As an example, consider the pairs (C_2, C_5) for which $C_5 \, C_2$ holds. We have $A(C_5) = \{C_5, C_1, C_2, C_6, C_3, C_0\} \subset A(C_2) = \{C_2, C_0\}$.

Using the asymmetric functions defined above we have

$$\sigma(C_5, C_2) = \frac{2}{2 + 0.4(4)} = \frac{5}{9}$$

$$\sigma(C_2, C_5) = \frac{2}{2 + 0.6(4)} = \frac{5}{11}$$

We can verify that $\sigma(C_5, C_2) > \sigma(C_2, C_5)$, as desired by human judgement.

2.2 Similarity Between Sets

The functions in Table 1 measure the "structural similarity" between items. We adapted S_{TV} and JS in the previous section for measuring "structural semantic similarity" on sets whose elements are concept terms. In this section we explain a method to calculate semantic similarity between two sets using the statistical functions "average" and "min-max". We illustrate our method below for max-min method. Let $A = \{c_1, c_2, \cdots c_m\}$ and $B = \{c'_1, c'_2, \cdots c'_n\}$ be the given sets of concepts from an ontology.

– For element $c_i \in A$ compute its similarity with every $c'_j \in B$ using Result 1. We have

$$\rho_i = \{\sigma(c_i, c'_j) | c'_j \in B\}$$

– Repeating the previous step for every $c_i \in A$ we get the sets $\rho_1, \rho_2, ..., \rho_m$.
– Calculate the minimum value min_i of each set ρ_i. That is, $min_i = minimum \{k | k \in \rho_i\}$. Hence we have calculated the set $Min = min_1, min_2, ..., min_m$. Calculate $m = maximum$ $\{k | k \in Min\}$. That is, m is the maximum of all the minimums.
– Define the set similarity as $\sigma(A, B) = m$.

Example 1. *Let $A = \{C_0, C_3\}$, and $B = \{C_4, C_6, C_7\}$ be two sets of concept terms taken from the Ontology in Fig. 1. The similarity values for the elements of these sets, computed using their vector models, are shown in Table 1. We have*

$$\rho_1 = \{\sigma(C_0, C_4), \sigma(C_0, C_6), \sigma(C_0, C_7)\} = \left\{\frac{1}{3}, \frac{1}{2}, \frac{5}{18}\right\}$$

$$\rho_1 = \{\sigma(C_3, C_4), \sigma(C_3, C_6), \sigma(C_3, C_7)\} = \left\{\frac{5}{12}, \frac{1}{2}, \frac{7}{19}\right\}$$

Hence, average $= 0.399$; $max - min = \frac{5}{18} = 0.278$, $min_m ax = {}^1 = 0.5$.

2.3 Implementation

We have implemented all the similarity function calculation methods and tested its performance efficiency. By inspection on the Table 1 and understanding the relatedness of concepts in Fig. 1 we could validity the results in that table. We combined the two Emotional ontology examples in [12], which has 46 concept terms, and computed 46 × 46 table of similarity values. We computed much larger similarity tables for the disease ontology and ATC codes ontology [13]. Based upon the validity of earlier results on the Table 1 we are assuming that the computed results using our similarity functions on larger ontology examples are valid. For these results, only domain experts will have the background knowledge to authentically validate our results. These results appear in the thesis work of Liu [10]. We use these results in Sects. 3 and in 4.

3   An Approach to Assess Drug-Drug Similarity

Many researchers [6, 14, 15] have proposed methods to calculate drug-drug similarity. All of them have taken only one aspect (feature/attribute) for modeling a drug. As examples, Zhang [16] considers *protein sequence* for each drug as the drug model, Ferdousi et al., [15] uses "biological element" as the attribute. As opposed to these models, our drug model is richer, includes five different attributes. Many of the attributes have ontology-based semantic support. The chosen attributes are *Drug Name, Cancer Names, ATC Codes, Dosage Strength,* and *Drug Side Effect*. Notice that we use only Brand Name (as Drug Name) in implementation, because we include in it the set of Generic names of that Brand name. Thus, we have a *vector* model with 5 components for a drug. The components of the vectors are attributes, arranged in a fixed order. To compare two drug vectors, we need to compare the corresponding components of the vectors. Because the attributes have different types we need different functions to "assess their similarity (closeness)". So, to emphasize the comparison at each attribute level we use the term "score" that measures the "similarity of a pair of attribute values", and we reserve the term "similarity" to assess the similarity of the entire drug vectors". We assign different weights $w_1, ..., w_5$ ($1 \leq w_i \leq 5$) to the attributes, in order to dis- criminate their level of significance in an experiment. These weights and types for these attributes are assigned by experts. Assume in the drug record the value of an attribute is r, and the user specifies the value q for that attribute. To integrate "user-level semantics for that attribute" we allow the user to specify a weight w for the attribute value, and specify either "MB" or "LB" for that attribute. The wish "More is better" of the user is conveyed through "MB". The meaning is "the user **prefers** a higher score assigned to the record in which r is maximum possible greater than q". Similarly, the wish of the user "Less is better" is conveyed through "LB". The meaning is "the user **prefers** to assign a higher score to the record in which r is the least possible amount less than q". The following scoring functions integrate these semantics with semantic distance functions to calculate similarity scores at attribute level.

Score for Drug Names: If there is no ontology support for drugs, and a drug may include any one of it's generic names the scoring function to compare two drug names r and q is defined as

$$score(r, q) = \begin{array}{l} 1 \; r = q \; or \; q \in \text{Synonym}(r) \\ 0 \; r /= q \; or \; q \notin \text{Synonym}(r) \end{array} \tag{4}$$

If an ontology support exists for drugs, then we calculate all the semantic distance measures defined in Sect. 2 for the pair (r, q). Under MB semantics, if $r > q$ then $score(r, q)$ for that record is to be assigned the maximum of the calculated measures. Under LB semantics, if $r < q$ then for that record $score(r, q)$ is to be assigned a higher value.

Score for Cancer Names & ATC Codes: Ontology support exists. So, for two different cancer names (ACT codes) we calculate all the semantic distance measures defined in Sect. 2 for the pair (r, q). Scores as explained before is assigned for MB and LB semantics.

Score for Dosage Type: The values r and q from two drug records are of numeric type. We project the distance function

$$S_{RC} = {}^{n}_{1} \frac{|a_i - b_i|}{max(a_i, b_i)}$$

on one attribute only.

Then we integrate LB and MB semantics in that projected function as shown below.

$$score(r, q) = \begin{array}{l} 1 \qquad r = q \\ \left| 1 - \frac{r-q}{q} \right|, r < q \\ \left| 1 + \frac{r-q}{q} \right|, r > q \end{array} \tag{5}$$

For LB semantics we just reverse $score$ functions defined for MB semantics.

$$score(r, q) = \begin{array}{l} 1 \qquad r = q \\ \left| 1 + \frac{r-q}{q} \right|, r > q \\ \left| 1 - \frac{r-q}{q} \right|, r > q \end{array} \tag{6}$$

Score for Side Effect: Side effect is recorded as a "string". The scoring function that compares "string" values will use only *Exact Match* (EM). So, for two strings r and q we define the scoring function as in Eq. 7.

$$score(r, q) = \begin{array}{l} 1 \; r = q \\ 0 \; r /= q \end{array} \tag{7}$$

Algorithm DS

Assume that $D = R_1, \ldots, R_n$ is a set of drug vectors and Q is query vector. Each R_i has 5 components. The query has 5 components, giving values for respective attributes, the weights assigned, and the semantic terms "MB" or "LB". The algorithm compares each component of the vector Q with the corresponding component of vector R_j. That is, it compares Q_i with R_{ji}, for $i = 1, \ldots, 5$. It applies the scoring function λ_i, as explained above, to the pair (Q_i, A_{ji}). The value $v_{ji} = \lambda_i(Q_i, A_{ji})$ is a measure of "closeness", consistent with the semantics and mode specified in the patient query structure. Next, it computes the weighted mean

$$s_j = \frac{\left(w_1 \times v_{j1} + w_2 \times v_{j2} + \cdots + w_5 \times v_{j5} \right)}{(w_1 + w_1 + \cdots + w_5)}$$

which gives the "similarity measure between the drug A_j and the target query Q. Having calculated the measures $s_1, s_2, \ldots, s_n$ for all drugs in the set D, the algorithm ranks the set of drug records in non-increasing order. So, the top of the ranked list is the "best match" for the target query.

A drug dataset consisting of 50 drugs was selected from Drug Bank to run our algorithm with one of the drug vector from the database chosen as the target query. All semantic distance measures were pre-computed and the similarity tables were input to Algorithm DS. The attribute weights were chosen as [1, 2, 4]. We identified from the ranked list of records the drugs that have "high similarity" and drugs that have "are close in ranking". We noticed that drugs that have low similarity and close to each other in the ranked list are those that share "few ATC codes", and drugs that have "high similarity" and "close to each other in ranking" are those that share "many ATC codes" and "some common side effects". Our observation make us believe that our Algorithm DS produces valid similarity results. Our algorithm runs efficiently on large datasets of drugs.

4 Using Similarity of Sets to Retrieve Relevant Datasets

In this section we discuss an application of the similarity calculation function for sets of concepts that we developed in Sect. 2. The application is in the discovery of *relevant datasets* in Big Data research domain. It is well known that AI & ML research community is one of the largest group of researchers who pursue data mining and knowledge discovery in many important application domains of national importance. They acknowledge [17, 18] that "finding relevant (suitable and accurate) datasets and understanding their structure" is the most important Data Management Step to be resolved before ML activities can begin. The notion of relevance has been defined differently by different research groups. It includes content semantics, context, scope, accuracy, and provenance (trustworthiness). The only two *dataset search engines* that are currently available for research community are Google [19] and Auctus [20]. Google engine displays a "list of metadata" chosen by the engine, and the user has to follow one of the links associated with it to access the dataset. Google and Auctus engines do not provide an option for users to input *semantic relevant metric and quality attributes and their metrics*. Auctus engine *generates a metadata* and tells the user to *either improve it or input their own metadata* for selecting datasets. The paper [20] states clearly that "automatically generated metadata may be incompatible with the actual dataset" it finds. Consequently, both Google and Auctus search engines do not meet the requirement of AI & ML research community in "finding relevant" datasets. The recent thesis work of Alaa Alsaig [11] has proposed a new approach for dataset search engine development using the similarity calculation function for sets of concepts that we have developed in Sect. 2.

Table 2. List of Quality Dimension Provided to Providers

Quality Dimension	Data Type	Value-Measurement	Required?
Volume	Numerical	gigabyte	Mandatory
Variety)	Nominal	{xml, cvs, text,..}	Mandatory
Velocity	Numerical	Number of days	Mandatory
Veracity	Categorical	{not known, acceptable, verified}	Optional
Value*	Numerical	Percentage	Mandatory
Release Year	Enumerate	{1995,..2050}	Mandatory
Availability	Interval	[2021,2023]	Optional
Reliability	Categorical	{low, medium, high}	Optional
Safety	Categorical	{low, medium, high}	Optional

The two most important descriptors used in [11] are *set of semantic terms (tags)*, and *quality attributes*. These two aspects of metadata descriptions are sufficient for similarity analysis. Assume that the set of metadata is organized in a database, and they can be accessed in a sequential indexing. For the ith metadata, The sets $TA_i = \{t'_{i1}, ..., t'_{im}\}$ which includes all the tags that are chosen from an ontology, and QV_i which includes values for all the quality attributes are associated. The quality attributes and their value types are shown in Table 2. The significance of the chosen set of attributes is that it includes the 5 most important Vs that characterize Big Data, and the trustworthiness attributes "timeliness (Release Year), Availability, Reliability, Safety". The attributes marked "mandatory" should be included and given a value (as specified in the table) in every metadata description. Both the ontology and Table 2 are shared by all users (ML or DM engineers) who will "query the database of metadata" through a rich user interface to the search engine. The user query has the structure $Q = [ST, (QV, W, B)]$, where $ST = (t_1, p_1), ... , (t_k, p_k))$ where t's are semantic terms from the ontology, and the ps are weights (semantic preference) associated with the semantic terms, QV is the quality vector in which each component is given a value for that attribute (as illustrated in the table), W is the weight vector whose components are weights for the respective QV components, $B = 0$ for LB semantics, $B = 1$ for MB semantics, $B = -1$ for no semantics. Algorithm DSE describes the essential steps of the search engine in extracting metadata from the database that "best match" user query. The search engine has access to the database and ontology in order to process the query $Q = [ST, (QV, W, B)]$.

Algorithm DSE

Let τ denote the threshold specified by the user to filter out those metadata which have "low semantic relevance". So, the algorithm will select the metadata j only if its "semantic relevance score as computed by the algorithm exceeds τ . This way algorithm respects "user-level judgement" in assessing semantic relevance.

1. *Assess Semantic Relevance & Filter Out:* For each metadata i the following steps are done. We modify the algorithm given in Sect. 2.2 to compute the score σ_i of similarity of ST (in the query) to each TA_i as follows:

   - From ST extract the set ST_{ct} of concept terms $\{t_1, \dots, p_k\}$.
   - Using Result 1, compute the similarity of $t_j \in ST_{ct}$ with every $t' \in TA_i$.

     We get $\sigma(t_j, t')$. For t_j the preference weight is p_j. Hence, we multiply the computed value by p_j to calculate the score of "closeness of t_j with $t'i_r$." Fixing t_j, this step is repeated for $r = 1, \dots, m$. We get the following set of weighted scores for t_j.

     $$\rho_j = \{\sigma(t_j, t'_{ir}) | r = 1, \cdots, m\}$$

   - Repeating the previous step for every $t_j \in ST_{ct}$ we get the sets $\rho_1, \rho_2, \dots, \rho_k$.
   - Calculate the minimum value min_i of each set ρ_i. That is, $min_i = minimum\ \{k | k \in \rho_i\}$. Hence we have calculated the set $Min = \{min_1, min_2, \dots, min_m\}$.
   - Calculate $m_i = maximum\ \{k | k \in Min\}$. That is, m is the maximum of all the minimums.
   - Define $\sigma(ST, TA_i) = m_i$.
   - If $m_i < \tau$, the ith metadata associated with TA_i is *not selected*. If $m_i \tau$ the ith metadata is selected.
   - We have now filtered out from the given dataset of metadata a set FS of metadata, and every metadata in FS is semantically relevant to user specified ST.
   - The above steps are repeated for every metadata tag set TA_i.

2. *Assess Quality Measure for each metadata in FS*

   - Assume that $|FS| = N$. Do the following step for $i = 1, \dots, N$. Compute the similarity score for the pair QV_i (of the ith metadata in FS) and QV. Vectors QV_i and QV have the same length 9, assuming unspecified fields will be treated as "0" (to be ignored). Algorithm DS given in Sect. 3 will be used here, with the weight vector W and semantics B as specified in Q. The result from Algorithm DS is the score λ_i, the similarity score for quality attributes.
   - Now we have the scores $\{\lambda_1, \dots, \lambda_N\}$. Rank the set FS of filtered metadata in the non-increasing order of their λ measures. So, the top of the ranked list is the "best match" metadata for the user query.
   - The dataset linked to each metadata in the ranked list can be requested from the dataset provider.

Example 2 *The concept terms are chosen from ontology in Fig. 1.*

Let $TA_1 = \{C_4, C_6\}$ and $TA_2 = \{C_1, C_3, C_5\}$ be the semantic terms associated respectively with metadata M_1 and M_2. Let ST in a user query be $\{(C_5, 3), (C_6, 2)\}$. So, we need to compare the set $\{(C_5, C_6)\}$ of semantic terms in the query with TA_1 and TA_2 and assess their weighted similarity score. We use the results from Table 2.

For M_1: We have to assess the similarity of $\{C_5, C_6\}$ with $\{C_4, C_6\}$. For term C_5, we look up from the table the similarity scores with the concept set $\{C_4, C_6\}$. We have $\left\{\frac{7}{12}, \frac{1}{2}\right\}$. We have to multiply these values with the preference weight 3 of C_5 (assigned by the user in the query). So, we get $\rho_1 = \left\{\frac{21}{12}, \frac{3}{2}\right\}$. Next, for term C_6, we look up from the table the similarity scores with the concept set $\{C_4, C_6\}$. We have $\left\{\frac{1}{2}, 1\right\}$. We have to multiply these values with the preference weight 2 of C_6 (assigned by the user in the query. So, we get $\rho_2 = \{1, 2\}$.

For M_2: Following similar steps, we calculate the set $\rho_3 = \left\{\frac{21}{15}, \frac{12}{9}, 3\right\}$ for C_5 similarity with $TA_2 = \{C_1, C_3, C_5\}$, and the set $\rho_4 = \{1, 1, 1\}$ for C_6 similarity with $TA_2 = \{C_1, C_3, C_5\}$. Below are the measures on relevancy under the three possible schemes.

- Average:
$$\sigma Average(ST, TA_1) = \frac{1.75 + 1.5 + 1 + 2}{4} = 1.5625$$
$$\sigma Average(ST, TA_2) = \frac{1.4 + 1.75 + 3 + 3}{4} = 2.26$$

- Max-Min:
$$\sigma_{Max-Min}(ST, TA_1) = max\{min\rho_1, min\rho_2\} = \frac{3}{2} = 1.5$$
$$\sigma_{Max-Min}(ST, TA_2) = max\{min\rho_3, min\rho_4\} = \frac{12}{9} = 1.75$$

- Min-Max:
$$\sigma_{Min-Max}(ST, TA_1) = min\{max\rho_1, max\rho_2\} = \frac{21}{9} = 1.75$$
$$\sigma_{Min-Max}(ST, TA_2) = min\{max\rho_3, max\rho_4\} = 3$$

The conclusion is, under all semantics metadata M_2 is "more relevant" than metadata M_1.

5 Conclusion

The significant contribution of our paper is the new family of semantic distance functions and their applications in Healthcare and Big Data. Our methods can be applied to selection and ranking problems in any domain, provided ontology is included and at- tributes (features) are assigned precise type definitions. By integrating domain-specific semantics and user judgement-level semantics in the definition of scoring functions we achieve a good level of domain accuracy in scoring function calculations that is acceptable to analysts (users). The methods that we have proposed must be empirically evaluated on large real-life datasets to assess their merits. Our future research continues in this direction, although we find it hard to get relevant datasets. We are hoping that ML and DM research community, who will have access to large data sources, can assess the merits of the semantic distance functions given in this paper.

References

1. Gini, G.: The qsar similarity principle in deep learning era: confirmation or revision. Springer Nat. **22**, 383–402 (2020)
2. Tversky, A.: Features of similarity. Psychol. Rev. **84**(4), 327–352 (1977)
3. Kulmanov, M., Smaili, F.Z., Guo, X., Hoehndorf, R.: Semantic similarity and machine learning with ontologies. Brief. Bioinform. **4**, 1–18 (2021)
4. El-Sappagh, S., Franda, F.A., et al.: Snomed ct standard ontology based on the ontology for general medical science. BMC Med. Inform. Decis. Mak. **18**(78), 1–19 (2018)
5. Daoui, A., Gherabi, N., Marzouk, A.: An enhanced method to compute the similarity between concepts of ontology. In: Noreddine, G., Kacprzyk, J. (eds.) International Conference on Information Technology and Communication Systems. ITCS 2017. Advances in Intelligent Systems and Computing, vol. 640. Springer, Cham (2018). 10.1007
6. Struckmann, S., Ernst, M., Fischer, S., Mah, M., Fuellen, G., M˙'oller, S.: Scoring functions for drug-effect similarity. Brief. Bioinform. **22**(3), 1–8 (2021)
7. Mabotuwana, T., Lee, M., Cohen-Solal, E.V.: An ontology-based similarity measure for biomedical data - application to radiology reports. J. Biomed. Inform. **46**, 857–868 (2013)
8. Harispe, S., Sa´nchez, D., Ranwez, S., Janaqi, S., Montmain, J.: A framework for unifying ontology-based semantic similarity measures: A study in the biomedical domain. Journal of Biomedical Informatics, pp. 38–53, 2014
9. Girardi, D., Wartner, S., Halmerbauer, G., Ehrenmu¨ller, H., Kosorus, H.: Using concept hierarchies to improve calculation of patient similarity. J. Biomed. Inform. **63**, 66–73 (2016)
10. Liu, Y.: Family of algorithms for patient similarity based on electronic health records, mas- ter of computer science thesis, Master's thesis, Concordia University, Montreal, Canada (2022). http://spectrum.library.concordia.ca
11. Alsaig, A.: A tight-coupling context-based framework for dataset discovery. Departmet of Computer Science and Software Engineering, Concordia University, Montreal, Canada, Ph.D. disser- tation (2023)
12. Larsen, R.R., Hastings, J.: From affective science to psychiatric disorder: Ontology as a semantic bridge. Front. Psych. **9**, 1–13 (2018)
13. Sketris, I.S., Metge, C.J., Ross, J.L., MacCara, M.E.: The use of the world health organization anatomical therapeutic chemical/defined daily dose methodology in Canada. Drug Inf. J. **38**(1), 15–27 (2004)
14. Huang, L., Luo, H., Yang, M., Wu, F., Wang, J.: Drug-drug similarity measure and its applications. Brief. Bioinform. **22**(4), 1–20 (2021)
15. Ferdousi, R., Safdari, R., Omidi, Y.: Computational prediction of drug-drug interactions based on drugs functional similarities. J. Biomed. Inform. **5**(1), 1–21 (2017)
16. Zhang, P., Wang, F., Hu, J., Sorrentino, R.: Towards personalized medicine: Leverag- ing patient similarity and drug similarity analytics. In: Proceedings of AMIA Joint Summits Transcience Science, pp. 132–136 (2014)
17. Polyzotis, N., Roy, S., Whang, S.E., Zinkevich, M.: Data lifecycle challenges in production machine learning: A survey. SIGMOD Record **47**(2), 17–28 (2018)
18. Paleyes, A., Urma, R., Lawrence, N.D.: Challenges in deploying machine learning: A survey of case studies. ACM Comput. Surv. (2022)
19. Noy, N., Burgess, M., Brickley, D.: Google dataset search: Building a search engine for datasets in an open web ecosystem. In: 28th Web Conference (2019)
20. Castelo, S., Rampin, R., Santos, A., Bessa, A., Chirigati, F., Freire, J.: Auctus: a dataset search engine for data discovery and augmentation. In: Proceedings of the VLDB Endowment, vol. 14, no. 12. VLDB Endowment, pp. 2791–2794 (2021)

A Multi-Scale Spatiotemporal Capsule Network for Epilepsy Seizure Detection

Wangliang Zhou[1], Yijie Pan[2], Hefan Zhou[1], Qingqing Chen[1], Jie Jiao[1], Meiyan Xu[1(✉)], and Peipei Gu[3]

[1] College of Computer Science, Minnan Normal University, Zhangzhou 363000, China
xmy2300@mnnu.edu.cn
[2] Eastern Institute for Advanced Study, Eastern Institute of Technology, Ningbo 315000, China
[3] Zhengzhou University of Light Industry, Zhengzhou 450000, China

Abstract. The electroencephalogram (EEG) signal is pivotal for the expert diagnosis of epilepsy in patients. However, experiential bias among these experts can sometimes lead to inconsistent judgment outcomes. To mitigate this, it is imperative to establish a comprehensive algorithm to aid in resolving this issue. This study introduces a novel deep learning architecture that integrates convolutional neural network (CNN) and capsule neural network (CapsNet) to provide end-to-end epilepsy diagnosis. Using CNN facilitates the extraction of both temporal and spatial information from EEG data. Subsequently, CapsNet analyses the resultant hybrid feature vector, enabling the categorization of interictal and ictal cases. The model was validated through its application to the CHB-MIT and SIENA public datasets for validation purposes. In the domain of seizure event detection, our model demonstrates the accuracy of 99.12% and 99.54%, the sensitivity of 89.97% and 90.93%, specificity of 99.27% and 99.59%, and F1 score of 77.15% and 77.27%, respectively. Furthermore, The CHB-MIT dataset was utilized for seizure onset detection, resulting in a sensitivity rate of 99.13% and a time delay of 9.28 s. Collectively, these results underline that our model adeptly extracts meaningful features from EEG datasets, ensuring accurate judgments.

Keywords: Capsule network · Convolutional neural network · Deep learning · Electroencephalogram · Seizure detection

1 Introduction

Epilepsy is identified as a pervasive and chronic neurological disorder, impacting an estimated global population of approximately 60 million [1]. The pathology originates from aberrant neuronal discharges in the cerebral region, culminating in transient perturbations in electrophysiological brain activity. Such manifestations encompass episodic loss of consciousness, convulsive episodes, and involuntary limb movements. The abrupt onset of these episodes leads to profound ramifications for affected individuals. Presently, the diagnostic evaluation of epilepsy largely hinges on the visual inspection of patients'

W. Zhou and Y. Pan—Contribute equally to this work.

electroencephalogram (EEG) by medical professionals [2]. The veracity of this diagnostic paradigm remains to be fully ascertained, with notable variations observed across medical evaluations. The infusion of artificial intelligence (AI) methodologies for the detection of epileptic seizures surfaces as a salient development in contemporary medical research, largely attributed to the monumental strides in AI domains. The integration of AI mechanisms not only holds promise for automating the seizure detection procedure but also for elevating its diagnostic precision [3].

In the realm of AI, machine learning techniques assume a pivotal role, particularly in discerning EEG seizures [4]. Over the past decade, a plethora of machine learning algorithms have emerged to tackle this intricate task. Alotaiby et al. [5] enhanced the common spatial pattern (CSP) method to distill features from EEG segments, subsequently leveraging SVM for classification purposes. Birjandtalab et al. [6] harnessed the Fourier transform technique to compute the power spectral density of EEG windows and utilized these computed metrics as features to feed into a random forest classifier. Yet, it's imperative to acknowledge that such feature extraction mandates a nuanced expertise. The stratified application of feature extraction might not resonate universally, given the inherent heterogeneity of EEG data across demography.

Deep learning has demonstrated an intrinsic capability to abstract high-level representations directly from raw signals [7]. Li et al. [8] leveraged CNNs to intuit multi-scale temporal and spectrum information from raw EEG. Additionally, they mitigated the issue of data imbalance by implementing the maximum mean difference loss. Albeit, this methodology uses only five EEG channels, which may result in the loss of important information. Thuwajit et al. [9] extracted time-domain receptive field information using multi-scale model. A spatiotemporal feature extractor is applied to different receptive fields, then a global pooling layer merges the features and feeds them into a linear layer for epileptic event categorization. Yet, the deployment of global average pooling inadvertently eclipses certain pivotal features.

To address the gaps that have been created by pooling layers, Sabour et al. [10] introduced capsule networks (CapsNet). Recent scholarly endeavors have documented the evolution and strategic implementation of capsule networks across various EEG paradigms. Building on this momentum, Chen et al. [11] refined EEG signals using a time-domain channel attention mechanism. Following this, CapsNet has been employed to perceive intricate feature interrelationships, optimized for fatigue-driven detection. In a similar vein, Wei et al. [12] presented a fusion of the Transformer and CapsNet, aiming to adeptly capture global information characteristics crucial for emotion detection. Theoretically speaking, CapsNet, with its ability to handle intricate spatial intricacies and its resilience to affine transformations, shows great promise in enhancing EEG signal feature extraction.

In this paper, we have introduced a cutting-edge, integrated end-to-end network architecture. Our rigorous benchmarking against two esteemed public datasets, which encompass both seizure events and seizure onsets detection, offers empirical evidence of our model's superiority. These assessments unequivocally highlight our model's enhanced performance metrics when contrasted with prevailing approaches.

The main contributions of the paper are as follows:

- We present a methodology for extracting spatiotemporal features by integrating multiple convolutional operations. This approach is designed to capture specific EEG signal characteristics within designated time intervals. Simultaneously, deep convolutions are employed to distinguish spatial characteristics that correspond to each temporal filter.
- We prompt a multi-scale module for the purpose of extracting features across different time windows, with the aim of enhancing the generalizability of the model. This particular strategy proves advantageous in effectively mitigating the observed signal variations that exist among individual patients.
- We introduce a pioneering approach for multi-channel seizure detection by integrating CNN and CapsNet. The intrinsic dynamic routing mechanism of CapsNet ensures efficient and robust feature propagation to higher hierarchical levels, mitigating potential data loss of critical information.

2 Materials and Methods

2.1 Data Preparation

The CHB-MIT [13] dataset features scalp EEG recordings from 23 pediatric patients. Conforming to the 10–20 international electrode placement standard, each recording sample is recorded at 256 Hz with a 16-bit resolution. Altogether, the dataset registers 198 epileptic seizure events. In our study, our focus narrows to those recordings detailing epileptic seizures. We harness 18 channels consistently available across patients. Worth noting, in the case of patient 12, three distinct recordings (chb12_27.edf, chb12_28.edf, and chb12_29.edf) deviate by featuring channels outside our selected spectrum, and thus we omit them from our evaluation.

The SIENA [14] dataset, curated by the Department of Neurology and Neurophysiology at the University of Siena, Italy, encompasses scalp EEG recordings spanning 14 patients. Consistent with the 10–20 international electrode placement standard, these recordings sample at 512 Hz. To harmonize with the CHB-MIT dataset's specifications, we resample the SIENA dataset down to 256 Hz. From the extensive dataset, we selected 29 channels consistently present across all patients. Notably, due to having only 21 channels, patient 10 does not feature in our study. Additionally, inconsistencies in the seizure timing annotations mandate the exclusion of patient 0 from our assessment.

2.2 Pre-processing

Tackling noise interference is indispensable in EEG signal processing, given its ubiquitous presence during data acquisition. In addressing this, our methodology harnesses a low-pass finite impulse response band-pass filter spanning 0–50 Hz, ensuring a meticulous eradication of unwarranted noise components. Subsequent to the filtering phase, we segment the data, opting for a 4s window length. Furthermore, by infusing a 2s overlap, we amplify the overall sample volume [8]. Maintaining a consistent sampling rate at 256 Hz, our formulated input data dimension stands at (N, 1024), where N corresponds to the channel count and 1024 pinpoints the sampling instances.

2.3 Model Architecture

The archetypal structure of our proposed multi-scale spatiotemporal capsule network (MSSTC-Net) is elegantly delineated in Fig. 1 At the outset, the Temporal Spatial Block is diligently tasked with extracting both temporal and spatial nuances from segmented EEG data. This foundational extraction then segues into the Multi-Scale Block, which is strategically designed to capture temporal information across multiple scales. Notably, to bolster the backpropagation efficacy, we incorporate a skip connection, which underpins the neural network's learning trajectory, ensuring an enhanced convergence rate. Culminating this orchestrated processing, we leverage the prowess of the capsule network, focusing on nuanced feature mapping, thus achieving the quintessential task of seizure detection.

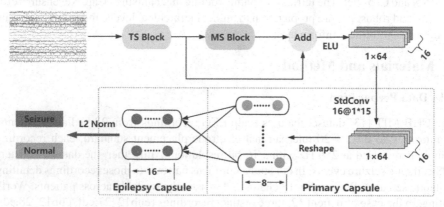

Fig. 1. Overall framework of MSSTC-Net.

Temporal-Spatial Block. In Fig. 2, our design features a trio of sequential convolutional blocks for time-domain feature extraction. These blocks use filters and kernels of sizes 8 and 15, respectively, harmonized with the exponential linear unit activation function and batch normalization. Next, an average pooling layer with a kernel size of 2 reduces dimensions and extracts receptive fields. After three iterations, the total receptive field spans approximately 128 units, roughly translating to 0.5 s. While [15] employs a convolutional block with a kernel size half the sampling rate for gleaning information above 2 Hz, noisy data poses challenges. Signal features extracted by large kernels sometimes miss the mark in completeness. By breaking these receptive fields into three smaller convolutions and incorporating more nonlinear functions, the design effectively addresses the complexities of EEG signals. The architecture then utilizes a depth-wise convolution [18] with a kernel size equivalent to the number of channels, extracting overarching spatial insights from the EEG. Consistent with previous steps, we implement an average pooling layer of size 2 to adjust the sampling rate. A notable advantage of depth-wise convolution is its efficiency in refining model parameters while capturing spatial details across diverse temporal filters.

Multi-Scale Block. In EEG signal analysis, using a consistent time convolution window across various patients often limits efficient feature extraction due to individual variances. Addressing this challenge, our model incorporates multi-scale architectures, echoing the successful outcomes from previous research [17]. Our approach skillfully discerns spatiotemporal dynamics over multiple scales employing depth-wise separable convolutions with three specific kernel sizes: 3, 7, and 15. Delving deeper, each branch commences with a depth-wise convolution following channel integration to isolate temporal features. This progression then follows a point-wise convolution, assimilating feature information through its designated filters. By arranging the trio of branches in line with feature map dimensions, a subsequent point-wise convolution marries these multi-scale feature maps. The result is an output with a feature map quantity mirroring the input. This consolidated output subsequently undergoes element-wise processing.

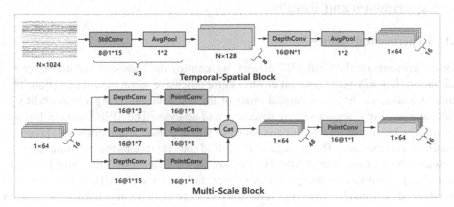

Fig. 2. A schematic illustration of the Temporal-Spatial Block and Multi-Scale Block.

Primary Capsule. The foundational layer of capsules is constructed using conventional convolution. Within this configuration, the kernel size is designated as 15, accompanied by 16 filters, and each capsule embodies a vector dimension of 8. Post-convolution, the resultant shape manifests as (batch, 16, 1, 64), which is subsequently reshaped to (batch, 128, 8). This is then subjected to the squash function, which effectively compresses the magnitude of elongated vectors to just below 1, while nearly nullifying the length of more diminutive vectors. The squash function is articulated as:

$$v_j = \frac{||s_j||2}{1 + ||s_j||^2} * \frac{s_j}{||s_j||^2} \tag{1}$$

where s_j represents the input vector of capsule j, v_j represents the output vector, and $||s_j||$ represents the l_2 norm of the vector.

Epilepsy Capsule. Inter-capsule communication is orchestrated through an algorithm termed dynamic routing. This iterative mechanism channels the low-level capsules toward their more active high-level counterparts. Detailed insights into this specific algorithm can be gleaned from [10]. In our configuration, we establish two digital capsule layers, denoted as interictal and ictal. The dimensionality of these digital capsule layers is fixed at 16. Within this framework, the magnitude of the vector in the digital capsule layer is computed to signify the probability of its associated category. The computation for margin loss is delineated as follows:

$$L_k = T_k * \max\left(0, m^+ - ||v_k||\right)^2 + \lambda(1 - T_k) * \max(0, ||v_k|| - m^-)^2 \qquad (2)$$

where T_k is 1 if the label k matches with the epilepsy capsule and 0 otherwise, m^+ the upper boundary is set to 0.9, and m^- the lower boundary is set to 0.1, λ is 0.5 prevents the mold length of the capsule from being too small during initial training.

3   Experiments and Results

3.1   Experimental Settings

For experiments on the CHB-MIT dataset, we employ the leave-one-record-out cross-validation (LOOCV) strategy, as it ensures comprehensive seizure event detection. This strategy maintains the chronological order of the test data, mirroring a real-world scenario and making it apt for seizure detection and analysis. The SIENA dataset has few recordings and the seizure duration is short, so we only used 5-fold cross-validation for seizure event detection. The average of the 5-fold data represents the outcome. In order to assess the performance of MSSTC-Net, we utilized four evaluation metrics: accuracy (Acc), sensitivity (Sen), specificity (Spec), and the F1 score (F1). In the context of imbalanced datasets, F1 score and sensitivity emerge as more insightful indicators for model evaluation.

The primary aim of seizure event detection is to distinguish between interictal and ictal states using EEG data, streamlining the labeling process for medical practitioners. For patients with epilepsy, the urgency of real-time seizure detection is paramount, necessitating instantaneous recognition and prompt alert generation. To mitigate false alarms, a classification is deemed accurate only when at least three consecutive epileptic episodes are detected. Two key metrics, sensitivity of onsets and latency, serve as performance evaluators. Sensitivity by onsets quantifies the ratio of correctly identified seizures to the overall seizure count. Meanwhile, latency denotes the temporal gap between the model's inaugural alert and the genuine inception of a seizure, as delineated by specialists. An exemplar of such detection, spanning from 2952s to 3048s for the chb01_03.edf file within the CHB-MIT dataset is depicted in Fig. 3.

3.2   Training Details

All experiments were implemented using Python v3.7.0 and Pytorch v1.8.1. All computational tasks were undertaken on an NVIDIA RTX2080Ti equipped with 11 GB of memory. We utilized the Adam optimizer with a 10^{-3} learning rate. The training epochs were limited to 100, and the batch size was set to 128. The final results are recorded as the last epoch of the test. Class weights were added to the loss function to balance the large difference between interictal and ictal samples.

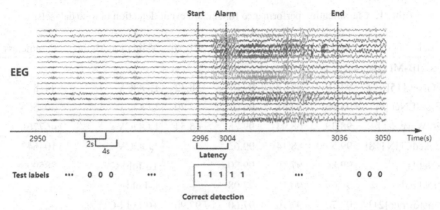

Fig. 3. Schematic diagram of seizure onset detection for file chb01_03.edf.

3.3 Results and Analysis

We employ two training strategies to evaluate the effectiveness of the proposed method. Table 1 lists the results of some state-of-the-art seizure event detection methods on the CHB-MIT dataset. The suggested model outperforms the previous methods in terms of accuracy, sensitivity, and specificity when using the k-fold strategy. The results show a significant difference in sensitivity between LOOCV and k-fold. The explanation behind this phenomenon may be attributed to two factors. Firstly, k-fold ensures that the number of data samples in each fold is balanced. Secondly, the training and testing data are not totally separated as there is an overlap in the sampling of samples. Hence, LOOCV presents a greater level of difficulty and realism. Under the LOOCV strategy, sensitivity is second to CE-stSENet [8], while accuracy and specificity are slightly inferior to StackedCNN [18], and F1 score the highest among the baseline methods with 77.15%. The trade-off between sensitivity and F1 score showed that the proposed model has a more stable detection ability.

The experiments of the SIENA dataset were conducted using the model code provided in the baseline methodology paper, ensuring consistent experimental circumstances. EEGNet [15] performed poorly overall, with an F1 score of only 55.32%, owing to its limited model parameters and weak fitting capacity. The sensitivity index of the suggested model has the greatest value among all models, with a percentage of 90.93%. This value surpasses that of the StackedCNN model by a margin of 12.03%. Furthermore, the F1 score also exhibits a leading margin of 2.1%. Although our model's accuracy and specificity may be slightly lower compared to other techniques, it consistently maintains stable identification performance.

Table 2 compares the seizure onset detection performance of the proposed model and baseline approach. The most effective deep learning model is StackedCNN, which achieves 99.31% sensitivity with 8.1s of latency. Overall, deep learning algorithms perform better than classical machine learning techniques, where our model outperforms most algorithms.

Table 1. Classification performance for seizure event detection on two datasets.

Model	Acc(%)	Sen(%)	Spec(%)	F1(%)	Validation Method	Parameters
A. CHB-MIT dataset						
EEGNet [15]	97.18	89.12	97.27	58.32	LOOCV	2418
CE-stSENet [8]	95.96	92.41	96.05	54.20	LOOCV	305566
EEGWaveNet [9]	98.39	68.94	99.25	65.54	LOOCV	46776
StackedCNN [18]	99.54	88.14	99.62	–	LOOCV	104642
LSNet [19]	99.80	97.10	99.80	–	10-fold-CV	28590
CNN [20]	96.69	96.19	97.08	–	k-Fold-CV	–
Transformer [21]	98.76	97.70	97.60	97.90	10-Fold-CV	–
Proposed	99.12	89.97	99.27	77.15	LOOCV	41192
	99.80	97.92	99.83	95.40	10-Fold-CV	
B. SIENA dataset						
EEGNet [15]	98.97	78.83	99.07	55.32	5-fold-CV	–
EEGWaveNet [9]	99.73	76.36	99.86	75.05	5-fold-CV	–
StackedCNN [18]	99.72	78.90	99.84	75.17	5-fold-CV	–
Proposed	99.54	90.93	99.59	77.27	5-fold-CV	–

Table 2. Classification performance for seizure onset detection on CHB-MIT dataset.

Model	Sensitivity by onset(%)	Latency(%)
CE-stSENet [8]	98.93	9.39
EMD, CSP+SVM [1]	98.47	–
StackedCNN [18]	99.31	8.1
DWT+RUSBoosted [22]	96.15	10.42
TQWT+CNN [23]	98.90	10.46
Proposed	99.20	9.29

4 Discussion

4.1 Analysis of Model Architecture

Influence of the Temporal Feature Extraction. To validate the rationality of the temporal convolution module design, we compare the performance of convolution with kernel size 128 with the proposed temporal convolution module on the CHB-MIT (SIENA) dataset. According to Table 3 results, the proposed temporal convolution module performs better, with improvements in accuracy, sensitivity, and specificity of 0.36% (0.24%), 2.80% (7.31%), and 0.36% (0.2%), respectively, while F1 score experiences a significant increase of 8.09% (9.1%). Figure 4 demonstrates the F1 score difference between the two models across patients in the CHB-MIT dataset. The graphs show that although a few patients perform slightly weaker in the proposed convolutional module, the majority of patients show nearly 2% to 7% performance improvement. In particular, in patient 6 and patient 16, the 128-size convolution scores only 4.7% and 1.68% in F1 score. The ictal and interictal sample ratios for patients 6 and 16 were 1:716 and 1:358, and the excessively large sample gaps prevented the single convolutional model from performing effective epileptic feature extraction when learning features. Instead, it is more likely to identify some of the noisy data from the interictal samples as seizures.

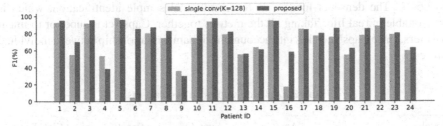

Fig. 4. Patient-specific parameters comparison of the single conv and proposed model.

Effect of the Multi-scale and Skip Connection. The multi-scale block and skip connection also play a crucial role in the model, and we demonstrate the impact by comparing the complete model with two simplified models designed. 1) single-scale convolution; 2) without skip connection. As shown in Table 3, the accuracy, sensitivity, specificity, and F1 score of the multi-scale model on the CHB-MIT (SIENA) dataset were 0.23% (0.08%), 0.76% (2.67%), 0.22% (0.07%), and 4.34% (5.83%) higher than those of the single scale model, respectively. This indicates that the features extracted by multi-scale models are of great help in detecting seizure events. In addition, compared to without using skip connection models, all indicators were improved on the CHB-MIT dataset, with accuracy, sensitivity, specificity, and F1 score increasing by 0.49%, 0.93%, 0.5%, and 2.73%, respectively. Sensitivity and F1 score increased by 1.92% and 3.31% on the SIENA dataset. Accuracy and specificity showed a slight decrease of 0.04% and 0.05%, respectively. By comparison, skip connections can help the model retain some important information and effectively improve it. In summary, the overall performance of the proposed model is superior to the simplified model, demonstrating the effectiveness of the multi-scale block.

Performance of the CapsNet. To demonstrate the effectiveness of capsule networks, we replaced the capsule network with a module combining a convolutional layer and a fully connected layer with an accompanying softmax layer. We observe that on the CHB-MIT dataset, CapsNet obtains an across-the-board performance improvement. In particular, accuracy, sensitivity, specificity, and F1 score are improved by 0.75%, 7.09%, 0.65%, and 3.18%, respectively. The confusion matrix shown in Fig. 5 also demonstrates that capsule networks outperform fully connected layer networks. On the SIENA dataset, the sensitivity metric of CapsNet improves even more significantly, with an increase

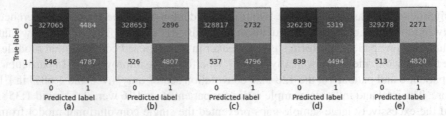

Fig. 5. Confusion matrixes on ablation study. (a) single conv(K = 128), (b) without skip connection, (c) single scale(K = 15), (d) densenet, (e) proposed.

of 17.64%. The densenet focuses more on interictal sample identification, which is unreasonable in real life. Taking all the metrics together, CapsNet is superior to linear classifiers, since CapsNet takes into account the dynamic relationship between individual features.

Table 3. Ablation studies on two datasets.

Model	Acc(%)	Sen(%)	Spec(%)	F1(%)
A. CHB-MIT dataset				
single conv(K = 128)	98.97	87.17	98.91	69.06
without skip connection	98.63	89.04	98.77	74.42
single scale(K = 15)	98.89	89.21	99.05	72.81
densenet	98.37	82.88	98.62	73.97
proposed	99.12	89.97	99.27	77.15
B. SIENA dataset				
single conv(K = 128)	99.30	83.62	99.39	68.15
without skip connection	99.58	89.01	99.64	73.96
single scale(K = 15)	99.46	88.26	99.52	71.44
densenet	99.79	73.29	99.95	78.35
proposed	99.54	90.93	99.59	77.27

5   Conclusion

In this paper, we delved into the nuanced spatiotemporal dynamics inherent to epilepsy, leading to the inception of the multi-scale spatiotemporal capsule network. Harnessing the strengths of both the inception and convolutional neural network architectures, we designed a sophisticated spatiotemporal feature extraction mechanism. Our findings underscored the enhanced efficacy of utilizing an ensemble of smaller convolutional kernels over singular larger counterparts in accurately discerning epilepsy-related spatiotemporal characteristics, signposting potential avenues for subsequent inquiries. Further enriching our model, the integration of a capsule neural network (CapsNet) facilitated a deeper synthesis and scrutiny of spatiotemporal patterns. This integration capitalized on CapsNet's adeptness at discerning subtle distinctions, particularly when specific features manifested in both ictal and interictal, bolstering the model's diagnostic acumen. Empirical evaluations across two datasets reaffirmed the salient efficacy and innovation underscored by our proposed approach in the realm of epilepsy detection.

Acknowledgments. This research was supported by the Fujian Provincial Natural Science Foundation (Grant No. 2023J01921), the Fujian Provincial Young and Middle-aged Teachers' Education Research Project (Grant No. JAT210265), the Young Tech Innovation Leading Talent Program of Ningbo City (Grant No. 2023QL008), and the Innovation Consortium Program for Green and Efficient Intelligent Appliances of Ningbo City (Grant No. 2022H002).

References

1. Li, C., et al.: Seizure onset detection using empirical mode decomposition and common spatial pattern. IEEE Trans. Neural Syst. Rehabil. Eng. **29**, 458–467 (2021)
2. Qiu, X., Yan, F., Liu, H.: A difference attention Resnet-LSTM network for epileptic seizure detection using eeg signal. Biomed. Signal Process. Control **83**, 104652 (2023)
3. Guo, J., et al.: Detecting high frequency oscillations for stereoelectroencephalography in epilepsy via hypergraph learning. IEEE Trans. Neural Syst. Rehabil. Eng. **29**, 587–596 (2021)
4. Tsiouris, K.M., Pezoulas, V.C., Zervakis, M., Konitsiotis, S., Koutsouris, D.D., Fotiadis, D.I.: A long short-term memory deep learning network for the prediction of epileptic seizures using eeg signals. Comput. Biol. Med. **99**, 24–37 (2018)
5. Alotaiby, T.N., Abd El-Samie, F.E., Alshebeili, S.A., Aljibreen, K.H., Alkhanen, E.: Seizure detection with common spatial pattern and support vector machines. In: 2015 International Conference on Information and Communication Technology Research (ICTRC), pp. 152–155 (2015)
6. Birjandtalab, J., Pouyan, M.B., Cogan, D., Nourani, M., Harvey, J.: Automated seizure detection using limited-channel eeg and non-linear dimension reduction. Comput. Biol. Med. **82**, 49–58 (2017)
7. Bengio, Y., Courville, A., Vincent, P.: Representation learning: A review and new perspectives. IEEE Trans. Pattern Anal. Mach. Intell. **35**(8), 1798–1828 (2013)
8. Li, Y., Liu, Y., Cui, W.G., Guo, Y.Z., Huang, H., Hu, Z.Y.: Epileptic seizure detection in eeg signals using a unified temporal-spectral squeeze-and-excitation network. IEEE Trans. Neural Syst. Rehabil. Eng. **28**(4), 782–794 (2020)
9. Thuwajit, P., et al.: Eegwavenet: Multiscale CNN-based spatiotemporal feature extraction for eeg seizure detection. IEEE Trans. Industr. Inf. **18**(8), 5547–5557 (2021)
10. Sabour, S., Frosst, N., Hinton, G.E.: Dynamic routing between capsules. Adv. Neural Inform. Process. Syst. **30** (2017)
11. Chen, C., Ji, Z., Sun, Y., Bezerianos, A., Thakor, N., Wang, H.: Self-attentive channel-connectivity capsule network for eeg-based driving fatigue detection. IEEE Trans. Neural Syst. Rehabil. Eng. **31**, 3152–3162 (2023)
12. Wei, Y., Liu, Y., Li, C., Cheng, J., Song, R., Chen, X.: Tc-net: A transformer capsule network for eeg-based emotion recognition. Comput. Biol. Med. **152**, 106463 (2023)
13. Shoeb, A.H.: Application of machine learning to epileptic seizure onset detection and treatment. Massachusetts Institute of Technology (2009)

14. Detti, P., Vatti, G., Zabalo Manrique de Lara, G.: Eeg synchronization analysis for seizure prediction: a study on data of noninvasive recordings. Processes **8**(7), 846 (2020)
15. Lawhern, V.J., Solon, A.J., Waytowich, N.R., Gordon, S.M., Hung, C.P., Lance, B.J.: Eegnet: a compact convolutional neural network for eeg-based brain-computer interfaces. J. Neural Eng. **15**(5), 056013 (2018)
16. Chollet, F.: Xception: deep learning with depthwise separable convolutions. In: Proceedings of the IEEE Conference on Computer Vision and Pattern Recognition, pp. 1251–1258 (2017)
17. Ding, Y., Robinson, N., Zhang, S., Zeng, Q., Guan, C.: Tsception: capturing temporal dynamics and spatial asymmetry from eeg for emotion recognition. IEEE Trans. Affect. Comput. (2022)
18. Wang, X., Wang, X., Liu, W., Chang, Z., Karkkainen, T., Cong, F.: One dimensional convolutional neural networks for seizure onset detection using long-term scalp and intracranial eeg. Neurocomputing **459**, 212–222 (2021)
19. Qiu, S., Wang, W., Jiao, H.: Lightseizurenet: A lightweight deep learning model for real-time epileptic seizure detection. IEEE J. Biomed. Health Inform. **27**(4), 1845–1856 (2022)
20. Cimr, D., Fujita, H., Tomaskova, H., Cimler, R., Selamat, A.: Automatic seizure detection by convolutional neural networks with computational complexity analysis. Comput. Methods Programs Biomed. **229**, 107277 (2023)
21. Zhao, Y., et al.: Interactive local and global feature coupling for eeg-based epileptic seizure detection. Biomed. Signal Process. Control **81**, 104441 (2023)
22. Shen, M., Wen, P., Song, B., Li, Y.: An eeg based real-time epilepsy seizure detection approach using discrete wavelet transform and machine learning methods. Biomed. Signal Process. Control **77**, 103820 (2022)
23. Shen, M., Wen, P., Song, B., Li, Y.: Real-time epilepsy seizure detection based on eeg using tunable-q wavelet transform and convolutional neural network. Biomed. Signal Process. Control **82**, 10456 (2023)

Improved ConvNeXt Facial Expression Recognition Embedded with Attention Mechanism

Yiteng Zhao[1,2], Lina Ge[1,2,3(✉)], Gaoxiang Cui[1,2], and Teng Fang[1,2]

[1] School of Artificial Intelligence, Guangxi Minzu University, Nanning 530000, China
66436539@qq.com
[2] Key Laboratory of Network Communication Engineering, Guangxi Minzu University, Nanning 530000, China
[3] Guangxi Key Laboratory of Hybrid Computation and IC Design Analysis, Nanning 530000, China

Abstract. Facial expression recognition (FER) is an emerging and important research field in the field of pattern recognition, with wide applications in safe driving, intelligent monitoring, and human-computer interaction. This article addresses the problems of insufficient key information extraction, low recognition accuracy, and easy overfitting in facial expression recognition, and proposes an ECA-ConvNeXt network based on transfer learning strategy and channel attention mechanism. Firstly, the weights of the pre-trained model are initialized using transfer learning on the FER 2013 dataset. Secondly, a series of data augmentation operations are performed on the facial images, allowing them to pass through the ECA-Net attention module of the network, enhancing the key information of the feature regions with high relevance to expressions and suppressing the interference of irrelevant regions in the feature maps. Finally, the inverse bottleneck layer, maximum pooling layer, global average pooling layer, and classification layer are sequentially passed into the network to accelerate the convergence speed and improve the expression recognition rate. Compared to the baseline network, the improved network achieved an accuracy of 72.86%, a recall rate of 72.04%, and a specificity of 64.15% on the FER 2013 dataset. Compared to the commonly used ResNet network and its improvement methods, the proposed ECA-ConvNeXt in this article achieved a 0.19% improvement in recognition accuracy.

Keywords: Transfer Learning · ConvNeXt · Attention

1 Introduction

In interpersonal communication, in addition to language, facial expression is also a very important way to express information. With the development of artificial intelligence, Facial Expression Recognition (FER) [1] technology has become a current research hotspot. The combination of facial expression recognition technology and machines can improve the efficiency and accuracy of recognition and provide support for facial

D.-S. Huang et al. (Eds.): ICAI 2023, CCIS 2014, pp. 89–100, 2024.
https://doi.org/10.1007/978-981-97-0903-8_10

expression recognition applications in the fields of medicine and automatic driving. In practical applications, facial expression recognition technology faces many challenges, such as the interference of the environment, the change of light, the influence of noise, and the complexity and diversity of expressions, which can significantly affect the effect of expression recognition [2]. In order to solve these problems, scholars have continuously proposed new deep learning algorithms to improve the recognition rate and generalization of facial expressions.

Methods for facial expression recognition are generally divided into traditional and deep learning methods. Traditional methods are mainly based on manually designed features, such as Gabor [3], LBP [4], HOG [5], to extract the appearance and motion information of facial images, and then use classifiers, such as SVM [6], KNN [7], to determine the class of facial expressions. Traditional facial expression recognition methods use hand-designed feature extractors, which tend to ignore the features that have a greater impact on classification when extracting features, leading to inaccurate classification results. Compared with traditional methods, deep learning methods have better generalization ability and robustness, and can handle facial expression recognition in complex situations such as different lighting, posture and occlusion, and are also the mainstream direction of current facial expression recognition technology. Since 2006, deep learning has received more and more attention from researchers due to its ability to adapt well to nonlinear feature weighting, and more and more classical network structures have been born on this basis, such as AlexNet [8], VGGNet [9], GoogLeNet [10], and ResNet [11], etc. Yusufu Tureke et al. [12] used AlexNet network as the basic network and applied training strategies such as global average pooling as well as batch normalization and achieved good prediction results on several different facial expression datasets. Kusuma et al. [13] used expression recognition method based on VGGNet network to improve the expression recognition rate. SHENGTAO G et al. [14] trained a model on residual network ResNet to train the model, with the help of shortcut in ResNet to solve the degradation phenomenon in deep neural network training, that is, with the increase of network layers, the accuracy of the model instead decreases.

When the face is affected by occlusion or other non-controllable factors, the recognition effect will be reduced, in order to improve the recognition effect, it is necessary to locate the effective facial coordinates more accurately, so as to reduce the introduction of non-relevant feature information. The traditional convolutional neural network cannot learn the structural information of the image, which leads to the model cannot capture some of the laws and relationships that exist in the image. Attention mechanism [15] it allows the model to focus on more important parts, thus improving the performance and efficiency of the model. Attention mechanism has been used with great success in several image vision tasks including image classification, target detection, semantic segmentation, etc. [16]. Wang et al. [17] proposed an efficient channel attention network model, ECA-Net, which enables local cross-channel interactions and highlights locally useful information about the samples, thus exhibiting superior recognition classification. Woo [18] et al. presented a model of ECA-Net in terms of the channel dimension and spatial dimension respectively to incorporate the attention mechanism thus obtaining CBAM. CBAM is a simple yet effective module that can be seamlessly integrated with any convolutional neural network without adding too much computational overhead. Hu et al. [19] proposed SE-Net, which uses the squeeze-and-excitation module to achieve dynamic inter-channel feature relabeling. This approach enhances the important features and suppresses the unimportant features, thus improving the accuracy of image recognition.

Through the above analysis, it is easy to see that the facial expression recognition based on deep learning can better solve the problem of low efficiency in traditional methods, but there are still problems that the network model is too complex, the recognition efficiency is low, and the generalization ability is not strong. To further improve the accuracy of facial expression recognition, this paper proposes an ECA-ConvNeXt facial expression recognition network incorporating the attention mechanism, and the main contributions include:

1. Using ConvNeXt as the backbone, an ECA-ConvNeXt facial expression recognition model incorporating the attention mechanism is proposed, which can effectively extract and utilize face features to improve the accuracy and robustness of expression recognition.
2. The transfer learning strategy uses the pre-trained model parameters as initial values to accelerate the convergence speed of the model, reduce the risk of overfitting, and improve the generalization ability of the model.
3. The ECA-Net module, an attention mechanism, amplifies the model's concentration on key channel features, empowering the network to self-assign weights to individual channel features and thereby enhance the network's learning potential.

2 Related Work

2.1 ConvNeXt

ConvNeXt [20] network is a pure convolutional neural network proposed by Facebook Artificial Intelligence Research Institute (FAIR, Facebook AI Research) in 2022. ConvNeXt is based on the ResNet network, inspired by Transform, and draws on Swim-Transform [21] network architecture and various state-of-the-art method strategies used in its training process. The ConvNeXt network mainly consists of four stage layers, each with a block stacking ratio of 3:3:9:3, while the Stem layer is replaced by a convolutional layer with a convolutional kernel of 4 and a step size of 4. ResNet uses a bottleneck structure in order to minimize the amount of computation, whereas ConvNeXt adopts the opposite idea, using an inverse bottleneck layer structure and increasing the number of channels in the intermediate layer to improve the expressive power of the network. In addition to these macro-scale improvements, ConvNeXt also fine-tuned some of the model's micro-architecture by replacing ReLU with GELU, reducing the use of activation and normalization functions, and using a 2×2 convolution with a step size of 2 for spatial down sampling. The model structure of ConvNeXt is shown in Fig. 1.

2.2 ECA-Net

Attention mechanisms can mimic human visual attention allocation, and existing research has shown that adding attention mechanisms to existing convolutional neural network frameworks or models can improve their performance. ECA-Net is based on

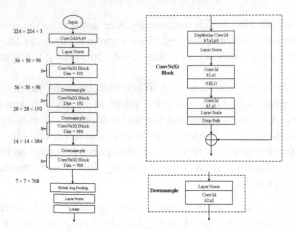

Fig. 1. ConvNeXt network structure

the channel attention mechanism, which utilizes one-dimensional convolution to extract the correlation between each channel and its neighboring channels to enhance feature representation. The core idea of ECA-Net is to achieve local cross-channel interactions by means of a One-dimensional convolution to achieve local cross-channel interactions, thus avoiding the use of downscaling and fully connected layers. The features are aggregated by global average pooling to obtain the global channel information, and the global average pooling formula is shown in (1):

$$g(X) = \frac{1}{WH} \sum_{i=1,j=1}^{W,H} X_{ij} \tag{1}$$

where X is the input feature map, W and H are the width and height, and $g(X)$ is the result of global average pooling for each channel.

The convolution kernel size K of ECA-Net is adaptively determined based on the channel dimension C, which is calculated as shown in (2):

$$k = \psi(C) = | \gamma \log_2(C) + \gamma b | \tag{2}$$

where γ and b are constants, $\gamma = 2$ and $b = 1$ are taken in this paper, and C is the channel dimension.

Then, a 1D convolution with convolution kernel size k is utilized to compute the channel weights and obtain the interdependencies between the channels. The specific convolution formula is shown in (3):

$$\omega = \sigma(C_1 D_k(y)) \tag{3}$$

where ω is the channel weight, σ is the sigmoid function, $C_1 D_k$ is the 1D convolution, and y is the result after global average pooling. Finally, the features with channel attention are obtained by performing dot product operation between the original input features and the channel weights.

2.3 Transfer Learning

Transfer learning [22] is a machine learning method that uses existing relevant knowledge to assist in learning new knowledge, which can improve the performance and generalization ability of the model, save training time and computational resources, and solve the problem of insufficient data or different distribution. A well-performing model needs a large amount of accurate data labeling information to be trained, otherwise it is easy to have underfitting problems, but in some fields, there is often not enough training data for the model to be adequately trained. Through transfer learning techniques, with the help of network parameter models that have been trained in other datasets, the dependence on the size of the dataset can be effectively reduced, so that the model can achieve good training results even when the dataset size is not large. One of the main purposes of transfer learning is to achieve parameter sharing and corresponding feature migration between different models, reducing the training cost while improving its generalization ability.

3 Model Construction

3.1 ECA-ConvNeXt Network Models

The overall architecture of the improved ECA-ConvNeXt network is shown in Fig. 2. The network model consists of the ConvNeXt module, the attention mechanism ECA-Net module, the inverse bottleneck layer, the maximum pooling layer and the global average pooling layer. Before the training starts, the ConvNeXt model parameters, which have been pre-trained in ImageNet, are used as initial weights and loaded into the network model framework with the help of Transfer Learning idea. After the training is completed, the unprocessed data from the original test set is input into the network model to successfully complete the classification.

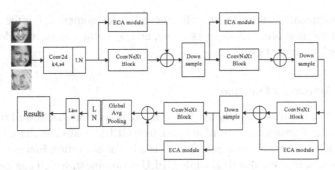

Fig. 2. The proposed network structure

3.2 Improvement of the Loss Function

Label smoothing regularization [23] is used in various tasks such as image classification, speech recognition and machine translation to improve the accuracy of deep learning models. Label smoothing regularization converts the original one-hot encoded label vector y into a soft label form y/, where each element of y/ has a non-zero probability value, instead of only one element being 1 and the others being 0. The advantage of this is that it prevents the model from overfitting to the correct class during training, while also increasing the model's attention to other classes, thereby improving the model's tolerance to noisy data and confusing categories. The specific conversion formula is as follows:

$$y_i' = (1 - \epsilon)y_i + \frac{\epsilon}{K} \tag{4}$$

where ϵ is a small positive number indicating the degree of smoothing.

3.3 AdamW Optimizer

The AdamW optimizer [24] makes some changes to the standard Adam optimizer, aiming to solve the problem of the Adam optimizer's sub-optimal handling of weight decay. Weight decay is a regularization method used to prevent overfitting, which makes the values of the model parameters as small as possible by adding the L2 paradigm of the model parameters as a penalty term in the loss function. The Adam optimizer adds a weight decay term to the gradient when performing weight updates, resulting in an unstable learning rate. In the AdamW optimizer, the weight decay term decays the weights individually before updating the parameters. This avoids the influence of the weight decay term on the gradient and improves the effectiveness of the Adam optimizer. The parameter update formula for the AdamW optimizer is as follows:

$$\begin{aligned} m_t &= \beta_1 m_{t-1} + (1 - \beta_1)\nabla L(\theta_{t-1}) \\ v_t &= \beta_2 v_{t-1} + (1 - \beta_2)(\nabla L(\theta_{t-1}))^2 \\ \theta_t &= \theta_{t-1} - \eta(\frac{1}{\sqrt{\widehat{v}_t}+\epsilon}\widehat{m}_t - \gamma\theta_{t-1}) \end{aligned} \tag{5}$$

where m_t is the mean, v_t is the estimate of the second-order moments, β_1 is the exponential decay rate of the first-order moment estimate, and β_2 is the exponential decay rate of the second-order moment estimate.

3.4 GELU Activation Function

Traditional CNN networks usually use ReLU as the activation function of the network, while the current Transformer type of network uses GELU (Gaussian Error Linear Unit) activation function in the mainstream. ReLU is a linear activation function, which has only two states, active and inactive, while GELU is nonlinear, which can capture more complex relationships between the inputs. ReLU is a linear activation function with only two states, active and inactive, while GELU is non-linear, which can capture more complex relationships between the inputs, and this non-linear property can help the neural network to better adapt to complex data distributions. Another feature of the GELU function is the smoothing, which has a gradient over the entire range of inputs and avoids the problem of vanishing gradients, whereas the ReLU has a gradient of zero in the case of negative inputs, which can lead to the problem of vanishing gradients.

Smoothness helps the model to propagate the gradient more stably during training, reducing the problems of gradient explosion and gradient vanishing.

Meanwhile, the GELU activation function incorporates the cumulative function of the Gaussian normal distribution, which improves the model's ability to fit independent random variables. For the GELU function with standard normal distribution, it is defined as follows:

$$GELU(x) = \frac{1}{2}x + \frac{1}{2}x\tanh\left(\sqrt{\frac{2}{\pi}}\left(x + 0.044715x^3\right)\right) \tag{6}$$

4 Experiment Analysis

4.1 Dataset

This experiment mainly uses a public dataset that is currently used in face expression recognition, the FER 2013 dataset [25]. The FER 2013 dataset contains about 30,000 face images with different expressions, each of which is 48×48 pixels in size. These images are categorized into seven expression categories, namely: anger, disgust, fear, happiness, sadness, surprise and neutral. This dataset is obtained by taking face images collected from the internet and manually labeling and filtering them. Facial expression recognition on this dataset is challenging because there are more mislabeled images of non-faces in this dataset and there are many watermarks and other noises in some of the samples. The expression images of this dataset are shown in Fig. 3.

Angry   Disgust   Fear   Happy   Sad   Surprise   Neutral

Fig. 3. FER 2013 dataset

Since the size of this dataset is relatively small, some data enhancement strategies can be adopted before training, and the basic data expansion methods include random geometric processing such as rotating, deflating and mirroring the original input photos. In addition to these basic data augmentation methods, this experiment uses some more complex data augmentation strategies, based on the theory or technique of deep learning, to perform more advanced transformations or combinations of images, which can further improve the performance and generalization ability of the model.

4.2 Experimental Methods and Environment Configuration

Experimental Design
Based on the size and attributes of the chosen FER 2013 dataset, a batch size of 64, 300 epochs, and an initial learning rate of 1e-3 have been established. Furthermore, a

learning rate decay strategy is implemented where a higher learning rate is applied to the top layers and a lower learning rate to the bottom ones. This technique enhances the model's convergence speed while preserving the crucial elements of the bottom layer. AdamW serves as the optimizer for training while optimization methods such as smooth label and EMA are incorporated. The model implements the cross-entropy function as its loss function. Additionally, the cosine annealing is utilized for continuous optimization of the learning rate to approach the global optimum value. This process culminates in the development of the facial expression recognition model.

Environment Configuration

This experiment utilizes the Pytorch 1.8.0 framework for training, verification, and testing facial expression recognition. The hardware environment consists of an Ubuntu18.04 operating system, an Intel Gold 5318Y processor, and an NVIDIA GeForce RTX 3080 graphics card. The software environment includes CUDA11.7, cuDNN8.9.2, and PyCharm2023 professional version.

4.3 Evaluation Criteria

To evaluate the classification effect of the network on facial expression recognition, this experiment uses Accuracy, Recall and Specificity together to evaluate the classification results, and these evaluation criteria are calculated based on the confusion matrix. Confusion matrix is a kind of index for judging the merits of a model and is often used to judge the merits of image classification models. In the real situation, the distribution of the predicted and true values of the confusion matrix is shown in Table 1.

Table 1. Classification index

		Predicted	
		Positive	Negative
Actual	Positive	TP	FP
	Negative	FN	TN

4.4 Result Analysis

The training curve of the ECA-ConvNeXt network model proposed in this paper on the Fer 2013 dataset is shown in Fig. 4, with a final accuracy of 72.69%. Observing the curves, it is found that with the increase in the number of iterations, the accuracy increases and the loss value decreases, and finally converges, it can be determined that the network model has strong generalization ability and robustness.

The confusion matrix in the test set is shown in Fig. 5. The confusion matrix reveals that the model predicts some categories better, such as happy, neutral, and surprised, with an accuracy of more than 90%, while negative expressions such as angry, disgusted, and

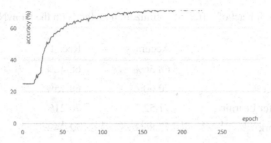

Fig. 4. Accuracy of change curve

fearful expressions are not so well recognized, due to the strong similarity of these expressions and the lack of differentiation of key facial features, which makes it difficult to differentiate them.

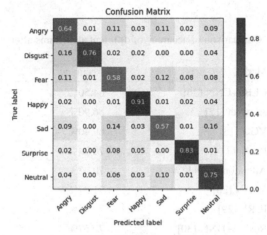

Fig. 5. Confusion matrix

To prove the effectiveness of the optimization method proposed in this paper, ablation experiments are conducted to obtain comparative results of its performance results as shown in Table 2. The results show that both ECA-Net and Transfer Learning can obtain a certain degree of performance improvement, and the improved network utilizes the ECA-Net attention mechanism to better mine local features and effectively integrate the correlation between these features, thus improving the accuracy of expression recognition.

4.5 Experimental Comparisons

To validate the effectiveness of the methods in this chapter, the proposed method is compared with the recent deep learning methods that conducted expression recognition experiments on the FER 2013 dataset, and the comparison results are shown in Table 3.

Table 2. The impact of different optimization methods on the ConvNeXt model

Model	Accuracy	Recall	Specificity
ConvNeXt	68.56%	68.42%	59.35%
ConvNeXt+ECA-Net	70.60%	68.15%	63.95%
ConvNeXt + Transfer Learning	71.52%	70.21%	63.17%
The proposed network	72.86%	72.04%	64.15%

The data specifies that the network proposed in this paper achieves an accuracy of 72.86% on the FER 2013 dataset, which exceeds the performance of other models. The model proposed in this paper uses ConvNeXt as the backbone network and introduces the attention mechanism and Transfer Learning strategy at the same time, which further improves the recognition rate of the model and proves that the improvement of ConvNeXt is effective.

Table 3. Comparison of accuracy of different algorithms after training

Model	Accuracy
CLBP+CNN [26]	64.50%
AlexNet [12]	66.90%
VGG [13]	69.40%
ResNet [14]	70.74%
Attention CNN [27]	70.02%
VSAN [28]	71.27%
ICRL [29]	72.36%
ResNet+DNN [30]	72.67%
The proposed network	72.86%

5   Conclusions

For facial expression recognition, based on the original ConvNeXt network, this paper proposes a method to improve the traditional convolutional neural network and conducts experimental verification on the FER 2013 dataset, which proves the feasibility and effectiveness of this paper's model through the ablation experiments and comparing it with the other commonly used convolutional networks and some researchers' improved networks. However, the model is not accurate enough to recognize some negative expressions, and future research will focus on how to reduce the error rate of classifying negative expressions. In addition, the model is currently trained only on the FER 2013 dataset, and in the next step, the model can be applied to various datasets, so that the model can be better adapted to the needs of real-world environments.

References

1. Michael Revina, I., Sam Emmanuel, W.R.: A survey on human face expression recognition techniques. J. King Saud Univ. Comput. Inform. Sci. **33**(6), 619–628 (2021). https://doi.org/10.1016/j.jksuci.2018.09.002
2. Xi, Z., et al.: Facial expression recognition of industrial internet of things by parallel neural networks combining texture features. IEEE Trans. Indust. Inform. **17**(4), 2784–2793 (2020)
3. Shen, L., Bai, L.: A review on gabor wavelets for face recognition. Pattern Anal. Appl. **9**, 273–292 (2006)
4. Zhao, G., Pietikainen, M.: Dynamic texture recognition using local binary patterns with an application to facial expressions. IEEE Trans. Pattern Anal. Mach. Intell. **29**(6), 915–928 (2007)
5. Wang, X., et al.: Feature fusion of HOG and WLD for facial expression recognition. In: Proceedings of the 2013 IEEE/SICE International Symposium on System Integration, pp. 227–332. IEEE (2013)
6. Luo, Y., et al.: Facial expression recognition based on fusion feature of PCA and LBP with SVM. Optik-Int. J. Light Electron Opt. **124**(17), 2767–2770 (2013)
7. Dino, H.I., Maiwan, B.A.: Facial expression classification based on SVM, KNN and MLP classifiers. In: 2019 International Conference on Advanced Science and Engineering (ICOASE), pp. 70–75. IEEE (2019)
8. Krizhevsky, A., et al.: ImageNet classification with deep convolutional neural networks. Commun. ACM **60**(6), 84–90 (2017)
9. Simonyan, K., Zisserman, A.: Very deep convolutional networks for large-scale image recognition. In: 3rd International Conference on Learning Representations (ICLR 2015), Computational and Biological Learning Society (2015)
10. Szegedy, C., et al.: Going deeper with convolutions. In: Proceedings of the IEEE Conference on Computer Vision and Pattern Recognition, pp. 1–9 (2015)
11. He, K., et al.: Deep residual learning for image recognition. In: Proceedings of the IEEE Conference on Computer Vision and Pattern Recognition, pp. 770–778 (2016)
12. Tureke, Y., Xu, W., Zhao, J.: AlexNet based facial expression classification. In: International Conference on Cloud Computing, Performance Computing, and Deep Learning (CCPCDL 2022). SPIE, vol. 12287, pp. 521–527 (2022)
13. Kusuma, G.P., et al.: Emotion Recognition on FER-2013 Face Images Using Fine-Tuned VGG-16. Adv. Sci. Technol. Eng. Syst. J. **5**(6), 315–322 (2020). DOI.org (Crossref), https://doi.org/10.25046/aj050638
14. Gu, S., et al.: Facial expression recognition based on global and local feature fusion with CNNs. In: 2019 IEEE International Conference on Signal Processing, Communications and Computing (ICSPCC), pp. 1–5. IEEE (2019). DOI.org (Crossref). https://doi.org/10.1109/ICSPCC46631.2019.8960765
15. Vaswani, A., et al.: Attention Is All You Need. Adv. Neural Inform. Process. Syst. **30** (2017)
16. Tian, C., et al.: Attention-Guided CNN for Image Denoising. Neural Networks **124**, 117–129 (2020)
17. Wang, X., et al.: ECA-ConvNeXt: a rice leaf disease identification model based on ConvNeXt. In: Proceedings of the IEEE/CVF Conference on Computer Vision and Pattern Recognition, pp. 6234–6242 (2023)
18. Woo, S., et al.: Cbam: convolutional block attention module. In: Proceedings of the European Conference on Computer Vision (ECCV), pp. 3–19 (2018)
19. Hu, J., et al.: Squeeze-and-excitation networks. In: Proceedings of the IEEE Conference on Computer Vision and Pattern Recognition, pp. 7132–7141 (2018)

20. Liu, Z., et al.: A Convnet for the 2020s. In: Proceedings of the IEEE/CVF Conference on Computer Vision and Pattern Recognition, pp. 11976–11986 (2022)
21. Liu, Z., et al.: Swin transformer: hierarchical vision transformer using shifted windows. In: Proceedings of the IEEE/CVF International Conference on Computer Vision, pp. 10012–10022 (2021)
22. Niu, S., et al.: A decade survey of transfer learning (2010–2020). IEEE Trans. Artific. Intell. 1(2), 151–66 (2020)
23. Yuan, L., et al.: Revisiting knowledge distillation via label smoothing regularization. In: Proceedings of the IEEE/CVF Conference on Computer Vision and Pattern Recognition, pp. 3903–11 (2020)
24. Loshchilov, I., Frank H.. Fixing Weight Decay Regularization in Adam (2018)
25. Han, B., et al.: Masked FER-2013: augmented dataset for facial expression recognition. In: 2023 IEEE Conference on Virtual Reality and 3D User Interfaces Abstracts and Workshops (VRW), pp. 747–48. IEEE (2023)
26. Moutan, M., et al.: A deep-learning-based facial expression recognition method using textural features. Neural Comput. Appl. 35(9), 6499–6514 (2023). Springer Link. https://doi.org/10.1007/s00521-022-08005-7
27. Shervin, M., et al.: Deep-emotion: facial expression recognition using attentional convolutional network. Sensors 21(9), 3046 (2021). DOI.org (Crossref). https://doi.org/10.3390/s21093046
28. Chen, J., et al.: Facial expression recognition based on the ensemble learning of CNNs. In: 2020 IEEE International Conference on Signal Processing, Communications and Computing (ICSPCC), pp. 1–5. IEEE (2020). Google Scholar. https://ieeexplore.ieee.org/abstract/document/9259543/
29. Xie, W., et al.: Adaptive weighting of handcrafted feature losses for facial expression recognition. IEEE Trans. Cybern. 51(5), 2787–2800 (2019)
30. Chen, Y., Hu, H.: Facial expression recognition by inter-class relational learning. IEEE Access 7, 94106–94117 (2019). DOI.org (Crossref). https://doi.org/10.1109/ACCESS.2019.2928983

A Domain Adaptation Deep Learning Network for EEG-Based Motor Imagery Classification

Jie Jiao[1] (iD), Yijie Pan[2], Hefan Zhou[1] (iD), Qingqing Chen[1] (iD), Wangliang Zhou[1] (iD), Peipei Gu[3], and Meiyan Xu[1(✉)] (iD)

[1] College of Computer Science, Minnan Normal University, Zhangzhou 363000, China
xmy2300@mnnu.edu.cn
[2] Eastern Institute for Advanced Study, Eastern Institute of Technology, Ningbo 315000, China
[3] Zhengzhou University of Light Industry, Zhengzhou 450000, China

Abstract. The correlation between neighboring electroencephalography (EEG) channels reveals brain signal interconnectedness, and how to represent this correlation is being studied. Simultaneously, variations in EEG signals among individuals may present difficulties in the model's ability to generalize across different individuals. A model may perform well on one person but not on others, limiting its reliability and generalizability in practical applications. We propose a domain adaptation-based deep learning network to address the issues above. Initially, the EEG data is transformed into a three-dimensional (3D) matrix to preserve the correlation between EEG channels, and subsequently, the spatial-temporal characteristics of the data are acquired by using the 3D convolution module. The spatial-feature map attention mechanism reinforces spatial features in the feature map, allowing the subsequent convolution module to learn spatial feature information. Finally, a domain adaptation strategy is employed for both single-source and multi-source domain scenarios. The objective of this strategy is to address the issue of variability in the EEG signal by minimizing the discrepancy between the source and target domains using a maximum mean discrepancy loss function. The proposed method was validated on two datasets, namely the BCIC IV 2a and OpenBMI datasets. We achieved an accuracy of 70.42% in an intra-subject OpenBMI experiment, which is 5.51% higher than the state-of-the-art approach. On the BCIC IV 2a dataset, we conducted intra-subject and inter-subject experiments, achieving accuracy results of 73.91% and 67.88%, respectively, which are 5.38% and 1.61% better than the state-of-the-art method.

Keywords: Brain machine interface · Attention mechanism · Motor imagery · Domain adaptation

1 Introduction

In recent times, the brain-computer interface (BCI) has emerged as a prominent subject of study, garnering significant attention due to its diverse applications within the domains of medical health and rehabilitation training. Motor imagery (MI) refers to the cognitive

---

J. Jiao and Y. Pan—contribute equally to this work.

phenomenon wherein individuals engage in the mental simulation of movement, specifically envisioning the motion of a particular body part without physically executing the corresponding action [1]. This phenomenon gives rise to alterations in the cerebral cortex, which can be recorded through electroencephalogram (EEG) signals [2]. The deciphering of potential alterations in the cerebral cortex resulting from MI has the capacity to convert biological signals into directives for the operation of external devices, thereby facilitating the implementation of BCI applications. The BCI technology has various practical applications, such as device movement control [3], stroke patient rehabilitation [4], and entertainment for healthy individuals [5]. Therefore, accurate decoding of EEG-based MI signals has become an important research topic.

Numerous machine learning techniques utilizing EEG signals have been proposed for the purpose of MI classification. For instance, Fang et al. [6] employed a band-pass filter and the common spatial pattern (CSP) algorithm to extract spatial features optimally. These features were then classified using a classification algorithm. Similarly, Ko et al. [7] utilized the fast Fourier transform and CSP algorithm to extract MI features from EEG data. Subsequently, three different classifiers were employed to classify the transformed EEG data. However, traditional frameworks require feature extraction and feature selection processes to be performed manually, resulting in significant workload and potential bias. The utilization of high-performance computing equipment has facilitated the widespread adoption of deep learning (DL), a technique that enables the direct extraction of features from data, commonly referred to as "end-to-end" [8]. The EEGNet framework, as described by Lawhern et al. [9], is a versatile DL architecture that employs three convolutional layers to extract both temporal and spatial patterns from EEG data. This framework has demonstrated strong performance across various experimental paradigms. The Filter-Bank Convolutional Network (FBCNet) model [10] utilizes a network architecture that incorporates multiple frequency bands. This design allows for the encoding of spectral-spatial discriminant information that is relevant to MI. Furthermore, in order to effectively leverage the capabilities offered by different dimensions of EEG, researchers have developed a novel three-dimensional (3D) representation of EEG [11]. This approach is complemented by the utilization of a multi-branch 3D convolutional neural network (CNN) and an associated classification strategy [12].

Recent research has indicated that DL techniques have exhibited notable benefits in the extraction of EEG features and the enhancement of classification accuracy [13]. Nevertheless, there are some factors that can contribute to variations in the EEG signal. These factors include minor changes in electrode placement, discrepancies in impedance between the electrodes and the skin, variations in head shape and size, divergent patterns of brain activity, and interference from brain activity unrelated to the task at hand. The phenomenon of variability in EEG signals among individuals or across multiple sessions within the same individual, resulting from a multitude of factors, is usually referred to as individual differences in EEG signals [14]. These variations among individuals result in notable disparities in the distribution of data used for training and testing the model. Consequently, applying the pre-trained model to a new individual becomes challenging. The practical implementation of EEG-based BCI DL algorithms is undoubtedly faced with challenges.

To solve the above-mentioned problems, a domain adaptation-based DL network called DADLNet is proposed in this paper. In order to more fully represent the spatial relationships between channels in EEG data, we employ a 3D matrix instead of the traditional EEG data representation. Subsequently, DADLNet uses 3D convolution to obtain temporal and spatial information from the data. To optimize the utilization of extracted information by the model, we propose an attention mechanism called spatial-feature map attention (SFMA). This mechanism enhances the model's ability to extract information in both the spatial and feature map dimensions and efficiently fuses features from both dimensions. In addition, we effectively mitigate the challenges posed by inter-session and inter-subject variability in MI-based EEG signals using the domain adaptation (DA) technique, which minimizes the difference between the source and target domains via the maximum mean difference (MMD) [15] loss function, thereby facilitating optimal adaptation of the model. The main contributions of this paper are summarised below:

- We propose a DL framework based on DA strategies. The framework targets the problem of inter-session and inter-subject differences and significantly improves the accuracy of MI decoding algorithms. More importantly, the framework demonstrates excellent performance on multiple datasets, proving its broad applicability and superiority.
- In order to further improve the feature extraction and representation abilities of the model, we introduce an attention mechanism that combines the features of the spatial domain and the dimension of the feature map.
- We propose a DA strategy for both single-source and multi-source domain scenarios to address individual differences in EEG signals.

2 Methods

2.1 3D Representation of EEG

This study employs 3D spatial-temporal representations of EEG data as the input for the proposed DADLNet. The acquisition of EEG information by electrodes placed in various regions on the electrode cap exhibits variability. Hence, it is worth noting that the data obtained from each electrode exhibits a spatial characteristic. However, in numerous studies [16, 17], MI-based EEG data has been transformed into a two-dimensional array (channel × time). In this representation, each column of the array corresponds to the temporal dimension of the EEG data, while each row represents the channel of the EEG. This approach proves advantageous in facilitating the acquisition of temporal features by networks, yet it compromises the preservation of the relative positional relationship among channels [18].

We used the 3D representation of EEG data suggested in [12] in order to fully utilize the spatial-temporal information of MI-based EEG data. First, we mapped the channels of the EEG data into a 3D array based on the electrode distributions shown in Fig. 1(a) and 1(b). The channels of the EEG data were mapped into a 3D array. The 2D matrix made up of n and m corresponds to the channel distribution of the EEG acquisition device, and the 3D array's l represents the temporal dimension of the EEG data. This 3D array representation keeps both the relative positional relationships between the channels and the temporal characteristics of the EEG data.

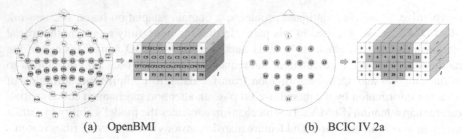

Fig. 1. EEG 3D representation. Subfigure (a): OpenBMI selects 31 channels. Subfigure (b): BCIC IV 2a selects 20 channels. l represents the temporal dimension. m and n represent the spatial dimension.

2.2 Architecture of DADLNet

The network architecture of the model we proposed is shown in Fig. 2. The DADLNet framework comprises two components, namely the feature extraction module and the DA module. The comprehensive details of each module will be elaborated upon in the subsequent subsections.

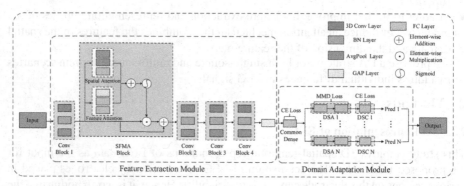

Fig. 2. DADLNet architecture. After each convolution operation, the sequence is batch normalization (BN), activation, average pooling (AvgPool), and then dropout.

Feature Extraction Module. The feature extraction module comprises two components, namely the Convolutional Block (Conv Block) and the Spatial-Feature Map Attention Block (SFMA Block). The Conv Block is composed of several layers, including a 3D convolutional (3D Conv) layer, a batch normalization (BN) layer, an exponential linear unit (ELU), and an average pooling (AvgPool) layer.

Convolution Block. Based on the 3D representation of EEG data, we designed a special spatial convolution process. In the Conv module, the convolution kernel size for the spatial dimension of the 3D Conv layer is set to [(2,2), (2,2), (1,2), (2,2)], while the step size is set to [(1,1), (2,2), (1,2), (2,2)]. This design takes into account the fact that the event-related desynchronization/event-related synchronization (ERD/ERS) phenomenon mainly occurs in brain regions corresponding to the execution of left-handed or right-handed MI. By using smaller convolutional kernels and step sizes, the network is able to learn spatial features within these regions more accurately while avoiding feature confusion between left and right brain regions. After processing by the first three 3D Conv modules, the channel features are explicitly divided into four regions: left of the central sulcus, right of the central sulcus, left of the parietal lobe, and right of the parietal lobe. The last Conv module is responsible for integrating these localized features. The feature map output from the 3D Conv layers in each Conv module is normalized by a BN layer. Next, regularization is performed using the ELU activation function, and the time dimension is downsampled by an AvgPool layer, aiming to reduce the amount of data while retaining key information. Finally, the dropout layer is applied to randomly deactivate some neurons with a certain probability, which not only helps to reduce the amount of computation but also enhances the robustness of the model and prevents overfitting. In this study, the rate of dropout was set to 0.5.

Spatial-Feature Map Attention Block. As shown in Fig. 2, the spatial attention mechanism [19] first performs AvgPool on the feature map dimension to reduce the computational complexity, and subsequently, AvgPool on the temporal dimension is utilized to reduce the temporal information. The final spatial attention matrix is generated by a fully connected (FC) layer. The feature map attention, on the other hand, first performs global average pooling (GAP) for each feature map, followed by a two-step Squeeze-Excite (SE) to obtain the attention weight parameters. The squeezing process uses a reduction ratio parameter r and an FC layer with a rectified linear unit (ReLU) activation function to reduce the number of channels to C/r ($r = 8$ in our model), which is then restored to its original size. Experiments demonstrate that the SE module is able to significantly improve performance with little additional computational cost [20]. We combine the spatial attention module with the SE module as a key part of feature extraction. After computing the spatial attention values and feature map attention values, we use element-by-element summation to merge these two attention values and process them through a sigmoid function to generate the final attention features. These features are multiplied by the original input and then added to the original input to get the final weighted features. This residual-like approach preserves the original information and helps the model propagate the gradient more efficiently.

DA Module. The DA module consists of a common FC layer, a Domain-Specific Adapter (DSA), and a Domain-Specific Classifier (DSC). First, we use an FC layer as a common layer, which serves to map the source and target domain data to a common feature space while extracting domain-invariant features in all domains. The structure of the DA module is shown in Fig. 2.

Domain-Specific Adapter. It consists of two FC layers. In the domain adapter, the data of the source and target domains is mapped to a separate potential feature space. In this potential space, we use MMD to measure the difference between the source and target domains. The MMD function can be defined as follows:

$$MMD_{(X^S,X^T)} = \left\| \frac{1}{N^S} \sum_{i=1}^{N^S} \Phi(x_i^S) - \frac{1}{N^T} \sum_{j=1}^{N^T} \Phi(x_j^T) \right\|_{\mathcal{H}}^2 \tag{1}$$

where X^S and X^T represent the source domain data and the target domain data respectively, N^S and N^T represent the vector lengths of X^S and X^T respectively. The function $\Phi(\cdot)$ represents a mapping of data points into the Reproducing Kernel Hilbert Space (RKHS) denoted by $\mathcal{H}$. The value of MMD can be regarded as the distance between X^S and X^T in this space. By reducing the MMD loss, the difference between the source domain and the target domain is narrowed, so that the domain adapter can better predict the target domain features.

Domain-Specific Classifier. It contains an FC layer, the activation function is sigmoid, and binary cross-entropy is used to measure the classification loss. DSC can make predictions about the target domain based on information from the current source domain. The specific definition of binary cross-entropy loss is:

$$\text{CE} = -\frac{1}{N} \sum_{i=1}^{N} y_i \cdot \log(p(y_i)) + (1 - y_i) \cdot \log(1 - p(y_i)) \tag{2}$$

where y_i represents the binary label 0 or 1, $p(\cdot)$ represents the output probability of y_i, and N represents the output dimension.

In the intra-subject experiment, we define data from the same subject, but from different sessions or conditions, as source and target domains. In this way, there is only one source domain data. In contrast, in inter-subject experiments, the data of the target subject is treated as the target domain, while the data of other subjects are treated as multiple independent source domains. As illustrated in Fig. 2, the DA module has the ability to dynamically adjust to the number of source domains adaptively, ensuring that the number of DSAs and DSCs always matches the number of source domains. This design can fully utilize the information from multiple source domains to further enhance the model performance.

2.3 Data Description

To assess the effectiveness of the proposed model, we compared DADLNet with other baseline methods on OpenBMI [21] and BCIC IV 2a [22].

OpenBMI: This dataset collected the EEG data of 54 healthy subjects (all right-handed, aged 24–35). EEG data were recorded using a device with 62 Ag/AgCl electrodes and a sampling rate of 1000 Hz. In this paper, we chose 31 channels (the selected channels are shown in Fig. 1a) in the motor region. The EEG signals were bandpass-filtered between 8 Hz and 30 Hz and downsampled from 1000 Hz to 400 Hz. The MI segments from 0 s to 4 s after the stimulus started were selected for analysis.

BCIC IV 2a: This dataset collected the EEG data of nine healthy subjects performing four categories (left hand, right hand, feet, and tongue) of MI tasks. EEG data were recorded using a device with 22 Ag/AgCl electrodes at a sampling frequency of 250 Hz. In this paper, we selected 20 channels (the selected channels are shown in Fig. 1b) and only used right-handed and left-handed MI task data. In order to ensure the same sampling frequency of the two datasets, the EEG data was upsampled from 250 Hz to 400 Hz, and the data were bandpass-filtered at 0.5 Hz and 100 Hz and notch-filtered at 50 Hz to suppress line noise. Also, select the 0 s to 4 s MI segment after stimulation for analysis.

2.4 Baseline Models

To verify the effectiveness of our proposed DADLNet, we compared it with several existing methods, including MIN2Net [23], EEG-adapt [24], Deep ConvNet [25], and EEGNet [9]. For the comparison, we used the hyper-parameters as described in their respective original papers.

2.5 Experimental Evaluation

Train Strategy. The model proposed in this study is implemented based on the TensorFlow framework, and the experiment is completed using an NVIDIA GeForce RTX 2080Ti GPU with 11 GB of memory. In order to reduce the time of model training, we adopted an early stop mechanism. When the validation loss of 30 consecutive epochs does not decrease, the model stops training. The optimizer chooses nadam ($lr = 0,001$, $beta = 0.9, 0.999$). We also use a multi-process training method to avoid the influence of the results of the previous fold on the subsequent training.

3 Result

This section presents the experimental results of the proposed DADLNet on two datasets.

3.1 MI Classification Result

First, we compared DADLNet with other methods in intra-subject experiments on two datasets, OpenBMI, and BCIC IV 2a. To evaluate the performance of the model, we chose four metrics, namely, accuracy, specificity, sensitivity, and F1 score, and the detailed experimental results are listed in Table 1. As can be seen from Table 1, DADLNet significantly outperforms the other compared methods in all metrics on the BCIC IV 2a dataset. In particular, compared with the best-performing EEGNet method, DADLNet shows a 5.38% increase in accuracy and a 7.41% increase in F1-score. Additionally, in comparison to other methods, its specificity and sensitivity have both significantly improved, particularly the specificity, which has increased by 6.92%. For the OpenBMI dataset, DADLNet improves its accuracy by 5.51% and F1-score by 5.06% compared to the outperforming comparison method. More notably, the sensitivity and specificity of DADLNet differed by 1.17%, while EEGNet showed the smallest difference in these two metrics among all the compared methods at 6.28%, which was significantly higher than DADLNet. This indicates that our proposed DADLNet exhibits a high category balance on the classification task of the OpenBMI dataset.

Second, we conducted inter-subject experiments on the BCIC IV 2a dataset and presented the results in Table 2. As seen in Table 2, DADLNet outperforms all the compared methods in terms of accuracy, reaching 67.88%, which is an improvement of 1.61% compared to the closest EEG-adapt method. In other metrics, DADLNet also performs very well, second only to some of the optimal methods. It is worth pointing out that while EEG-adapt achieves the highest sensitivity of 69.74%, DADLNet performs even better in specificity, at 71.52%. Meanwhile, DADLNet scores higher in accuracy, sensitivity, and F1-score compared to the method with the highest specificity. This indicates that our proposed model has higher robustness and adaptability compared to other methods.

Table 1. Classification Performance (mean ± SD) for the intra-subject on OpenBMI and BCIC IV 2a compared to baseline methods. SD denotes standard deviation. Bold denotes the best numerical values.

Dataset	Method	Accuracy (%)	Sensitivity (%)	Specificity (%)	F1-score (%)
BCIC IV 2a	EEGNet	68.53 ± 15.57	67.89 ± 20.34	69.17 ± 14.89	65.76 ± 19.24
	MIN2Net	62.73 ± 12.83	64.48 ± 16.07	60.09 ± 14.04	62.73 ± 13.48
	EEG-adapt	64.51 ± 13.88	71.42 ± 18.30	57.59 ± 18.16	65.19 ± 15.64
	Deep ConvNet	60.22 ± 7.27	62.85 ± 12.09	57.78 ± 8.50	60.29 ± 9.12
	DADLNet	**73.91** ± 11.28	**71.79** ± 12.69	**76.09** ± 10.64	**73.17** ± 11.91
OpenBMI	EEGNet	64.48 ± 16.03	67.62 ± 18.71	61.34 ± 20.37	64.01 ± 17.69
	MIN2Net	59.83 ± 13.40	67.60 ± 16.31	52.50 ± 17.78	62.20 ± 13.28
	EEG-adapt	64.91 ± 15.92	68.70 ± 23.89	61.11 ± 26.51	64.53 ± 19.91
	Deep ConvNet	57.76 ± 12.51	62.09 ± 14.29	53.43 ± 16.02	58.34 ± 13.03
	DADLNet	**70.42** ± 12.44	**69.85** ± 14.98	**71.02** ± 12.67	**69.59** ± 13.60

Table 2. Classification Performance (mean ± SD) for the inter-subject on BCIC IV 2a compared to baseline methods. SD denotes standard deviation. Bold denotes the best numerical values.

Dataset	Method	Accuracy (%)	Sensitivity (%)	Specificity (%)	F1-score (%)
BCIC IV 2a	EEGNet	64.61 ± 8.67	61.01 ± 22.63	68.22 ± 17.27	59.66 ± 18.06
	MIN2Net	59.23 ± 7.18	45.22 ± 21.47	**73.24** ± 19.25	47.89 ± 15.25
	EEG-adapt	66.27 ± 7.90	**69.74** ± 11.55	62.79 ± 11.52	**67.12** ± 8.83
	Deep ConvNet	61.74 ± 5.92	54.65 ± 14.30	68.83 ± 9.51	56.86 ± 10.78
	DADLNet	**67.88** ± 7.27	64.15 ± 10.96	71.52 ± 5.52	66.19 ± 9.07

4 Discussion

4.1 Transfer Learning

In this section, we focus on the performance of the models with and without DA (w/o DA) on different datasets. As shown in Table 3, on the OpenBMI and BCIC IV 2a datasets, the model using the DA strategy outperforms the w/o DA model in all metrics. Specifically, for the OpenBMI dataset, the DA model improves accuracy by 3.16%, specificity by 5.20%, and F1-score by 2.45% relative to the w/o DA model. These data clearly reflect the importance of the DA strategy in improving the overall performance of the model. More notably, the DA model has a more balanced performance in terms of specificity and sensitivity, which implies that the DA strategy is able to handle both types of MI classification in a more balanced manner. Similarly, on the BCIC IV 2a dataset, the DA strategy also brings significant performance improvements to the model.

Additionally, the inter-subject experiment results in Table 4 show that the DA model performed better than the w/o DA model, showing a 6.85% increase in accuracy and

Table 3. Classification Performance (mean ± SD) for the intra-subject experimental results for DA and w/o DA on OpenBMI and BCIC IV 2a. Bold denotes the best numerical values.

Dataset	Method	Accuracy (%)	Sensitivity (%)	Specificity (%)	F1-score (%)
OpenBMI	DA	**70.42** ± 12.44	**69.85** ± 14.98	**71.02** ± 12.67	**69.59** ± 13.60
	w/o DA	67.26 ± 14.49	68.71 ± 14.98	65.82 ± 12.67	67.14 ± 13.60
BCIC IV 2a	DA	**73.91** ± 11.28	**71.79** ± 12.69	**76.09** ± 10.64	**73.17** ± 11.91
	w/o DA	71.86 ± 12.55	70.22 ± 20.64	73.51 ± 10.21	69.71 ± 17.19

Table 4. Classification Performance (mean ± SD) for the inter-subject experimental results for DA and w/o DA on BCIC IV 2a. SD denotes standard deviation. Bold denotes the best numerical values.

Dataset	Method	Accuracy (%)	Sensitivity (%)	Specificity (%)	F1-score (%)
BCIC IV 2a	DA	**67.88** ± 7.27	**64.15** ± 10.96	**71.52** ± 5.52	**66.19** ± 9.07
	w/o DA	61.03 ± 7.64	60.57 ± 15.00	61.50 ± 13.58	59.06 ± 10.81

a 7.13% increase in F1-score. Compared with the results of the intra-subject experiment, the performance gain of the DA model in the inter-subject experiment is even more pronounced. This highlights the effectiveness of the DA strategy in dealing with the variability of data across subjects. When comparing the performance of models, the standard deviation (SD) can offer supplementary insights to evaluate the relative reliability of each model. Although models may have similar average performance, the model with the smaller SD is generally regarded as superior due to its lower performance fluctuations. Further analyzing the SD in Tables 3 and 4, we can find that the DA model has a lower SD compared to the w/o DA model, which suggests that the use of the DA strategy not only improves the performance of the model but also enhances its robustness and ensures that a consistent performance can be obtained in a wide range of contexts.

4.2 Attention

In order to validate the effectiveness of the SFMA mechanism proposed in this paper, we discuss it on the BCI IV 2a dataset. The specific experimental setup included: 1) using only spatial attention mechanisms (Only Spa); 2) using only feature map attention mechanisms (Only Fm); 3) not using any attention mechanisms at all (No Atten); and 4) using both spatial and feature map attention mechanisms (Proposed). The detailed results of the experiments are listed in Table 5.

It is clear from Table 5 that the method proposed in this study significantly outperforms the other schemes in terms of average accuracy, with the largest accuracy improvement reaching 3.24%. More specifically, Only Spa achieved the highest accuracy on Subject 1 and Subject 3; Only Fm performed best on Subject 4; and the method combining both attention mechanisms achieved the best performance on Subjects 2, 5, 6, 7, 8, and 9, especially on Subject 5, where the accuracy improvement was 10.30%

Table 5. Intra-subject classification accuracy (%) of different attention mechanism schemes on the BCIC IV 2a. Bold denotes the best numerical values.

Method	Subject									Mean
	1	2	3	4	5	6	7	8	9	
No Atten	74.94	50.42	86.71	56.79	54.78	58.35	71.61	87.11	76.90	68.62
Only Spa	**75.49**	51.29	**88.26**	57.24	53.89	58.04	73.25	86.58	76.74	68.98
Only FM	75.26	52.01	86.35	**57.61**	55.00	58.76	72.43	87.43	76.02	68.99
Proposed	74.12	**52.84**	86.85	55.99	**65.30**	**62.43**	**77.75**	**89.00**	**82.49**	**71.86**

(Only Fm). On the contrary, the method No Atten failed to achieve the best performance in all subjects.

Overall, by combining spatial and feature map attention mechanisms, we succeeded in enhancing the model's ability to represent features in both spatial and feature map dimensions, thereby significantly improving the decoding performance of MI signals.

5   Conclusion

In this study, we proposed a deep learning network based on domain adaptation (DA) that aimed to fully learn the spatial characteristics of motor imagery (MI) while effectively solving the individual differences present in electroencephalography (EEG) signals. To preserve the correlation among adjacent channels in the EEG data, we opted to depict it as a three-dimensional matrix. To thoroughly investigate and comprehend this correlation, we additionally devised an attention mechanism that integrates both spatial and feature map dimensions. Following experimental verification, this approach that combines feature map and spatial attention mechanisms could significantly improve the model's capacity for learning and representation, offering helpful insights for further research in the area of MI. Furthermore, through the implementation of the DA strategy, our model showcased exceptional proficiency in effectively addressing differences among individuals. The efficiency and reliability of our proposed method were further supported by experimental results obtained from two distinct datasets.

Acknowledgment. This research was supported by the Fujian Provincial Natural Science Foundation (Grant No. 2023J01921), the Fujian Provincial Young and Middle-aged Teachers' Education Research Project (Grant No. JAT210265), the Young Tech Innovation Leading Talent Program of Ningbo City (Grant No. 2023QL008), and the Innovation Consortium Program for Green and Efficient Intelligent Appliances of Ningbo City (Grant No. 2022H002).

References

1. Kwak, Y., Kong, K., Song, W.J., Kim, S.E.: Subject-invariant deep neural networks based on baseline correction for EEG motor imagery BCI. IEEE J. Biomed. Health Inform. **27**(4), 1801–1812 (2023)

2. Zhang, Y., Ding, W.: Motor imagery classification via stacking-based takagi–sugeno–kang fuzzy classifier ensemble. Knowl.-Based Syst. **263**, 110292 (2023)
3. Ai, J., Meng, J., Mai, X., Zhu, X.: Bci control of a robotic arm based on ssvep with moving stimuli for reach and grasp tasks. IEEE J. Biomed. Health Inform. (2023)
4. Al-Qazzaz, N.K., Alyasseri, Z.A.A., Abdulkareem, K.H., Ali, N.S., Al-Mhiqani, M.N., Guger, C.: EEG feature fusion for motor imagery: a new robust framework towards stroke patients rehabilitation. Comput. Biol. Med. **137**, 104799 (2021)
5. Amini, M.M., Shalchyan, V.: Designing a motion-onset visual evoked potential-based brain-computer interface to control a computer game. IEEE Trans. Games (2023)
6. Fang, H., Jin, J., Daly, I., Wang, X.: Feature extraction method based on filter banks and riemannian tangent space in motor-imagery BCI. IEEE J. Biomed. Health Inform. **26**(6), 2504–2514 (2022)
7. Ko, L.W., et al.: Multimodal fuzzy fusion for enhancing the motor-imagery-based brain computer interface. IEEE Comput. Intell. Mag. **14**(1), 96–106 (2019)
8. Zhu, H., Forenzo, D., He, B.: On the deep learning models for EEG-based brain-computer interface using motor imagery. IEEE Trans. Neural Syst. Rehabil. Eng. **30**, 2283–2291 (2022)
9. Lawhern, V.J., Solon, A.J., Waytowich, N.R., Gordon, S.M., Hung, C.P., Lance, B.J.: EEGNet: a compact convolutional neural network for EEG-based brain-computer interfaces. J. Neural Eng. **15**(5), 056013 (2018)
10. Mane, R., et al.: FBCNet: a multi-view convolutional neural network for brain-computer interface. arXiv preprint, 2104.01233 (2021)
11. Gao, D., Wang, K., Wang, M., Zhou, J., Zhang, Y.: SFT-net: a network for detecting fatigue from EEG signals by combining 4d feature flow and attention mechanism. IEEE J. Biomed. Health Inform. (2023)
12. Zhao, X., Zhang, H., Zhu, G., You, F., Kuang, S., Sun, L.: A multi-branch 3D convolutional neural network for EEG-based motor imagery classification. IEEE Trans. Neural Syst. Rehabil. Eng. **27**(10), 2164–2177 (2019)
13. Chen, D., et al.: Scalp EEG based pain detection using convolutional neural network. IEEE Trans. Neural Syst. Rehabil. Eng. **30**, 274–285 (2022)
14. Cui, J., Lan, Z., Sourina, O., Müller-Wittig, W.: EEG-based cross-subject driver drowsiness recognition with an interpretable convolutional neural network. IEEE Trans. Neural Networks Learn. Syst. (2022)
15. Zhang, X., Miao, Z., Menon, C., Zheng, Y., Zhao, M., Ming, D.: Priming cross-session motor imagery classification with a universal deep domain adaptation framework. Neurocomputing **556**, 126659 (2023)
16. Zhang, D., Chen, K., Jian, D., Yao, L.: Motor imagery classification via temporal attention cues of graph embedded EEG signals. IEEE J. Biomed. Health Inform. **24**(9), 2570–2579 (2020)
17. Altaheri, H., Muhammad, G., Alsulaiman, M.: Dynamic convolution with multi-level attention for eeg-based motor imagery decoding. IEEE Internet Things J. 1 (2023)
18. Li, A., Wang, Z., Zhao, X., Xu, T., Zhou, T., Hu, H.: MDTL: a novel and model-agnostic transfer learning strategy for cross-subject motor imagery BCI. IEEE Trans. Neural Syst. Rehabil. Eng. **31**, 1743–1753 (2023)
19. Jia, Z., Lin, Y., Cai, X., Chen, H., Gou, H., Wang, J.: Sst-emotionnet: spatial-spectral-temporal based attention 3d dense network for EEG emotion recognition. In: Proceedings of the 28th ACM International Conference on Multimedia. pp. 2909–2917 (2020)
20. Hu, J., Shen, L., Sun, G.: Squeeze-and-excitation networks. In: Proceedings of the IEEE Conference on Computer Vision and Pattern Recognition, pp. 7132–7141 (2018)
21. Lee, M.H., et al.: EEG dataset and OpenBMI toolbox for three BCI paradigms: An investigation into BCI illiteracy. GigaScience **8**(5), giz002 (2019)

22. Tangermann, M., et al.: Review of the BCI competition IV. Front. Neurosci. p. 55 (2012)
23. Autthasan, P., et al.: Min2net: end-to-end multi-task learning for subject-independent motor imagery EEG classification. IEEE Trans. Biomed. Eng. **69**(6), 2105–2118 (2021)
24. Zhang, K., Robinson, N., Lee, S.W., Guan, C.: Adaptive transfer learning for EEG motor imagery classification with deep convolutional neural network. Neural Netw. **136**, 1–10 (2021)
25. Schirrmeister, R.T., et al.: Deep learning with convolutional neural networks for EEG decoding and visualization. Hum. Brain Mapp. **38**(11), 5391–5420 (2017)

T-GraphDTA: A Drug-Target Binding Affinity Prediction Framework Based on Protein Pre-training Model and Hybrid Graph Neural Network

Yijia Wu[1], Yanmei Lin[1], Yuzhong Peng[1,2(✉)], Ru Zhang[1], and Li Cai[3]

[1] Key Lab of Scientific Computing and Intelligent Information Processing, Nanning Normal University, Nanning 530000, Guangxi, China
jedison@163.com
[2] Guangxi Academy of Sciences, Nanning 530007, Guangxi, China
[3] School of Software, Yunnan University, Kunming 650000, Yunnan, China

Abstract. Drug-target affinity (DTA) prediction is an important task in computer-aided drug design and drug repositioning, which can speed up drug development and reduce resource consumption. Researchers have explored some deep learning-based methods to improve DTA prediction in recent years, demonstrating the great potential of deep learning in DTA prediction. They have developed several molecular representation learning methods for drug compounds in deep learning-based DTA prediction methods. However, most of the existing deep learning-based DTA prediction models use one-hot encoding-based methods for protein representation learning, or use recursive neural network-based methods for learning feature representations from raw protein sequences. These may affect the ability of the DTA prediction model to learn the potential features of the protein, thus weakening the predictive power of the model. To tackle this problem, we developed a novel protein pre-training method (PTR) for protein representation learning, then proposed a DTA prediction framework, called Transformer-Graph drug-target affinity prediction (T-GraphDTA), based on PTR and hybrid graph neural network. The hybrid graph neural network is mainly responsible for molecular presentation learning of drugs. Extensive experiments were conducted on four benchmark datasets of drug-target binding affinity, comparing T-GraphDTA against state-of-the-art models. The experimental results show that T-GraphDTA achieves significantly better performance than state-of-the-art models on all four benchmark datasets. It indicates that T-GraphDTA is expected to be an excellent practical tool for predicting the affinity of drug-target pairs.

Keywords: drug-target interaction · binding affinity · pre-trained model · graph convolutional neural network · deep learning

1 Introduction

Studies have shown that applying deep neural networks to predict DTA can yield good results [1]. To train low-dimensional representations of drug and protein sequences for DTA prediction, researchers have used a variety of deep neural networks and their

D.-S. Huang et al. (Eds.): ICAI 2023, CCIS 2014, pp. 113–123, 2024.
https://doi.org/10.1007/978-981-97-0903-8_12

variants, including deep feedforward neural network (DFNN) [2, 3], convolutional neural network (CNN) [4–6], stacked auto-encoder (SAE) [7], recursive neural network (RNN) [8–10], and graph neural network (GNN) [11, 12, 33]. For example, Öztürk et al. [11] proposed the deep learning model DeepDTA that uses only sequence information of both targets and drugs to predict drug-target interaction binding affinities. Abbasi et al. [8, 34–37] proposed DeepCDA, which combines convolutional layers and long short-term memory (LSTM) layers to efficiently encode local and global temporal patterns for deep cross-domain complex drug-protein affinity prediction. Shrimon Mukherjee et al. [10, 38] proposed a novel architecture DeepGLSTM based on graph convolutional network (GCN) and LSTM, which predicts binding affinity values between the FDA-approved drugs and the viral proteins of SARS-CoV-2. However, most of the DTA prediction models used one-hot encoding representation for proteins that is commonly learned features by a CNN with one-dimensional convolutional layers. These models use one-dimensional convolutional layers and global pooling operations to roughly aggregate features, which may result in the loss of a large amount of useful information. Some works used RNN-based methods to learn protein representation for raw protein sequences, which may lose some important position information of amino acids in the protein. In addition, the tertiary structure of proteins does not always exist in a reliable form, resulting in a graphical representation of proteins that does not work well.

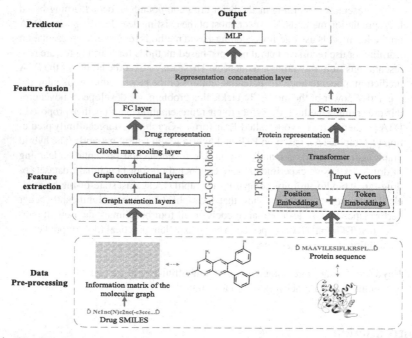

Fig. 1. The flowchart and architecture of the proposed T-GraphDTA framework. T-GraphDTA consists of four modules including the data pre-processing module, feature extraction module, feature fusion module, and predictor.

2 Method

2.1 Overview of T-GraphDTA

To effectively predict drug-target affinity, we develop the novel framework, T-GraphDTA, mainly consisting of a protein sequence pre-training model, a hybrid graph neural network, a concatenation layer, several fully connected layers, and a Multi-layer Perceptron Network (MLP). Figure 1 shows the flowchart and architecture of T-GraphDTA, which consists of four major modules: (1) Data pre-processing. The data pre-processing module is in charge of pre-processing the drug data represented in SMILES strings and constructing the corresponding data structure of molecular graphs. (2) Feature extraction. The feature extraction module is mainly in charge of learning features from molecular graphs of drugs and protein sequences. Drug features are learned by a hybrid graph neural network, called GAT-GCN, based on a graph attention network (GAT) and GCN, while protein features are learned by the Transformer-based protein pre-training model PTR. (3) Feature fusion. The feature fusion module integrates and optimizes the output feature representations from GAT-GCN and PTR. (4) Predictor. This module mainly contains an MLP, which is responsible for predicting the affinity values of drug-target pairs based on the fused features, and finally outputting them. We will describe each module in detail below.

2.2 Data Pre-processing

Compounds can be described by molecular graphs with atoms as nodes and bonds as edges. Therefore, one can use machine learning algorithms to process drug compound data in the form of graph data and learn drug features to perform DTA prediction tasks. For this purpose, we construct the corresponding molecular graph of each drug based on its SMILES string, which reflects the structural information and the interatomic interactions. We use the cheminformatics toolbox RDKit to calculate the relevant properties of compounds to construct related information matrixes of the drug molecular graphs. In these molecular graph data, each node's information can be mapped into a multidimensional binary feature vector, which expresses five pieces of information: the atom symbol, the number of adjacent hydrogens, the number of adjacent atoms, the implicit value of the atom, and whether the atom is in an aromatic structure. T-GraphDTA does not require the processing of the raw protein data in the data pre-processing module. Because we treat protein sequences as texts in natural language and present a Transformer-based protein pre-training model to learn protein features in T-GraphDTA.

2.3 Feature Extraction for Proteins

In recent years, with the development of deep learning, Transformer-based large-scale pre-trained models (PTMs) have achieved great success in natural language processing (NLP) and visual analytics. Large-scale PTM can efficiently capture rich knowledge from large amounts of labeled and unlabeled data and store them in the model with many parameters. These large number of parameters with rich implicit knowledge can be fine-tuned to specific tasks, thus benefiting various downstream tasks. Protein sequences and textual language data have some similar properties, which provide favorable conditions for applying language pre-training models to protein representation learning [14].

Inspired by these, we developed a Transformer-based protein pre-training model, called PTR, to learn protein features for the DTA prediction task in this work. PTR mainly consists of N Encoder blocks and N Decoder blocks, as shown in Fig. 2.

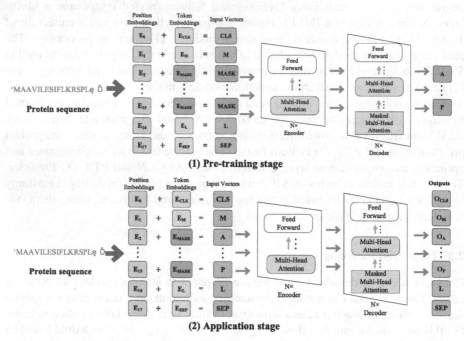

(1) Pre-training stage

(2) Application stage

Fig. 2. PTR model can be divided into two stages: pre-training stage and application stage.

In the pre-training phase, each original protein sequence is divided into several sub-sequences in character units in the first step. For each protein sequence, a certain percentage of characters are masked, and then a prediction is made for the masked part based on information from the sequence context. In this way, PTR is able to identify the dependencies between the masked and unmasked portion of protein sequences after extensive training, which results in a more accurate protein representation. In the application phase, DTA prediction is a downstream task of the protein pre-training model. Similar to the pre-training phase, proteins are first partitioned into subsequences that are then encoded and fed into the model. The huge number of parameters and contextual relationships in the protein sequences learned in the pre-training phase are used to extract the protein features. Contextual relevance information is mapped to each character in the sequence. Finally, the feature matrix output from the final layer of PTR is used as the protein representation.

2.4 Feature Extraction Module for Drugs

Because T-GraphDTA uses molecular graphs to represent drugs, it needs to design a method that can efficiently learn and extract drug features from molecular graphs. GCN models can extract feature information from a given graph by capturing local structures based on the input graph information [16]. However, GCN treats each node equally, which is not conducive to the information extraction of core nodes. On the other hand, GAT can assign different weights for each neighboring node to identify the more important core nodes. The self-attention mechanism [17] of GAT is used to aggregate the neighboring nodes, achieving adaptive matching of weights for different neighbors. Therefore, we developed the hybrid graph neural network GAT-GCN that combines GCN and GAT to obtain a better ability to learn drug features.

The implementation of GAT-GCN is described as follows. To start with, the feature extraction module takes the nodes of the drug molecule graph as input. Each node in the molecular graph is linearly transformed by the weight matrix W. The node attention coefficients are then calculated for each pair of existent edges. For each input node i in the molecular graph, the attention coefficient of i with respect to each first-order neighbor node can be calculated by the following equations:

$$h = \left\{ \vec{h}_1, \vec{h}_2, \ldots, \vec{h}_N \right\} \tag{1}$$

$$e_{ij} = F(W\vec{h}_i, W\vec{h}_j) \tag{2}$$

where h, N, e, and W are the hidden feature representation of neighbor nodes, the number of the neighbor nodes, the attention coefficients, and the weight matrix, respectively. $F(\cdot)$ is a single-layer feedforward neural network. The magnitude of attention coefficients indicates the importance of node j to node i. These attention coefficient values are then normalized by using the *softmax* function, which is used to calculate the output features of the node.

$$a_{ij} = softmax(e_{ij}) \tag{3}$$

$$\vec{h}_i'' = \sigma \left(\sum_{j \in N_i} a_{ij} W\vec{h}_i \right) \tag{4}$$

where $a_{ij}, \sigma(\cdot)$ and $\vec{h}_i''$ are the normalized weight coefficient, the nonlinear activation function, and the feature representation of node i, respectively. The GAT layer aggregates the information of neighboring nodes by assigning attention coefficients based on the importance of the nodes. Thus after processing in the GAT layer, each node feature in the molecular graph is abstracted and contains a lot of high-level features of the molecular graph. Then, the abstracted feature matrix $A \in R^{N*C}$ (N: a set of N nodes, C: : the number of per-node features) of these nodes is fed into the subsequent GCN layers with the *ReLu* function. The multi-layer GCN takes the abstracted feature matrix A as input. The GCN layer propagation rules are defined as:

$$H^{l+1} = ReLu(H^l, A) \tag{5}$$

where H^l is the input to the l-th layer. Finally, the final feature representation vector for the drug is calculated by a global max pooling layer.

2.5 Feature Fusion

The feature vectors of drugs and proteins generated in the feature extraction module are fused in the feature fusion module. Following the feature extraction module, the fully connected layer was also used to convert the drug feature f_d vector learned from the GAT-GCN block and the protein feature vector f_p learned from the PTR block to 128 dimensions. Then the vector f_d and the vector f_p were concatenated, to obtain an integrated vector $f_{con} = [f_d; f_p]$. Finally, the output vector f_{con} is the high-level representation of the drug-protein pair, which will be fed into the predictor to predict the drug-target affinity value.

2.6 Predictor

T-GraphDTA uses an MLP which consists of two fully connected layers on its top to predict drug-target affinity values and output results. The MLP can be formulated as follows:

$$y = \sigma(W_i \cdot z + b_h) \tag{6}$$

where z, W_i and b_h are the input vector, the weight matrix of the input and output layer, and the bias vector of the corresponding layer, respectively. y is the predicted affinity value of the drug-target pair.

3 Experimental Result and Analysis

To evaluate the performance of T-GraphDTA, we conducted extensive experiments on four publicly available benchmark datasets of drug-target binding affinities, comparing T-GraphDTA against several state-of-the-art models.

3.1 Datasets and Evaluation Metrics

Following the previous works [6, 18–24], the most used datasets and evaluation metrics in the community of drug-target affinity prediction are used to evaluate the performance of the models in this work.

1) Datasets: The benchmark datasets include Davis [18], Kiba [19], Metz [20], and DTC [21] used in this work.
2) *Evaluation metrics:* The evaluation metrics used in this work are Mean Square Error (MSE) and Concordance Index (CI), as shown in Eqs. (10) and (11).

$$MSE = \frac{1}{n} \sum\nolimits_{i=1}^{n} (\ddot{y}_i - \bar{\bar{y}}_i)^2 \tag{7}$$

$$CI = \frac{1}{C} \sum\nolimits_{y_i > y_j} h(p_i - p_j) \tag{8}$$

For *MSE*, $\ddot{y}$ is the predicted value, $\overline{\overline{y}}$ is the actual value, and n is the sample size. For CI, p_i is the predicted value for its larger affinity y_i, p_j is the predicted value for its smaller affinity y_j, C is a normalization constant, and $h(x)$ is a step function, e.g.:

$$h(x) = \begin{cases} 1 & , x > 0 \\ 0.5 & , x = 0 \\ 0 & , x < 0 \end{cases}$$

Note that for drug-target affinity prediction, higher CI is better while lower MSE is better.

3.2 Baselines

To verify the advantage of our model, we evaluated T-GraphDTA against 9 state-of-the-art models. The state-of-the-art models have traditional machine learning-based models including KronRLS [23, 24] and SimBoost [25], and deep learning-based models including DeepDTA [6], DeepGLSTM [10], WideDTA [26], AttentionDTA [27], GANsDTA [28], GraphDTA [29], SAG-DTA [32] and DeepGS [30].

3.3 Experimental Setup

Following the SAG-DTA [32], for each dataset, we use 80% of the data samples to train the model and the 20% as a benchmark test set to test the model. Our experiments were performed on a GPU server with an NVIDIA GeForce RTX 3090 graphics card with 24GB of memory.

Note that all performance results of the baseline models in this work are cited from their corresponding original papers.

3.4 Results and Analysis

Results on the Davis and Kiba datasets: Table 1 shows the prediction results of T-GraphDTA and baseline models on the Davis datasets. As can be seen from Table 1, T-GraphDTA achieves 0.193 and 0.906 in terms of MSE and CI values, respectively, achieving the best results among all compared models. The best MSE and CI values obtained by the baseline models on the Davis dataset are 0.209 (SAG-DTA) and 0.903 (SAG-DTA), respectively. The MSE obtained by T-GraphDTA is 7.65% more than the state-of-the-art results, respectively.

Table 2 shows the prediction results of T-GraphDTA and baseline models on the Kiba datasets. As can be seen from Table 2, T-GraphDTA achieves 0.124 and 0.900 in terms of MSE and CI values, respectively, winning the best results among all compared models. DeepGLSTM achieved the best MSE (0.130) and the best CI (0.897) in the state-of-the-art models on the Kiba dataset. Compared to the state-of-the-art, T-GraphDTA achieved a 4.61% improvement in terms of MSE and a slightly higher CI of 0.003.

In summary, experimental comparisons show that T-GraphDTA outperforms the state-of-the-art models for all evaluation metrics on all benchmark datasets.

Table 1. Comparison of methods on the Davis dataset.

Model	Drug	Protein	MSE	CI
KronRLS [23, 24]	Pubchem-Sim	Smith-Waterman	0.379	0.871
SimBoost [25]	Pubchem-Sim	Smith-Waterman	0.282	0.873
WideDTA [26]	CNN	CNN	0.262	0.886
GANsDTA [28]	GNN	CNN	0.276	0.881
DeepGS [30]	Smi2Vec	Prot2Vec	0.252	0.880
DeepGLSTM [10]	GCNs	Bi-LSTM	0.232	0.895
GraphDTA [6]	GCN	1D CNN	0.254	0.880
GraphDTA [6]	GAT-GCN	1D CNN	0.245	0.881
GraphDTA [6]	GAT	1D CNN	0.232	0.892
GraphDTA [6]	GIN	1D CNN	0.229	0.893
SAG-DTA [32]	Graph (HierPool)	CNN	0.212	0.901
SAG-DTA [32]	Graph (GlobPool)	CNN	0.209	0.903
Our T-GraphDTA	GAT-GCN	PTR	**0.193**	**0.906**

Table 2. Comparison of methods on the Kiba dataset.

Model	Drug	Protein	MSE	CI
KronRLS [23, 24]	Pubchem-Sim	Smith-Waterman	0.411	0.782
SimBoost [25]	Pubchem-Sim	Smith-Waterman	0.222	0.836
WideDTA [26]	CNN	CNN	0.179	0.875
GANsDTA [28]	GNN	CNN	0.224	0.866
DeepGS [30]	Smi2Vec	Prot2Vec	0.193	0.860
DeepGLSTM [10]	GCNs	Bi-LSTM	0.133	0.897
GraphDTA [6]	GCN	1D CNN	0.139	0.889
GraphDTA [6]	GAT-GCN	1D CNN	0.139	0.891
GraphDTA [6]	GAT	1D CNN	0.179	0.866
GraphDTA [6]	GIN	1D CNN	0.147	0.882
SAG-DTA [32]	Graph (HierPool)	CNN	0.131	0.893
SAG-DTA [32]	Graph (GlobPool)	CNN	0.130	0.892
Our T-GraphDTA	GAT-GCN	PTR	**0.124**	**0.900**

4 Conclusion

We proposed a novel drug-target binding affinity prediction framework with even limited biology and chemistry knowledge, called T-GraphDTA, which is based on the Transformer and graph neural network. In the T-GraphDTA framework, we developed a Transformer-based pre-trained protein model (PTR) to learn protein features from many raw protein sequences and a hybrid graph neural network (GAT-GCN) to learn drug features from molecular graphs. We compared the performance of the proposed model against those of nine state-of-the-art models on four benchmark datasets. Experimental results show that T-GraphDTA outperforms the state-of-the-art models on all the datasets across all evaluation metrics.

Although T-GraphDTA is excellent compared to existing models, T-GraphDTA makes less use of biological and chemical expertise and experience in studying drug-target interaction. Numerous studies in the past have shown that there is a great deal of biological and chemically relevant expertise and experience useful in predicting drug-target interactions. Therefore, for future work, we will study to improve the model by exploiting more related expertise and experience in biology and chemistry.

Acknowledgements. This work was supported in part by the National Natural Science Foundation of China (#62262044, #U22A2039), and Natural Science Foundation of Guangxi Province (#2023GXNSFAA026027), the Project of Guangxi Chinese medicine multidisciplinary crossover innovation team (#GZKJ2311). Yijia Wu and Yanmei Lin contributed equally to this work and should be considered co-first authors.

References

1. Lee, H., Kim W.: Comparison of target features for predicting drug-target interactions by deep neural network based on large-scale drug-induced transcriptome data. Pharmaceutics (11), 377 (2019)
2. Peng, J., Li, J., Shang, X.: A learning-based method for drug-target interaction prediction based on feature representation learning and deep neural network. BMC Bioinform. (21), 394 (2020)
3. Azzopardi, J., Ebejer, J.-P.: LigityScore: convolutional neural network for binding-affinity predictions. Bioinformatics 38–4(2021)
4. Shim J., Hong, Z. Y., Sohn, I., Hwang, C.: Prediction of drug-target binding affinity using similarity-based convolutional neural network. Sci. Rep. (11), 4416 (2021)
5. Rifaioglu, A.S., Atalay, R.C., Kahraman, D.C., Doan, T., Atalay, V.J.B.: MDeePred: Novel Multi-Channel protein featurization for deep learning based binding affinity prediction in drug discovery. Bioinformatics (37), 693–704 (2020)
6. Ozturk, H., Ozgur, A., Ozkirimli, E.: DeepDTA: deep drug-target binding affinity prediction. Bioinformatics (34), i821–i829 (2018)
7. Wang, L., et al.: A Computational-based method for predicting drug-target interactions by using stacked autoencoder deep neural network. J. Comput. Biol. (25), 361–373 (2018)
8. Abbasi, K., Razzaghi, P., Poso, A., Amanlou, M., Ghasemi, J. B., Masoudi-Nejad, A.: DeepCDA: deep cross-domain compound-protein affinity prediction through LSTM and convolutional neural networks. Bioinformatics (36), 4633–4642 (2020)

9. Yuan, W., Chen, G., Chen, C.Y.: FusionDTA: attention-based feature polymerizer and knowledge distillation for drug-target binding affinity prediction. Brief. Bioinform. (23), 506 (2022)

10. Mukherjee, S., Ghosh, M., Basuchowdhuri, P.J.A.E.-P.: DeepGLSTM: Deep Graph Convolutional Network and LSTM based approach for predicting drug-target binding affinity. Proceedings of the 2022 SIAM International Conference on Data Mining (SDM), pp. 729–737 (2020)

11. Nguyen, T.M., Nguyen, T., Le, T.M., Tran, T.: GEFA: early fusion approach in drug-target affinity prediction. IEEE/ACM Trans. Comput. Biol. Bioinform. (19), 718–728 (2022)

12. Yang Z., Zhong, W., Zhao, L., Chen, C. Yu-Chian: MGraphDTA: deep multiscale graph neural network for explainable drug-target binding affinity prediction. Chem. Sci. (13), 816–833 (2022)

13. Bento A.P., et al.: An open source chemical structure curation pipeline using RDKit. J. Cheminform (12), 51 (2020)

14. Rives, A., et al.: Biological structure and function emerge from scaling unsupervised learning to 250 million protein sequences. Proc. Natl. Acad. Sci. USA (118), 15 (2021)

15. Goldberg, Y., Levy,O.: word2vec Explained: deriving Mikolov et al.'s negative-sampling word-embedding method. arXiv (2014)

16. Welling, M., Kipf, T.N.: Semi-supervised classification with graph convolutional networks. International Conference on Learning Representations (2017)

17. Vaswani, A., et al.: Attention Is All You Need. Advances in neural information processing systems (2017)

18. Davis, M. I., et al.: Comprehensive analysis of kinase inhibitor selectivity. Nat. Biotechnol. (29), 1046–1051 (2011)

19. Tang, J., et al.: Making sense of large-scale kinase inhibitor bioactivity data sets: a comparative and integrative analysis. J. Chem. Inf. Model (54), 735–43 (2014)

20. Metz, J.T., Johnson, E.F., Soni, N.B., Merta, P.J., Kifle, L., Hajduk, P.J.: Navigating the kinome. Nat, Chem, Biol (7), 200–202 (2011)

21. Tang, J., et al.: Drug target commons: a community effort to build a consensus knowledge base for drug-target interactions. Cell Chem. Biol. (25), 224–229 (2018)

22. Gönen, M., Heller, G.: Concordance probability and discriminatory power in proportional hazards regression. Biometrika (92), 965–970 (2005)

23. Cichonska, A., et al.: Computational-experimental approach to drug-target interaction mapping: A case study on kinase inhibitors. PLoS Comput. Biol. (13), e1005678 (2017)

24. Cichonska, A., et al.: Learning with multiple pairwise kernels for drug bioactivity prediction. Bioinformatics (34), i509–i518 (2018)

25. He, T., Heidemeyer, M., Ban, F., Cherkasov, A., Ester, M.: SimBoost: a read-across approach for predicting drug-target binding affinities using gradient boosting machines. J. Cheminform. (9), 24 (2017)

26. Öztürk, H., Ozkirimli, E., Özgür, A.J.A.E.-P.: WideDTA: prediction of drug-target binding affinity. arXiv (2019)

27. Zhao, Q., Duan, G., Yang, M., Cheng, Z., Li, Y., Wang, J.: AttentionDTA: drug-target binding affinity prediction by sequence-based deep learning with attention mechanism. IEEE/ACM Trans. Comput. Biol. Bioinform. (2022)

28. Zhao, L., Wang, J., Pang, L., Liu, Y., Zhang, J.: GANsDTA: predicting drug-target binding affinity using GANs. Front Genet. (10), 1243 (2019)

29. Nguyen, T., Le, H., Quinn, T.P., Nguyen, T., Le, T.D., Venkatesh, S.: GraphDTA: predicting drug-target binding affinity with graph neural networks. Bioinformatics (37), 1140–1147 (2021)

30. Lin, X.J.A.E.-P.: DeepGS: Deep Representation Learning of Graphs and Sequences for Drug-Target Binding Affinity Prediction. arXiv(2003)

31. Xu, K., Hu, W., Leskovec, J., Jegelka, S.J.A.E.-P.: How powerful are graph neural networks? In: 2019 international conference on learning representations (2019)
32. Zhang, S., Jiang, M., Wang, S., et al.: SAG-DTA: Prediction of Drug-Target Affinity Using Self-Attention Graph Network. Multidisciplinary Digital Publishing Institute (2021)
33. Zhang, H., Zhou, S., Zhang, K., Guan, J.: Residual similarity based conditional independence test and its application in causal discovery. Proc. AAAI Conf. Artific. Intell. **36**(5), 5942–5949 (2022)
34. Zhang, H., Zhou, S., Yan, C., Guan, J., Wang, X.: Recursively learning causal structures using regression-based conditional independence test. Proc. AAAI Conf. Artific. Intell. **33**(01), 3108–3115 (2019)
35. Zhang, H., Zhou, S., Yan, C., Wang, X., Zhang, J., Huan, J.: Learning causal structures based on divide and conquer. IEEE Trans. Cybern. **52**(5), 3232–3243 (2022)
36. Peng, Y., Zhang, Z., Jiang, Q., Guan, J., Zhou*, S.: TOP: towards better toxicity prediction by deep molecular representation learning. In: 2019 IEEE International Conference on Bioinformatics and Biomedicine (BIBM), pp. 318–325. IEEE (2019)
37. Peng, Y., Zhang, Z., Jiang, Q., Guan, J., Zhou, S.: TOP: A deep mixture representation learning method for boosting molecular toxicity prediction. Methods **179**(1), 55–64 (2020)
38. Peng, Y., Lin, Y., Jing, X., Zhang, H., Huang, Y., Luo, G.: Enhanced graph isomorphism network for molecular ADMET properties prediction. IEEE Access **8**(1), 168344–168360 (2020)

Imputation of Compound Property Assay Data Using a Gene Expression Programming-Based Method

Hongliang Zhou[1], Yanmei Lin[1(✉)], Nan Chen[1], and Yuzhong Peng[1,2(✉)]

[1] Key Lab of Scientific Computing and Intelligent Information Processing,
Nanning Normal University, Nanning 5300001, Guangxi, China
`ymlin20160714@163.com, jedison@163.com`
[2] Guangxi Academy of Sciences, Nanning 530007, Guangxi, China

Abstract. Compound property assays are an important part of drug development, but incomplete data may occur for a variety of reasons. To deal with these incomplete data and improve the success rate of drug development, researchers often need to effectively impute the missing data. Therefore, this paper proposes a gene expression programming-based method, called GEP-CPI, for imputing missing compound property assay data. In GEP-CPI, the missing data imputation model is expressed by the parse tree of a chromosome, and then the optimal missing data imputation model is mined by iterative evolution of the chromosome population. Experimental results on three compound property assay related datasets demonstrates that the proposed method generally outperforms the state-of-the-art methods in imputing missing data of compound property assays.

Keywords: Gene Expression Programming · Missing Imputation · Compound Property Assay

1 Introduction

Missing data is a pervasive problem across various disciplines and fields. Extracting knowledge from databases with missing data is a challenge for researchers in the related field. Given that most data mining algorithms struggle to handle incomplete datasets effectively, it becomes necessary to interpolate the missing data [1–6].

Missing data imputation methods can be categorized into three types based on the sources of information that they rely on: univariate statistical analysis-based methods, multivariate statistical analysis-based methods, and machine learning-based methods [7]. Among these, machine learning-based methods utilize machine learning to construct mappings relationship or probability models between the target attribute and other attributes to impute missing values. Examples include K-Nearest Neighbors (KNN), Artificial Neural Network (ANN), Support Vector Machines (SVM), Random Forests (RF) [8]. These methods can deal with complex and nonlinear data features, exhibiting of generalization and robustness. However, they require tuning of multiple parameters and hyperparameters, and have high demands for both the quality and quantity of training

© The Author(s), under exclusive license to Springer Nature Singapore Pte Ltd. 2024
D.-S. Huang et al. (Eds.): ICAI 2023, CCIS 2014, pp. 124–135, 2024.
https://doi.org/10.1007/978-981-97-0903-8_13

data. For example, some researchers utilized the KNN to estimate missing speed data on UTIS [9] and missing precipitation data [10]. Some researchers have employed RF to impute forest volume [11] and the lawn length of lawnmowers [12] and missing values in other field [13]. Several studies have utilized ANNs for imputing missing values in datasets [14–20]. Nouvo et al. [21] used fuzzy c-means for data interpolation. Wang et al. [22] used SVM for filling missing medical data.

Compound property assay is crucial in drug development, but the assay data may be incomplete for numerous factors. This incompleteness manifests as unknown or unreliable attribute values for certain compounds. Data missing can impact the integrity and quality of data, increase the complexity of data analysis and mining, result in inaccurate or unreliable outcomes, thereby diminishing the utility of the data [23]. However, traditional machine learning-based methods often not well do in the imputation of compound property assay data. Recently, the issue of imputation of compound property assay has attracted the attention of the chemical community. Some researchers have proposed some deep learning-based methods for missing data imputation. For example, Irwin et al. [24] used a convolutional neural network (CNN) to populate image or chemical structure data, and then used a generative adversarial network (GAN) to generate missing data. Whitehead et al. [25] utilized Deep Neural Network (DNN) to impute missing values in assay bioactivity data, aiming to improve the reliability and accuracy of the imputation process. Whitehead et al. [26] developed methods based on sparse and noisy data to impute missing compound activities, enhancing the accuracy and completeness of activity predictions. However, deep learning-based methods often entail learning a substantial number of parameters (ranging from tens of thousands to billions) from training samples and fine-tuning multiple hyperparameters. These methods require high-quality and high-quantity training data, as well as significant computational resources, typically GPU servers. To address the problems of the above-mentioned missing imputation methods, this work aims to develop a better non-deep learning-based missing value imputation scheme.

Gene Expression Programming (GEP) is a powerful evolutionary algorithm that combines genotype and phenotype. It has been successfully applied to various data mining knowledge discovery and optimization problems [27, 28]. This work introduces GEP to solve the imputation problem in compound property assay, and propose a Gene Expression Programming-based Compound Property Imputation method (GEP-CPI). GEP-CPI utilizes gene expression programming to effectively impute in the missing data. By iteratively evolving the chromosome population, GEP-CPI mines the optimal solutions for compound property assay data. Experiments were conducted on three datasets to validate the effectiveness of the proposed method. Experimental results show that GEP-CPI generally outperforms other methods in imputing missing compound property assay data.

2   Overview of Gene Expression Programming

GEP is a powerful evolutionary algorithm that combines genotypes and phenotypes, inheriting the advantages of Genetic Algorithms and Genetic Programming. GEP encodes individuals into genes, which are later encoded into various expression trees in evaluating individuals. Afterwards, these expression trees are decoded to obtain the functional expression of the corresponding chromosome. By assessing an individual's fitness, we can calculate the degree to which their expression is effective in solving the problem. By creating an initial population and then performing genetic manipulations to iteratively evolve, the individuals that provide the optimal solutions can eventually be found. In GEP, a chromosome consists of one or more genes, where genes are a symbolic string composed of a series of function symbols and terminal symbols. Each gene in GEP is divided into two parts: the head and the tail. The "head" consists of function symbols and terminal symbols, while the "tail" can only contain terminal symbols. The relationship between the tail length t and the head length h needs to satisfy as follows:

$$t = h * (n - 1) + 1 \tag{1}$$

where, n represents the maximum number of operands in the set of function operators.

The GEP chromosomes consist of genotypic and phenotypic forms. The GEP has a straightforward, linear, and compact chromosome structure that facilitates genetic operations. Furthermore, this coding method helps to avoid the generation of invalid gene structures during genetic operations, thus improving the efficiency of the algorithm. Taking the simple mathematical expression (2) as an example.

$$x^2 + y^2 \tag{2}$$

GEP's gene decoding method is a hierarchical traversal of the phenotypic ET from top to bottom and from left to right. This process produces K-expression (genotype). Conversely, decoding the K-expression in a reverse process allows you to obtain the corresponding ET. By traversing the expression tree in an inorder traversal, one can obtain the mathematical expression corresponding to the chromosome (Figs. 1 and 2).

1	2	3	4	5	6	7
+	*	*	x	x	y	y

Fig. 1. Genotype example figure.

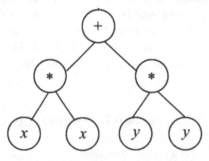

Fig. 2. Example of phenotype illustration

The primary process of the GEP is similar to the traditional genetic algorithm and genetic programming. It evolved by a population composed of individuals through multiple generations of genetic operations to ultimately discover the optimal individual consequently which can be mapped to the final solution to the problem. For the specific execution process of the GEP, please refer to reference [29].

3   GEP-Based Method for Imputing Missing Data of Compound Properties

3.1   Problem Description

Utilizing known properties to impute in missing attributes for compound properties is a widely used and effective method. The basic idea of this method is that we can use the already available attribute information to infer and fill in the missing attributes. As shown in Eq. (3):

$$V = f(x, y, z...) \tag{3}$$

Equation (3) represents the formula for imputing missing assay compound properties, where V represents the missing attribute, and $x, y, z...$ represent known attributes. The key to apply Eq. (3) is to determine the mapping relationship $f()$ between V and $x, y, z....$. The derivation of the function $f()$ for this model involves optimizing a multi-parameter nonlinear model. Once $f(\cdot)$ is determined, we can use it to impute in missing compound property assay data.

3.2   The GEP-CPI Method

Basic Ideas of GEP-CPI. The basic ideas of GEP-CPI is to treat the missing unit data attributes in compound property assay as the target attributes. Next, all available data information is utilized to determine the exact mapping relationship between the data attributes of the training set and the target attributes. In this context, every individual in the GEP serves as a candidate solution for this mapping relationship. Iterative optimization is performed using genetic evolution strategies [30], such as mutation operators, crossover operators and selection operators, until the optimal mapping relationship is identified. Finally, one can use the known data and the best mapping relationship to complete the missing imputation of the target attribute. In a word, GEP-CPI achieves individual evolution and optimization through operations such as mutation and recombination to efficiently find the optimal solution to a problem.

Gene and Individual Design. "GEP encoding" refers to the technique and procedure for converting the potential solutions of a problem from their representation space into the search space compatible with the GEP. To impute missing data of compound property assays, we design the gene structure and encoding method for GEP-CPI:

Definition 1: (Gene) Denoted as $G = \{H, T\}$. H is the gene's head, composed of elementary function symbols and mathematical operators, the encoding represents the operation method of the parameter variable. T is the gene's tail, consisting of the parameter variable. Its encoding represents the known compound property assay data that has been explicitly defined, the length of the gene GL is: $GL = h + t$.

Definition 2: (Individual) Denoted as $C = \{G, ET, K, S\}$, G represents genes, ET represents expression trees, K represents the expression of genes in ET, S is the fitness value of an individual for a specific dataset.

Definition 3: (Population) A population is a collection of n individuals, defined as $P = \{C_1, C_2, \ldots, C_n\}$.

GEP-CPI is powerfully adaptive, automatically adjusting the structure and parameters of an individual to different problems and environments.

Individual Evaluation. In the optimization process of GEP-CPI, the reasonable selection of the fitness function is the foundation for accurately imputing missing data of compound property assays. In GEP-CPI, each individual is a potential candidate solution for the given problem. To evaluate individual fitness, the specific requirement is to measure the difference between the predicted value and the true value of a candidate solution. Therefore, this paper uses a fitness function based on Mean Squared Error (MSE), as shown in Eq. (4):

$$E = \sum_{i=1}^{n} (P_i - T_i)^2 \tag{4}$$

where E represents Mean Squared Error, n is the number of data sample in the experimental dataset, P is the predicted value, and T is the true value.

3.3   GEP-CPI Process

The process description of the proposed GEP-based method for compound property assay data imputation is as follows:

Algorithm 1

Input: Population size (*pSize*) , maximum evolutionary generations *N*, terminal set *Ts*, Function symbol set *Fs*, gene head length   , gene tail length *t*, probabilities for various genetic operators, dataset.

Output: The best individual *Cbest*.

Step:

Step 1: Use the Correlation analysis method to calculate the correlation coefficients between different compound properties.

Step 2: Remove data attributes that have low relevance to the target attribute.

Step 3: Normalize the dataset.

Step 4: Generate the first generation of individuals randomly and initialize the population.

Step 5: Perform the chromosome decoding operation on every individual in the current population to obtain the corresponding mathematical expression.

Step 6: Use equation (4) to calculate the fitness of each individual.

Step 7: Sort the individuals in the current population based on their fitness values to identify the best individual.

Step 8: If the best individual satisfies the stopping condition, then proceed to step 12.

Step 9: If the best individual does not satisfy the stopping condition, then go to step 10.

Step 10: Perform genetic operation on the population for every individual using the selection method described in reference [30], then go to step 5.

Step 11: Output the mathematical expression represented by the current best individual, and the algorithm terminates.

4 Experiment and Results Analysis

4.1 Experimental Setup

Dataset. Three benchmark datasets including QM8, ESOL, and Lipophilicity are used to evaluate the performance of the comparative methods in this work. The statistics of these benchmark datasets is shown in Table 1.

The QM8 dataset includes more than 20,000 organic molecules. Each molecule is represented by the Cartesian coordinates of the atoms and the corresponding quantum mechanics (QM) properties. The dataset contains 12 properties for each molecule, encompassing properties such as energy, enthalpy, free energy, dipole moment, polarizability, heat capacity, zero-point vibrational energy, and more.

The ESOL dataset contains solubility data for 1,128 compounds, including molecular weight, octanol-water partition coefficient (logP), polar surface area, and more. These physicochemical properties can use for predicting the solubility of compounds.

The Lipophilicity dataset provides experimental results of the octanol/water distribution coefficient (logD at pH 7.4) for 1,144 compounds. Solubility and lipophilicity are fundamental physicochemical properties crucial for understanding how molecules interact with solvents and cell membranes.

Table 1. Dataset Information

Dataset	Compounds Number	Compound Properties
QM8	21786	12
ESOL	1128	9
Lipophilicity	1144	5

Evaluation Metrics. The evaluation metric used in this work is the Mean Squared Error described in Sect. 3.2.2, which can assess the performance of missing imputation methods.

Baseline Model. To assess the performance of GEP-CPI in imputing missing data of compound property assays, GEP-CPI compared with five methods including RF [11–13], Multiple Imputation (MI), Feedforward Neural Network (FNN) [16–18], SVM [22] and DNN [25]. RF is an ensemble learning model based on decision trees. It is trained using training data acquired through random sampling. It combines multiple decision trees for learning and prediction, aiming to enhance both the stability and prediction accuracy of the algorithm. MI is a method used to handle missing data by imputing values. The fundamental idea is to estimate missing data values by interpolating calculation from known data points. This method has the capability to predict not only one-dimensional data but also high-dimensional data. FNN can learn and represent complex nonlinear patterns through multiple hidden layers and numerous neurons. By integrating multiple hidden layers and nonlinear activation functions, FNN effectively extract useful features from raw input data. Compared to FNN, DNN have a deeper network structure. DNN exchange and iteration of information multiple times within the network, enabling the processing of more complex nonlinear relationships and feature representations. SVM can perform classification and regression tasks on high-dimensional data by mapping the data into a higher-dimensional feature space and constructing an optimal hyperplane within that space.

Parameter Configuration. GEP parameters iteration count is 200, population size is 100, Gene head length is 7, Mutation rate is 0.1, Crossover rate is 0.1, Training set sample count is 100, Selection algorithm is Tournament Selection.

MI max_iter parameter (the maximum number of interpolations rounds to be executed before the last round of calculation) is taken as 10.

RF parameters: Number of classifiers is 10, Maximum depth of decision trees is 5, Minimum samples per leaf node is 1.

Parameters of the SVM: Linear kernel function, Penalty coefficient is 100, Kernel coefficient is 0.1, Acceptable error range is 0.1.

The parameters of the FNN: 64 and 32 neurons in 6 input layers and 2 hidden layers, respectively, using ReLU activation function, linear activation function in the output layer, mean square error in the loss function, Adam in the optimizer, 100 model iterations, and 16 batch sizes.

The parameters of the DNN, consistent with reference [25].

4.2 Experimental Results and Analysis

Experimental results of GEP-CPI comparing against other missing data imputation methods on three common public datasets are shown in Table 2. Comparison results in Table 2 show that GEP-CPI generally outperforms other methods in imputing missing data of compound properties assay. The main reason may be solutions generated by the GEP often have a prominent level of interpretability, which means they can clearly explain the meaning and function of each gene and gene combination. This helps in gaining a deeper understanding of the problem's essence and the effectiveness of the solutions. Besides GEP-CPI, although MI perform well on the QM8 dataset, they are not as effective as FNN, DNN, and RF on the ESOLS dataset. DNN outperforms the FNN in imputing missing data on these three commonly used public datasets due to the multi-layer structure of DNN that enables layer-by-layer abstraction and feature extraction on complex data.

Table 2. Experimental results of optimal parameters for each comparative method

Model	QM8	ESOL	Lipophilicity
DNN	2.21	**0.94**	0.8
FNN	2.73	1.3	0.9
SVM	2.32	1.7	0.86
RF	2.77	1.1	0.84
MIA	2.18	1.39	0.81
GEP-CPI	**2.13**	**1.03**	**0.79**

4.3 The Impact of Key Parameters of GEP-CPI

To optimize GEP-CPI, we investigated the effects of tournament and roulette wheel selection operators, various mutation rates, and different gene lengths on both the optimal solution and the average optimal solution. In this paper, the method of controlling

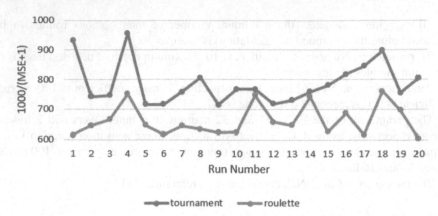

Fig. 3. The effect of two selection operators of GEP-CPI.

variables is employed to explore the results of the impact of various key parameters of the GEP algorithm. Figure 3, Fig. 4, and Fig. 5 represent the impact of various selection operators, mutation rates, and gene lengths of GEP-CPI on the same dataset (QM8) respectively. The vertical axis of each figure represents the effectiveness of the GEP-CPI for imputing missing data, with closer values to 1000 indicating better performance. The horizontal axis represents the number of experiments.

Figure 3 represents the impact of various selection operators of GEP-CPI under the same conditions. As shown in Fig. 3, GEP-CPI performs better in compound property prediction when using the tournament selection operator. The tournament selection operator tends to favor individuals with higher fitness during the selection process. Because the tournament selection operator only chooses the better performing individuals for reproduction and evolution, it helps preserve excellent gene combinations and solutions. Additionally, the tournament selection operator introduces randomness into the competition, meaning that the individuals selected in each tournament are not entirely deterministic. This randomness increases the diversity of the population, prevents falling into local optima, and enhances the exploration capability of the population.

Figure 4 represents the impact of different mutation rates of GEP-CPI under the same conditions. As shown in Fig. 4, when the mutation rate parameter is 0.1, GEP-CPI performs better in composite attribute prediction. The mutation rate refers to the probability of mutations occurring in the gene mutation operation. Different mutation rates can affect the algorithm's exploration capability and convergence speed. When the mutation rate is low, the probability of mutation operations occurring is small. This may result in slower convergence because there are fewer changes in the population, limiting the ability to explore new gene combinations and solutions. When the mutation rate is high, the probability of mutation operations occurring is larger, which helps increase the diversity of the population and encourages the algorithm to search the solution space more extensively. However, a high mutation rate may cause the algorithm to be unstable because the mutation operation may produce invalid individuals. If the mutation rate is moderate, the algorithm's exploratory capability and convergence speed can be balanced. In addition, an appropriate moderate mutation rate can increase diversity in the

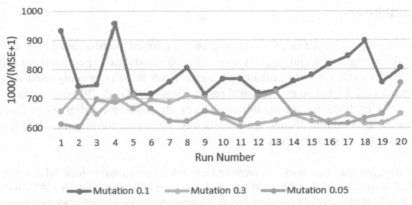

Fig. 4. The effect of three mutation rates of GEP-CPI.

population, helping to avoid falling into local optima and promoting global exploration of the solution space.

Figure 5 represents the impact of different gene head lengths of GEP-CPI under the same conditions. It can be observed from Fig. 5 that GEP-CPI achieves the best missing data imputation performance when the gene head length parameter is 7. In GEP-CPI, gene length refers to the number of nodes in the gene expression tree, which determines the individual's expressive power. Different gene lengths can have varying effects on the algorithm's search capability and representation capability. When genes are short in length, they limit the ability of individuals to express themselves. This may result in individuals only being able to express simpler solutions, making it challenging to solve complex problems. When gene length is long, the individual's expressive power is strong, the search space is large, but convergence becomes difficult. In the case of moderate gene length, individuals have strong expressive power and can represent moderately complex solutions. Moderate gene length is suitable for most common problems and offers a good balance between search capability and computational efficiency.

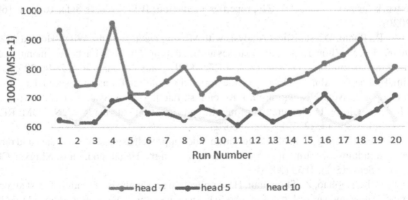

Fig. 5. The impact of different gene header lengths of GEP-CPI.

5 Conclusion

This work proposed a gene expression programming-based method called GEP-CPI for imputing missing compound property assay data. We conducted experiments comparing GEP-CPI with other missing imputation methods on three commonly used datasets to evaluate GEP-CPI. The experimental results show that GEP-CPI outperforms other comparative methods in imputing missing data of compound properties assay. This also demonstrates the validity of applying GEP for missing imputation in compound property assay datasets to improve accuracy.

Acknowledgements. This work was supported in part by the National Natural Science Foundation of China (#62262044), and Natural Science Foundation of Guangxi Province (#2023GXNS-FAA026027), the Project of Guangxi Chinese medicine multidisciplinary crossover innovation team (#GZKJ2311).

References

1. Zhang, H., Zhou, S., Zhang, K., Guan, J.: Residual similarity based conditional independence test and its application in causal discovery. In: Proceedings of the AAAI Conference on Artificial Intelligence, vol. 36, no. 5, pp. 5942–5949 (2022)
2. Zhang, H., Zhou, S., Yan, C., Guan, J., Wang, X.: Recursively learning causal structures using regression-based conditional independence test. In: Proceedings of the AAAI Conference on Artificial Intelligence, vol. 33, no. 01, pp. 3108–3115 (2019)
3. Zhang, H., Zhou, S., Yan, C., Wang, X., Zhang, J., Huan, J.: Learning causal structures based on divide and conquer. IEEE Trans. Cybern. **52**(5), 3232–3243 (2022)
4. Peng, Y., Zhang, Z., Jiang, Q., Guan, J., Zhou, S.: TOP: towards better toxicity prediction by deep molecular representation learning. In: 2019 IEEE International Conference on Bioinformatics and Biomedicine (BIBM), pp. 318–325. IEEE (2019)
5. Peng, Y., Zhang, Z., Jiang, Q., Guan, J., Zhou, S.: TOP: A deep mixture representation learning method for boosting molecular toxicity prediction. Methods **179**(1), 55–64 (2020)
6. Peng, Y., Lin, Y., Jing, X., Zhang, H., Huang, Y., Luo, G.: Enhanced graph isomorphism network for molecular ADMET properties prediction. IEEE Access **8**(1), 168344–168360 (2020)
7. Little, R., Rubin, D.: Statistical Analysis with Missing Data, 2nd edn. Wiley, Hoboken (2019)
8. Liu, K., Hu, X., Zhou, H.: Feature analyses and modeling of lithium-ion battery manufacturing based on random forest classification. IEEE/ASME Trans. Mechatron. **6**, 2944–2955 (2021)
9. Kim, E., Bae, G., Ahn, G.: A study on the imputation solution for missing speed data on UTIS by using adaptive k-NN algorithm. J. Korea Inst. Intell. Transp. Syst. **3**, 66–77 (2014)
10. Sahoo, A., Ghose, D.: Imputation of missing precipitation data using KNN, SOM, RF, and FNN. Soft. Comput. **12**, 5919–5936 (2022)
11. Ma, T., Hu, Y., Wang, J.: A novel vegetation index approach using sentinel-2 data and random forest algorithm for estimating forest stock volume in the Helan mountains, Ningxia, China. Remote Sens. **15**(7), 1853 (2023)
12. Zushida, K., Haohao, Z., Shimamur, H.: Application and analysis of random forest algorithm for estimating lawn grass lengths in robotic lawn mower. Int. J. Mech. Eng. Appl. (1), 6 (2021)
13. Rahman, M., Islam, M.: Missing value imputation using decision trees and decision forests by splitting and merging records: two novel techniques. Knowl.-Based Syst. **53**, 51–65 (2013)

14. Che, Z., Purushotham, S., Cho, K.: Recurrent neural networks for multivariate time series with missing values. Sci. Rep. **8**(1), 6085 (2018)
15. Phiwhorm, K., Saikaew, C., Leung, C.: Adaptive multiple imputations of missing values using the class center. J. Big Data **9**(1), 52 (2022)
16. Chen, J., Huang, H., Tian, F.: A selective bayes classifier for classifying incomplete data based on gain ratio. Knowl.-Based Syst. **21**(7), 530–534 (2008)
17. Johnson, T., Isaac, N., Paviolo, A.: Handling missing values in trait data. Glob. Ecol. Biogeogr. **30**(1), 51–62 (2021)
18. Fei, K., Li, Q., Zhu, C.: Non-technical losses detection using missing values' pattern and neural architecture search. Int. J. Electr. Power Energy Syst. **134**, 107410 (2022)
19. Dinh, D., Huynh, V., Sriboonchitta, S.: Clustering mixed numerical and categorical data with missing values. Inf. Sci. **571**, 418–442 (2021)
20. Zhang, Y., Wang, Y., Gong, D.: Clustering-guided particle swarm feature selection algorithm for high-dimensional imbalanced data with missing values. IEEE Trans. Evol. Comput. **26**(4), 616–630 (2021)
21. Di, N.: Missing data analysis with fuzzy C-Means: a study of its application in a psychological scenario. Expert Syst. Appl. **6**, 6793–6797 (2011)
22. Wang, J., Li, D., Zhang, H.: An improvement of support vector machine imputation algorithm based on multiple iteration and grid search strategies. In: 2020 IEEE International Conference on Informatics, IoT, and Enabling Technologies (ICIoT), pp. 538–543 (2020)
23. Kengkanna, A., Ohue, M.: Enhancing Model Learning and Interpretation Using Multiple Molecular Graph Representations for Compound Property and Activity Prediction. arXiv preprint arXiv:2304.06253 (2023)
24. Irwin, B., Levell, J., Whitehead, T.: Practical applications of deep learning to impute heterogeneous drug discovery data. J. Chem. Inf. Model. **6**, 2848–2857 (2020)
25. Whitehead, T., Irwin, B., Hunt, P.: Imputation of assay bioactivity data using deep learning. J. Chem. Inf. Model. **3**, 1197–1204 (2019)
26. Whitehead, T., Irwin, B., Hunt, P.: Imputing compound activities based on sparse and noisy data. In: The American Chemical Society (ACS), p. 257 (2019)
27. Sarir, P., Chen, J., Asteris, P.: Developing GEP tree-based, neuro-swarm, and whale optimization models for evaluation of bearing capacity of concrete-filled steel tube columns. Eng. Comput. **37**, 1–19 (2021)
28. Ren, L., Wang, N., Pang, W.: Modeling and monitoring the material removal rate of abrasive belt grinding based on vision measurement and the gene expression programming (GEP) algorithm. Int. J. Adv. Manuf. Technol. **120**(1–2), 385–401 (2022)
29. Ferreira, C.: Gene expression programming: a new adaptive algorithm for solving problems. Complex Syst. (2), 87–129 (2001)
30. Changan, Y., Yuzhong, P., Xiao, Q.: Principles and Applications of Gene Expression Programming Algorithm. China Science Publishing, Beijing (2010)

Identification of Parkinson's Disease Associated Genes Through Explicable Deep Learning and Bioinformatic

Yuxin Zhang[1,2], Xiangrong Sun[1,2], Peng Zhang[3], Xudan Zhou[1,2], Xiansheng Huang[1], Mingzhi Zhang[1], Guanhua Qiao[4], Jian Xu[1], Ming Chen[5], and Wei Shu[1,2(✉)]

[1] College of Intelligent Medicine and Biotechnology, Guilin Medical University, Guilin, China
shuwei7866@126.com
[2] Key Laboratory of Medical Biotechnology and Translational Medicine of the Education Department of Guangxi Province, Guilin Medical University, Guilin, China
[3] Department of Neurology, Affiliated Hospital of Guilin Medical University, Guilin, China
[4] School of Basic Medicine, Guilin Medical University, Guilin, China
[5] State Key Laboratory for Chemistry and Molecular Engineering of Medicinal Resources, School of Chemistry and Pharmacy, Guangxi Normal University, Guilin, China
chenmingprotein@mailbox.gxnu.edu.cn

Abstract. Weutilized interpretable deep learning methodologies to discern critical genes and latent biomarkers associated with Parkinson's disease (PD). Gene expression data were collected from the GEO dataset, subjected to rigorous differential expression analysis to curate genes for subsequent scrutiny. Based on the P-Net and PASNet models, we have developed a pathway-related deep learning model that integrates PD-associated gene expression data with established biological pathways. This method has yielded satisfactory results, manifesting an Area Under the Curve (AUC) of 0.73 and an F1 score of 0.71, thereby efficaciously discriminating PD patients and bestowing novel insights into the pertinent biological pathways. Through interpretable deep learning models, we have identified potential biomarkers (XK, PDK1, TUBA4B, TP53) and their associated biological pathways (innate immune system, hemostasis, G protein-coupled receptor signaling pathway) related to Parkinson's disease. The importance of these genes has been validated through external datasets and UPDRS III scores. Of particular significance is the XK gene, also known as Kell blood group precursor, and numerous XK gene mutations have been linked to the McLeod syndrome which exhibits symptomatic similarities with PD. Taken together, we identified several PD associated genes by explicable deep learning and bioinformatics methods, and XK gene was demonstrated a close correlation to PD.

Keywords: Parkinson's Disease · Deep Learning · Gene Expression Analysis · Biomarkers · XK Gene

© The Author(s), under exclusive license to Springer Nature Singapore Pte Ltd. 2024
D.-S. Huang et al. (Eds.): ICAI 2023, CCIS 2014, pp. 136–146, 2024.
https://doi.org/10.1007/978-981-97-0903-8_14

1 Introduction

Parkinson's disease (PD) has emerged as an increasingly pervasive neurodegenerative ailment on a global scale, afflicting in excess of six million individuals, and its incidence continues to rise steadily [1, 2]. The crux of the PD quandary lies in the progressive degeneration of dopaminergic neurons, setting forth a domino effect of pathological transformations, encompassing the accretion of α-synuclein protein and the consequential loss of cells in various cerebral regions [3]. PD manifests as a constellation of symptoms, including tremors, muscular rigidity, bradykinesia, and a conspicuous deterioration in motor function [4]. Present therapeutic interventions are largely oriented towards alleviating these symptomatic burdens, yet they fall short of providing efficacious remedies to arrest or retard dopaminergic neuronal degeneration. Consequently, a more profound comprehension of the molecular mechanisms underlying PD and novel biomarkers discovery became exigent. These would offer the prospect of early diagnosis, treatment modalities, prognostic evaluations, and the potentiality of groundbreaking therapeutic modalities.

Efficient medical science data processing and the extraction of informative characteristics is very important for the quest for a more profound comprehension of diseases and the development of efficacious therapeutic modalities. The exploitation of data mining and machine learning methodologies has been harnessed for the analysis of disease-related data, ushering in novel avenues for the diagnosis and treatment of maladies [5]. Yet, given the intricate nature of PD, conventional statistical analysis techniques grapple with the comprehensive capture of multigenic risk factors, thus compelling the imperative for more robust tools to confront this challenge. With the relentless enhancement in computational capabilities, the deployment of deep learning artificial intelligence models in the prediction of genetic risk ushers in fresh possibilities to disentangle the multifaceted etiology of neurodegenerative disease [6]. Consequently, the deployment of interpretable deep learning neural network models to ascertain and validate potential biomarkers for PD emerges as a matter of profound practical significance. In this investigation, we employed an interpretable deep learning neural network models to dissect potential associated genes of Parkinson's disease.

2 Materials and Methods

2.1 Data Acquisition for Parkinson's Disease

In the Gene Expression Omnibus (GEO) database, datasets were meticulously selected based on stringent criteria: specimens derived from individuals afflicted by Parkinson's disease (PD) with samples from their healthy counterparts, all sourced from peripheral blood. Ultimately, three datasets namely, GSE99039 [7], GSE57475 [8], and GSE6613 [9] were deemed suitable. GSE99039 was partitioned into a training set and a test set, allocating 80% for model training and 20% for model performance evaluation. These datasets encompass UPDRS scores for PD patients, facilitating the exploration of correlations between core genes and clinical manifestations. Furthermore, GSE57475 and GSE6613 served as external validation datasets to authenticate hub genes. Raw data or sequence matrix files were adeptly procured and processed, with the selection of probes bearing the highest average expression values for the annotation of genes endowed with multiple matching probes, duly adorned with homologous gene symbols. For in-depth information on these datasets, please refer to Table 1.

Table 1. Basic information of the Datasets Used

Study ID	Platform	# Probes	Sample size(n)		Age (mean ± SD)		Sex N (% male)		Hoehn-Yahr (mean ± SD)
			PD	CT	PD	CT	PD	CT	
GSE6613	GPL96	12,403	50	22	69.4 ± 8.4	64.4 ± 10.7	39 (78%)	11 (50%)	2.3 ± 0.7
GSE57475	GPL6947	19,223	93	49	62.8 ± 9.5	61.4 ± 9.6	62 (67%)	26 (53%)	2.0 ± 0.5
GSE99039	GPL570	20,188	205	233	62 ± 11.0	58 ± 30.1	95 (46%)	75 (32%)	1.8 ± 0.9
Total	–	51,814	348	304	–	–	196 (56%)	112 (37%)	–

2.2 Methodology Overview

Our computational workflow unfolds across three pivotal stages:

  (i) The Preprocessing Phase, where differentially expressed genes are methodically culled through differential expression analysis.
 (ii) The Model Construction Phase, marked by the deployment of interpretable models, namely PASNet [10] and P-Net [11], to craft intricate, sparse deep learning networks attuned to Parkinson's disease-associated genes and pathways.
(iii) Lastly, machine learning techniques come into play, meticulously selecting hub genes, whose efficacy is subsequently validated using external datasets and clinical phenotype scores. Figure 1 illustrates a schematic representation of our comprehensive workflow.

2.3 Analysis of Differential Gene Expression

The GSE99039 data underwent a logarithmic transformation and normalization, followed by dimensionality reduction through Principal Component Analysis (PCA) [12], illuminating the dispersion of data. Subsequent to data preprocessing, differential gene expression (DGE) analysis concerning Parkinson's disease and their healthy counterparts within GSE99039 was carried out employing the "limma" package in R [13], with results being adeptly visualized. Our stringent selection criteria encompassed |LogFC| > 0.25 and a P-value less than 0.05.

2.4 Formulation of Deep Learning Neural Network Models

We constructed an intricate deep learning network model closely intertwined with Parkinson's disease pathways, predicated upon the PASNet and P-Net models. This model encompasses five distinct strata: the input layer (gene layer), the pathway layer, the

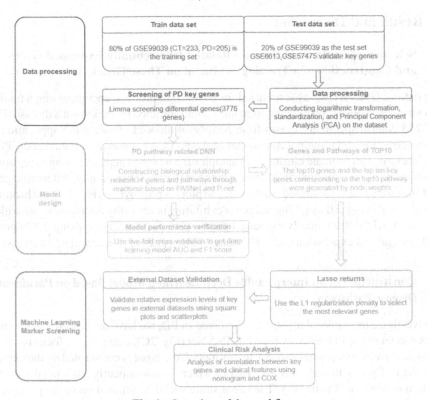

Fig. 1. Overview of the workflow

hidden layers, the initial hidden layer, and the out-put layer. Following data preprocessing, we culled 3,776 genes for the training dataset and gathered 972 genes associated with pathways from the Reactome [14] databases to form the input and pathway layers, respectively. We harnessed established gene-pathway relationships to construct a mask table, judiciously constricting the interconnections between the gene and pathway layers. Choosing Adam as the optimizer and applying dropout and L2 regularization serves the dual purpose of optimizing model performance and preventing overfitting.

2.5 Development of Clinical Risk Prediction Models Anchored in Putative Biomarkers

The putative biomarkers prognosticated by our model were harnessed as indices for predicting the onset of the disease, underpinning the construction of comprehensive disease risk prediction curves. Leveraging the "rms" package in R, we painstakingly engineered clinical diagnostic models, complete with Receiver Operating Characteristic (ROC) curve area under the curve (AUC) computation and the generation of calibration curves to comprehensively gauge the diagnostic precision of our model. Furthermore, Decision Curve Analysis (DCA) [15] plots were meticulously fashioned, serving as a litmus test for the effectiveness of the clinical diagnostic model.

3 Result and Discussion

3.1 Selection of Parkinson's Disease-Related Differentially Expressed Genes and Construction of a Training Set Based on These Genes

The dataset GSE99039 was scrutinized for expression profiles, encompassing a total of 438 samples, with 205 originating from individuals afflicted by Parkinson's disease (PD) and 233 control specimens drawn from peripheral blood. Following the application of batch correction and principal component analysis (PCA), it was discerned that the PCA graph revealed an intimate clustering of samples from both groups, denoting exceptional reproducibility and minimal disparities in data similarity. Subsequently, differential gene expression analyses, illustrated via the volcano plot (as portrayed in Fig. 2A) and heatmap (as indicated in Fig. 2B), highlighted genes exhibiting noteworthy inter-group disparities. A total of 3,776 differentially expressed genes were unveiled, comprising 1,579 genes with upregulated expression and 2,197 genes demonstrating downregulated expression.

3.2 Construction of an Interpretable Deep Learning Model Based on Parkinson's Disease Pathways

To investigate the molecular pathways involved in PD, we have developed a neural network model of the PD pathway based on PASNet (Fig. 2C), centering its focus upon the biological pathways germane to PD. In this model, the input is constituted by the expression data of genes linked with the disease, which is subsequently associated with the stratum of biological pathways. The latent strata within the model serve the purpose of extracting abstract, high-level features from the stratum of pathways, thereby enhancing the model's capacity to encapsulate non-linear expressions and interpretability. In the endeavor to gauge the model's prognostication performance, we calibrated the learning rate to 8e-05, the L2 regularization coefficient to 1e-06, and nEpochs to 6000. Employing a five-fold cross-validation approach on the data pertaining to PD and control samples was instrumental in fortifying the robustness of our findings. The model's training and validation processes yielded loss values over the course of its operation, as delineated in Fig. 2D, with the training loss continuously diminishing and the validation loss stabilizing after 3000 iterations. On the test set, it achieved an AUC of 0.73 (as exhibited in Fig. 2F), an F1 score of 0.71, a true negative rate (TN) of 70.21%, and a true positive rate (TP) of 73.17% (depicted in Fig. 2E). In comparison to conventional bioinformatics and deep learning methodologies, interpretable deep learning models tethered to pathways exhibited exceptional aptitude in managing gene expression data, especially when grappling with its sparsity and the extraction of concealed signals within this intricate domain. Furthermore, deep learning methods accommodated an expansion in sample size and dimensions, fostering more extensive investigations. To counterbalance the inherent opaqueness of deep neural networks, we conscientiously incorporated prior biological knowledge pertaining to gene-pathway associations, allowing for the identification of key genes and pathways underpinning PD. An analysis of the relevance of each node involved scrutinizing the weights of the trained model, thus enabling the identification of principal pathways and their affiliated genes. The top ten of these pathways encompassed

Signal Transduction [16], Immune System [17], Metabolism of Proteins, Gene Expression (Transcription), RNA Polymerase II Transcription [18], Adaptive Immune System [19], Generic Transcription Pathway, Disease, Post-translational Protein Modification and Innate Immune System [20]. Most of these pathways, notably the immune response, inflammation, signal transduction, transcriptional processes, and protein metabolism, have previously been documented in the scientific literature as being germane to the etiology of Parkinson's disease. Consequently, we singled out core genes, signified by their substantial weights and recurrent occurrences, as plausible biological markers associated with PD.

3.3   Identification of Biomarkers for Parkinson's Disease Diagnosis

In the quest to unearth potential biomarkers within peripheral blood tissues for the diagnosis of Parkinson's disease (PD), our focus gravitated toward the top 10 genes, endowed with significant weights, in conjunction with the core pathways and their respective genes. By amalgamating these entities, we were able to pinpoint 34 genes of paramount relevance. The model yielded an expression matrix which was comprised of genes inherently associated with pathways. Leveraging the Lasso regression algorithm for the purpose of variable selection concerning PD, the introduction of L1 regularization served to compress a portion of gene coefficients to zero, thus facilitating feature selection. The meticulous determination of the optimal lambda value, denoted as lambda.1se (as visualized in Fig. 3A and Fig. 3B), led us to the revelation of 12 non-zero regression coefficients pertaining to genes implicated in PD. These genes were subsequently subjected to a validation process to ascertain their differential expression within the training set, as illuminated in Fig. 3C. The vast majority of these genes exhibited highly significant differences, notable examples being CRTAM [21, 22], INTS12, KIR2DS2 [23, 24], NPPB, PDK1 [25], TP53 [26, 27], TUBA4B, ZNF267. The ensuing correlation analysis between UPDRS III scores within the GSE99039 samples and the expression levels of genes (as portrayed in Fig. 4A–D) accentuated a noteworthy positive correlation, particularly regarding the XK gene and the motor function of patients. The validation of these findings within external validation sets (GSE57475 and GSE6613) corroborated the veracity of our results (refer to Fig. 4E–F), thereby paving the way for these distinctive genes to emerge as promising biomarkers.

XK is an X-linked gene encoding XK protein, a hypothetical membrane transporter of unknown function that can form a complex by linking to endothelin-3 converting enzyme Kell through a single disulfide bond, and the main function of the XK-KELL complex is to participate in the stability, morphology, and functional regulation of red blood cells. The expression of the Kell system antigen is partially controlled by XK, and the lack of XK results in decreased expression of the Kell antigen [28]. The morphology of red blood cells in Parkinson's disease is also abnormal, and the expression level of XK gene in PD shows a down-regulation situation, which may be due to the downregulation of XK leading to downregulation of the function of the XK-KELL complex, resulting in abnormal red blood cell morphology.

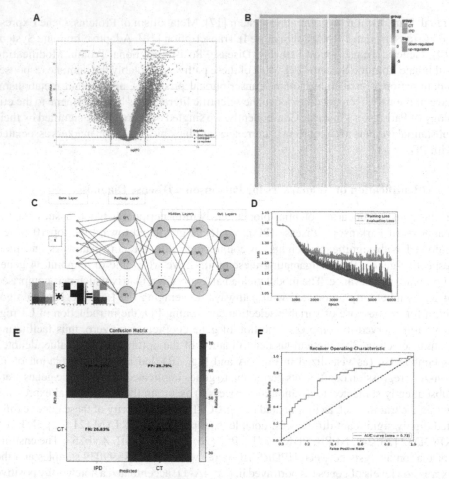

Fig. 2. Differential Expressed Genes (DEGs) screening and Model Architecture and the Predictive Performance of the constructed model. (A–B) A volcano plot and A heatmap illustrates the differential genes between Parkinson's disease and normal controls. (C) Model Structure: The model architecture consists of a gene layer (input layer), which incorporates biological priors, hidden layers representing other biological processes, and an output layer representing both PD and normal states. Candidate genes and pathways are identified based on weights. (D) Training Set Loss: The training set loss continues to decrease, while the test set loss tends to be flat, indicating that the model is in an underfitting state. (E–F) Evaluation of the performance of the model: The model had a true negative rate (TN) of 70.21%, a true positive rate (TP) of 73.17%, and an area under the curve (AUC) of 0.73 for ROC analysis on the validation set.

3.4 Establishment and Evaluation of a Risk Score Prediction Model

To uncover the interplay between the risk of developing the disease and its prognostic outcome, we formulated a nomogram, as exemplified in Fig. 5A, harnessing the "Rms" package. The receiver operating characteristic (ROC) [29] area under the curve of the clinical model stood at an impressive 0.8369 (as seen in Fig. 5B), affirming its aptitude

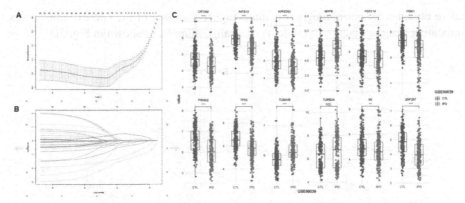

Fig. 3. Screening of Potential Biomarkers Related to Parkinson's Disease (PD). (A) Using cross-validation, we computed the optimal λ with the minimum average error and The λ value of the simplest model is obtained within a range of variance. (B) The dynamic process of variable filtering of the LASSO algorithm is shown in Fig. As λ increases, the estimated parameters shrink accordingly, and the parameter values of the final variables are compressed to 0, indicating that they are excluded from the model. (C) Gene expression level analysis. On the GSE99039 dataset, there were significant differences in gene expression levels in 9 of the 12 genes between the PD group and the control group (***$p < 0.001$).

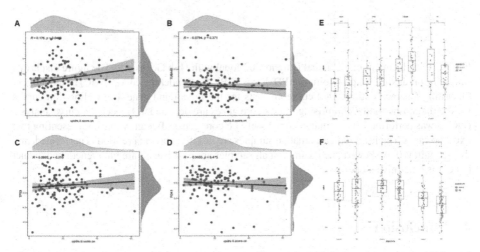

Fig. 4. Validation of Correlation Analysis Based on the External Datasets GSE6613 and GSE57475. (A–D) Correlation of Core Genes (XK, TP53, TUBA4B and PDK1) with Clinical Features (UPDRS III scores). (E–F) Validation of selected key genes in the external datasets GSE6613 and GSE57475, where XK and TUBA4B exhibit differential expression.

for predictive analytics. Moreover, the calibration curve, seen in Fig. 5C, showcased the remarkable congruence between observed and predicted risk associated with Parkinson's disease, substantiating the clinical diagnostic model's high accuracy. In addition, through the judicious application of decision curve analysis (DCA), The net benefit curve obtained by our nomogram is much higher than that of the two extreme curves, indicating that the diagnostic model is clinically valuable, as shown in Fig. 5D.

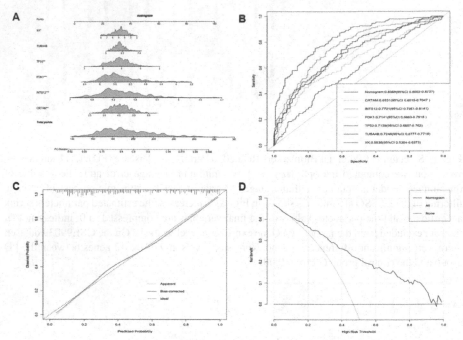

Fig. 5. Establishment of a Clinical Diagnostic Model with Hub Genes. (A) The figure displays a line chart predicting the probability of PD disease. (B) Area under the curve (AUC) of the Subject Operating Characteristic (ROC) curve analysis for the model and gene. (C) Calibration curves for the diagnostic model comprising the six core genes are depicted. (D) Decision curve analysis (DCA) was performed on the diagnostic model of 6 core genes. Two gray lines, representing two extreme cases. The level indicates that all samples are negative, no intervention is performed, and the net gain is 0. A skewed one means that all samples are positive, all are intervened, and the net benefit is a negative slope.

4   Conclusion

In the present study, we proffer an intelligible deep learning framework rooted in PAS-Net for the multifaceted genetic analysis of PD. Our model attains an area under the curve (AUC) of 0.73 for the discrimination of PD-afflicted patients. Moreover, through the conduction of pathway-level examinations to elucidate the deep learning model's outcomes, we discern interconnections between genes of susceptibility and pathways intrinsic to PD pathogenesis. While neural network models may be deployed for polygenic risk assessment in the context of PD, there remains a scope for augmentation in model performance, predominantly attributed to inherent model underfitting.

To ameliorate the precision of disease classification, we proffer an initial recommendation involving the amplification of the sample size within the classification model, thereby enabling a more encompassing encapsulation of the genetic underpinnings of the ailment. Additionally, given that gene expression data derived from assorted batches and platforms can impinge upon model precision, a more expansive PD patient gene expression dataset is advocated to furnish a holistic panorama of genes associated with the ailment.

In summation, by means of the integration of bioinformatics and deep learning methodologies, we have ascertained and authenticated four genes linked to PD, with a pronounced focus on the XK gene, deemed pivotal in the pathogenesis of McLeod syndrome and essential in maintaining homeostasis within the realms of the immune and nervous systems. McLeod syndrome disease is an exceedingly rare neurodegenerative malady bereft of efficacious therapeutic modalities, and clinical management is largely confided to the sphere of supportive care, centered on the regulation of seizures, cardiac anomalies, and psychiatric conditions. However, the efficacy of interventions for its choreiform motility impairments may be suboptimal. The potential nexus of this ailment with PD opens uncharted avenues for the management of McLeod syndrome. These genes may be pivotal actors in the inception and progression of PD, potentially offering innovative biomarkers for the diagnosis and surveillance of PD.

Acknowledgment. We would like to express our heartfelt gratitude to the National Natural Science Foundation of China for providing the financial support through grant No. 32060157 and 82360098, Central Guiding Local Science and Technology Development Fund Projects (ZY20230103), Graduate research project of Guilin Medical University No. GYYK2022020, which made this study possible.

References

1. GBD 2016 Neurology Collaborators. Global, regional, and national burden of neurological disorders, 1990–2016: a systematic analysis for the Global Burden of Disease Study 2016. Lancet Neurol. 18, 459–480 (2019)
2. Dorsey, E.R., Sherer, T., Okun, M.S., Bloem, B.R.: The emerging evidence of the Parkinson pandemic. J. Parkinsons Dis. **8**, S3–S8 (2018)
3. Tysnes, O.-B., Storstein, A.: Epidemiology of Parkinson's disease. J. Neural Transm. **124**, 901–905 (2017)
4. Clarke, C.E.: Parkinson's disease. BMJ **335**, 441–445 (2007)
5. Rauschert, S., Raubenheimer, K., Melton, P.E., Huang, R.C.: Machine learning and clinical epigenetics: a review of challenges for diagnosis and classification. Clin. Epigenetics **12**, 51 (2020)
6. Zhou, X., Chen, Y., Ip, F.C.F., Jiang, Y., Cao, H., Lv, G., et al.: Deep learning-based polygenic risk analysis for Alzheimer's disease prediction. Commun. Med. **3**, 49 (2023)
7. Shamir, R., Klein, C., Amar, D., Vollstedt, E.-J., Bonin, M., Usenovic, M., et al.: Analysis of blood-based gene expression in idiopathic Parkinson disease. Neurology **89**, 1676–1683 (2017)
8. Locascio, J.J., Eberly, S., Liao, Z., Liu, G., Hoesing, A.N., Duong, K., et al.: Association between α-synuclein blood transcripts and early, neuroimaging-supported Parkinson's disease. Brain **138**, 2659–2671 (2015)
9. Scherzer, C.R., Eklund, A.C., Morse, L.J., Liao, Z., Locascio, J.J., Fefer, D., et al.: Molecular markers of early Parkinson's disease based on gene expression in blood. Proc. Natl. Acad. Sci. U.S.A. **104**, 955–960 (2007)

10. Hao, J., Kim, Y., Kim, T.-K., Kang, M.: PASNet: pathway-associated sparse deep neural network for prognosis prediction from high-throughput data. BMC Bioinform. **19**, 510 (2018)
11. Elmarakeby, H.A., Hwang, J., Arafeh, R., Crowdis, J., Gang, S., Liu, D., et al.: Biologically informed deep neural network for prostate cancer discovery. Nature **598**, 348–352 (2021)
12. Ringnér, M.: What is principal component analysis? Nat. Biotechnol. **26**, 303–304 (2008)
13. Ritchie, M.E., Phipson, B., Wu, D., Hu, Y., Law, C.W., Shi, W., et al.: Limma powers differential expression analyses for RNA-sequencing and microarray studies. Nucleic Acids Res. **43**, e47 (2015)
14. Jassal, B., Matthews, L., Viteri, G., Gong, C., Lorente, P., Fabregat, A., et al.: The reactome pathway knowledgebase. Nucleic Acids Res. **48**, D498-503 (2020)
15. Vickers, A.J., Holland, F.: Decision curve analysis to evaluate the clinical benefit of prediction models. Spine J. **21**, 1643–1648 (2021)
16. Farkas, S., et al.: Signal transduction pathway activity compensates dopamine D_2/D_3 receptor density changes in Parkinson's disease: a preliminary comparative human brain receptor autoradiography study with [^{3}H]raclopride and [^{35}S]GTPγS. Brain Res. **9**(1453), 56–63 (2012)
17. Tansey, M.G., Wallings, R.L., Houser, M.C., Herrick, M.K., Keating, C.E., Joers, V.: Inflammation and immune dysfunction in Parkinson disease. Nat. Rev. Immunol. **22**(11), 657–673 (2022)
18. Bastide, M.F., Bido, S., Duteil, N., Bézard, E.: Striatal NELF-mediated RNA polymerase II stalling controls l-dopa induced dyskinesia. Neurobiol. Dis. **85**, 93–98 (2016)
19. Harms, A.S., Ferreira, S.A., Romero-Ramos, M.: Periphery and brain, innate and adaptive immunity in Parkinson's disease. Acta Neuropathol. **141**, 527–545 (2021)
20. Schlachetzki, J.C., Winkler, J.: The innate immune system in Parkinson's disease: a novel target promoting endogenous neuroregeneration. Neural Regen. Res. **10**(5), 704–706 (2015)
21. Sulzer, D., et al.: T cells from patients with Parkinson's disease recognize α-synuclein peptides. Nature **546**(7660), 656–661 (2017)
22. Takeuchi, A., et al.: CRTAM determines the CD4+ cytotoxic T lymphocyte lineage. J. Exp. Med. **213**(1), 123–138 (2016)
23. Earls, R.H., Lee, J.K.: The role of natural killer cells in Parkinson's disease. Exp. Mol. Med. **52**(9), 1517–1525 (2020)
24. Saulquin, X., Gastinel, L.N., Vivier, E.: Crystal structure of the human natural killer cell activating receptor KIR2DS2 (CD158j). J. Exp. Med. **197**(7), 933–938 (2003)
25. Vallée, A., Lecarpentier, Y., Guillevin, R., Vallée, J.-N.: Thermodynamics in neurodegenerative diseases: interplay between canonical WNT/Beta-catenin pathway-PPAR gamma, energy metabolism and circadian rhythms. Neuromolecular Med. **20**, 174–204 (2018)
26. Lu, T., Kim, P., Luo, Y.: Tp53 gene mediates distinct dopaminergic neuronal damage in different dopaminergic neurotoxicant models. Neural Regen. Res. **12**, 1413–1417 (2017)
27. He, Z.-Q., Huan, P.-F., Wang, L., He, J.-C.: Paeoniflorin ameliorates cognitive impairment in Parkinson's disease via JNK/p53 signaling. Metab. Brain Dis. **37**, 1–14 (2022). https://doi.org/10.1007/s11011-022-00937-2
28. Daniels, G.L., Weinauer, F., Stone, C., Ho, M., Green, C.A., Jahn-Jochem, H., et al.: A combination of the effects of rare genotypes at the XK and KEL blood group loci results in absence of Kell system antigens from the red blood cells. Blood **88**, 4045–4050 (1996)

Enzyme Turnover Number Prediction Based on Protein 3D Structures

Yuhao He[1], Yizhen Wang[1], Yanyun Zhang[1,2], Yongfu Yang[3], Li Cheng[1,2(✉)],
and Daniyal Alghazzawi[4]

[1] School of Computer Science and Information Engineering, Hubei University,
No. 368 Youyi Road, Wuhan 430062, Hubei, China
chengli@hubu.edu.cn
[2] Key Laboratory of Intelligent Sensing System and Security (Hubei University)
Ministry of Education, Wuhan, China
[3] School of Mathematics and Statistics, Hubei University, No. 368 Youyi Road, Wuhan 430062,
Hubei, China
[4] Faculty of Computing and Information Technology (FCIT), King AbdulAziz University
(KAU), Jeddah 21589, Saudi Arabia

Abstract. Protein function prediction has long been a widely discussed task in the field of synthetic biology, and it is of paramount importance for gaining a deeper understanding of the roles and interactions of proteins within living organisms. Since the 3D structure data of proteins obtained experimentally are far less in quantity than the corresponding protein sequence data, most experiments related to protein function prediction currently rely on using protein sequences as training data, although 3D protein structures contain much more information. Here, an enzyme turnover number prediction model (PSKcat) is proposed based on 3D protein structures. PSKcat takes protein PDB files as input, represents proteins using a modified pre-trained model called GearNet-Edge for 3D protein structures, and combines graph neural network to characterize the substrates involved in enzyme reactions. In order to verify the effectiveness of the model, several enzyme reaction datasets were constructed, and multiple groups of comparative experiments were conducted. The experimental results demonstrate the feasibility of using 3D protein structures for enzyme function prediction, which opens up avenues for further exploration of the applications of 3D protein structures in the future.

Keywords: Graph Neural Network · Pretraining model · 3D Protein structures · Enzyme turnover number prediction

1 Introduction

Protein function prediction, as one of the important downstream tasks in proteomics, provides valuable insights into various research areas within the field of synthetic biology [1], metabolic engineering [2, 3], and genome editing [4]. Proteomics is a technology

---

Y. He and Y. Wang—Contributed equally to this work and should be considered co-first authors.

D.-S. Huang et al. (Eds.): ICAI 2023, CCIS 2014, pp. 147–158, 2024.
https://doi.org/10.1007/978-981-97-0903-8_15

application that involves identifying and quantifying the overall protein in cells, tissues, or organisms. It complements other "omics" technologies such as genomics and transcriptomics, shedding light on the identity of proteins in organisms and providing insights into the structures and function of specific proteins [13]. Proteomic data, serving as a pivotal component in protein function prediction, comprises protein sequence, structure, expression levels, and modification information. Among these, protein sequence information is the most widely employed.

Protein sequence is an essential component of proteomics data with various practical applications, including protein function prediction [14], drug design, drug target identification [15], and gene editing [16]. They provide strong support for protein function prediction tasks, such as enzyme function prediction. Numerous works have been conducted in the area of enzyme function prediction. Researchers used protein sequences in previous studies with relatively small datasets to extract information about amino acid pairs, distribution, and basic features. Subsequently, they employed classical machine learning algorithms like Bayesian methods [5], random forests [6], and support vector machines (SVM) [7] for protein function prediction. With the rapid development of artificial intelligence, many deep learning algorithms have been increasingly adopted by researchers in the field of synthetic biology. Tsubaki et al. [8] proposed an end-to-end representation learning approach using graph neural networks (GNN) and convolutional neural networks (CNN) for interaction prediction between compounds and proteins. Li et al. [9] modified this approach and introduced a deep learning model named DLKcat to predict the values of enzyme turnover number (K_{cat}). K_{cat} is critical for understanding cellular metabolism, protein allocation, and physiological diversity, as it represents the maximum rate at which an active site of an enzyme can convert substrate molecules in a unit of time. DLKcat used the amino acid sequence of enzymes and one substrate from the reaction as the input for the entire model. It introduced an attention mechanism to assign weights to different substrates and used a convolutional neural network (CNN) to encode protein information. Kroll et al. [10] introduced the TurNuP model, which incorporated details of the entire reaction, allowing this approach to maintain some level of generalizability even when dealing with enzymes with sequence identity below 40%.

While these efforts have yielded certain achievements, most of the existing work in this field has primarily relied on using protein sequence as input data to perform various tasks in proteomics. In contrast, there has been less emphasis on using the 3D structures. The three-dimensional protein structures encompass the protein's overall folding, spatial structures, and topology, providing much richer information than the one-dimensional structures. The current 3D structural information for many proteins is still lacking experimental determination. For instance, while the UniProt database contains over 227M protein sequences [17], the Protein Data Bank (PDB) holds only 210K experimentally determined protein structures. This means that the quantity of protein structure lags behind datasets in other machine learning domains by several orders of magnitude [12]. Only recently did Hermosilla et al. [11] introduce a novel contrastive learning framework for 3D protein structure representation learning. This phenomenon where researchers have rarely used the 3D structures in their studies can likely be attributed to two possible reasons. First, it may be due to the inherent difficulty in experimentally determining protein structures, making it challenging for researchers to obtain protein 3D structure datasets that meet their training requirements. Second, in certain contexts, using 3D protein structures may not yield the expected benefits when considering the results. Hence, in specific situations, researchers may consider it unnecessary to incorporate protein 3D structure information into protein function prediction.

To validate our hypothesis, we have proposed a deep learning approach named PSKcat for predicting the K_{cat} values of enzyme reactions. In contrast to previous work, we contemplate utilizing 3D protein structures rather than protein sequences and employing them as input for our model. To capture information about enzymes, we employ the GearNet-Edge model [12] and graph neural networks (GNN) to encode 3D protein structural information and substrate information from enzyme reactions. This allows us to test whether using the 3D protein structures is superior to using protein sequences. In this work, we make the following contributions:

- We collected a dataset of 16,838 enzyme reaction data from the Brenda, Sabio-RK, and UniProt databases. After filtering, we augmented the dataset using AlphaFold, resulting in 1,633 protein structure files (PDB) for training.
- We employed a fine-tuned GearNet model to encode protein three-dimensional structures and introduced this information into the DLKcat model.
- We have demonstrated that using protein structure information is effective for predicting K_{cat} values and can achieve results similar to or better than conventional sequence-based methods in this task.

2 Methods

2.1 Data Acquisition

Construction of the Enzyme Reaction Dataset Dec-11k with UniProt ID. We utilized a dataset of 16,838 enzyme reaction records containing EC numbers, substrate SMILES, protein sequences, and K_{cat} values from the Sabio-RK and BRENDA databases (see Fig. 1). Subsequently, we extracted 2,226 unique UniProt IDs and their corresponding protein sequences from this dataset. Next, we aligned the protein sequence data with the enzyme reaction dataset using a pairwise sequence alignment method. After filtering, we obtained an enzyme reaction dataset with 11,419 entries, each associated with a unique UniProt ID. These records encompass 1,633 distinct proteins. Finally, we used these protein identifiers to retrieve the corresponding protein structure files from the Protein Data Bank (PDB).

Sequence Alignment and Data Clean. First, we successfully searched for a portion of experimentally determined real PDB data in the RCSB-PDB [21] database. For the remaining proteins for which real PDB data could not be obtained, we turned to the AlphaFold dataset. Thanks to the impressive protein structure prediction capabilities of AlphaFold2 [18], many proteins lacking real structures can be reliably predicted through deep learning methods. However, there were some issues encountered when searching for data in the RCSB-PDB database:

- Some enzymes in the enzyme reaction dataset are short-peptide sequences without structural information. For this subset of data, we directly removed them.

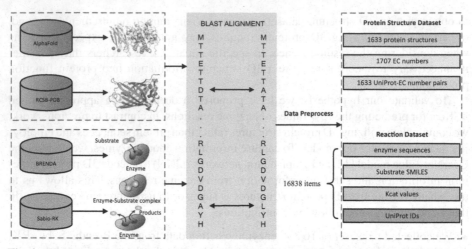

Fig. 1. The data preprocessing workflow encompasses the acquisition of reaction data from Sabio-RK and Brenda databases, along with the retrieval of actual protein structures data from RCSB PDB and predicted protein structures data from the AlphaFold database. Ultimately, a multifaceted selection process is employed to obtain the desired enzyme reaction dataset and protein structures dataset.

- A single protein in the RCSB-PDB database often corresponds to multiple PDB records, which originate from different experiments. Therefore, it is necessary to select the most closely matching record. Using the BLAST Alignment [22], we aligned the protein's UniProt ID with the unique PDB structure information.
- The PDB files obtained by experiments may not necessarily represent the complete protein structures, they might only target a specific chain or a very small portion of the sequence. Moreover, it may lead to the usage of structures in model training that do not pertain to the catalytic region, failing to characterize the entire protein's information and causing information loss. For these proteins, we conducted a new search for structural information in the AlphaFold database.
- In addition, there is a subset of PDB files obtained from experiments that may have issues, such as format errors, abnormal atom, or residue numbering. These issues can potentially lead to errors during the parsing of PDB files using RDKit [23], resulting in parsing failures. To prevent that, we have implemented a simple parser to preprocess PDB files. This parser extracts only essential information, including amino acid sequences and atomic coordinates, effectively avoiding parsing errors.
- Among the previous 16,838 data entries, there were instances where certain proteins may have been split or merged into other UniProt IDs. As a result, it became impossible to retrieve data using the original UniProt IDs. We addressed this issue through manual curation, obtaining new UniProt IDs and their corresponding PDB structures.

Constructing the Protein Structures Dataset, Dst-1.6k. After these processing steps, we extracted all 1,707 non-redundant EC numbers from the enzyme reaction dataset. Simultaneously, we generated labels by associating each protein with its corresponding EC numbers. Finally, we accurately filtered out the PDB data corresponding to each protein and combined it with the files associated with UniProt ID and EC numbers. This compilation resulted in the creation of the protein structures dataset, Dst-1.6k, containing all the necessary PDB files for our study.

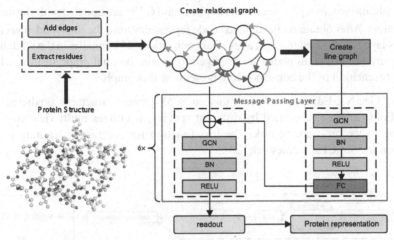

Fig. 2. The architecture diagram of the GearNet-Edge model illustrates its methodology, where GearNet-Edge encodes protein structural information by constructing residue-level interaction graph and line graph. For the representation of these two types of graphs, a 6-layer GCN is employed in the training process. Finally, the model aggregates node features by summing them and taking the average, thereby transforming them into graph features.

2.2 Pre-trained Protein Structure Encoder

We opted for a pre-training approach to first perform unsupervised learning on a large volume of proteins and then fine-tune our structure dataset. We selected the GearNet-Edge model proposed by Zhang et al. [12] for pre-training, the model architecture of GearNet-Edge is depicted in the diagram as shown in the figure (see Fig. 2).

Create Relational Graph. Differing from small molecule structure pre-training models [19], which use atoms as nodes and chemical bonds between atoms as edges to construct a relationship graph for structural representation, GearNet-Edge uses the α-carbon atom to represent amino acid residues and employs it as the graph node, denoted as f_i. Subsequently, three different types of directed edges are constructed as edges in the relationship graph, denoted as (i,j,r). These three types of edges are sequential edges, radius edges, and K-nearest neighbor edges.

Following node construction and directed edge creation, we ultimately obtain the graph $G = \{V, E, R\}$, where V, E, and R are represent nodes, directed edges, and edge types, respectively. We use (i, j, r) to denote a directed edge from node i to node j with type r, where $i, j \in V$.

Create Line Graph. In addition to characterizing protein structures by constructing the relational graph G between nodes, GearNet-Edge also constructs a line graph [27], denoted as $G^{edge} = \{V^{edge}, E^{edge}, R^{edge}\}$, to represent relationships between edges.

Message Passing Layer. After constructing these two graphs, GearNet-Edge uses GCN [24] to obtain protein representations. Graphs G and G^{edge} are updated with similar GCN parameters. After obtaining the updated node representations, the final hidden vector $h_i^{(l)}$ for this layer is obtained through a residual connection [25]. Finally, in the readout step, the feature vectors of all nodes are averaged to obtain the final graph feature, which is the representation of the corresponding protein for this graph.

The GearNet-Edge model pre-trains on 805k protein structures predicted in the AlphaFold database, classified by different species. It utilizes multi-view contrastive learning as the pre-training task. The loss function for contrastive learning is set up based on the SimCLR framework [20].

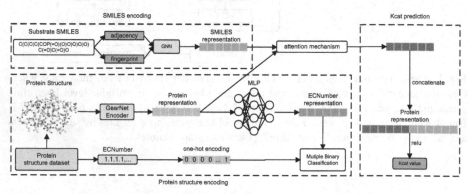

Fig. 3. Using the GearNet-Edge model to encode protein structures, then encoding substrate SMILES with a Graph Neural Network (GNN), applying an attention mechanism to both, and finally predicting the K_{cat} value.

2.3   Calculating K_{cat} Values

Protein Structures Encoding. Our method is named PSKcat (Protein Structures K_{cat}) (see Fig. 3). First, we extract protein structure data and EC numbers separately from the structure dataset. Each EC number is represented using a 1,707-dimensional one-hot vector, denoted as v_{ec}, and served as the training target. Then, we fine-tune the pre-trained GearNet-Edge using the protein structures, representing every protein as a 3,072-dimensional tensor. Starting from the first training round, we obtain representations of proteins and update these representations in each epoch. After fine-tuning, we extract the representations for all proteins, which are subsequently used in the downstream training process.

We consider the training of the protein structures dataset as a downstream task for EC number prediction. The objective of this task is to predict the EC number for different proteins. The EC number determines the catalytic role of a protein in reactions, signifying its function and characteristics. EC number prediction is treated as a multi-label binary classification task, where a protein may belong to one or more EC codes, and an EC number may correspond to one or more proteins. Each EC number has two mutually exclusive subcategories, and we establish a binary classifier for each EC number to independently predict the positive and negative categories of the EC number.

The protein representation vectors obtained from GearNet-Edge are processed using a Multi-Layer Perceptron (MLP) and used in conjunction with v_{ec} to calculate the cross-entropy loss, subsequently updating the model parameters.

Substrate SMILES Encoding. After completing the EC numbers prediction task, all trained protein vectors are retrieved. First, the molecular structures are extracted from the SMILES, and the molecule is converted into an undirected graph in the form of a molecular graph, with atoms as nodes and chemical bonds as edges. Then, the adjacency matrix for the molecule is constructed. Additionally, the Weisfeiler-Lehman algorithm [26] is employed to generate molecular fingerprints from the molecular graph through iterative traversal of each node.

The molecular fingerprint vectors, along with the adjacency matrix, are used as input for training the Graph Neural Network (GNN). At each GNN iteration layer, updated hidden vectors represent molecular fingerprint information after each update:

$$h^l = M_A \sigma \left(GNN \left(v_{fp} \right) \right) \quad c^l = h^l + v_{fp} \tag{1}$$

v_{fp} represents the representation vector of the substrate molecular fingerprint, σ is the non-linear activation function (in this case, ReLU), and M_A is the adjacency matrix of the substrate molecule's undirected graph. h^l is the hidden vector obtained after the l-th layer of GNN training. At this stage, a residual connection is used to add h^l to v_{fp}, resulting in the final intermediate vector c^l.

K_{cat} Value Prediction. The obtained protein structure representation vector v_{ps} and substrate representation vector v_{smiles} are used to calculate attention scores with an attention mechanism. Initially, the inner product of these two vectors is computed. The resulting matrix is then passed through a hyperbolic tangent (tanh) function, which compresses the linear transformation results into the range of $[-1, 1]$ to produce the weight matrix W_a. Subsequently, this weight matrix is multiplied by the substrate representation vector to obtain the updated protein representation. Finally, the updated protein representation $v_{protein}$ and v_{smiles} are concatenated, and a non-linear activation function (ReLU) is applied to predict the K_{cat} value for the current reaction.

3 Experiments

3.1 Dataset

In the preceding sections, we've constructed two enzyme reaction and protein structure datasets: Dec-11k and Dst-1.6k. Additionally, we obtained 24,616 enzyme catalysis reaction data and using the processing methods detailed in Sect. 1.1, we obtained a dataset with added UniProt IDs, totaling 14,309 data entries, which we refer to as Dec-14k. Dec-14k contains 1,930 distinct proteins and 1,130 EC numbers. With this data, we created a new protein structure dataset named Dst-1.9k.

Furthermore, to investigate the impact of protein structural information predicted by AlphaFold on protein representation learning, we acquired two datasets consisting entirely of structure information predicted by AlphaFold. These datasets correspond to proteins in Dst-1.6k and Dst-1.9k and are named Dst-1.6k-AlphaFold and Dst-1.9k-AlphaFold, respectively. The sources and quantities of data for these four protein structure datasets are detailed in Table 1. Data sources and quantities of each dataset.

Table 1. Data sources and quantities of each dataset.

	D_{st}-1.6k	D_{st}-1.9k	D_{st}-1.6k-AlphaFold	D_{st}-1.9k-AlphaFold
RCSB-PDB	820	954	0	0
AlphaFold	813	977	1633	1930

3.2 Splitting the Dataset

To confirm whether using protein structures for feature representation and K_{cat} value prediction is as effective as or even better than using protein sequences, the DLKcat was used as a baseline, and it was compared with our approach. The DLKcat encodes protein features using protein sequences. It was trained on SMILES and protein sequences from the Dec-14k, and Dec-11k datasets, with a training-to-validation-to-testing data split ratio of 8:1:1. For the comparative analysis using our approach, in the case of Dec-14k, we used protein structures from both Dst-1.6k and Dst-1.6k-AlphaFold for protein feature encoding.

3.3 Training the Datasets

First, we attempted to introduce protein 3D structure information into the DLKcat model to explore the effectiveness of incorporating protein structure information for K_{cat} value prediction. In the Dec-11k dataset, there are 820 proteins with real structural information. We constructed a dataset named Dst-820-PDB. This dataset is associated with 7,371 enzyme reaction data records, forming a sub-enzyme reaction dataset called Dec-7k. We used these data to train the model, and the results were compared to models using only sequence information (see Fig. 4).

After validating the effectiveness of incorporating real protein structures, we aimed to investigate whether protein structure information predicted by AlphaFold2 would introduce biases in K_{cat} value predictions relative to real protein structures. We replaced all the structural files in the Dst-820-PDB dataset with the predicted structural files, creating a dataset named Dst-820-AlphaFold. The enzyme reaction dataset remained

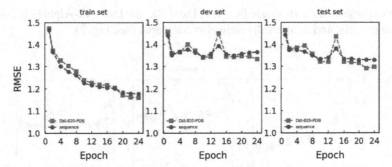

Fig. 4. PSKcat and DLKcat employ the Dec-7k reaction dataset, and PSKcat is trained with the Dst-820-PDB protein structure dataset. The Root Mean Square Error (RMSE) for training is shown in three separate plots for the training,validation, and test set. The red and the green dashed line represents DLKcat and PSKcat respectively. Both models converge to approximately 1.1 in the training set.

the same, and models were trained using both Dst-820-PDB and Dst-820-AlphaFold structures in conjunction with the Dec-7k dataset (see Fig. 5).

From these experiments, we found that there is little difference in predictive performance between using predicted structure information and real structure information. This suggests the reliability of the AlphaFold2 protein structure prediction model. Since only a fraction of proteins have experimentally determined structures, we can use AlphaFold to search for predicted protein structures to add to our dataset. Therefore, we expanded the remaining proteins in Dec-11k based on Dst-820-PDB, resulting in Dst-1.6k. To further validate the credibility of protein structures in the AlphaFold database, we replaced all the real structures in Dst-1.6k with predicted structures to create Dst-1.6k-AlphaFold. We compared the results of models trained on these two structure datasets and those trained using sequence information (see Fig. 6).

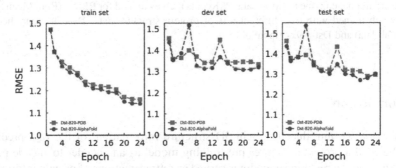

Fig. 5. PSKcat utilizes the Dec-7k reaction dataset for training and is subsequently evaluated based on the RMSE (Root Mean Square Error) when trained with two different protein structures datasets, Dst-820-AlphaFold and Dst-820-PDB.

The expansion of data to create Dec-14k, Dst-1.9k, and Dst-1.9k-AlphaFold followed a similar process, and their results were also compared (see Fig. 7).

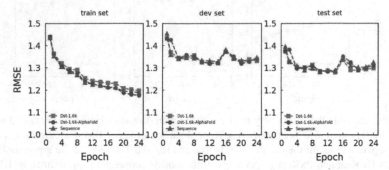

Fig. 6. PSKcat and DLKcat are trained using the Dec-11k reaction dataset. In the case of PSKcat, RMSE (Root Mean Square Error) values are evaluated when it is trained with two different protein structure datasets: Dst-1.6k and Dst-1.6k-AlphaFold.

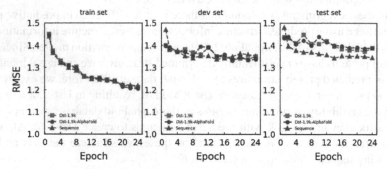

Fig. 7. PSKcat and DLKcat are trained using the expanded Dec-14k reaction dataset, which includes additional enzyme reaction data. PSKcat is then evaluated for RMSE (Root Mean Square Error) when trained with two different sets of protein structure data: Dst-1.9k (enriched with additional data) and Dst-1.9k-AlphaFold.

4   Conclusion

In this work, we introduced protein 3D structure information for the K_{cat} prediction task. We used a protein structures pre-training model as an encoder to encode protein structures, and the resulting encodings served as representations of protein information, which were then applied to the specific task. We addressed a series of issues encountered during structure data acquisition with various solutions, and we tackled the problem of insufficient real structural data by incorporating predicted structural data from the AlphaFold database. Through a series of experiments, we validated the effectiveness of using protein structure information for protein representation and applying it to the

K_{cat} value prediction task. Furthermore, these experiments indirectly demonstrated the high credibility of protein structures predicted by AlphaFold2, which can be utilized in various downstream tasks.

Acknowledgement. This work was supported by the National Key Technology Research and Development Program of China (2022YFA0911800).

References

1. Li, S., An, J., Li, Y., et al.: Automated high-throughput genome editing platform with an AI learning in situ prediction model. Nat. Commun. **13**(1), 7386 (2022)
2. Zelezniak, A., Vowinckel, J., Capuano, F., et al.: Machine learning predicts the yeast metabolome from the quantitative proteome of kinase knockouts. Cell Syst. **7**(3), 269–283.e6 (2018)
3. Kim, G.B., Kim, W.J., Kim, H.U., et al.: Machine learning applications in systems metabolic engineering. Curr. Opin. Biotechnol. **64**, 1–9 (2020)
4. Doudna, J.A., Charpentier, E.: The new frontier of genome engineering with CRISPR-Cas9. Science **346**(6213), 1258096 (2014)
5. Radivojević, T., Costello, Z., Workman, K., et al.: A machine learning automated recommendation tool for synthetic biology. Nat. Commun. **11**(1), 4879 (2020)
6. Li, G., Rabe, K.S., Nielsen, J., et al.: Machine learning applied to predicting microorganism growth temperatures and enzyme catalytic optima. ACS Synth. Biol. **8**(6), 1411–1420 (2019)
7. Limbu, S., Dakshanamurthy, S.: A new hybrid neural network deep learning method for protein-ligand binding affinity prediction and de novo drug design. Int. J. Mol. Sci. **23**(22), 13912 (2022)
8. Tsubaki, M., Tomii, K., Sese, J.: Compound–protein interaction prediction with end-to-end learning of neural networks for graphs and sequences. Bioinformatics **35**(2), 309–318 (2019)
9. Li, F., Yuan, L., Lu, H., et al.: Deep learning-based k cat prediction enables improved enzyme-constrained model reconstruction. Nat. Catal. **5**(8), 662–672 (2022)
10. Kroll, A., Rousset, Y., Hu, X.P., et al.: Turnover number predictions for kinetically uncharacterized enzymes using machine and deep learning. Nat. Commun. **14**(1), 4139 (2023)
11. Hermosilla, P., Ropinski, T.: Contrastive representation learning for 3d protein structures. arXiv preprint arXiv:2205.15675 (2022)
12. Zhang, Z., Xu, M., Jamasb, A., et al.: Protein representation learning by geometric structures pretraining. arXiv preprint arXiv:2203.06125 (2022)
13. Aslam, B., Basit, M., Nisar, M.A., et al.: Proteomics: technologies and their applications. J. Chromatogr. Sci. 1–15 (2016)
14. Zhao, J., Yan, W., Yang, Y.: DeepTP: a deep learning model for thermophilic protein prediction. Int. J. Mol. Sci. **24**(3), 2217 (2023)
15. Hu, T.M., Hayton, W.L.: Architecture of the drug–drug interaction network. J. Clin. Pharm. Ther. **36**(2), 135–143 (2011)
16. Wang, Z., Masoomi, A., Xu, Z., et al.: Improved prediction of smoking status via isoform-aware RNA-seq deep learning models. PLoS Comput. Biol. **17**(10), e1009433 (2021)
17. Paysan-Lafosse, T., Blum, M., Chuguransky, S., et al.: InterPro in 2022. Nucleic Acids Res. **51**(D1), D418–D427 (2023)
18. Jumper, J., Evans, R., Pritzel, A., et al.: Highly accurate protein structures prediction with AlphaFold. Nature **596**(7873), 583–589 (2021)

19. Zaidi, S., Schaarschmidt, M., Martens, J., et al.: Pre-training via denoising for molecular property prediction. arXiv preprint arXiv:2206.00133 (2022)

20. Chen, T., Kornblith, S., Norouzi, M., et al.: A simple framework for contrastive learning of visual representations. In: International Conference on Machine Learning, pp. 1597–1607. PMLR (2020)

21. Berman, H.M., et al.: The protein data bank. Nucleic Acids Res. 28(1), 235–242 (2000)

22. Ye, J., McGinnis, S., Madden, T.L.: BLAST: improvements for better sequence analysis. Nucleic Acids Res. 34(suppl_2), W6–W9 (2006)

23. Landrum, G., et al.: RDKit: open-source cheminformatics (2006). http://www.rdkit.org

24. Kipf, T.N., Welling, M.: Semi-supervised classification with graph convolutional networks. arXiv preprint arXiv:1609.02907 (2016)

25. He, K., Zhang, X., Ren, S., et al.: Identity mappings in deep residual networks. In: Leibe, B., Matas, J., Sebe, N., Welling, M. (eds.) Computer Vision–ECCV 2016, Part IV, pp. 630–645. Springer, Cham (2016). https://doi.org/10.1007/978-3-319-46493-0_38

26. Shervashidze, N., Schweitzer, P., Van Leeuwen, E.J., et al.: Weisfeiler-lehman graph kernels. J. Mach. Learn. Res. 12(9) (2011)

27. Harary, F., Norman, R.Z.: Some properties of line digraphs. Rendiconti del circolo matematico di palermo 9, 161–168 (1960)

Computer Vision

Challenges in Realizing Artificial Intelligence Assisted Sign Language Recognition

Prashan Premaratne$^{(\boxtimes)}$ ⓘ, Peter James Vial ⓘ, and Sibghat Ulla

University of Wollongong, North Wollongong, NSW 2522, Australia
prashan@uow.edu.au

Abstract. Many publications tout the ability to develop or address certain aspects of research which tries to solve an existing problem. However, some approaches would appear to solve a certain aspect of a problem, but not the real problem at hand. In the context of a challenging real problem, such approach would simply deceive the researcher into extrapolating the existing capabilities but would not offer any practical realization of the real problem. Computer vision-based sign language recognition is one such problem. With our research into hand gesture recognition of dynamic gestures which can easily be compared to different sign languages present in many parts of the world, certain aspects such as static hand sign recognition has no part to play in dynamic hand gesture recognition or in sign language recognition. This article tries to reach out to the readers and researchers to highlight why sign language recognition is currently not making any progress despite enormous inroads into objects detection in realtime using artificial intelligent tools such as YOLO algorithms.

Keywords: Hand Gestures · Sign Language · Artificial Intelligence

1 Introduction

Sign language is a communication mode between individuals who have lost their hearing yet could see. Some individuals are born with hearing or lose hearing during their life due to ailments or accidents. It is estimated that every day, 31 children are born in the USA along with hearing impairment [1]. Since the development of Artificial Intelligence and due to the ability to many machine-learning assisted systems to support humans in day-to-day tasks, many tend to believe that machines could also soon assist people with hearing loss to communicate through sign language. However, there exists unsurmountable challenges presently that hinders machine recognition of sign language.

Most of the challenges are due to the inability of the modern computer vision systems to accurately capture hand-shoulder-face signs in order to process them as part of sign language. These challenges are mainly due to vision systems inability to separate hand, fingers, shoulders, elbows and face from other body parts and from the background accurately. The resolution of the separated parts can also pose a big challenge as having lower resolution fingers will make it difficult for fingers and their postures to be accurately separated and tracked. This is shown in Fig. 1. Which depicts that the separated body

D.-S. Huang et al. (Eds.): ICAI 2023, CCIS 2014, pp. 161–168, 2024.
https://doi.org/10.1007/978-981-97-0903-8_16

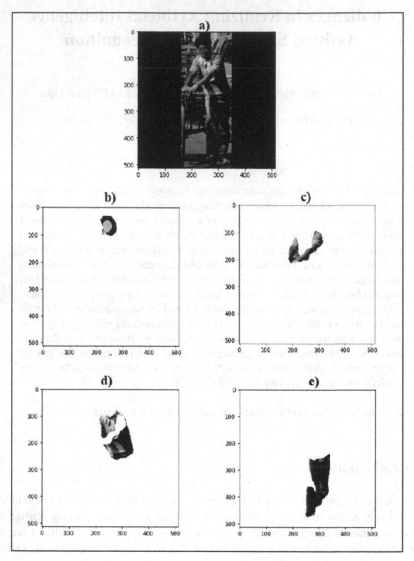

Fig. 1. Separation of body parts using skin segmentation and the deficiency in the clarity of such separation as evident by [2].

parts have very low resolution, their separation from other body parts and background are not 'clean'.

In sign language recognition, the details to be recognized for sign interpretation includes

- Finger postures in three dimensions and tracking of these gestures when hand signs are posted dynamically over few seconds

- Recognizing the start and end of a word or sentence
- Subtle variations between signers in implementing (signing) words or sentences
- Recognizing face or facial impressions and combining them with related hand signs
- Recognizing elbow and shoulder movements and realizing their relationship in words, sentences or other moods
- How the mood of a signer may confuse a recognition system.

These are some of the obvious sign language related challenges. When it comes to interpreting facial moods, any artificial system would have enormous difficulty as facial expressions would also depend on the community. As it happened in many deep neural network-based systems, training a system of very specific data confined to a very specific ethnicity would make completely opposite classifications when different data are used. Hence, AI systems are no wiser than many other systems in development.

2 Evidence of Dynamic Gestures and the Mistakes of Interpreting Them Using Computer Vision

2.1 Evidence of 'Start' and 'End' Issues

Today due to recent pandemic, many researchers have increasingly used zoom or other types video conferencing tools which offer the ability to provide a virtual background for video conferencing. These tools have been quite accurate in separating the person from the background and include a virtual background for the communication. Despite this ability, it is quite obvious that sudden movement would disrupt the virtual background and reveal the normally cluttered backgrounds that people try to avoid seen by the other parties. This indicates that even under controlled environments, the technology is not mature enough to adequately separate the user from the background, unless sudden movements are avoided.

In capturing a video scene which should be taking place continuously when a machine is requiring input, a 'signer' (user of a sign language) would not specify to another user of sign language that he/she intends to start communication. He/she simply starts communication naturally and the other person interprets the meaning and reacts and communicate accordingly. However, this scenario is way too complicated for a machine to understand. Video data involves minimum of 15 frames per second to typically 30 frames per second to capture details of motion. Yet, when processing such large amount of data, the system also has to detect and separate the face, hands (both hands), elbow and torso as signers use multiple body parts to convey a message as was shown in Fig. 1. Not only these but also the synchronism of these parts working together to define the word, sentence or the mood. If the machine fails to recognise the 'start' of this word, sentence or the mood, it will not be able to interpret any later image frames as part of this communication. Many researchers have failed to realise the depth of this problem. Currently, Google has supported Kaggle which is a mobile phone app that makes use of user input video streams to develop a database to decipher Sign Language. If a correctly separated sign language word, sentence or a mood as video frames are available, they may have significance in training a neural network for deep learning approaches. However, this does not still solve the much bigger challenge of a system realising when a communication is going to start. To address this, it is possible to setup sign language communication specifically meant for machine interaction. In this concept, a signer would deliberately carry out an action to notify the machine that a new communication is about to start. Then the machine captures all subsequent sections of the video and start assessing the frames and look for body parts associated with the communication. Then the user has to finally issue another command to notify that the communication has ended. Then the machine will be able to process the video and perhaps be able to process the data to extract the meaning.

Yet, this type of deliberate 'start' and 'end' signing will undoubtedly discourage using machine for interaction. In a typical communication, there would be many sentences, many moods and many words and separating them with 'start', 'end' commands so often will undoubtedly 'kill' the communication.

Figure 1 clearly shows the challenge in separating a person's face, hands and other body parts to interpret a sign language communication and then use the synchronisation of each body part with others to interpret the meaning. When looking at these body parts of Fig. 1 after extraction using computer vision, one would realize that these parts are so unclear that they will not be used in a neural network-based system to interpret their actions. Figure 2 also shows yet another challenge in skin segmentation to capture body parts. As the figure would show, skin segmentation sometimes fails and would lead to unreliability of a system that is based on skin detection, compounding already difficult problem of capturing dynamic gestures.

Fig. 2. Failure of skin segmentation to separate skin and non-skin regions [2]

Not only that, their dynamic motion has to be equally captured accurately and the process becomes almost impossible to be accurate or even processed. Figure 3. Indicates the complexity of dynamic gestures in its simplest form. If one would analyse the facial expressions within these few static images along would indicate the complexity of the recognition process. If skin segmentation is used, it is possible to capture most of the hand movement not in occlusion however, simple change of clothes would present yet another challenge.

Fig. 3. The dynamic complexity of sign language interpretation [3]

Figure 4 shows our own work published in 2007 as part of 'Hand Gesture Recognition for Control Application'. In this work, static gestures or simple hand signs were captured and processed in realtime, with great success. However, this great success was due to our own design in selecting the best 10 hand gestures that would not 'clash' with other potential gestures. We carefully eliminated number of gestures so that there wont be any potential clashes in gestures when appearing quite close to each other. A good example is to avoid 3 finger gesture when two finger gesture is used. However, another reason for great success was using Hu moments, a well-established feature extraction method with many invariant properties. Yet, looking at Fig. 4 shows how fragile the captured image in the middle column. These images with noise are then filtered using morphological approaches such as 'erosion', 'dilation', 'opening' and 'closing' to remove and fill noise affected regions so that they appear as in last column.

As shown in Fig. 5, after morphological filtering and normalisation, these filtered regions were used for extracting 'Hu moments' so that ten such gestures could be uniquely separated even with different orientations.

The simplicity of the above approach clearly highlights what is needed in a dynamic gesture. These challenges can be stated as follows:

- Gesture signing orientation (people will sign certain horizontal motions in an inclined angle)
- Lighting imperfections would create much noisier sections of arms, faces, other body parts that the recognising system will be unable to deal with the input
- Occlusions will prevent the capturing system of recognising the signs as previously known
- Physical differences in hands and arms may complicate any deep learning-based training system
- Clothing hampers the body part recognition

Original Image	Skin Segmentation Image	Normalised Image

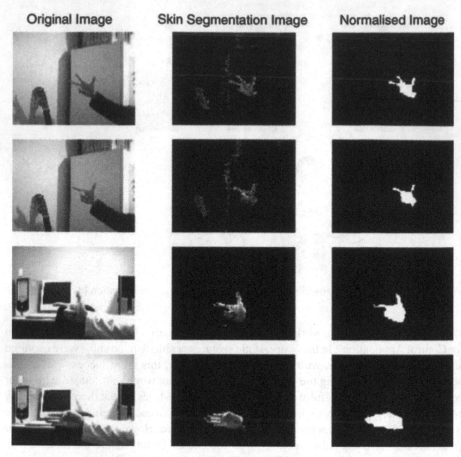

Fig. 4. Static signs or hand gesture-based control system developed in 2007 [4]

- Despite many skin segmentation approaches work well, yet they still suffer from inaccuracies under different dark skin colors

These are some of the most obvious obstacles in sign language detection when a dynamic gesture tracking method is envisioned.

3   The Advantages of a Glove Based System

It is quite evident that computer vision-based system with the current state of developments is difficult to achieve. Hence, realizing a different sign language system based on a sensor-based glove has been realized [5]. The system is reported to capable of posting 50 words. However, it should be stated that 50 words would not realise in communication but a good start. Yet, it is impossible to envision this is going to improve as the subtle differences in certain words prevent systems from correctly interpreting them. Our work in 2005 realised a world's first consumer electronics control system based on hand

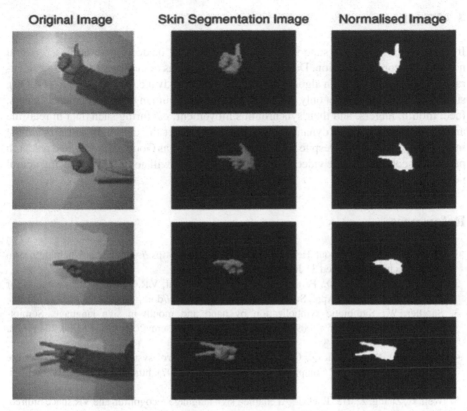

Fig. 5. Normalized image after applying morphological filtering related to Fig. 4. [4].

gestures with recognition of 10 commands with 100% accuracy using neural networks [4, 6–10]. However, we started with about 30 hand signs and through experimentation, removed 20 gestures due to their clash with the final 10 gestures the system was capable of recognizing. This clearly demonstrated that neural network-based systems or any other deep learning systems would not fare better due to inherent similarity of many gestures to others. Hence, realizing a deep learning-based sign language recognition system is difficult to attain for the foreseeable future. Some work recently published give the notion of AI based sign language recognition however without any evidence and based on simple concepts [11]. Many argue that due to success of algorithms such as YOLO (YOLO5 and YOLO6) being able to label objects in images so accurately, the next natural step is the action recognition in video. However, this is indeed difficult to achieve when one interprets a small video clip, each frame has many objects and when considering humans, hands, face, eyes, legs, torso have to be separated and tracked continuously and their motions over time to be interpreted. This is almost an impossible challenge to be surmounted at the modern computer vision related AI.

4 Conclusion

It is important to clearly state what is feasible with AI or deep learning based neural networks in computer vision. Despite image labelling has demonstrated very high accuracy using object detection algorithms such as YOLO (advanced YOLO5 and YOLO6), sign language relies on not only finding objects such as human body parts such as hands, face, mouth, fingers, and their synchronous movement, capturing such data in realtime and following individual dynamic movements to extract the communication is almost impossible at this stage. Despite large organisations such as Google has initiated research paths with collecting more video data, dynamic tracking will not be realized using neural networks.

References

1. Data and Statistics About Hearing Loss in Children. https://www.cdc.gov/ncbddd/hearin gloss/data.html. Accessed 31 July 2023
2. Leite, M., Parreira, W.D., Fernandes, A.M.d.R., Leithardt, V.R.Q.: Image segmentation for human skin detection. Appl. Sci. **12**, 12140 (2022). https://doi.org/10.3390/app122312140
3. Sandler, W.: Symbiotic symbolization by hand and mouth in sign language. Semiotica **2009**(174), 241–275 (2009). https://doi.org/10.1515/semi.2009.035. PMID: 20445832; PMCID: PMC2863338
4. Premaratne, P., Nguyen, Q.: Consumer electronics control system based on hand gesture moment invariants. IET Comput. Vision **1**(1), 35–41 (2007). https://doi.org/10.1049/iet-cvi:20060198
5. Wen, F., Zhang, Z., He, T., et al.: AI enabled sign language recognition and VR space bidirectional communication using triboelectric smart glove. Nat. Commun. **12**, 5378 (2021). https://doi.org/10.1038/s41467-021-25637-w
6. Premaratne, P., Yang, S., Vial, P., Ifthikar, Z.: Dynamic hand gesture recognition using centroid tracking. In: Huang, D.S., Bevilacqua, V., Premaratne, P. (eds.) Intelligent Computing Theories and Methodologies, pp. 623–629. Springer, Cham (2015). https://doi.org/10.1007/978-3-319-22180-9_62
7. Premaratne, P., Yang, S., Zou, Z., Vial, P.: Australian sign language recognition using moment invariants. In: Huang, D.S., Jo, K.H., Zhou, Y.Q., Han, K. (eds.) Intelligent Computing Theories and Technology, pp. 509–514. Springer, Heidelberg (2013). https://doi.org/10.1007/978-3-642-39482-9_59
8. Premaratne, P., Ajaz, S., Premaratne, M.: Hand gesture tracking and recognition system for control of consumer electronics. In: Huang, D.-S., Gan, Y., Gupta, P., Gromiha, M.M. (eds.) ICIC 2011. LNCS (LNAI), vol. 6839, pp. 588–593. Springer, Heidelberg (2012). https://doi.org/10.1007/978-3-642-25944-9_76
9. Yang, S., Premaratne, P., Vial, P.: Hand gesture recognition: an overview. In: Proceedings of 2013 5th IEEE International Conference on Broadband Network and Multimedia Technology, IEEE IC-BNMT 2013, pp. 63–69 (2013)
10. Premaratne, P.: Human Computer Interaction Using Hand Gestures. Springer, Singapore (2014). https://doi.org/10.1007/978-981-4585-69-9
11. Papastratis, I., Chatzikonstantinou, C., Konstantinidis, D., Dimitropoulos, K., Daras, P.: Artificial intelligence technologies for sign language. Sensors **21**, 5843 (2021). https://doi.org/10.3390/s21175843

Efficient and Accurate Document Parsing and Verification Based on OCR Engine

Ruoyan Dong[1], Kexian Zhang[1], Xiangbo Wang[2], Qiang Xue[3(✉)], and Qingyun Tan[3]

[1] Information Center of Guizhou Power Grid Corporation, Guiyang, China
[2] Southern Power Grid Supply Chain (Guizhou) Co., Ltd., Guiyang, China
[3] Colorful Guizhou Digital Technology Co., Ltd., Guiyang, China
xueqiang2017@163.com

Abstract. This paper is dedicated to efficiently and accurately extracting, parsing, and verifying various types of materials such as business licenses and qualification certificates from electronic documents like images, scans, and PDFs within bid documents. Leveraging an OCR engine and well-trained models with strong error correction capabilities, the accuracy of OCR in bid document processing for Guizhou Power Grid Company is significantly improved. This system automatically extracts bid documents of various formats from different sources, precisely parses and verifies key information within them. Through a visual interface, evaluation experts can pinpoint issues related to key material information in bid documents accurately. Experimental results demonstrate that our system accurately extracts crucial information from bid documents of different formats, thereby reducing review and verification time. Our research holds substantial value and promising application prospects. The system has the potential to lower labor costs and enhance the efficiency and fairness of the bidding process.

Keywords: Key Information in Bid Documents · Information Extraction · OCR Engine · Robust Error Correction · Multi-format

1 Introduction

With the rapid development of the internet, electronic bid documents [1] are gradually replacing the traditional paper-based bid documents in the bidding process. The emergence of electronic bid documents has made intelligent auditing of bid information feasible. The scrutiny of key information within bid contents [2] is a vital task in bid evaluation, aimed at identifying potential discrepancies in materials like business licenses and qualification certificates, ensuring fairness, accuracy, and effectiveness in bid outcomes. However, due to the diverse origins and complex nature of bid documents, manual scrutiny is often time-consuming and error-prone.

This paper aims to design an efficient and accurate system for parsing and verifying individual documents based on OCR engines [3]. This system automatically extracts key

Supported by Intelligent Bidding Evaluation Assistance Platform based on Deep Learning (Project Number: 066700KK52210003) developed by Guizhou Power Grid Limited Liability Company.

information from electronic bid documents such as images, scans, and PDFs using various OCR engines. It then analyzes and verifies this key information, assisting evaluation experts in efficiently and accurately identifying inadequate document information within bids. By incorporating OCR engine technology, we can significantly reduce evaluation time, enhance the quality of assessment, and prevent the selection of bids containing inadequate material information.

The significance of this study lies in providing an intelligent solution for extracting, parsing, and verifying key information within bid documents to address the challenges and issues currently encountered in the bid evaluation process. By designing an efficient and accurate system for parsing and verifying individual documents based on OCR engines, we can effectively and accurately extract, parse, and audit various material information within bid documents, thereby enhancing OCR accuracy in the field of tender document processing. The integration of OCR technology can significantly reduce the time required for bid qualification review, thereby increasing efficiency and reducing labor costs.

This research employs robust error correction [4] on the extracted key information from bid documents, greatly enhancing the accuracy of bid review, reducing the risk of oversight or errors, and identifying potential falsification of crucial bid information. This ensures fair and impartial bid outcomes. Through a visual interface, evaluators can accurately identify potential errors in key information, facilitating precise error localization. Through the design and implementation of the document parsing and verification system, we will provide novel technological support for the assessment of key bid information, thereby driving the development and progress of the bidding industry.

2 Related Work

2.1 OCR Technology

OCR (Optical Character Recognition) is a commonly used natural language processing technology that converts text within images into editable text formats. OCR consists of two main steps: text detection [5] and text recognition [6]. It enables the extraction of text from scanned documents, images captured by cameras, and PDF files. In the context of the efficient and accurate document parsing and verification system for bid documents, different OCR engines can be employed to extract text from bid documents of various formats, such as business licenses and qualification certificates, thereby facilitating the analysis and verification of errors within key material information of bid documents.

2.2 Enhancing OCR Error Correction

The accuracy of OCR is influenced by various factors, including poor image quality (such as scanning resolution and noise) and mismatches between the training instances of character image classifiers and the representation of characters in printed documents (such as fonts, sizes, and spacing) [7]. Due to significant format disparities in bid documents from different sources, employing OCR technology alone for text extraction of their key material information may lead to issues like text loss and character recognition errors. This paper introduces enhanced OCR error correction [8], an area that has seen considerable research aimed at automatically rectifying OCR recognition errors. An early and informative survey can be found in [9], while methods specific to Arabic OCR are summarized in [10] and compiled in [11]. In this study, a Seq2Seq model [12] is adopted to train word and syntax correction models, employing both character-level and word-level language models as well as dictionaries for error correction of OCR engine recognition.

Despite the widespread application of OCR technology and OCR error correction techniques in various domains, there still exist challenges and limitations. The substantial variations in content and formats of bid documents from different sources make it difficult for OCR technology to precisely locate key material information within bid document texts, and the quality of extracted text is often subpar. As a result, this paper proposes an efficient and accurate document parsing and verification system based on OCR engines. This system possesses robust error correction capabilities, enhancing the accuracy of OCR text extraction. It aids bid document review by accurately extracting, parsing, and verifying key material information within bid documents.

3 Method

As a significant AI tool, OCR technology has the potential to enhance operational efficiency for enterprises, reducing labor and time costs. Establishing an intelligent OCR recognition platform has become a crucial initiative across various industries to foster smart strategies and growth. The workflow of our OCR recognition system is illustrated in Fig. 1.

3.1 Image Preprocessing

Image preprocessing involves the preparation of images, scans, PDFs, and other electronic files. It primarily employs image processing techniques to extract required feature information. The extraction of key information from various materials like business licenses and qualification certificates within bid documents is influenced by diverse factors, leading to variations in image quality and interference from various unknown elements. Prior to commencing the OCR recognition task, the OCR detection and text recognition system necessitates a series of preprocessing operations to enhance the computer's speed and accuracy in recognizing text. The preprocessing steps in this paper encompass grayscale conversion, binarization, noise reduction, and skew correction, all aimed at enhancing the accuracy of text recognition.

3.2 Selection and Configuration of OCR Engines

Tesseract, an optical character recognition engine maintained by Google, is an open-source OCR engine. It supports text detection in multiple languages. However, if its built-in Simplified Chinese language library is directly used for detecting materials like business licenses and qualification certificates, its recognition rate may not meet industrial application standards. This is because it is trained on a vast range of text content, making its training samples diverse. In contrast, a self-trained OCR engine

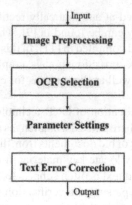

Fig. 1. Workflow Diagram of the OCR Recognition System

is more tailored. Its internal network can learn patterns that are more aligned with materials such as business licenses and qualification certificates. Therefore, this paper offers different OCR engines for the recognition of materials like business licenses and qualification certificates. Users can choose the appropriate OCR engine based on their needs and characteristics, followed by configuration and parameter adjustments, to achieve high accuracy in document parsing.

3.3 Model Training

This paper offers a personalized selection of OCR engines, which requires training different OCR engines. The training process is shown in Fig. 2. To retrain the model and create language libraries specifically for recognizing business licenses, the detailed process is as follows:

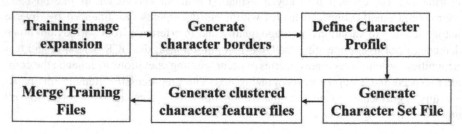

Fig. 2. Model Training Flow Chart

1) Training Image Augmentation: Due to the limited volume of training data, model convergence is challenging. This paper expands the training dataset by randomly shuffling the text within the training images. Ultimately, a training dataset of 400 images and a test dataset of 158 images are obtained. All training images are merged into the.tif format.

2) Character Box Generation and Adjustment: The borders of training data are generated and fine-tuned using the Tess Box Editor developed in Java, ensuring the integrity of characters within each box.
3) Defining Character Configuration File: To describe character attributes, a font properties file is defined, containing character-related information. As the attributes of business license text are relatively consistent, this paper sets all attributes uniformly to 0.
4) Generating.tr Training Files
5) Generating Character Set File
6) Generating Clustered Character Feature File
7) Merging Training Files: After the synthesis of training files, a new language library is created, specifically tailored to business licenses.

The process for training OCR models for other materials like qualification certificates follows a similar procedure.

3.4 Enhanced Error Correction Capability

In this study, a Seq2Seq model, as illustrated in Fig. 3, is employed to train word and syntax correction models. The task of text correction can be viewed as a transformation process between different sequences, where the original sentence serves as the source utterance, and the correct sentence is the target utterance. Hence, the Seq2Seq model can be introduced as a sequence transformation model for text correction. The underlying structure of the Seq2Seq model consists of an Encoder-Decoder network model. The Encoder encodes the input text sequence, transforming it into a vector representation of fixed length. The Decoder decodes this vector representation of fixed length obtained from the Encoder and converts it into an output sequence.

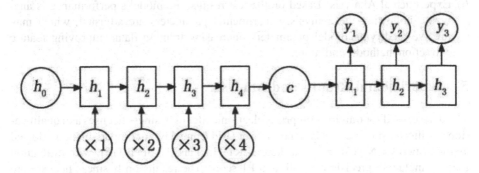

Fig. 3. Structure of the Seq2Seq Model

4 Experimental Design

The dataset used to train the OCR engine models consists of electronic files of business licenses and qualification certificates provided by Guizhou Power Grid Company. The business license dataset comprises 558 images, with 400 images used for training and

158 images for testing. The qualification certificate dataset comprises 487 images, with 341 images used for training and 146 images for testing.

The evaluation metrics employed in this study are as follows:

Precision: Precision refers to the ratio of correctly recognized characters by the OCR system to the total recognized characters by the system. It measures the accuracy of the system in character recognition. A higher precision indicates a greater probability of correct recognition by the system.

Recall: Recall refers to the ratio of correctly recognized characters by the OCR system to the actual number of existing characters. It measures the completeness of character recognition by the system. A higher recall implies the system's ability to correctly recognize more existing characters.

F1 Score: The F1 score is a composite metric that balances precision and recall. It represents the harmonic mean of precision and recall, calculated as: F1 = 2 * (Precision * Recall)/(Precision + Recall). The F1 score ranges from 0 to 1, with higher values indicating better system performance. Experimental Procedure:

1) Data Collection: All data for this experiment originates from electronic files of business licenses and qualification certificates provided by Guizhou Power Grid Company.
2) Data Preprocessing: This step involves operations like noise reduction, binarization, rotation correction, and image enhancement on the images.
3) Feature Extraction: Useful features are extracted from the images of each character. Common feature extraction methods include algorithms based on shape, texture, edges, and more.
4) Model Training: The OCR model is trained using the training dataset.
5) Model Testing: The trained OCR model is evaluated using the test dataset. Evaluation metrics include precision, recall, and F1 score.
6) Experimental Analysis: Based on the test results, the model's performance is analyzed. Following the analysis, experimental parameters are adjusted, which may involve modifying model parameters, increasing training data, improving feature extraction methods, and more.

5   Experimental Results and Analysis

The dataset used for training comprises electronic files of business licenses and qualification certificates provided by Guizhou Power Grid Company. A comparison is conducted against Spell GCN [13], Soft-Masked BERT [14], and FASpell [15], with evaluation metrics including precision, recall, and F1 score. The results on business licenses are presented in Table 1.

The results on qualification certificates are presented in Table 2.

The experimental results indicate that our proposed models achieved higher precision and recall on business licenses compared to FASpell by 24.7 and 21.6 percentage points respectively, Spell GCN by 22.2 and 13.7 percentage points respectively, and Sof-Masked BERT by 20.8 and 32.7 percentage points respectively. On qualification certificates, our proposed models exhibited precision and recall improvements of 22.3 and 17.9 percentage points over FASpell, 23.9 and 24.9 percentage points over Spell GCN, and

Table 1. Results on Business Licenses

Method	Accuracy(%)	Recall(%)	F1 Score
FASpell	67.3	61.3	0.64
Spell GCN	68.7	42.3	0.52
Sof-Masked BERT	64.8	53.4	0.59
Ours	89.5	75.0	0.82

Table 2. Results on Qualification Certificates

Method	Accuracy(%)	Recall(%)	F1 Score
FASpell	65.3	59.3	0.62
Spell GCN	63.7	52.3	0.57
Sof-Masked BERT	74.8	63.4	0.69
Ours	87.6	77.2	0.82

12.8 and 13.8 percentage points over Sof-Masked BERT. These results demonstrate the effectiveness of our approach in character recognition.

From the above experimental results, it can be observed that our method exhibits significant potential for application, showcasing markedly improved recall and precision compared to the contrasted methods. Favorable results were achieved in the recognition of both business licenses and qualification certificates. Given the limitations of our dataset, we have focused the experiments on business licenses and qualification certificates, lacking experiments on other types of documents.

6 Application Cases and Discussions

Currently, several researchers have leveraged OCR technology in invoice recognition and achieved promising outcomes. Siek [16] introduced an OCR system developed using deep learning algorithms and convolutional neural networks. This system streamlines certain steps in the manual payment approval workflow, expediting payment verification and confirmation processes. On the test dataset, the system achieved 100% accuracy in detecting trace numbers, approval codes, and nominal designations. The resulting OCR system serves as a reliable and accurate tool for addressing payment verification challenges in real-world business applications.

With the development of the Internet and the increasing adoption of paperless office practices, electronic bidding systems have become vital tools for organizations engaging in project procurement. Applying OCR technology to the bidding field offers an efficient solution to prominent challenges in engineering projects. Reliable technical support for bid document information retrieval is accompanied by a pressing practical need. The intelligent recognition and discrimination designed in this paper significantly enhance operational efficiency.

7 Conclusion

This paper introduces an efficient and accurate document parsing and auditing system based on OCR engines. The system accomplishes the extraction of key information from bid documents of various formats, along with the analysis and rectification of existing errors, thereby enhancing the error correction capability in bid document reviews. The system holds significant potential for widespread application, particularly within the bidding industry. It aids bid evaluation experts in precisely pinpointing errors in bid document content, preventing misjudgments, and ensuring fair and impartial bidding outcomes. Future enhancements and extensions will further elevate the system's performance and functionalities, driving advancements and progress in this field.

References

1. Santoso, D.S., Bourpanus, N.: Moving to e-bidding: examining the changes in the bidding process and the bid mark-up decisions of thai contractors. J. Financ. Manag. Prop. Constr. **24**(1), 2–18 (2019)
2. Jang, Y., Son, J., Yi, J.S.: Classifying the level of bid price volatility based on machine learning with parameters from bid documents as risk factors. Sustainability **13**(7), 3886 (2021)
3. Geetha, M., Pooja, R., Swetha, J., Nivedha, N., Daniya, T.: Implementation of text recognition and text extraction on formatted bills using deep learning. Int. J. Contrl. Automat. **13**(2), 646–651 (2020)
4. Chen, M., Ge, T., Zhang, X., Wei, F., Zhou, M.: Improving the efficiency of grammatical error correction with erroneous span detection and correction. arXiv preprint arXiv:2010.03260 (2020)
5. Bartz, C., Yang, H., Meinel, C.: STN-OCR: a single neural network for text detection and text recognition. arXiv preprint arXiv:1707.08831 (2017)
6. Su, Y.M., Peng, H.W., Huang, K.W., Yang, C.S.: Image processing technology for text recognition. In: 2019 International Conference on Technologies and Applications of Artificial Intelligence (TAAI), pp. 1–5. IEEE (2019)
7. Kissos, I., Dershowitz, N.: OCR error correction using character correction and feature-based word classification. In: 2016 12th IAPR Workshop on Document Analysis Systems (DAS), pp. 198–203. IEEE (2016)
8. Mokhtar, K., Bukhari, S.S., Dengel, A.: OCR error correction: state-of-the-art vs an NMT-based approach. In: 2018 13th IAPR International Workshop on Document Analysis Systems (DAS), pp. 429–434. IEEE (2018)
9. Kukich, K.: Techniques for automatically correcting words in text (abstract). In: ACM Annual Computer Science Conference: Proceedings of the 1993 ACM Conference on Computer Science, vol. 16 (1993)
10. Magdy, W., Darwish, K.: Arabic OCR error correction using character segment correction, language modeling, and shallow morphology. In: Proceedings of the 2006 Conference on Empirical Methods in Natural Language Processing, pp. 408–414 (2006)
11. Märgner, V., El Abed, H.: Guide to OCR for Arabic scripts. Springer, London (2012). https://doi.org/10.1007/978-1-4471-4072-6
12. Gu, S., Lang, F.: A Chinese text corrector based on seq2seq model. In: 2017 International Conference on Cyber-Enabled Distributed Computing and Knowledge Discovery (CyberC), pp. 322–325. IEEE (2017)
13. Cheng, X., et al.: Spellgcn: incorporating phonological and visual similarities into language models for Chinese spelling check. arXiv preprint arXiv:2004.14166 (2020)

14. Zhang, S., Huang, H., Liu, J., Li, H.: Spelling error correction with soft-masked bert. arXiv preprint arXiv:2005.07421 (2020)
15. Hong, Y., Yu, X., He, N., Liu, N., Liu, J.: Faspell: a fast, adaptable, simple, powerful Chinese spell checker based on DAE-decoder paradigm. In: Proceedings of the 5th Workshop on Noisy User-generated Text (W-NUT 2019), pp. 160–169 (2019)
16. Ghosh, S.K., Samanta, S., Hirani, H., da Silva, C.R.V.: Effective waste management and circular economy

Intelligent Comparison of Bidding Documents Based on Algorithmic Analysis and Visualization

Kexian Zhang[1], Ruoyan Dong[1], Yu Lu[2], Haoheng Tan[2], and Qiang Xue[3(✉)]

[1] Information Center of Guizhou Power Grid Corporation, Guiyang, China
[2] Guizhou Power Grid Co., Ltd., Guiyang, China
[3] Colorful Guizhou Digital Technology Co., Ltd., Guiyang, China
xueqiang2017@163.com

Abstract. This paper aims to achieve intelligent comparison of bidding documents from different sources and identify potential bid-rigging situations. In response to possible irregularities and unfair practices in the bidding process, we design and implement a system based on algorithmic analysis and visualization. The system automatically parses bidding documents from various sources and displays the differences between them. Through algorithmic analysis and a visual interface, evaluation experts can quickly identify potential bid-rigging situations. Experimental results demonstrate that our system effectively reduces evaluation time and improves the accuracy of evaluation results. Our research holds significant value and promising applications. This system can reduce labor costs while enhancing the efficiency and fairness of the bidding process. Furthermore, through intelligent comparison technology, we can promptly detect violations and ensure fair bidding outcomes.

Keywords: Intelligent Comparison · Bidding Documents · Bid-rigging · Text Parsing · Text Comparison

1 Introduction

Bidding documents [1] are application files submitted by suppliers to the procurement party in competitive bidding processes. The comparison of bidding document contents [2] is a crucial task in bid evaluation, aiming to identify potential bid-rigging situations and ensure fair and impartial bidding outcomes. However, due to the diverse sources and complex nature of bidding documents, manual comparison is often time-consuming and prone to errors. This paper aims to design a system based on algorithmic analysis and visualization that can automatically parse bidding documents from different sources and provide a user-friendly interface to display the differences, assisting evaluation experts in conducting fast and efficient text comparisons. By introducing intelligent comparison [3] technology, we can significantly reduce the evaluation time, improve the quality of evaluations, and mitigate the potential risks of bid-rigging.

Supported by Intelligent Bidding Evaluation Assistance Platform based on Deep Learning (Project Number: 066700KK52210003) developed by Guizhou Power Grid Limited Liability Company.

With the rapid development of information technology, electronic bidding documents [4] have gradually replaced traditional paper-based documents as the primary form in the bidding process. Electronic bidding documents offer advantages such as convenience, efficiency, and environmental friendliness. However, their diversified sources and formats present new challenges for comparing document contents. Currently, manual comparison is still the prevailing method in bid evaluation. Evaluation experts need to manually compare various sections of bidding documents, searching for potential similarities or repetitions to determine the existence of bid-rigging activities. However, this traditional manual comparison approach is not only time-consuming and error-prone, but also incapable of handling large amounts of data and complex document formats.

The significance of this research lies in providing an automated [5], intelligent solution for comparing bidding document contents to address the existing problems and challenges faced in the bidding evaluation process. By designing a system based on algorithmic analysis [6] and visualization [7], we can achieve several improvements. Firstly, time and cost savings can be realized. Introducing intelligent comparison technology can greatly reduce the evaluation time, thereby improving efficiency and reducing labor costs. Secondly, accuracy can be enhanced. Automatic parsing and comparison of bidding document files can avoid human errors and omissions, increasing the accuracy of evaluation results. Furthermore, the risk of bid-rigging can be mitigated. By detecting potential bid-rigging situations, we can help the procurement party identify potential irregularities and ensure fair and impartial bidding outcomes. Lastly, enhanced visualization display can be provided. Offering a user-friendly interface to showcase document differences allows evaluation experts to intuitively understand and compare bidding document contents from different sources. This research will fill the gap in the field of bidding document comparison and provide an effective solution for more efficient, accurate, and fair results in bid evaluation. Through the design and implementation of an intelligent comparison system, we aim to provide new technological support for bidding document evaluations, driving the development and progress of the bidding industry.

2 Related Work

2.1 Text Parsing Techniques

Text parsing is a crucial step in achieving the comparison of bidding document contents. In recent years, significant progress has been made in the field of Natural Language Processing (NLP) to transform textual data into structured information. In the context of parsing bidding document contents, NLP techniques can be used to identify and extract key information such as bidding requirements, pricing terms, delivery dates, etc. Additionally, Information Extraction techniques [8] can be employed to extract important information from unstructured bidding text. This includes subtasks like Named Entity Recognition [9] and Relation Extraction [10], which help identify and extract key entities and their relationships within the bidding documents.

2.2 Text Comparison Techniques

Text comparison is a critical step in identifying differences between bidding documents and detecting potential bid-rigging situations. The following are commonly used text comparison techniques:

Text matching techniques: Based on similarity or distance measurement methods, these techniques compare the similarity between two texts. Common text matching algorithms include cosine similarity, Jaccard similarity, and edit distance. In recent years, deep learning techniques such as Convolutional Neural Networks (CNN) and Recurrent Neural Networks (RNN) have achieved significant advancements in text matching.

Difference comparison techniques: These techniques aim to find specific differences between two texts and highlight areas of divergence. Common difference comparison methods include Longest Common Subsequence (LCS) [11] and Minimum Edit Distance [12]. Furthermore, tree-based algorithms like Tree Edit Distance [13] are widely applied for comparing bidding document contents with hierarchical structures.

2.3 Text Comparison Techniques

Text parsing and comparison techniques find extensive applications in various fields. Here are some application cases in the realm of information comparison: In software development processes, different versions of source code need to be compared to identify changes and errors. Text parsing and difference comparison techniques are used for detecting differences and similarities between code [14]. File version control systems [15] often employ text comparison techniques to compare different versions of documents or source code, keeping a record of modification history. This aids team members in tracking and managing file changes. News organizations require comparison of news articles from different sources to verify factual accuracy and consistency in reporting. Text comparison techniques help identify and rectify inconsistencies.

Despite the wide-ranging applications of text parsing and comparison techniques, there are still challenges and limitations: Bidding documents from different sources may have varying structures, formats, and language styles. Thus, handling this diversity becomes necessary during the parsing and comparison process. Bidding documents typically contain substantial textual content, requiring efficient algorithms and resource management for parsing and comparison of lengthy texts. Ambiguities or vague expressions may exist within bidding documents, introducing difficulties during the parsing and comparison process. Therefore, an automated and intelligent approach to bidding document comparison is of utmost importance.

3   Method

After being trained on massive amounts of data, the pre-trained model ERNIE has demonstrated excellent feature extraction capabilities. Drawing inspiration from transfer learning, we leverage the semantic information learned by ERNIE from vast data to assist in the intelligent comparison of bidding document content. We utilize the ERNIE Sentence-PairBERT model to achieve efficient and accurate text matching. The system flowchart is shown in Fig. 1.

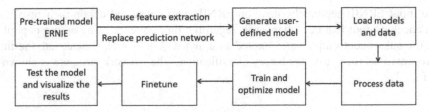

Fig. 1. System Flowchat

3.1 Data Preprocessing and Model Design

Before integrating ERNIE into text comparison, the primary step is data pre-processing. During this stage, we meticulously segment the textual content of each bidding document that will be used for training, dividing it into hierarchical paragraphs, sentences, or even more fine-grained text units. This processing provides a favorable foundation for sentence-level comparison. Each pair of texts to be compared is cleverly combined into a sentence pair, where one sentence originates from a specific bidding document and the other from another bidding document. For example, suppose we have two bidding documents, referred to as Document A and Document B. We aim to compare the differences in text between these two documents. We take a sentence from Document A as the first sentence of the sentence pair and the corresponding sentence from Document B as the second sentence of the sentence pair. In this way, we obtain a sentence pair where one sentence comes from Document A and the other from Document B. The same approach is applied to construct other text pairs to be compared, which are then fed into the model for comparative analysis.

In the design of the intelligent comparison, we employ the ERNIE model to implement the Chinese bidding document comparison task. With the pre-trained weights, we employ the model's sentence-pair classification task to obtain descriptions of closely related sentences. For each pair of sentences, we need to transform their textual content into a suitable input format for the model. We add special tokens in the model, such as "[CLS]" (start token for classification tasks) and "[SEP]" (sentence separation token to indicate boundaries between different sentences). Additionally, the text needs to be accurately segmented into words, which are then converted into corresponding word vectors. In this task, we establish a well-defined binary classification task where positive examples represent two sentences with similar semantics, while negative examples imply that the semantics between these two sentences are dissimilar. The intelligent document comparison process is illustrated in Fig. 2. In the framework of the ERNIE model, the input of sentence pairs is passed through multiple layers of transformer encoders within the model. These encoders aim to capture contextual information of sentences perfectly, reflecting their inherent meanings accurately. Once encoding is completed, the extracted features are inputted into fully connected layers for the classification task. The output of the classification task often manifests as a probability value between 0 and 1, which implicitly represents the measure of similarity between sentences. However, the model parameters of ERNIE are very large, resulting in a very large computational load and unsatisfactory prediction speed. In response to this issue, the network results adopted a sense bert structure. Sense bert adopts the network structure of Siamese. Query and

Title input ERNIE separately, share an ERNIE parameter, and obtain their respective sequences_Output feature. Afterwards, regarding the sequence_ The output is pooled, and the subsequent outputs are denoted as u and v. Afterwards, concatenate the three representations (u, v, u-v) for binary classification. The network structure is shown in the Fig. 3.

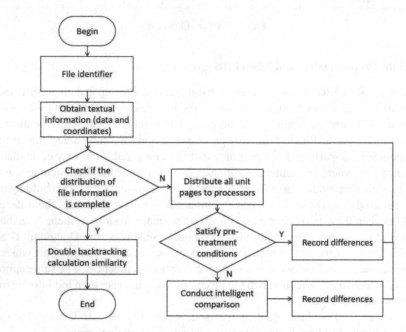

Fig. 2. The intelligent document comparison process

3.2 Similarity Measurement and Threshold Determination

The output of the classification task can be used to measure the similarity between two sentences. A higher probability value indicates a greater semantic similarity between sentences. To determine the existence of differences, a threshold can be set. Probability values exceeding this threshold are considered similar, while those below it are regarded as dissimilar.

3.3 Visualization and Result Analysis

Visualizing the comparison results provides an intuitive representation of the differences between bidding documents. In the visualization interface, similar portions can be highlighted, and detailed differences can be presented. Evaluators can quickly identify potential bid-rigging situations through this method, enabling more targeted assessment and decision-making.

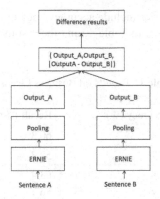

Fig. 3. The model adopts a sense bert structure

4 Experimental Design

The dataset used to train the Sentence-Pair model consists of electronic files of business licenses and qualification certificates provided by Guizhou Power Grid Company. The business license dataset contains 558 images, with 400 images used as the training set and 158 images used as the test set. The qualification certificate dataset contains 487 images, with 341 images used as the training set and 146 images used as the test set. We evaluate the system's performance in terms of difference detection accuracy, recall rate, F1 score, etc.

The experimental design includes steps such as data preprocessing, model training, and testing.

Data Collection: All data for this experiment is sourced from electronic files of business licenses and qualification certificates provided by Guizhou Power Grid Company.

Data Preprocessing: This involves operations such as denoising, binarization, rotation correction, and image enhancement.

Feature Extraction: Useful features are extracted from each character's image. Common feature extraction methods include algorithms based on shape, texture, edges, etc.

Model Training: The Sentence-Pair model is trained using the training dataset.

Model Testing: The trained Sentence-Pair model is evaluated using the test dataset. Evaluation metrics include accuracy, recall rate, F1 score, etc.

Experimental Analysis: Based on the test results, the performance of the model is analyzed. Experimental parameters are adjusted accordingly, including tuning model parameters, increasing training data, improving feature extraction methods, etc.

5 Experimental Results and Analysis

The dataset composed of electronic files of business licenses and qualification certificates provided by Guizhou Power Grid Company was used for training. A comparison was made with SRP-TF-IDF [16], TF-IDF-Simhash [17], TextRank+ [18], and our proposed method. The comparison metrics include accuracy, recall rate, and F1 score. The results on business licenses are shown in Table 1, and the results on qualification certificates are shown in Table 2.

Table 1. Results on Business Licenses

Method	Accuracy (%)	Recall (%)	F1 Score
SRP-TF-IDF	65.3	60.3	0.63
TF-IDF-Simhash	63.7	52.3	0.57
TextRank+	68.8	63.4	0.66
Ours	92.5	79.3	0.88

The experimental results demonstrate that our proposed model achieves significantly higher accuracy and recall rates compared to SRP-TF-IDF, TF-IDF-Simhash, and TextRank+ methods. On business licenses, our model improves the accuracy and recall rates by 27.2%, 19.0% compared to SRP-TF-IDF, and by 28.8%, 27.0% compared to TF-IDF-Simhash. Compared to TextRank+, it improves the accuracy and recall rates by 23.7% and 15.9% respectively. On qualification certificates, our model improves the accuracy and recall rates by 26.2%, 27.7% compared to SRP-TF-IDF, and by 19.1%, 20.2% compared to TF-IDF-Simhash. Compared to TextRank+, it improves the accuracy and recall rates by 20.0% and 21.5% respectively. These results indicate the effectiveness of our method in identifying document content. From the above experimental results, it can be concluded that our method shows great potential compared to other methods, with significantly higher recall and accuracy rates. It achieves good performance in recognizing business licenses and qualification certificates. Due to the limited nature of our dataset, we only conducted experiments on business licenses and qualification certificates, lacking experiments on other types of documents.

Table 2. Results on Qualification Certificates

Method	Accuracy (%)	Recall (%)	F1 Score
SRP-TF-IDF	59.6	45.9	0.52
TF-IDF-Simhash	66.7	53.4	0.59
TextRank+	65.8	52.1	0.58
Ours	85.8	73.6	0.79

6   Application Cases and Discussions

During the bidding process, there may be differences in the tender documents submitted by different vendors. The system can assist evaluation experts in quickly comparing the documents, identifying possible bid rigging or collusion situations, thus ensuring fair competition and transparent bidding. In the legal field, contract review requires comparing different versions of contracts to identify modifications. The system can be used for automated contract review, helping lawyers and legal teams accurately capture changes in contract terms. In the academic and publishing sectors, the system can be used to detect text similarity to avoid plagiarism or infringement.

In the context of bid document evaluation, the system can quickly and accurately compare the tender documents from different vendors, highlighting possible bid rigging or collusion situations. Evaluation experts can clearly see the differences between the documents through a visual interface, enabling faster judgment. In contract review, the system can highlight differences in contract terms across versions, helping lawyers quickly identify modifications.

Intelligent document comparison has significant potential for future applications. The automation of comparison and intelligent prompts can greatly improve the efficiency of manual comparisons and reduce human errors. In fields such as bidding and contracts, the system can help decision-makers understand text differences more quickly and accurately, enabling informed decisions. Besides text comparison, similar technologies can be applied in other domains such as code comparison and image similarity analysis. With the development of deep learning technology, the performance of models can be further improved, enabling more accurate comparison and analysis. The system can be expanded to support multilingual comparison, meeting global demands.

7 Conclusion

This paper proposes a system based on algorithm parsing and visualization that achieves intelligent comparison of tender document content from different sources and identifies potential bid rigging or collusion situations. The system has broad application prospects and can assist evaluation experts in the bidding industry to conduct fast and efficient text comparisons, ensuring fair and just bidding outcomes. Future improvements and expansions will further enhance the system's performance and functionality, driving the development and progress of this field.

References

1. Tanjung, R.A., Festiyed, F., Mayasari, T.: Meta-analysis of the influence of group investigation type cooperative models on student's competence in physics learning. Pillar Phys. Educ. **15**(3), 156–163 (2022)
2. Han, B., Baldwin, T.: Lexical normalisation of short text messages: Makn sens a# twitter. In: Proceedings of the 49th Annual Meeting of the Association for Computational Linguistics: Human Language Technologies, pp. 368–378 (2011)
3. Vani, K., Gupta, D.: Integrating syntax-semantic-based text analysis with structural and citation information for scientific plagiarism detection. J. Am. Soc. Inf. Sci. **69**(11), 1330–1345 (2018)
4. Gelbukh, A.: Computational Linguistics and Intelligent Text Processing, CICLing 2006, vol. 3878. Springer, Heidelberg (2006)
5. Hu, Z., Havrylov, S., Titov, I., Cohen, S.B.: Obfuscation for privacy-preserving syntactic parsing. arXiv preprint arXiv:1904.09585 (2019)

6. Johnson, T.: Intelligent interface for managing data content and presentation (2006). US Patent App. 10/520,018
7. Belhareth, Y., Latiri, C.: Sentiment forecasting based on past textual content and deep learning architectures. Int. J. Intell. Inf. Database Syst. **15**(4), 377–397 (2022)
8. Sharma, D.: Intelligent content priority assignment (2023), US Patent 11,617,005
9. Barry, J., Mohammadshahi, A., Wagner, J., Foster, J., Henderson, J.: The DCUEPFL enhanced dependency parser at the IWPT 2021 shared task. arXiv preprint arXiv:2107.01982 (2021)
10. Sboev, A., Rybka, R., Moloshnikov, I., Gudovskih, D.: Syntactic analysis of the sentences of the Russian language based on neural networks. Procedia Comput. Sci. **66**, 277–286 (2015)
11. Choi, Y.S.: Tree pattern expression for extracting information from syntactically parsed text corpora. Data Min. Knowl. Disc. **22**, 211–231 (2011)
12. Srivastava, S., et al.: Semantic modeling and machine learning-based generation of conceptual plans for manufacturing assemblies (2020), US Patent App. 16/387,976
13. Li, J., Huang, Y., Chen, X., Fu, Y.G.: Semi-supervised node classification via semiglobal graph transformer based on homogeneity augmentation. Parallel Process. Lett. **33**(01n02), 2340008 (2023)
14. Tinner, W., Theurillat, J.P.: Uppermost limit, extent, and fluctuations of the timberline and treeline ecocline in the swiss central alps during the past 11,500 years. Arct. Antarct. Alp. Res. **35**(2), 158–169 (2003)
15. Liu, Y., Hu, G.: Mapping the field of english for specific purposes (1980–2018): a co-citation analysis. Engl. Specif. Purp. **61**, 97–116 (2021)
16. Zhuohao, W., Dong, W., Qing, L.: Keyword extraction from scientific research projects based on srp-tf-idf. Chin. J. Electron. **30**(4), 652–657 (2021)
17. Zhang, X., He, D.: Similar document recognition technology based on the improved simhash algorithm. Comput. Sci. Appl. **10**(02) (2020)
18. Li, W., Zhao, J.: Textrank algorithm by exploiting wikipedia for short text keywords extraction. In: 2016 3rd International Conference on Information Science and Control Engineering (ICISCE), pp. 683–686. IEEE (2016)

Image Denoising Method with Improved Threshold Function

Xueqing Li, Caixia Deng, Shasha Li$^{(\boxtimes)}$, and Lu Pi

Harbin University of Science and Technology, Harbin 150080, China
48001724@qq.com

Abstract. Since remote sensing image are created uniquely, noise is invariably present. This can degrade the image quality and hinder further processing of the picture. For this reason, image denoising is a crucial step in the image processing process. The limitations of the traditional threshold functions in practical applications, as well as the fact that the threshold functions in previous studies were not continuous and did not discuss the type of noise. Therefore, a new adjustable continuous threshold function is constructed based on existing threshold functions and is used for denoising images with different kinds of noise. Simulation experiments demonstrate that wavelet threshold denoising using the new threshold function outperforms current threshold functions and methods for images with salt and pepper, Gaussian, and speckle noise. Moreover, it effectively filters out noise while retaining more detail. This provides a feasible method for wavelet threshold denoising and can be applied to images containing different noises.

Keywords: Noise · Image denoising · Remote sensing image · Threshold function

1 Introduction

With the development of remote sensing technology, remote sensing image is used in numerous vital areas, including natural disaster prevention and geological exploration. Long-range imaging and motion blur can impact the quality of remote sensing image, and untreated image data can result in subpar target detection performance [1]. Hence, image preprocessing is critical to address these issues [2]. Image denoising has been the subject of research by many academics. Some of these methods include adaptive image denoising based on diffusion equation and deep learning [3], new crop image denoising based on improved wavelet domain SVD [4], and wavelet threshold denoising based on improved threshold function [5, 6]. The wavelet transform is a multiresolution analysis technique that combines the frequency and time domains to accurately describe the signal's multiscale properties [7]. Wavelet threshold shrinkage denoising was first introduced by Donoho et al. in 1995 [8]. Denoising remote sensing image using wavelet threshold techniques improves the quality and clarity of the images and enables more accurate analysis of geographic and environmental data. The basic principle of wavelet threshold denoising is to judge whether the signal is noise by selecting an appropriate threshold. Therefore, the selection of the threshold function is essential.

D.-S. Huang et al. (Eds.): ICAI 2023, CCIS 2014, pp. 187–199, 2024.
https://doi.org/10.1007/978-981-97-0903-8_19

The two categories of traditional threshold functions are hard and soft threshold functions. Hard threshold function produce oscillating reconstructed signals at the threshold point [9], whereas soft threshold function provide reconstructed signals that consistently diverge from the original signal. Wang Y and Jing-Yi L et al. proposed the improved threshold functions. Literature 5 still has an issue with discontinuity, and the two papers do not provide a more detailed discussion of the types of noise. This study introduces a new continuous threshold function that is adjustable and close to the hard threshold function. Denoising images that contain three distinct types of noise using various methods. Simulation studies show that the denoising effect of the threshold function proposed in this study is better than the other methods mentioned in the paper. Consequently, the wavelet threshold denoising method effectively denoises images containing multiple noises.

2   Principle of Wavelet Threshold Denoising

The wavelet threshold denoising algorithm is shown in Table 1.

Table 1. Wavelet threshold denoising algorithm.

Algorithm. Wavelet threshold denoising algorithm
Input: Noisy image
Output: Denoised image
1. Setting the wavelet basis function, the number of transform layers, and the threshold function
2. Perform the wavelet transform and obtain the wavelet coefficients c and scale factors s
3. Calculation the threshold *th*
4. If *abs(c(i,j))* < *th*, **then**
$c(i,j) = 0$
End if
5. Wavelet inverse transform to get denoised image

3   Threshold Functions Available

3.1   Traditional Threshold Functions

Traditional threshold functions are categorized into hard and soft threshold functions, and their expressions are as follows

$$\hat{\omega}_{j,k} = \begin{cases} \omega_{j,k}, & |\omega_{j,k}| \geq \lambda \\ 0, & |\omega_{j,k}| < \lambda \end{cases} \tag{1}$$

$$\hat{\omega}_{j,k} = \begin{cases} sign(\omega_{j,k})(|\omega_{j,k}| - \lambda), & |\omega_{j,k}| \geq \lambda \\ 0, & |\omega_{j,k}| < \lambda \end{cases} \tag{2}$$

where $\omega_{j,k}$ is the original wavelet coefficients, while $\hat{\omega}_{j,k}$ is the new wavelet coefficients obtained after threshold processing, $sign(\cdot)$ is the symbolic function, and λ denotes the threshold.

The images of the traditional threshold functions are displayed (see Fig. 1).

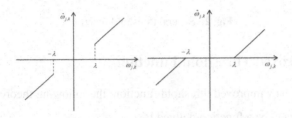

Hard threshold function   Soft threshold function

Fig. 1. The traditional threshold functions.

3.2 Improved Threshold Functions Available

The expressions for the threshold functions given in Literatures 5 and 6 are in order

$$\hat{\omega}_{j,k} = \begin{cases} sign(\omega_{j,k})[|\omega_{j,k}|^2 - (\lambda e^{-(|\omega_{j,k}|-\lambda)/k})^2]^{1/2}, & |\omega_{j,k}| \geq \lambda \\ a\omega_{j,k}, & |\omega_{j,k}| < \lambda \end{cases} \tag{3}$$

$$\hat{\omega}_{j,k} = \begin{cases} sign(\omega_{j,k})\left\{|\omega_{j,k}| - \dfrac{\lambda}{\exp^3[\alpha(|\omega_{j,k}|-\lambda)/\lambda]}\right\}, & |\omega_{j,k}| \geq \lambda \\ 0, & |\omega_{j,k}| < \lambda \end{cases} \tag{4}$$

where λ is the threshold. The thresholds are in order $\lambda = \sigma\sqrt{2\ln N}\big/\ln(j+1)$ and $\lambda = \sigma\sqrt{2\ln N}\big/\log_2(j+1)$. j represents the number of decomposition layers, σ is the noise standard deviation, N is the total number of wavelet coefficients in the image. k, a, and α are the adjustable parameters, where $k > 0$ and $a \in (0.05, 0.5)$ in Literature 5, and α can be taken as an arbitrary real number in Literature 6. $\omega_{j,k}$ and $\hat{\omega}_{j,k}$ are the original wavelet coefficients and new wavelet coefficients after threshold processing, respectively.

The above several threshold functions are illustrated in graph (see Fig. 2).

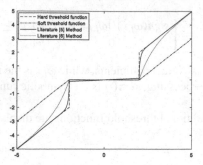

Fig. 2. Several threshold functions.

4 New Improved Threshold Function

To construct the new improved threshold function, the following theorem is given.

Theorem. Let $f(x)$ be a function defined by

$$f(x) = \begin{cases} sign(x)(|x| - \dfrac{\lambda}{e^{(2\beta+1)(|x|-\lambda)^\beta}}), & |x| \geq \lambda \\ 0, & |x| < \lambda \end{cases} \tag{5}$$

Then the function $f(x)$ is a continuous odd function with asymptote $y = x$, where $\beta > 0$ and $\lambda > 0$.

Proof. The domain of the function $f(x)$ is $(-\infty, +\infty)$, and there is

$$f(-x) = \begin{cases} sign(-x)(|-x| - \dfrac{\lambda}{e^{(2\beta+1)(|-x|-\lambda)^\beta}}), & |-x| \geq \lambda \\ 0, & |-x| < \lambda \end{cases}$$

$$= -f(x)$$

Then the function $f(x)$ is an odd function. Considering continuity next, we have

$$\lim_{x \to \lambda^+} f(x) = \lim_{x \to \lambda^+} (x - \frac{\lambda}{e^{(2\beta+1)(x-\lambda)^\beta}}) = 0, \quad \lim_{x \to \lambda^-} f(x) = 0$$

So $\lim\limits_{x \to \lambda^+} f(x) = \lim\limits_{x \to \lambda^-} f(x) = f(\lambda) = 0$, the function $f(x)$ is continuous at $x = \lambda$. Since $f(x)$ is an odd function, similarly, $f(x)$ is continuous at $x = -\lambda$. $f(x)$ is continuous when $|x| > \lambda$, and $f(x) = 0$ is continuous when $|x| < \lambda$, it follows that $f(x)$ is continuous on $(-\infty, +\infty)$.

The asymptote of $f(x)$ is $y = x$, in fact

$$\lim_{x \to +\infty} \frac{f(x)}{x} = 1 - \lim_{x \to +\infty} \frac{\lambda}{xe^{(2\beta+1)(x-\lambda)^\beta}} = 1, \quad \lim_{x \to -\infty} \frac{f(x)}{x} = 1 + \lim_{x \to -\infty} \frac{\lambda}{xe^{(2\beta+1)(-x-\lambda)^\beta}} = 1$$

From the function (5), a new threshold function can be constructed as follows

$$\hat{\omega}_{j,k} = \begin{cases} sign(\omega_{j,k})(|\omega_{j,k}| - \dfrac{\lambda}{e^{(2\beta+1)(|\omega_{j,k}|-\lambda)^\beta}}), & |\omega_{j,k}| \geq \lambda \\ 0, & |\omega_{j,k}| < \lambda \end{cases} \tag{6}$$

Here, β is an adjustable parameter with $\beta > 0$. $\omega_{j,k}$ and $\hat{\omega}_{j,k}$ are the original wavelet coefficients and the processed wavelet coefficients. λ represents the threshold, it is chosen as $\lambda = \sigma\sqrt{2\ln N} \Big/ \log_2(j + 1)$. Furthermore, j represents the number of decomposition layers, σ is the standard deviation of the noise, and the total number of wavelet coefficients is N.

From Theorem, the new threshold function (6) is a continuous function with tunability, ultimately approaching the hard threshold function (see Fig. 3).

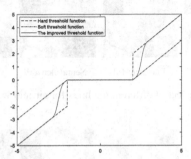

Fig. 3. The new threshold function in this paper.

5   Simulation Experiments

This study selected three photographs, chemical plant, airfield, and airfield2, from the standard image processing test set. A sym4 wavelet basis is taken, and the number of decomposition layers is set to 3. Gaussian, salt and pepper, and speckle noise were added to the image. Matlab is used for the simulation studies. This work used the improved threshold function (6), the threshold functions in Literatures 5 and 6, and the hard and soft threshold functions to denoise the noisy image. Since neural network is a popular technique for image denoising, this article also employs the method to achieve a comparison. Peak signal-to-noise ratio (PSNR), Root Mean Square Error (RMSE), Structural Similarity Index Measure (SSIM), Coefficient of Correlation (CoC), and degree of distortion are some objective evaluation criteria used to examine the denoised images. In general, better denoising and better preservation of the original image's details are associated with higher PSNR, SSIM, and CoC values and lower RMSE and distortion values. In this paper, $\beta = 4$ is chosen to perform simulation experiments. The simulation results are presented in Tables 2, 3, 4, 5, 6, 7, 8, 9 and 10. To be able to provide more details of the results of the simulation experiments, the images were enlarged locally (see Figs. 4, 5, 6, 7, 8, 9, 10, 11 and 12).

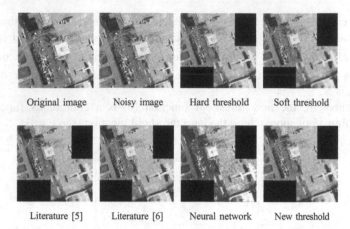

Fig. 4. Denoising effect of different methods for airfield with Gaussian noise.

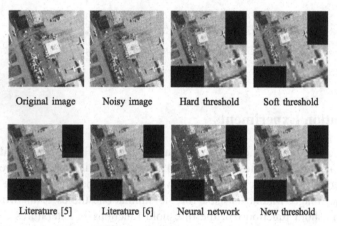

Fig. 5. Denoising effect of different methods for airfield with salt and pepper noise.

The application of the method described in this paper and other methods have the phenomenon that the detailed information is regarded as noise and removed, as shown in Figs. 4, 5, 6, 7, 8, 9, 10, 11 and 12. Tables 2, 3, 4, 5, 6, 7, 8, 9 and 10 objectively demonstrate that the improved threshold function in this study outperforms the traditional threshold functions, the methods in Literatures 5 and 6, and the neural network method in denoising images with different types of noise. However, for some images, the denoised image appears more blurred because the threshold chosen in this work is relatively high, causing many real detail coefficients to be incorrectly identified as noise, resulting in a loss of detail.

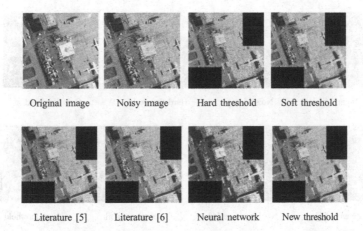

| Original image | Noisy image | Hard threshold | Soft threshold |

| Literature [5] | Literature [6] | Neural network | New threshold |

Fig. 6. Denoising effect of different methods for airfield with speckle noise.

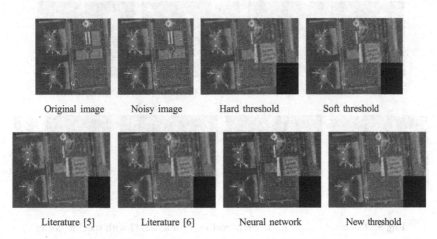

| Original image | Noisy image | Hard threshold | Soft threshold |

| Literature [5] | Literature [6] | Neural network | New threshold |

Fig. 7. Denoising effect of different methods for airfield2 with Gaussian noise.

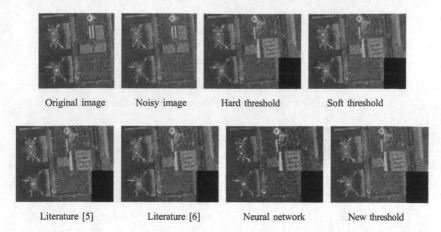

Fig. 8. Denoising effect of different methods for airfield2 with salt and pepper noise.

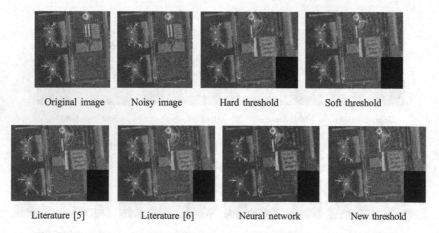

Fig. 9. Denoising effect of different methods for airfield2 with speckle noise.

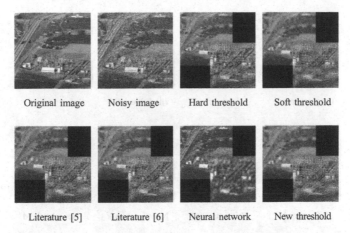

Fig. 10. Denoising effect of different methods for Chemical plant with Gaussian noise.

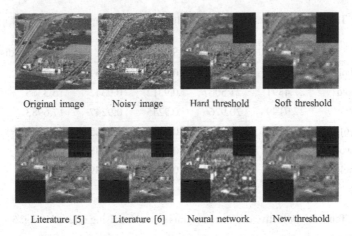

Fig. 11. Denoising effect of different methods for Chemical plant with salt and pepper noise.

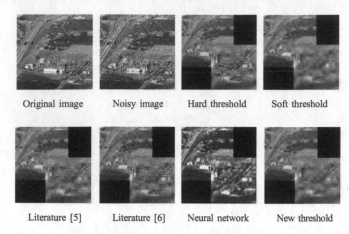

Fig. 12. Denoising effect of different methods for Chemical plant with speckle noise.

Table 2. Objective evaluation results of the denoising effect for Fig. 4.

Methods	RMSE	PSNR	SSIM	CoC	Degree of distortion
Hard threshold	24.4341	20.3709	0.9162	0.9157	18.7888
Soft threshold	21.4391	21.5067	0.9312	0.9342	16.3365
Literature [5]	22.9199	20.9266	0.9245	0.9247	17.6983
Literature [6]	23.2995	20.7839	0.9226	0.9225	18.0559
Neural network	31.7304	18.1013	0.8849	0.8888	25.4228
New threshold	**21.1394**	**21.6289**	**0.9339**	**0.9359**	**16.1316**

Table 3. Objective evaluation results of the denoising effect for Fig. 5.

Methods	RMSE	PSNR	SSIM	CoC	Degree of distortion
Hard threshold	28.1000	19.1567	0.8807	0.8841	20.2081
Soft threshold	25.0945	20.1392	0.8990	0.9111	17.9323
Literature [5]	26.4405	19.6854	0.8912	0.8983	18.7980
Literature [6]	27.2692	19.4174	0.8857	0.8910	19.6696
Neural network	40.9355	15.8888	0.8185	0.8272	33.2507
New threshold	**24.9870**	**20.1765**	**0.9005**	**0.9115**	**17.8638**

Table 4. Objective evaluation results of the denoising effect for Fig. 6.

Methods	RMSE	PSNR	SSIM	CoC	Degree of distortion
Hard threshold	30.4573	18.4570	0.8752	0.8746	22.6103
Soft threshold	23.8725	20.5729	0.9175	0.9194	18.0059
Literature [5]	25.3304	20.0580	0.9099	0.9101	19.1525
Literature [6]	26.8006	19.5679	0.9005	0.9002	20.2244
Neural network	41.2500	15.8223	0.8695	0.8940	33.9370
New threshold	**23.8427**	**20.5837**	**0.9184**	**0.9198**	**17.9752**

Table 5. Objective evaluation results of the denoising effect for Fig. 7.

Methods	RMSE	PSNR	SSIM	CoC	Degree of distortion
Hard threshold	20.3463	21.9611	0.8459	0.8432	15.5269
Soft threshold	16.2102	23.9351	0.8863	0.8900	11.9172
Literature [5]	17.3915	23.3241	0.8774	0.8755	12.8429
Literature [6]	18.4660	22.8033	0.8667	0.8637	13.8826
Neural network	27.8105	19.2466	0.7911	0.8063	22.5362
New threshold	**16.1021**	**23.9932**	**0.8894**	**0.8916**	**11.8510**

Table 6. Objective evaluation results of the denoising effect for Fig. 8.

Methods	RMSE	PSNR	SSIM	CoC	Degree of distortion
Hard threshold	31.0449	18.2910	0.6691	0.6666	20.8806
Soft threshold	17.3719	23.3338	0.8687	0.8830	12.9831
Literature [5]	17.9974	23.0266	0.8657	0.8708	13.1779
Literature [6]	18.8531	22.6232	0.8571	0.8581	13.8383
Neural network	32.1473	17.9879	0.6805	0.6860	24.0093
New threshold	**17.2874**	**23.3762**	**0.8716**	**0.8836**	**12.9132**

Table 7. Objective evaluation results of the denoising effect for Fig. 9.

Methods	RMSE	PSNR	SSIM	CoC	Degree of distortion
Hard threshold	18.1897	22.9343	0.8696	0.8667	13.2862
Soft threshold	17.7567	23.1436	0.8696	0.8683	12.6171

(*continued*)

Table 7. (*continued*)

Methods	RMSE	PSNR	SSIM	CoC	Degree of distortion
Literature [5]	18.2899	22.8866	0.8657	0.8630	13.1746
Literature [6]	18.4025	22.8333	0.8650	0.8621	13.3961
Neural network	21.5748	21.4519	0.7911	0.8063	22.5362
New threshold	**17.6629**	**23.1896**	**0.8717**	**0.8701**	**12.5669**

Table 8. Objective evaluation results of the denoising effect for Fig. 10.

Methods	RMSE	PSNR	SSIM	CoC	Degree of distortion
Hard threshold	23.8033	20.5981	0.8486	0.8464	18.5770
Soft threshold	22.9953	20.8980	0.8485	0.8468	17.8518
Literature [5]	24.2012	20.4540	0.8393	0.8367	18.8603
Literature [6]	23.9156	20.5572	0.8445	0.8420	18.6724
Neural network	31.7050	18.1082	0.8335	0.8539	25.9428
New threshold	**22.9322**	**20.9219**	**0.8505**	**0.8486**	**17.8049**

Table 9. Objective evaluation results of the denoising effect for Fig. 11.

Methods	RMSE	PSNR	SSIM	CoC	Degree of distortion
Hard threshold	23.0040	20.8947	0.8472	0.8466	17.2296
Soft threshold	20.6926	21.8145	0.8610	0.8769	15.6167
Literature [5]	21.5405	21.4657	0.8558	0.8631	15.9929
Literature [6]	21.8489	21.3422	0.8559	0.8593	16.3704
Neural network	31.8263	18.0751	0.7583	0.7595	25.3802
New threshold	**20.5910**	**21.8573**	**0.8634**	**0.8777**	**15.5290**

Table 10. Objective evaluation results of the denoising effect for Fig. 12.

Methods	RMSE	PSNR	SSIM	CoC	Degree of distortion
Hard threshold	26.8539	19.5507	0.8072	0.8044	19.2849
Soft threshold	20.6442	21.8348	0.8662	0.8733	15.0919
Literature [5]	21.1105	21.6408	0.8647	0.8675	15.2351

(*continued*)

Table 10. (*continued*)

Methods	RMSE	PSNR	SSIM	CoC	Degree of distortion
Literature [6]	23.0200	20.8887	0.8463	0.8451	16.6446
Neural network	29.9261	18.6098	0.8514	0.8705	24.7627
New threshold	**20.5646**	**21.8684**	**0.8679**	**0.8743**	**15.0444**

6 Conclusions

Due to the unique imaging technique used for remote sensing imagery, the image is not immune to noise. It has a substantial impact on the subsequent processing of the image, making image pre-processing and denoising essential. In this paper, a continuous threshold function with adjustability has been constructed to improve upon the traditional threshold functions as well as the previously enhanced ones. This function gradually approaches the hard threshold function. Metrics such as PSNR and RMSE are employed to objectively validate the feasibility of selecting this threshold function. The application of this function has a good effect on the denoising of images containing Gaussian noise, salt and pepper noise, and speckle noise, which is better than other threshold functions mentioned in the paper. There were individual images in the experiment that became blurrier after denoising. Future research will choose a better threshold to solve this problem.

Acknowledgements. This work was supported in part by the National Natural Science Foundation of China (Grant No. 11871181).

References

1. Wang, X., Wu, Y., Ming, Y., et al.: Remote sensing imagery super resolution based on adaptive multi-scale feature fusion network. Sensors **20**(4), 1142 (2020)
2. Qi, B., Shi, H., Zhuang, Y., et al.: On-board, real-time preprocessing system for optical remote-sensing imagery. Sensors **18**(5), 1328 (2018)
3. Ma, S., Li, L., Zhang, C.: Adaptive image denoising method based on diffusion equation and deep learning. J. Robot. 1–9 (2022)
4. Wang, R., Cai, W., Wang, Z.: A new method of denoising crop image based on improved SVD in wavelet domain. Secur. Commun. Netw. 1–11 (2021)
5. Wang, Y., Xu, C., Wang, Y., et al.: A comprehensive diagnosis method of rolling bearing fault based on CEEMDAN-DFA-improved wavelet threshold function and QPSO-MPE-SVM. Entropy **23**(9), 1142 (2021)
6. Jing Yi, L., Hong, L., Dong, Y., et al.: A new wavelet threshold function and denoising application. Math. Probl. Eng. (2016)
7. Liu, X.L., Liu, Z., Li, X.B., et al.: Wavelet threshold de-noising of rock acoustic emission signals subjected to dynamic loads. J. Geophys. Eng. **15**(4), 1160–1170 (2018)
8. Donoho, D.L.: De-noising by soft-thresholding. IEEE Trans. Inf. Theory **41**(3), 613–627 (1995)
9. Xia, J., Qiao, X., Li, Z., et al.: Application of semi-airborne frequency domain electromagnetic data based on improved ant-colony-optimized wavelet threshold denoising method. IEEE Access **10**, 129163–129175 (2022)

FasterPlateNet: A Faster Deep Neural Network for License Plate Detection and Recognition

Lei Huang[1], De Shuang Huang[2,3], Yuan Yuan Chen[1], Yu Zhong Peng[1,2(✉)], Chao Wang[3], and Jianping Liao[1(✉)]

[1] Guangxi Key Laboratory of Human-Computer Interaction and Intelligent Decision-Making, School of Computer and Information Engineering, Nanning Normal University, Nanning 530100, Guangxi, China
jedison@163.com, ljp021916@163.com
[2] Guangxi Academy of Sciences, Nanning 530007, Guangxi, China
[3] School of Electronic and Information Engineering, Tongji University, Shanghai 201804, China

Abstract. License plate recognition is an important technology for vehicle management. However, the existing methods based on traditional image processing or deep learning have limitations in accuracy and efficiency. In this paper, we propose a novel method for license plate detection and recognition, called FasterPlateNet. FasterPlateNet consists of two stages: detection localization and character recognition. In the detection localization stage, it employs a backbone network with stacked C3_Faster modules and a one-stage object detection algorithm with a multi-scale feature fusion pyramid to extract multi-scale features of the license plate, and enhances the resolution and global feature dependency of the feature map by using the content-aware feature reassembly (CARAFE) algorithm and the exposed visual center (EVC) module. In the character recognition stage, it adopts a character recognition network with a convolutional neural network and a connectionist temporal classification loss function, which can directly output the character sequence from the license plate image without character segmentation. The experimental results on the CPPD dataset and its subsets demonstrate that our method achieves 98.8% and 98.5% accuracy in detection localization and recognition respectively. This method has great potential and value in practical applications.

Keywords: License plate recognition · deep neural network · object detection · license plate localization

1 Introduction

Automobiles are vital for daily transportation and social economic development. Each vehicle has a unique license plate number for identification. License plate recognition, an essential component of intelligent transportation systems, has various applications in vehicle management, traffic safety, violation monitoring, etc.

D.-S. Huang et al. (Eds.): ICAI 2023, CCIS 2014, pp. 200–208, 2024.
https://doi.org/10.1007/978-981-97-0903-8_20

This paper addresses license plate recognition, Various object detection algorithms have been proposed for this task, which fall into two types: two-stage detection and one-stage detection. Two-stage detection representative examples are RCNN [1], FasterR-CNN [2], MaskR-CNN [3], etc. One-stage detection is faster and simpler than two-stage detection algorithms. Among them, You Only Look Once (YOLO) [4] is one of the most popular one-stage detection algorithms. It has multiple versions from V2to V7 [5, 6], DAMO-YOLO [7], Single Shot MultiBox Detector (SSD) [8] etc.

We review two categories of license plate recognition (LPR) methods: traditional and modern. Traditional methods use image processing techniques to preprocess, extract features, segment, and recognize the input image for LPR. Modern methods use deep learning techniques to learn the feature representation of license plates and characters in images, and output the recognition results directly. They can improve accuracy and speed of recognition, and adapt to different scenarios and images. However, these methods also have drawbacks: they need tedious and complex network design and tuning. Therefore, both traditional and modern methods have limitations.

This paper proposes a novel license plate recognition method based on deep learning and one-stage object detection, which aims to improve the performance of LPR methods. The main contributions of this paper are:

1. We proposed C3_Faster, a novel convolutional network module that combines C3 and PConv concepts. It extracts image features effectively.
2. We introduced a PAFPN, a multi-scale feature fusion pyramid to extract multi-scale features of the license plate, by using the content-aware feature reassembly (CARAFE) algorithm and the exposed visual center (EVC) module.
3. We presented a lightweight PlateNet for character recognition based on CNN + CTC, which has a simple network architecture, small parameter size, and fast inference speed.

2 Methodology

2.1 Overview of FasterPlateNet

We present FasterPlateNet, a model for license plate detection and recognition. It consists of four main components: BackBone, Neck, Head, and PlateNet (Fig. 1).

2.2 Network Backbone of Faster PlateNet

2.2.1 C3_Faster Based on Partial Convolution

Figure 2(a) shows the C3_Faster structure, with three parts: Conv, Faster_block, and Concat. Faster_Block extracts high-level features; Conv1 and Conv2 reduce input channels; Conv3 increases output channels.

We can reduce unnecessary calculations and costs. A recent method called partial convolution (PConv) [9] does this. Figure 2(c) shows the PConv structure, which reduces redundant calculations and memory access and extracts spatial features better. Equation (1) shows that PConv also has lower memory access.

$$h \times w \times 2c_p + k^2 \times c_p^2 \approx h \times w \times 2c_p \tag{1}$$

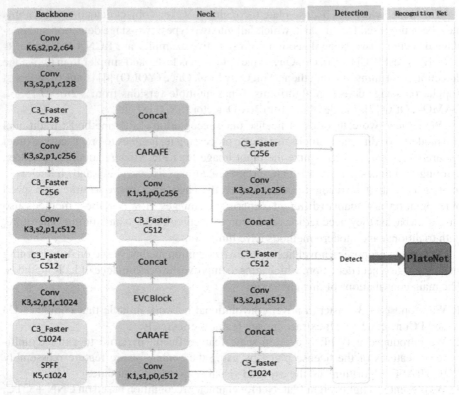

Fig. 1. The network framework of FasterPlateNet. From left to right, it consists of Backbone, Neck, Head, and PlateNet.

PConv costs $h \times w \times 2c_p + k^2 \times c_p^2 \approx h \times w \times 2c_p$, where $h, w > k$. When $r = 1/4$, PConv is 1/4 of regular convolution, reading and writing data from some channels, not all. This lowers memory bandwidth and speeds up the network.

2.3   Multi-scale Fusion Neck

Neck, a key part of multi-scale feature fusion, uses FPN + PAN [10]. EVC [11] and CARAFE [12] modules improve the dependency and upsampling of features (Fig. 3).

Figure 4 shows the EVCBlock structure, with two parallel parts: lightweight MLP and learnable LVC. MLP captures global dependency of deep features, and LVC preserves local region features. MLP has two residual blocks, each with a depthwise convolution block and a channel convolution block. LVC has two parts: encoding and scaling factor. The encoding method of LVC is as follows:

$$e_k = \sum_{i=1}^{N} \frac{e^{-s_k \|x_i - b_k\|^2}}{\sum_{j=1}^{K} e^{-s_k \|x_i - b_k\|^2}} (x_i - b_k) \tag{2}$$

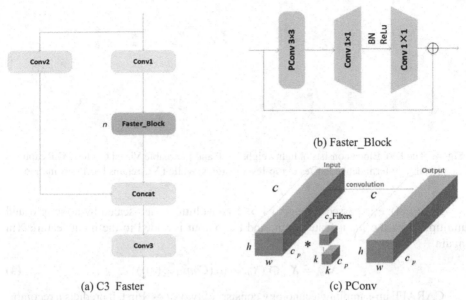

Fig. 2. The structure of C3_Faster. (a) C3_Faster consists of Conv, Concat, and Faster_Block; (b) consists of PConv, Conv, BN and Relu; (c) PConv is the part that participates in convolution operations.

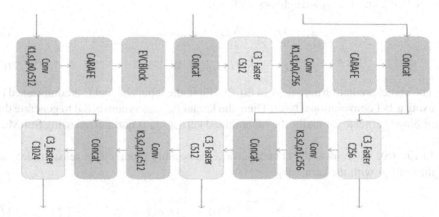

Fig. 3. The Neck network. The Neck is composed of Conv, C3_Faster, Concat, EVCBlock, and CARAFE.

where, x_i represents the i-th pixel point, b_k represents the k-th learnable encoding position. $x_i - b_k$ is the offset position of each x_i relative to b_k. e_k is transformed into e as shown in Eq. (3).

$$e = \sum_{k=1}^{K} \text{Relu}(\text{BN}(e_k)) \tag{3}$$

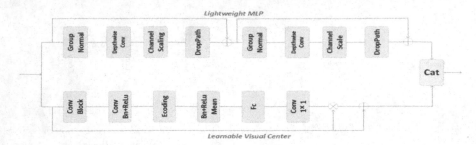

Fig. 4. The EVCBlock consists of lightweight MLP and Learnable Visual Center. MLP captures the global long-term dependencies of top-level features, while LVC retains local information.

In Eq. (4), e is passed through a 1×1 convolution, then scaled by a factor σ and multiplied by the input feature Xin, and the output is added to the input feature Xin again.

$$X_{out} = X_{in} \oplus (X_{in} \otimes (\sigma (Conv_{1\times1}(e)))) \tag{4}$$

CARAFE up-sampling technology consists of two steps. First, it predicts a recombination kernel for each target based on its content. Then, it recombines the features using the predicted kernel. The internal kernel prediction module ψ predicts the position kernel for location l' based on its neighbor χ_l, while ϕ is the content-aware recombination module that combines $\chi_{l'}$'s neighbors with $w_{l'}$.

$$W_{l'} = \psi(N(\chi_l, k_{encoder})) \tag{5}$$

$$\chi'_{l'} = \varphi(N(\chi_l, k_{up}), W_{l'}) \tag{6}$$

The kernel prediction module ψ in Eq. (5). First, the input channel C is compressed to C_m using a 1x1 convolutional layer. Then, the kernel $k_{encoder}$ is convolved to generate the recombined kernel k_{up}. Finally, the recombined kernel k_{up}^2 is normalized using SoftMax [13].

In Eq. (6), where ϕ is the content-aware reassembly module that reassembles the neighbor of χ_l with the kernel $W_{l'}$.

$$\chi'_{l'} = \sum_{n=-r}^{r} \sum_{m=-r}^{r} W_{l'(n,m)} \cdot \chi_{(i+n,j+m)} \tag{7}$$

where $r = \lfloor k_{up}/2 \rfloor$, for a target location l' and the corresponding square region $N(x_l, k_{up})$ centered at $l = (i, j)$, the reassembly is shown in Eq. (7).

2.4 Detection Head

The detection head is used to determine the position and size of the license plate. This paper directly uses the detection head of YOLOV8 [14]. The detection head of YOLOv8 is a decoupled head structure that separates the classification and regression branches and uses Anchor-Free method.

2.5   License Plate Recognition Network PlateNet

This paper proposes PateNet, PateNet consists of two parts: a convolutional neural network (CNN) [15] that extracts character features from input images, and a connectionist temporal classification (CTC) [16] loss function that decodes feature sequences to obtain the final license plate number. The structure of the license plate recognition network is shown in Fig. 5, in which CNN comprises multiple convolutional layers, activation layers, and maximum pooling layers.

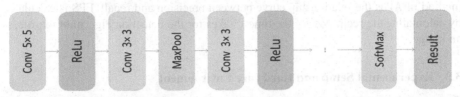

Fig. 5. The character feature extraction network consisting of a CNN network. The network structure mainly consists of Conv, Relu, MaxPool, and SoftMax, with a total of 30 layers for character feature extraction.

3   Experimental Results and Analysis

3.1   Dataset Introduction

The CCPD [17] dataset consists of several subsets, among which ccpd_base is split into training and validation sets with an 8:2 ratio; the rest of ccpd_challenge, ccpd_db, ccpd_fn, cppd_np, ccpd_rotate, ccpd_tilt, and ccpd_weather are used as test sets.The dataset is shown in Table 1.

Table 1. Description of different sub-datasets in CCPD

Type	Num	Illustrates
ccpd_base	199998	Normal license plate
ccpd_challenge	10006	More challenging
ccpd_db	20001	Darker or brighter light
ccpd_fn	19999	Farther or closer to the camera
ccpd_rotate	9998	Horizontal tilt 20–50°vertical tilt -10–10°
ccpd_tilt	10000	Horizontal tilt 15–45°vertical tilt 15–45°
ccpd_weather	9999	License plates for rainy, snowy, or foggy days
Total: 283,037 license plates		

3.2 Evaluation Metrics and Baseline Models

3.2.1 Evaluation Indicators

Precision, Average Precision (AP) [18], and Frames Per Second (FPS) [19].
The Precision is formulated as follows:

$$Precision = \frac{TP}{TP + FP} \tag{8}$$

The higher the precision, the more accurate the detection algorithm. The calculation method of AP is the relationship curve between precision and recall. FPS is calculated by calculating the reciprocal of the time it takes for the detection algorithm to process an image.

3.3 Experimental Setup and Hardware Environment

We optimize our model using SGD, with an initial learning rate of 0.001.We resize all input images to 640 × 640 pixels.We performed experiments on a server with an Nvidia GPU Tesla A100 80 GB PCIe and 48 GB RAM for data processing and validation.

3.4 Experimental Results

3.4.1 License Plate Test Results

The evaluation metrics for the detection models were frames per second (FPS) and average precision (AP). The license plate detection performance of each comparison algorithm is shown in Table 2.

Table 2. Vehicle license plate detection and positioning results

Methods	FPS	AP	Base	DB	FN	Rotate	Tilt	Weather	Challenge
Cascade classifier [20]	32	47.2	55.4	49.2	52.7	0.4	0.6	51.5	27.5
SSD300 [8]	40	94.4	99.1	89.2	84.7	95.6	94.9	83.4	93.1
YOLO9000 [5]	42	93.1	98.8	89.6	77.3	93.3	91.8	84.2	88.6
Faster-RCNN [2]	15	92.9	98.1	92.1	83.7	91.8	89.4	81.8	83.9
TE2E [21]	3	94.2	98.5	91.7	83.8	95.1	94.5	83.6	93.1
RPnet [17]	61	94.5	99.3	89.5	85.3	94.7	93.2	84.1	92.8
MTLP [22]	65	95.8	–	–	–	–	–	–	–
Ours	83	98.8	99.6	93.6	96.6	99.4	99.2	99	99

Note: The Base (100k), DB, FN, Rotate, Tilt, Weather, and Challenge results in the table are all expressed in Precision. AP is the average of the accuracy of the subsets DB, FN, Rotate, Tilt, Weather, Challenge and Base (100k). FPS is the average frame rate of each subset

Table 2 presents the results of license plate detection and localization. Our method detection and localization adopts a one-stage structure based on PConv to design the C3_Faster module, which has a high speed of 83 FPS/s and balances performance and efficiency, surpassing the benchmark algorithm.

Table 3. License plate recognition results, HC represents Holistic-CNN [23]

Methods	FPS	AP	Base	DB	FN	Rotate	Tilt	Weather	Challenge
Cascade classifier + HC	29	58.9	69.7	67.2	69.7	0.1	3.1	52.3	30.9
SSD300 + HC	35	95.2	98.3	96.6	95.9	88.4	91.5	87.3	83.8
YOLO9000 + HC	36	93.7	98.1	96.0	88.2	84.5	88.5	87.0	80.5
Faster-RCNN + HC	13	92.8	97.2	94.4	90.9	82.9	87.3	85.5	76.3
TE2E	3	94.4	97.8	94.8	94.5	87.9	92.1	86.8	81.2
RPnet	61	95.5	98.5	96.9	94.3	90.8	92.5	87.9	85.1
MTLPR	64	96.7	–	–	–	–	–	–	–
our	78	98.5	99.6	97.0	95.2	93.2	93.4	96.1	96.3

Note: The Base(100k), DB, FN, Rotate, Tilt, Weather, and Challenge results in the table are all expressed in Precision. AP is the average of the accuracy of the subsets DB, FN, Rotate, Tilt, Weather, Challenge and Base (100k). FPS is the average frame rate of each subset

3.4.2 License Plate Character Recognition

The results of license plate character recognition are shown in Table 3. Since the average precision of license plate detection and localization is 98.5%, our method is faster than other detection and localization methods, reaching 78FPS/s, and the recognition adopts convolution as the backbone to design the whole network, so our method has some advantages in speed.

4 Conclusion

In this work, we proposed an end-to-end method called FasterPlateNet for license plate detection and recognition. The detection and localization module can detect and locate license plates in different environments accurately and quickly. We evaluated the method on the CCPD dataset and its subsets, and compared it with the state-of-the-art models in terms of accuracy and efficiency. FasterPlateNet contributes a new idea and method to the field of license plate detection and recognition.

References

1. Girshick, R.: Fast R-CNN. In: 2015 IEEE International Conference on Computer Vision (ICCV), pp. 1440–1448 (2015)
2. Ren, S., He, K., Girshick, R., Sun, J.: Faster R-CNN: towards real-time object detection with region proposal networks. IEEE Trans. Pattern Anal. Mach. Intell. 1137–1149 (2017)
3. He, K., Gkioxari, G., Dollár, P., Girshick, R.: Mask R-CNN. In: 2017 IEEE International Conference on Computer Vision (ICCV), pp. 2980–2988 (2017)
4. Redmon, J., Divvala, S., Girshick, R., Farhadi, A.: You only look once: unified, real-time object detection. In: 2016 IEEE Conference on Computer Vision and Pattern Recognition (CVPR), pp. 779–788 (2016)
5. Redmon, J., Farhadi, A.: YOLO9000: better, faster, stronger. In: 2017 IEEE Conference on Computer Vision and Pattern Recognition (CVPR), pp. 6517–6525 (2017)

6. Wang, C.-Y., Bochkovskiy, A., Yuan, H., Liao, M.: YOLOv7: trainable bag-of-freebies sets new state-of-the-art for real-time object detectors. arXivpreprint arXiv:2207.02696 (2022)
7. Xu, X.Z., Jiang, Y.Q., Chen, W.H., Huang, Y.l., Zhang, Y., Sun, X.Y.: DAMO-YOLO: A Report on Real-Time Object Detection Design. arXivpreprint arXiv:2211.15444 (2023)
8. Liu, W., et al.: SSD: single shot MultiBox detector. In: European Conference on Computer Vision (ECCV), pp. 21–37 (2016)
9. Chen, J., et al.: Run, don't walk: chasing higher FLOPS for faster neural networks. In: 2023 IEEE/CVF Conference on Computer Vision and Pattern Recognition (CVPR), pp. 12021–12031 (2023)
10. Lin, T.-Y., Dollár, P., Girshick, R., He, K., Hariharan, B., Belongie, S.: Feature pyramid networks for object detection. In: 2017 IEEE Conference on Computer Vision and Pattern Recognition (CVPR), pp. 936–944 (2017)
11. Quan, Y., Zhang, D., Zhang, L., Tang, J.: Centralized feature pyramid for object detection. IEEE Trans. Image Process. 4341–4354 (2023)
12. Wang, J., Chen, K., Xu, R., Liu, Z., Loy, C.C., Lin, D.: CARAFE: Content-Aware ReAssembly of FEatures: In: 2019 IEEE/CVF International Conference on Computer Vision (ICCV), pp. 3007–3016 (2019)
13. Hilbe, J.M.: Generalized linear models. International Encyclopedia of Statistical Science, pp. 591–596 (1987)
14. Reis, D., Kupec, J., Hong, J., Daoudi, A.: Real-Time Flying Object Detection with YOLOv8. arXivprepring arXiv:2305.09972 (2023)
15. LeCun, Y., et al.:Backpropagation applied to handwritten zip code recognition. Neural Comput. 541–551 (1989)
16. Graves, A., Fernández, S., Gome, F., Schmidhuber, J.: Connectionist temporal classification: labelling unsegmented sequence data with recurrent neural networks. In: Proceedings of the 23rd International Conference on Machine Learning (ICML), pp. 369–376 (2006)
17. Xu, Z., et al.: Towards end-to-end license plate detection and recognition: a large dataset and baseline. In: Computer Vision – ECCV, pp. 261–277 (2018)
18. Rumelhart, D.E., McClelland, J.L.: Learning internal representations by error propagation. In: Parallel Distributed Processing: Explorations in the Microstructure of Cognition: Foundations, pp. 318–362 (1987)
19. Lewis, H.R.: A statistical interpretation of term specificity and its application in retrieval. Classic Papers of Computer Science, pp. 339–347 (1972)
20. Wang, S.-Z., Lee, H.-J.: A cascade framework for a real-time statistical plate recognition system. IEEE Trans. Inf. Forensics Secur. 267–282 (2007)
21. Li, H., Wang, P., Shen, C.: Towards end-to-end car license plates detection and recognition with deep neural networks. arXiv preprint arXiv:1709.08828 (2017)
22. Wang, W., Yang, J., Chen, M., Wang, P.: A light CNN for end-to-end car license plates detection and recognition. IEEE Access 173875–173883 (2021)
23. Lin, S., Ji, R., Chen, C., Tao, D., Luo, J.: Holistic CNN compression via low-rank decomposition with knowledge transfer. Pattern Anal. Mach. Intell. 2889–2905 (2019)

An Improved Seq-Deepfake Detection Method

Zhenrong Deng[1], Kang You[1], Rui Yang[1(✉)], Xinru Hu[1], and Yuren Chen[2]

[1] Guangxi Key Laboratory of Images and Graphics Intelligent Processing,
Guilin University of Electronic Technology, Guilin 541004, China
792481404@qq.com

[2] Guangxi Construction Industry Mostly, Guangxi, China

Abstract. Facial processing technology's ability to generate realistic human faces poses significant societal risks when exploited maliciously. Deep face fraud detection relies on deep learning to meticulously scrutinize the manipulation sequence of fake faces, uncovering deceptive traces. This study focuses on Detecting Sequential DeepFake Operations (Seq-DeepFake), transforming the face detection task into an image-to-sequence exploration. To enhance detection accuracy, this paper introduces a Seq-DeepFake detection method. The Seq-DeepFake Transformer model's activation function is refined, incorporating the Rectified Randomized Leaky Unit (RReLU) to address learning rate challenges associated with negative input values. Furthermore, diverse attention mechanism modules are integrated into the backbone network, forming the innovative CLSP-Resnet-50 model. Experimental results demonstrate the efficacy of the enhanced Seq-DeepFake model, employing two evaluation metrics on a deepfake dataset, showcasing improved accuracy. Comparative analysis against other real and fake face detection methods substantiates the effectiveness of the Seq-DeepFake model.

Keywords: face fake detection · facial attribute manipulation detection · facial component manipulation detection

1 Background

Realistic face forgery techniques, especially the recent deep learning-driven methods [1], have attracted widespread social attention, such as media (i.e., images and videos, etc.) that fake faces in a way that deceives the human eye. Recent technological advances have made it easier to create hyper-realistic videos, now known as "deep fakes," that use face-swapping technology and leave few traces of manipulation [2]. Deep learning models can generate hyper-realistic facial images, which are visually indistinguishable from real images.

Face detection is crucial to the development of face recognition [3], expression recognition [4], tracking and classification. Early research on face detection [5, 6] mainly focused on the design of handcrafted features and used traditional machine learning algorithms to train effective classifiers for detection and recognition [7]. In face related research, face reconstruction and tracking is a well-studied field [8], which is the basis of face editing methods. The face can emphasize as well as alone convey a message, and it plays a central role in human communication. The current facial manipulation methods can be divided into two categories: facial expression manipulation and facial component manipulation. One of the most prominent facial expression manipulation techniques is the method of Thies et al. [9], called Face2Face. It only uses simple hardware to realize the real-time transfer of one person's facial expression to another person. This technology has brought great challenges to the authenticity of face recognition.

In response to this series of threats, this paper improves on the existing Seq-DeepFake technology, aiming to generate corresponding face detection sequences according to different face image attributes and components, hoping to provide help in further face image restoration, and improve the detection accuracy and restoration accuracy.

2 Related Work

In recent years, deep learning-based algorithms have developed rapidly in object detection, and face detection methods based on deep convolutional neural networks [10] have been extensively studied.

Google proposed a neural network architecture Transformer based on a self-attention mechanism, which has demonstrated excellent performance in realizing sequence-to-sequence NLP tasks [11]. This method has been widely used in fields such as face recognition. The cross-attention mechanism can be used to study image processing, and many major breakthroughs have been made in society in recent years. These technologies bring many references to face detection technology.

Compared with the existing deepfake detection tasks, Ziwei et al. proposed a detection operation sequence, using a specific data set, converted the detection Seq-DeepFake operation into a specific image-to-sequence task, and realized face detection through the SeqFakeFormer module. And based on the detected facial operation sequence, it provides a basis for further restoring the original face, and its superiority has been proven through a large number of quantitative and qualitative experiments. Ziwei et al. considered two different facial manipulation techniques, one is facial component manipulation [12] and the other is facial attribute manipulation [13].

Facial component manipulation. It adopts the StyleMapGAN proposed in the article to conduct the facial component operation by utilizing the potential spatial dimension in gan for real-time image editing [12], Different replacement sequences will obtain different facial operation results.

Facial attribute operation. It uses the fine-grained facial editing method proposed by Talk-to-Edit [13] to generate different pictures based on different hidden vectors in the hidden space, Potential codes sampled from StyleGAN trained on FFHQ data set [14] are used to generate original images. After each attribute randomly replaces the original face, GIQA algorithm is used to filter low-quality samples.

Based on the above detection model [15], several improved methods are proposed and tested on the original data set to verify that the detection accuracy can indeed be improved.

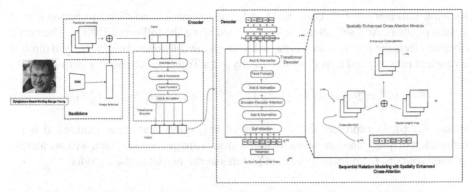

Fig. 1. This is a SeqFakeFormer Figure. The face image is first obtained, and then the face image is input into the convolutional neural network CNN. Combined with the position coding function, the spatial information in the image is extracted by learning the features of the operation area, and then their spatial relations are extracted by a self-attention module in the encoder. The feature output of the encoder is used as part of the input of the decoder to build a detection sequence relationship model and recognize facial features based on the sequence. The decoder integrates a spatially enhanced cross-attention module, which is beneficial to improve attention on features.

3 SeqFakeFormer Network Model Structure

The Seq-DeepFake pape [15] proposes a Seq-DeepFake Transformer (SeqFakeFormer) that includes spatial relation extraction, face sequential relation modeling with spatially enhanced cross-attention (Fig. 1).

3.1 Resnet Extraction Features

In image processing, resnet is used for feature extraction. The deeper the deep learning layer, the better its expressive ability in theory, but after the depth reaches a certain level, increasing the number of layers will not improve the classification performance [16]. Considering this factor, the experiment in this paper performs convolution operation under the resnet-50 network, the network convergence speed is moderate, and the classification performance and accuracy can also achieve the desired effect.

3.2 Spatial Relationship Feature Extraction

CNN is a deep learning model commonly used in image recognition. Features in images can be extracted through operations such as convolution and pooling. In order to obtain the detailed features of the facial area, a convolutional neural network (CNN) can be used to perform multi-layer convolution operations on the input image. Through the feature map f^{ori}=CNN(x), the input image is extracted and converted, and the features of the facial operation area are learned from it to extract the spatial information features. $f^{ori} \in R^{C \times H \times W}$ where H, W are the matrix height and width, respectively, and C is the number of channels of the feature map.

With transformer architecture unchanged, location coding features are added to expand the visual feature mapping f^{ori} to obtain feature mapping f^{pos} with spatial location information. f^{pos} Uses K, Q and V to extract the relationship between each spatial position. And self-attention is calculated using the following Eq. (1). The vector obtained from the previous step is passed through the full connection layer, then through a residual network and LayerNorm to finally get a Transformer encoder output.

$$f_i^{seq} = \text{Softmax}\left(K_i^T Q_i \sqrt{d}\right)V_i, f_i^{seq} = \text{Concat}(f_1^{seq}, \dots, f_D^{seq}) \tag{1}$$

where K_i, Q_i, V_i represent the i-th group of key, query and value features, d is the dimension of query and key, and a total of d groups are generated. Then, we concatenate all the groups to form spatially related features as the output of the encoder.

3.3 Spatial Augmented Cross-Attention Sequence Relationship Modeling

Before the Transformer decoder processes the data, the facial sequence to be processed is sent to the Tokenizer, and an SOS token and an EOS token are inserted at the beginning and end of the sequence, respectively, to obtain an operation sequence Stok $\in$ RC*(N + 2). Then, this sequence is input into Transformer decoder, and combined with part of the output of Transformer encoder, the sequence is decoded by using the autoregressive mechanism. Due to the short length of the operation sequence Stok and limited information, in order to effectively extract spatial region features, the original model used a sequence relationship modeling method with spatially enhanced cross attention.

The autoregressive mechanism is integrated into the above cross-attention process, and then the decoded sequence with sequential relationship features processed by transformer decoder is fed into FFN to obtain the prediction score of each operation. Finally, we jointly train the CNN, transformer encoder, and decoder to minimize the cross-entropy loss between each class score and the corresponding operational annotations in the sequence.

4 Improved Seq-DeepFake Detection Fake Restoration Sequence Model

In order to improve the detection accuracy, this paper improves the original Seq-DeepFake model (see Fig. 2).

4.1 Improved Activation Function

The original Seq-DeepFake model uses the Relu activation function in the transformer decoder part and the MLP module. This paper proposes an improved method to modify the activation function used in the model. ReLU: This is a non-linear correction function that removes all x values below 0 and replaces them with 0. RReLU function: A new type of convolutional neural network activation function, which is modified on the basis of ReLU function to better solve the problem of neuron death in the negative interval of ReLU function.

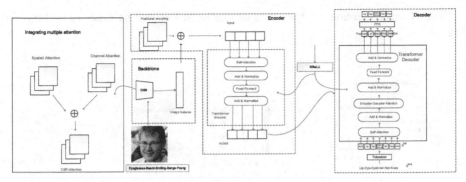

Fig. 2. The face image is first acquired, and then the face image is input into the improved convolutional neural network CNN, where in the backbone network resnet-50, multiple attention mechanism modules are integrated to form a new CLSP-resnet-50 model.

The comparison between the ReLU activation function and the RReLU activation function is shown in Fig. 3:

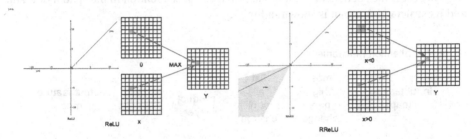

Fig. 3. Comparison of ReLU activation function and RReLU activation function. The slope of negative values is random during training but fixed during testing. The beauty of RReLU is that during the training session, ai is randomly drawn from a uniform distribution $U(I,u)$, which is fixed during the testing session.

In this paper, we refer to the RReLU function and make some improvements to introduce an improved function between the input features and the hidden layer.

4.2 Introducing Multiple Attention Mechanism Modules

We often add attention mechanisms to backbone networks, such as SENet, which is a novel network architecture that can improve the representation ability of the network by modeling the interdependence between the channels of the feature map [17].

Spatial Attention mechanism: Generate and score the mask of the space, which represents the Spatial Attention Module.

In this paper, a variety of attention mechanism modules are cited and added to the backbone network, which strengthens the attention to useful features and greatly improves the ability to extract useful information.

The channel attention mechanism is similar to SENet, and its structure is shown in Fig. 4:

Fig. 4. Channel attention mechanism structure diagram

Although the structure is similar, it differs from senet in that it applies both average pooling and Max pooling operations to spatially compress the input features. To get two one-dimensional vector outputs, two pooling operations can be used. The obtained weights are added to the output feature map to obtain the final result feature map.

Then, it is the spatial attention module that extracts attention in the spatial domain, and its structural diagram is shown in Fig. 5.

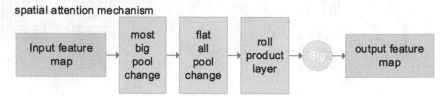

Fig. 5. Structural diagram of spatial attention module

To derive the spatial dimension attention feature values, the sigmoid activation function can be used to calculate the final output feature map. The feature map is: $F_{avg}^s \in R^{1*H*W})$ and $F_{max}^s \in R^{1*H*W}$, the mathematical formula of this part is as follows:

$$M_{SP}(F) = \sigma\left(f^{7\times7}([Avg(F); Max(F)])\right) = \sigma\left(f^{7\times7}\left(\left[F_{avg}^s; F_{max}^s\right]\right)\right) \quad (2)$$

In this paper, on the original Resnet-50 original model, a variety of attention mechanisms are added. As mentioned earlier, after the input feature map is preprocessed, it will also go through layer1, layer2, layer3, and layer4. Each layer contains multiple bottlenecks. The improvement of this paper is to introduce multiple attention mechanisms after the last bottleneck of each layer. The improved CLSP-Resnet-50 part structure is shown in Fig. 6:

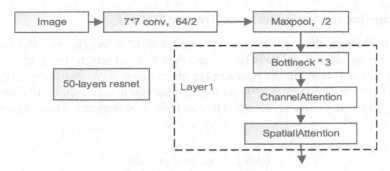

Fig. 6. Partial structure diagram of CLSP-Resnet-50

5 Experiments

5.1 Introduction to Data

This article uses the deepfake data set to set 26 types of operation sequences, and the length of each sequence is from 1 to 5. The dataset is divided into two types, one is facial component manipulation and the other is facial attribute manipulation. The first type includes a total of 35,166 operating face images, and the proportions of 1–5 operating sequences of different lengths are: 20.48%, 20.06%, 18.62%, 20.88%, and 19.96%. The division ratio of training set, verification set and test set is 8:1:1, that is, 28132 training sets, 2813 verification sets and 2813 test sets. The second type includes a total of 49,920 operating face images, and the proportion of 1–5 operating sequences of different lengths is 20%. The division ratio of training set, verification set and test set is 8:1:1, that is, 41600 training sets, 4160 verification sets and 4160 test sets. The data set is shown in Fig. 7.

Fig. 7. Schematic diagram of data set division

5.2 Experimental Environment and Training Strategy

For the transformer, this experiment uses 2 encoders plus 2 decoder layers with 4 attention heads. The initial learning rate is $1e-3$, and the CNN part sets the initial learning rate to $1e-4$. Let $\lambda = 4$. For the training plan, the warm-up strategy used is 20 epochs, the total number of epochs is 170, and the learning rate is decreased by 10% every 50 epochs. The basic parameter settings of true and false face sequence detection are shown in Table 1.

Table 1. Basic parameter table

Paramerers	Value
Batch size	32
lr_backbone	1e-4
Leraning rate	1e-3
Epoch	170

The hardware environment of this experiment uses Intel(R) Xeon(R) W-2265 CPU @ 3.50GHz CPU, NVIDIA RTX A4000 GPU, and 16G video memory. The software environment adopts the operating system Ubuntu 16.04, the programming language is python 3.6, and the deep learning framework Pytorch 1.10.0.

5.3 Evaluation Indicators

For true and false face detection, there are two evaluation indicators for reference.

- Fixed Accuracy (Fixed- acc): Given the prediction fixed N length (N = 5), if the length of the "no operation" class is less than N, it will be filled into the annotation sequence, which can be maintained between the prediction and annotation sequence Train with the same length [15]. The first type of evaluation is to compare each action class in the predicted sequence with its corresponding annotation to calculate the evaluation accuracy.

- Adaptive accuracy (Adaptive-acc): Since facial manipulations can be detected through sequential information, such as the initial SOS mark and EOS mark, facial manipulation sequences with an adaptive length can be detected by this method. The second type of evaluation makes it possible to compare predicted operations with annotations within a maximum number of steps of operations ($N \leq 5$). This will make such assessments more focused on operational accuracy.

5.4 Experimental Results and Analysis

After training, each training 10 epochs is used as a group, and the accuracy achieved by the current model is tested according to the evaluation index, and the detection accuracy change curve of facial attribute operation and facial component operation can be obtained, as shown in Fig. 8.

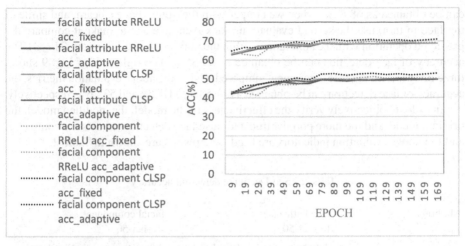

Fig. 8. Changes in detection accuracy of facial attribute operations and component operations

It can be seen from Fig. 8 that the detection accuracy of facial attribute operations and facial component operations increases slowly with the increase of training times, and it is close to saturation when the training reaches 170 epochs, and the evaluation accuracy fluctuates back and forth within a certain range. Under the two detection benchmarks, the detection accuracy of Fixed-Acc is higher than that of Adaptive-Acc, indicating that the detection of Adaptive-Acc is more difficult.

This paper has made two improvements, one is to improve the rrelu activation function, and the other is to integrate multiple attention mechanisms. According to these two improvements, training is performed to obtain an improved model. Taking the fusion of multiple attention mechanisms as an example, the following briefly introduces the detection effect of the modified model on fake face pictures. (see Fig. 9).

Fig. 9. Operation sequence detection effect based on facial attributes and Detection effect based on facial component operation sequence

The left half of Fig. 9 shows three images, which are the original picture and two pictures after the facial attributes have been tampered with. It can be seen that when we only tamper with the expression of the original face to smile, using the first evaluation index Fixed Accuracy, the fixed detection length is one, and the accuracy of face detection can be obtained as 68.88%; when we tamper with the youth, bangs, beard, and smile of the face in turn, use the second evaluation index Adaptive-acc to make it compare the predicted operation with the annotation within the maximum operation step (N ≤ 4).The accuracy of face detection can be obtained as 49.85%. The right half of Fig. 9 shows three images with the face component tampered. Using the above evaluation metrics, the accuracy of face detection can be obtained as 71.54%, 71.52% and 53.46%, respectively.

In order to objectively verify the effectiveness of the model, the modified model, the original model and the more popular true and false face detection models are compared, and the above evaluation indicators are used. The results are shown in Table 2.

Table 2. Seq-Deepfake detection accuracy

Methods	facial attribute Resnet-50		facial component Resnet-50	
	Adaptive-acc	Fixed-acc	Adaptive-acc	Fixed-acc
Original	48.54	68.07	47.89	67.73
Multi-Cls	46.00	66.66	50.57	69.65
DETR	47.99	67.62	59.84	69.75
Transformers + rrelu	49.75	68.88	50.79	69.61
CLSP-resnet-50	49.84	68.87	53.46	71.51

In the above two tables, the two evaluation indicators used are Fixed-Acc and Adaptive-Acc respectively. The left half of Table 2 lists the detection accuracy of operation detection based on face attributes. It can be seen that the detection accuracy of the improved model is better than that of the original model. Based on the improved activation function, Fixed-Acc increased by 0.8%, and Adaptive-acc increased by 1.21%. Based on the fusion of multiple attention mechanisms, Fixed-Acc increased by 0.81%, and Adaptive-acc increased by 1.3%. The right half of Table 2 lists the detection accuracy of operation detection based on face component. It can be seen that the improved model detection performance is better than the original model detection accuracy, and the improved accuracy is greater than that based on facial attribute operation detection accuracy. Based on the improved activation function, Fixed-Acc increased by 1.88%, and Adaptive-acc increased by 2.9%. Based on the fusion of multiple attention mechanisms, Fixed-Acc increased by 5.57%, and Adaptive-acc increased by 3.78%. Under both detection benchmarks, the detection accuracy of Fixed-Acc is higher than that of Adaptive-Acc, which verifies that detecting continuous face operations with adaptive length is much more difficult than detecting simplified versions with fixed length.

In Table 2, it is also compared with the accuracy of Multi-Cls and DETR models based on facial attribute operation and facial component operation respectively. It can be seen that the detection accuracy of the improved model is better than other models and shows better performance than other models.

6 Conclusion

Based on the existing DeepFake research [15], this paper proposes two improved methods for detecting real and fake face operation sequences, aiming to achieve higher performance. Based on the Seq-DeepFake dataset [15], the task of detecting real and fake faces is changed from image processing to image-to-sequence tasks. This paper improves the activation function of the original Seq-DeepFake model, and integrates multiple attention mechanisms into the Seq-DeepFake model, which greatly improves the detection performance. When we have obtained the correct face sequence, we can try to restore the manipulated and tampered face. We define the face restoration task as, given a sequentially processed facial image, process the tampering process reversely according to the sequence to obtain an image as close as possible to the original image. It is hoped that the improved method proposed in this paper can provide reference for more deep fake face detection tasks in the future.

Acknowledgments. This work was partially supported by the National Natural Science Foundation of China (No. 6202780103), by the Guangxi Science and Technology Project (No. AB22035052), Guangxi Key Laboratory of Image and Graphic Intelligent Processing Project (Nos. GIIP2211, GIIP2308), by the Innovation Project of GUET Gurduate Education (No. 2023YCXB09).

References

1. Fried, O., et al.: Text-based editing of talking-head video. ACM Trans. Graph. (TOG) **38**(4), 1–14 (2019)
2. Westerlund, M.: The emergence of deepfake technology: a review. Technol. Innov. Manage. Rev. **9**(11), 39–52 (2019). https://doi.org/10.22215/timreview/1282
3. Deng, J., Guo, J., Xue, N., Zafeiriou, S.: Arcface: additive angular margin loss for deep face recognition. In: Proceedings of the IEEE/CVF Conference on Computer Vision and Pattern Recognition, pp. 4690–4699 (2019)
4. Zeng, N., Zhang, H., Song, B., Liu, W., Li, Y., Dobaie, A.M.: Facial expression recognition via learning deep sparse autoencoders. Neurocomputing **273**, 643–649 (2018)
5. Viola, P., Jones, M.J.: Robust real-time face detection. Int. J. Comput. Vision **57**, 137–154 (2004)
6. Dalal, N., Triggs, B.: Histograms of oriented gradients for human detection. In: 2005 IEEE Computer Society Conference on Computer Vision and Pattern Recognition (CVPR'05), vol. 1, pp. 886–893. IEEE (2005)
7. Lin, K., et al.: Face detection and segmentation based on improved mask r-cnn. Discret. Dyn. Nat. Soc. **2020**, 1–11 (2020)
8. Zollhofer, M., et al.: State of the art on monocular 3d face reconstruction, tracking, and applications. In: Computer Graphics Forum, vol. 37, pp. 523–550. Wiley Online Library (2018)
9. Thies, J., Zollhofer, M., Stamminger, M., Theobalt, C., Niesner, M.: Face2face: real-time face capture and reenactment of RGB videos. In: Proceedings of the IEEE Conference on Computer Vision and Pattern Recognition, pp. 2387–2395 (2016)
10. Ranjan, R., Patel, V.M., Chellappa, R.: Hyperface: a deep multi-task learning framework for face detection, landmark localization, pose estimation, and gender recognition. IEEE Trans. Pattern Anal. Mach. Intell. **41**(1), 121–135 (2017)

11. Vaswani, A., et al.: Attention is all you need. In: Advances in Neural Information Processing Systems, vol. 30 (2017)

12. Kim, H., Choi, Y., Kim, J., Yoo, S., Uh, Y.: Exploiting spatial dimensions of latent in gan for real-time image editing. In: Proceedings of the IEEE/CVF Conference on Computer Vision and Pattern Recognition, pp. 852–861 (2021)

13. Jiang, Y., Huang, Z., Pan, X., Loy, C.C., Liu, Z.: Talk-to-edit: Fine-grained facial editing via dialog. In: Proceedings of the IEEE/CVF International Conference on Computer Vision, pp. 13799–13808 (2021)

14. Karras, T., Laine, S., Aila, T.: A style-based generator architecture for generative adversarial networks. In: Proceedings of the IEEE/CVF Conference on Computer Vision and Pattern Recognition, pp. 4401–4410 (2019)

15. Shao, Rui, Tianxing, Wu., Liu, Ziwei: Detecting and recovering sequential deepfake manipulation. In: Avidan, S., Brostow, G., Cissé, M., Farinella, G.M., Hassner, T. (eds.) Computer Vision – ECCV 2022, pp. 712–728. Springer Nature Switzerland, Cham (2022). https://doi.org/10.1007/978-3-031-19778-9_41

16. He, K., Zhang, X., Ren, S., Sun, J.: Deep residual learning for image recognition. In: Proceedings of the IEEE Conference on Computer Vision and Pattern Recognition, pp. 770–778 (2016)

17. Roy, S.K., Dubey, S.R., Chatterjee, S., Baran Chaudhuri, B.: Fusenet: fused squeeze-and-excitation network for spectral-spatial hyperspectral image classification. IET Image Proc. 14(8), 1653–1661 (2020)

Multimodal Depression Recognition Using Audio and Visual

Xia Xu[✉], Guanhong Zhang, Xueqian Mao, and Qinghua Lu

Department of Artificial Intelligence and Big Data, Hefei University, Hefei 230000, China
xuxia090078@163.com

Abstract. Depression, as one of the prominent challenges in the field of world-wide psychological health, affects the quality of life and psychological well-being of hundreds of millions of people. Due to its high prevalence, recurrence and strong association with other health problems, early diagnosis and treatment are crucial. With advances in technology, audio and visual data are increasingly recognized as biomarkers for the identification of depression. However, it should be noted that many existing studies focus primarily on a single modality, often overlooking the potential complementarity between different modalities. In this context, this study proposes an advanced approach that integrates convolutional neural networks (CNN) and bidirectional long short-term memory networks (BiLSTM) with attention mechanisms, with the objective of extracting more profound features from speech data. For facial expressions, a hybrid model comprising temporal convolutional networks (TCN) and long short-term memory networks (LSTM) is utilized. Furthermore, to achieve a seamless integration of different modalities, we design a cross-attention fusion strategy that allows speech and facial information to be integrated into a unified framework. Our methodology's efficacy is confirmed by the experimental findings on the E-DAIC dataset, in which the multimodal fusion strategy demonstrates higher precision and reliability in detecting depression compared to a single modality.

Keywords: Multimodal fusion · Facial features · Speech signal

1 Introduction

Depression has evolved into a major global public health challenge [1]. An astounding number of more than 280 million people worldwide suffer from depression, according to data compiled by the World Health Organization (WHO) [2]. However, this figure may be just the tip of the iceberg because many people still hesitate to openly discuss their mental health issues [3]. What is even more concerning is that the outbreak of the COVID-19 pandemic has further exacerbated the number of people with depression. As a result, early identification of people with depression, timely treatment, and effective disease management have become urgent priorities in today's society.

In recent years, many researchers have conducted in-depth studies on the application of speech recognition in the field of depression. Depressed individuals frequently exhibit speech characteristics, including pauses, low intonation, and a sluggish speech rate, as demonstrated by these studies [4]. For instance, Rejaibia and colleagues suggested an audio recognition method that uses convolutional neural networks to process Mel frequency cepstral coefficients (MFCC) and pitch features. The research results showed that MFCC works well for detecting depression [5]. Additionally, he and his team employed an innovative approach by processing speech signals, extracting improved spectrogram features, and utilizing the eGeMAPS (Extended Geneva minimalistic acoustic parameter set) feature set. They achieved outstanding results through feature fusion in deep convolutional networks [6]. Furthermore, Huang and colleagues introduced a deep learning method for depression classification using audio signals in the 2016 AVEC (Audio/Visual Emotion Challenge). This approach used MFCC features from audio signals and CNN networks, LSTM networks, and fully connected layers for the prediction of depression [7]. These studies provide promising approaches for the early identification and monitoring of depression.

Moreover, depression can be identified based on its visible characteristics. In an early study, Girard et al. [8] examined the manual and reflexive facial expressions of depressed clinical patients during semi-structured clinical interviews. The aim of this research was to explore the facial expression characteristics of people with depression to understand if there are noticeable differences in their emotional expressions. Patients exhibiting severe symptoms of depression are more likely to verbalize feelings of disdain and smile less, according to the study. This suggests that they may have unique patterns of emotional expression compared to normal individuals. Regarding facial behavior modalities, Pampouchidou et al. [9] summarized a series of widely used and effective facial feature extraction methods. However, given the dynamic nature of facial expression activity, the application of temporal facial dynamics information is considered more effective than relying solely on static information. Gavrilescu et al. [10] used facial action units (AU) to describe the features used for the recognition of depression, which helps to gain a deeper understanding of the deep connection between depression and facial emotion.

In fact, the fusion of multimodal data provides more valuable information for the recognition of depression [11]. Currently, many researchers are dedicated to using multimodal approaches to assess the condition of individuals with depression. Meng et al. [12] used visual and audio data in their research. They utilized motion history histograms to capture dynamic information from visual data and then fused it with audio features. Using partial least squares regression, they effectively predicted the severity of depression using these multimodal characteristics. Alghowinem et al. [13] used head pose and motion data, including parameters such as yaw, roll, and pitch, as well as static characteristics to identify depression, offering a motion and posture-based analysis method for depression. In 2019, Williamsons assessed the severity of depression by extracting vocal pronunciation coordination from audio and video signals and training a predictive model using coordination features. This approach combines auditory and visual cues, helping to provide a more accurate understanding of the emotional state of individuals with depression [14].

Previous research has had some success with single-modal approaches, but they have problems like not having enough information and being easily affected by noise. This makes emotion prediction systems that rely on single-modalities hard to make reliable and accurate, among other things. Additionally, some studies have focused on extracting features from static images or single video frames, neglecting dynamic information. Depression often manifests itself as changes in emotions and mood, and considering temporal information and dynamic features may be more beneficial for accurate identification of depression. A unique multimodal emotion recognition model that integrates information from the visual and auditory modalities is therefore proposed in this paper. Various model architectures are compared to further enhance the extraction of meaningful information. The objective of this paper is to achieve highly precise and robust emotion recognition while ensuring excellent generalization performance.

2 Multimodal Depression Recognition Method

2.1 The Multimodal Depression Recognition Framework

The multimodal depression recognition framework is shown in Fig. 1. First, we preprocess the simultaneously obtained facial behavior data and speech signals. Next, we extract features from the preprocessed data and then obtain a multimodal feature set through different multimodal fusion methods. Then, these multimodal features are fed into a classifier to complete the classification processing of depression. Finally, the classification results are the output. Figure 1 clearly shows the entire depression recognition process.

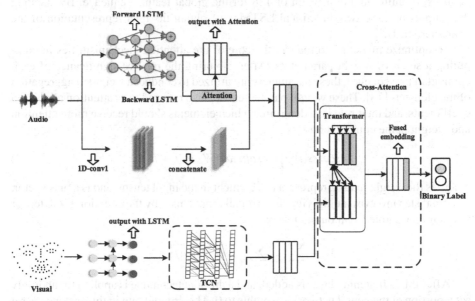

Fig. 1. To deeply extract emotional information, we use a combination of CNN and BiLSTM with attention mechanisms to train audio features. Additionally, we construct a combination model of TCN + LSTM that is specifically designed to further extract visual features. Finally, by applying the cross-attention fusion strategy, the outputs of both modalities are organically integrated together to achieve accurate recognition of depression.

2.2 Depression Recognition from Audio

Mel Frequency Cepstral Coefficients Features. Lower-order MFCCs are more significant for tasks involving emotion prediction and paralinguistic voice analysis, according to studies [15, 16]. In this study, the Librosa library was used to extract MFCC features from speech signals. First, the speech signals were segmented into small time windows, and the Fourier transform was applied to each window to obtain spectral information. Then, by mapping the spectral information into the Mel frequency space, a series of MFCC coefficients were obtained, which reflect the energy distribution of speech signals at different frequencies [17]. To obtain a representation of the entire audio sample, we performed mean pooling on all MFCC coefficients of the windows.

BiLSTM Model with Attention Mechanism. The sequence of speech characteristics is represented as, where T denotes the quantity of frames in the speech and represents the feature vectors at time t. Each neuron in the LSTM layer receives the input feature at time t and the output of all neurons from the previous time step t-1. The following describes the update to the internal concealed state in LSTM:

$$h_t = f_\theta(h_{t-1}, S_t) \tag{1}$$

The hidden state at time step t is represented by h_t, and the LSTM function with weight parameters θ is denoted by f_θ. In this work, each directional LSTM uses 64 neurons, resulting in a dimension of 128 for the global feature sequence. By stacking the outputs of these two directional LSTMs, we obtain the final representation of the characteristic H.

To optimize model performance, the core of the attention mechanism lies in computing a series of weight parameters. After capturing the relative significance of each element in the sequence, these parameters are utilized to conduct a weighted aggregation of the elements [18]. These weight parameters are also referred to as attention allocation coefficients, and their role is to determine which elements should receive more attention and weight in the computation

$$scores[i][j] = softmax(W_{ij} * H + b_j) \tag{2}$$

where is the weight matrix, represents an element in the input tensor, and is a bias vector. The final step involves multiplying the original input tensor by the attention score tensor to obtain a weighted sum output tensor:

$$M = \sum_{i=1}^{n} \sum_{j=1}^{m} scores[i][j] * H \tag{3}$$

After this, a flattening layer is added, and a dropout technique is applied to randomly set a portion of the neural network's weights to 0. The dropout rate in this instance is set at 0.3. The layers that are fully connected are then linked. Finally, the softmax function can be used to obtain the final prediction results and the probability distribution for each class.

CNN Framework. A convolutional layer performs convolution on the extracted MFCC matrix using a size filter. The values of k are 3, 4, and 5, respectively. The convolution layer has the same number of convolution kernels: 128. The width of the convolution kernel is the same as the dimension of the audio feature vector d. The convolution kernel $\omega \in Rh*d$. For each convolution calculation $c_i = ReLU(\omega \cdot v_{i:i+h-1}) + b$, where ReLU is a nonlinear activation function and $b \in R$ is a bias term, c_i represents the local audio feature obtained through the convolution operation. The length of the S sequence is n, and the stride is set to 1, so the window slides n-h + 1 times. The convolution summary result is $C_1 = [c_1, c_2, \dots, c_{n-h+1}]$. During the convolution calculation process, set the padding to "same" to ensure that the input and output dimensions are consistent. The output of different channel CNN structures is fused through the concatenate function $C = concatenate([C_1, C_2, C_3], \quad axis = -1)$. At the same time, add a constraint to add the index L2 norm with a coefficient of 0.05, which can appropriately improve overfitting during network training. Finally, fuse spatial features and context features by splicing layers to obtain the fused feature vector $S_{cat} = C, M$ for classification.

2.3   Depression Recognition from Visual

This section provides a novel method for detecting depression from visual data using a TCN and LSTM model hybrid. Unlike previous studies, this research adopts the collaborative work of TCN and LSTM to better handle various dependencies in time series data.

The original data is linearly converted using min-max normalization to map it into the range [0,1]. Equation (4) illustrates the transformation function.

$$x^* = \frac{x - min}{max - min} \tag{4}$$

where max represents the data's highest value while min represents its lowest. Which then serves as the input for the model.

LSTM Framework. LSTM networks provide good handling of sequential problems by employing three gate architectures to mitigate challenges related to long-term dependencies and gradient vanishing in neural networks. The three gate structures are schematically represented in Fig. 2 below:

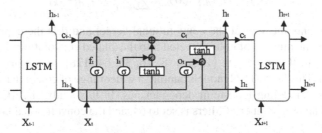

Fig. 2. The architecture of LSTM model is characterized by the unit inputs at different time steps, denoted as X_{t-1}, X, and X_{t+1} for time $t - 1, t$, and $t + 1$ correspondingly. The unit outputs h_{t-1}, h and h_{t+1} are associated with each other. The hidden unit memory at time t-1, t, and t+1are denoted as c_{t-1}, c and c_{t+1} respectively.

Subsequently, the input data is also processed by LSTM with a neuron number of 256 and the hidden state of each time step in the output sequence is obtained. TCN processes the LSTM output in more detail. The block diagram in Fig. 1 clearly shows the structure of LSTM + TCN.

TCN Framework. TCN [19], a deep learning model for processing time series data, excels at capturing contextual information and achieves good performance in multiple tasks, including action segmentation [20], action localization [21], and emotion recognition [22]. Facial expression changes in visual features belong to time series model translation, where $X = (x_1, x_2, \cdots, x_t)$ denotes the input sequence and $Y = (y_1, y_2, \cdots, y_t)$ denotes the output sequence. There exists a mapping relationship f between them. To ensure that the TCN model depends only on past data at each time step and is not disturbed by future data, it adopts a causal convolution method. The causal convolution formula for the input sequence X is as follows:

$$(F * X)(x_t) = \sum_{k=1}^{K} f_k X_{t-K+k} \tag{5}$$

The filter is denoted by $F = (f_1, f_2, \cdots, f_k)$, while the input sequence is denoted by $X = (x_1, x_2, \cdots, x_t)$. Causal convolution is a critical convolution operation in TCN, with the goal of enabling convolution operations to use only the data from the past at each time step. This is achieved by zero-padding on the left side of the input sequence to maintain the length of the input sequence unchanged. This padding strategy ensures that the convolution kernel considers only the current time step and the previous data when performing sliding calculations, without exceeding the current time step. This design enables TCN to model long-term dependencies in time series data and contributes to improving accuracy. In addition, TCN uses Dilated Convolution to further expand the network's receptive field without using pooling operations. Spiking convolutional neural networks use a dilation rate to enable the convolution kernel to perform convolution on the input sequence in a hopping manner, effectively expanding the receptive field. For a one-dimensional input sequence X and a one-dimensional convolutional kernel, the dilation convolution operation F is defined as:

$$F(x_t) = (F *_d X)(x_t) = \sum_{k=1}^{K} f_k X_{t-d(K-k)} \tag{6}$$

where k represents the size of the convolutional kernel and d is the expansion factor used to control the number of holes injected into the dilated convolution. The expansion factors chosen in this paper are [1, 2, 4, 8, 16, 32, 64, 128], which are powers of 2 added upward. This helps TCN models capture a wider range of contextual information, particularly for modeling long-term dependencies. In this study, the TCN network's convolutional layer's number of filters is set to 64, and the convolutional kernel's size is set to 3.

Finally, the fully connected layer is replaced with a global plane pooling layer that uses less parameters, in order to further process features and output, extra convolution and global average pooling operations are carried out after stacking numerous residual blocks.

2.4 Different Fusion Methods

In multimodal training research, this study investigates the impact of several multimodal fusion techniques on the efficacy of depression recognition. The topic is examined through a sequence of experimental analyses. For the fusion strategy, three methods are explored, as follows:

Concatenation Fusion. By concatenating the facial behavior feature set with the voice feature set, a fused feature set is formed.

$$X_{fuse} = \left[F_{cat}^1, F_{cat}^2, \cdots, S_{cat}^1, S_{cat}^2, \cdots \right] \tag{7}$$

Addition Fusion. This method element-wise adds two input elements to generate a new output.

$$X_{Add} = [F_{cat}, S_{cat}] \tag{8}$$

Cross-Attention Mechanism Fusion. For each data source, the original attention weights $E \in \mathbb{R}^{M \times N}$ are calculated based on their abstract representations. Matrix E represents the operation of the dot product between the feature sets. Through SoftMax operation, normalized attention weights $\alpha_{ij} = \frac{e^{E_{ij}}}{\sum_{k=1}^N e^{E_{ik}}}$ are obtained. Using the normalized weights, the voice features are weighted and finally, the weighted voice features and facial features are concatenated.

3 Dataset

The E-DAIC used in this article is an extended DAIC-WOZ dataset, which includes 275 participants who recorded conversations with a virtual interviewer named Ellie. Among these participants, 81 were diagnosed with depression, and 194 were not. The audio data were recorded at a sampling rate of 16 kHz, and the duration of each audio clip ranged from 7 to 33 min. Due to privacy concerns, the original video data is not publicly available, but the extracted data from the interview videos was provided through Open-Face. Furthermore, the dataset includes labels labeled by doctors based on participants' PHQ-8 scores, where 0 indicates non-depression and 1 indicates depression, which can be used for depression classification tasks.

3.1 Visual Features

Visual cues are derived primarily from the extraction of facial key points or raw video data, capturing subtle changes in facial expressions that are then used to estimate the presence of depression. These facial features correspond to each time slot in the interview, recorded at each timestamp, with an interval of 0.3334 s between each timestamp. To better prepare the data for classification analysis, we first focused on the "success" flag in the data preprocessing stage, where 0 represents failure to capture and 1 represents successful capture.

Furthermore, to better handle data and improve interpretability, this paper splits the data into multiple parts, each containing 900 rows of data, which is equivalent to cutting every 30 s based on the calculation of time frames.

3.2 Audio Features

Given the inherent raw qualities of the acquired data, it is imperative to prioritize measures that guarantee the correctness and validity of the data. So, this paper removes the interviewer's voice from the audio data.

When processing audio data, this paper tried using a noise reduction library to reduce noise, but unfortunately, it resulted in more silent sections. Therefore, this article manually cuts audio files using Audacity audio editing software to ensure more accurate audio feature extraction results. To ensure that each dialogue segment contains sufficient voice information, dialogue segments with a duration less than 1 s and long periods of silence are excluded. Finally, to better extract features, each valid audio file is split into audio fragments with a duration of 30 s without overlap.

4 Experiment and Results

4.1 Results of Depression Detection Using Audio Features

This paper utilizes various models to assess the efficacy of Audio unimodality in the context of depression recognition. The impact of speech modality on this recognition process is examined and presented in Table 1.

Table 1. The results of different models in Audio

Audio			
Models	Precision	Recall	F1
LSTM	0.738	0.7261	0.732
BiLSTM	0.7581	0.7447	0.7513
Atten BiLSTM	0.7547	0.7633	0.759
CBLAN	**0.7685**	**0.7878**	0.778

Table 1 demonstrates that the "CBLAN" (CNN + BiLSTM-Attention) model, which combines CNN and BiLSTM-Attention, exhibits superior classification performance when compared to the other three models. It obtains a precision of 76.85% and an F1 score of 77.8%, which is 1.9% higher than the model without CNN.

This indicates that the "CBLAN" model has excellent capabilities in understanding and extracting key features from the input data, as well as in capturing correlations between them. The attention mechanism behind it allows the model to dynamically focus on important information parts, which helps to better distinguish different categories.

4.2 Results of Depression Recognition Using Visual Features

To evaluate the effectiveness of facial expression behavior in the recognition of depression, this paper proposes a new model structure that combines the architecture of

TCN and LSTM. The study additionally conducts a comparison of various models, as displayed in Table 2.

Table 2. The results of different models in Visual

Visual			
Models	Precision	Recall	F1
LSTM	0.724	0.7818	0.7518
CNN	0.5781	0.5511	0.5643
TCN	0.648	0.8	0.716
LSTM + TCN	**0.814**	**0.8279**	**0.8209**

In Table 2, TCN have demonstrated significant advantages over LSTM in terms of training time, convergence speed, and performance evaluation. And it is evident that the model LSTM + TCN performs exceptionally well in the classification task, achieving a precision of 81.4% and an F1 score of 82.09%, which is 6.91% higher than the model without LSTM. This finding implies that the LSTM + TCN model has outstanding capabilities for processing data and capturing temporal information.

4.3 Effectiveness of Different Fusion Methods

After obtaining the best unimodal depression recognition models for speech and facial expressions, this article adopts several different fusion strategies to evaluate differences in depression recognition performance under different fusion strategies.

Table 3. The results of different fusion methods in Audio & Visual

Audio &Visual			
Fusion method	Precision	Recall	F1
Concatenation	0.7915	0.8457	0.8214
Add	0.7891	**0.864**	0.8249
Cross-Attention	**0.8152**	0.8479	**0.8312**

Multimodal fusion performs better than unimodal approaches in depression recognition tests, according to Tables 1, 2, and 3 results. In particular, using the cross-attention mechanism in multimodal fusion achieves the best performance with an F1 score of 83.12%.

This finding highlights the importance of multimodal information because it can integrate information from different data sources to provide a more comprehensive context, helping to improve the accuracy of depression recognition. The cross-attention mechanism may help models better understand and utilize the correlation between different modalities, further improving recognition performance.

5 Conclusions

Recognizing depression is of significant practical importance in helping clinical doctors in diagnosis and patients in self-diagnosis. This study conducted an in-depth exploration of the two main unimodalities, speech and facial expressions, based on the E-DAIC dataset and constructed various network models to recognize depression. After careful comparison, the "CBLAN" model based on speech and the LSTM + TCN model based on facial expressions showed promising performance. Furthermore, this paper adopted a cross-attention mechanism to organically integrate these two modalities, constructing an efficient multimodal recognition model.

It should be noted that recognizing depression faces many challenges. Restrictions on patient privacy, limited and difficult-to-obtain public datasets, and sample imbalances may bias experimental results. This encourages further in-depth strategies, like data augmentation, to be explored in the future and pre-processing strategies for data sets to further improve model accuracy. Furthermore, combining more modality information, such as text information, can comprehensively enhance the accuracy of depression recognition.

Acknowledgement. The authors acknowledge the Key Research and Development Plan of Anhui Province (202104d07020006), the Natural Science Foundation of Anhui Province (2108085MF223), University Natural Sciences Research Project of Anhui Province (KJ2021A0991), the Key Research and Development Plan of Hefei (2021GJ030).

References

1. Hammar, Å., Ronold, E.H., Rekkedal, G.Å.: Cognitive impairment and neurocognitive profiles in major depression—a clinical perspective. Front. Psychiatry **13**, 764374 (2022)
2. WHO: Depression key facts. World Health Organization (2023). https://www.who.int/newsroom/fact-sheets/detail/depression
3. Schumann, I., Schneider, A., Kantert, C., Löwe, B., Linde, K.: Physicians' attitudes, diagnostic process and barriers regarding depression diagnosis in primary care: a systematic review of qualitative studies. Fam. Pract. **29**, 255–263 (2012)
4. World Health Organization. Depression and Other Common Mental Disorders: Global Health Estimates. World Health Organization (2017)
5. Mundt, J.C., Vogel, A.P., Feltner, D.E., Lenderking, W.R.: Vocal acoustic biomarkers of depression severity and treatment response. Biol. Psychiat. **72**(7), 580–587 (2012)
6. Rejaibi, E., Komaty, A., Meriaudeau, F., Agrebi, S., Othmani, A.: MFCC-based recurrent neural network for automatic clinical depression recognition and assessment from speech. Biomed. Signal Process. Control **71**, 103107 (2022)
7. He, L., Cao, C.: Automated depression analysis using convolutional neural networks from speech. J. Biomed. Inform. **83**, 103–111 (2018)

8. Ma, X., Yang, H., Chen, Q., Huang, D., Wang, Y.: Depaudionet: an efficient deep model for audio based depression classification. In: Proceedings of the 6th International Workshop on Audio/Visual Emotion Challenge, pp. 35–42 (2016)
9. Girard, J.M., Cohn, J.F., Mahoor, M.H., Mavadati, S., Rosenwald, D.P.: Social risk and depression: evidence from manual and automatic facial expression analysis. In: 2013 10th IEEE International Conference and Workshops on Automatic Face and Gesture Recognition (FG), pp. 1–8. IEEE (2013)
10. Pampouchidou, A., et al.: Automatic assessment of depression based on visual cues: a systematic review. IEEE Trans. Affect. Comput. **10**(4), 445–470 (2017)
11. Gavrilescu, M., Vizireanu, N.: Predicting depression, anxiety, and stress levels from videos using the facial action coding system. Sensors **19**(17), 3693 (2019)
12. Ramachandram, D., Taylor, G.W.: Deep multimodal learning: a survey on recent advances and trends. IEEE Signal Process. Mag. **34**(6), 96–108 (2017)
13. Meng, H., Huang, D., Wang, H., Yang, H., Ai-Shuraifi, M., Wang, Y.: Depression recognition based on dynamic facial and vocal expression features using partial least square regression. In: Proceedings of the 3rd ACM International Workshop on Audio/Visual Emotion Challenge, pp. 21–30 (2013)
14. Alghowinem, S., Goecke, R., Wagner, M., Parkerx, G., Breakspear, M.: Head pose and movement analysis as an indicator of depression. In: 2013 Humaine Association Conference on Affective Computing and Intelligent Interaction, pp. 283–288. IEEE (2013)
15. Williamson, J.R., Young, D., Nierenberg, A.A., Niemi, J., Helfer, B.S., Quatieri, T.F.: Tracking depression severity from audio and video based on speech articulatory coordination. Comput. Speech Lang. **55**, 40–56 (2019)
16. Bone, D., Lee, C.C., Narayanan, S.: Robust unsupervised arousal rating: a rule-based framework with knowledge-inspired vocal features. IEEE Trans. Affect. Comput. **5**(2), 201–213 (2014)
17. Eyben, F., Weninger, F., Schuller, B.: Affect recognition in real-life acoustic conditions-a new perspective on feature selection. In: Proceedings INTERSPEECH 2013, 14th Annual Conference of the International Speech Communication Association, Lyon, France (2013)
18. Zhai, S.P., Yang, Y.Y.: Bilingual text sentiment analysis based on attention mechanism Bi-LSTM. Comput. Appl. Softw. **36**(12), 251–255 (2019)
19. Bai, S., Kolter, J.Z., Koltun, V.: An empirical evaluation of generic convolutional and recurrent networks for sequence modeling. arXiv preprint arXiv:1803.01271 (2018)
20. Lea, C., Flynn, M.D., Vidal, R., Reiter, A., Hager, G.D.: Temporal convolutional networks for action segmentation and detection, pp. 156–165 (2017)
21. Chao, Y.W., Vijayanarasimhan, S., Seybold, B., Ross, D.A., Deng, J., Sukthankar, R.: Rethinking the faster R-CNN architecture for temporal action localization. In: Proceedings of the IEEE Conference on Computer Vision and Pattern Recognition, pp. 1130–1139 (2018)
22. Khorram, S., Aldeneh, Z., Dimitriadis, D., McInnis, M., Provost, E.M.: Capturing long-term temporal dependencies with convolutional networks for continuous emotion recognition. arXiv preprint arXiv:1708.07050 (2017)

Functional Semantics Analysis in Deep Neural Networks

Ben Zhang[1,2], Gengchen Li[1,2], and Hongwei Lin[1,2(✉)]

[1] School of Mathematical Sciences, Zhejiang University, Hangzhou, China
[2] State Key Lab. of CAD & CG, Zhejiang University, Hangzhou, China
hwlin@zju.edu.cn

Abstract. Deep neural networks (DNNs) have achieved remarkable success in various domains, yet their lack of interpretability remains a critical limitation. To address this challenge, functional networks have emerged as an interpretable framework for understanding the internal workings of DNNs. Functional networks examine the statistical dependencies between activation values of neurons, thereby unraveling the functional organization of DNNs. In this work, we propose the classified functional network, which enables the analysis of the functional organization within DNN models specific to different classes of data. By introducing the distance metric between classified functional networks, we present the semantic map and hierarchical clustering as tools to delve into the functional semantic relationships within DNNs. Our results demonstrate that models exhibit similar functional organizations for classes with similar semantics. These observed semantic relationships arise from the similarity between functional connectivities, as opposed to the similarity between activation values. Furthermore, our experiments demonstrate the existence of hierarchical functional semantic relationships within DNNs. These insights into the functional organization of DNNs not only deepen our understanding of models but also provide potential avenues for enhancing their interpretability.

Keywords: Deep Neural Network · Functional Network · Semantic Map

1 Introduction

Deep neural networks (DNNs) have emerged as powerful models for solving complex problems in various domains, such as computer vision [5, 14] and natural language processing [13]. DNNs have achieved remarkable advancements, yet they suffer from a critical limitation, the lack of interpretability. The inability to understand and explain the internal workings of DNNs hampers their broader adoption [16].

To address this challenge, researchers have directed their attention towards exploring the interpretability of DNNs [9, 12, 15]. Among the various approaches proposed to uncover the inner workings of these models, functional networks have emerged as a promising framework for enhancing interpretability [15]. Functional networks examine the statistical dependencies between activation values of neurons. By breaking down the layered structure of DNNs, functional networks pave the way for graph-theoretic

© The Author(s), under exclusive license to Springer Nature Singapore Pte Ltd. 2024
D.-S. Huang et al. (Eds.): ICAI 2023, CCIS 2014, pp. 232–243, 2024.
https://doi.org/10.1007/978-981-97-0903-8_23

analysis and topological data analysis in understanding and interpreting DNNs behavior [2, 15, 17].

Building upon these advances, this study introduces the concept of classified functional networks of DNNs to explore the functional organizations of models for specific classes of data. To achieve this, we divide the dataset into sub-datasets labeled with distinct classes and construct classified functional networks accordingly. We define the classified functional distance metric to quantify the similarity between classified functional networks. Furthermore, we investigate the impact of different datasets on the functional patterns observed in DNNs.

By comparing the similarity of classified functional networks, we create a semantic map of classes to capture the semantic relationships within DNNs. The results show that models exhibit similar functional organization for classes with similar semantics.

Notably, our experiment demonstrates that the semantic relationships observed primarily result from the similarity between functional connectivities rather than the activation values alone. Finally, we reveal the functional semantic hierarchy within DNNs by introducing average functional distances between sup-classes.

By exploring the classified functional networks of DNNs, this work enhances our understanding of the working mechanisms and internal functional structures of DNNs.

The rest of the paper is organized as follows. Section 2 provides the construction of classified functional networks and the definition of functional distances between them. In Sect. 3, we present our experiments for exploring functional semantic relationships at the class level and sup-class level, and we investigate whether the semantic relationships observed in classified functional networks extend to activation patterns. Section 4 presents our conclusions and future work.

1.1 Related Work

The exploration of functional networks has garnered significant attention in recent research. Researchers have used these functional networks to illuminate the internal functional structures of DNNs, drawing inspiration from brain functional networks [15]. The exploration of functional networks has yielded valuable insights, such as the small-world properties exhibited in functionality of DNNs [15]. Graph theory and persistent homology have been employed to explain the rationale behind regularization methods [15]. Moreover, some studies have modeled functional networks as simplicial complexes and investigated the relationship between topological structures and generalization [1, 2]. Functional networks have also aided in the detection of Trojan neural networks [17] and the analysis of category relationships within models using community and centrality analysis [6]. These investigations exemplify the potential and achievements of functional networks in elucidating the inner workings of DNNs.

In the context of measuring the dissimilarity between functional networks, the field of neuroscience has put various metrics [11]. These metrics include the Hamming distance [3], graph edit distance [4], SimiNet algorithm [10], DeltaCon algorithm [7], and more. Inspired by the representational similarity analysis [9], we employ the cosine distance between the functional connectivities. The cosine distance measures the dissimilarity of the overall importance of functional connectivities in the different classified functional networks. By quantifying the dissimilarity, we can effectively assess the functional semantic relationships within DNNs.

2   Construction of Classified Functional Networks

In this section, we will present the construction of classified functional networks for the DNN M and the definition of functional distances between them. Consider a dataset $S = \{(x_i, y_i)\}$, where x_i represents a sample and y_i represents its label. Let S^l denote the subset of S that consists of samples with the label l, defined as $S^l = \{(x_i, y_i)|(x_i, y_i) \in S, y_i = l\}$.

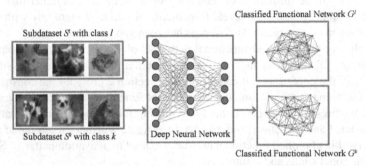

Fig. 1. Flowchart for the construction of classified functional networks.

As depicted in Fig. 1, within the context of the DNN M and the dataset S^l, the pairwise feature similarities between the neurons are computed to generate the classified functional network $G^l(V, E, W^l)$ of DNN for the l th class.

Moreover, the functional distance $d_{l,k}$ can be obtained by comparing two classified functional networks, $G^l(V, E, W^l)$ and $G^k(V, E, W^k)$. This distance quantifies the differences in functionality when the same model M processes data with labels l and k.

For certain datasets, such as CIFAR-100, semantic hierarchies exist. CIFAR-100 consists of 20 super-classes and 100 classes, with each super-class containing 5 classes. One example is the super-class "people", which includes classes like "baby", "boy", "girl", "man", and "woman". To evaluate the semantic relationship between two super-classes, the average functional distance across all classified functional networks within the two super-classes is defined.

Extracting Classified Activation Patterns. All samples in the sub-dataset S^l are fed into the model M consisting of m neurons. The model M generates an activation pattern vector $(a^l_{i,1}, a^l_{i,2}, \ldots, a^l_{i,m})$ for each sample $(x_i, y_i) \in S^l$, where $a^l_{i,j}$ represents the activation value of the j th neuron. For the convolutional layer, we consider the convolutional kernels as neurons and take the averages of the corresponding feature maps as their activation values. By considering all n_l samples, we create a classified activation pattern matrix $A^l = (a^l_{i,j})$ with dimensions $1 \le i \le n_l$ and $1 \le j \le m$. The matrix captures the extracted features of the model from the sub-dataset and records the information processing.

Calculating Functional Connectivity. Common measures of statistical dependencies between two variables include the Pearson correlation coefficient [1, 2, 15] and the Spearman correlation coefficient [6]. The former only captures the linear relationship between two variables, while the latter measures the degree of any monotonic relationship, either linear or non-linear. In this work, we utilize the Spearman correlation coefficient to measure the functional connectivity between neurons.

Given pairwise data denoted as $P = \{p_1, p_2, \ldots, p_n\}$ and $Q = \{q_1, q_2, \ldots, q_n\}$, we rank the data individually in ascending order, and the Spearman correlation coefficient is computed using the formula:

$$Spearman(P, Q) = 1 - \frac{6 \sum d_i^2}{(n^3 - n)} \tag{1}$$

where d_i represents the difference between the ranks of q_i and p_i.

To evaluate the functional connectivity between neurons, we focus on the activation patterns within the classified activation pattern matrix A^l. Each column of A^l denoted as $A_j^l = (a_{1,j}^l, a_{2,j}^l, \ldots a_{n_l,j}^l)$ represents the activation values of the j th neuron for all samples with label l. By calculating the absolute value of the Spearman correlation coefficient between A_i^l and A_j^l, we quantify the strength of functional connectivity between neurons v_i and v_j, denoted as $f_{i,j}^l$:

$$f_{i,j}^l = \left| Spearman(A_i^l, A_j^l) \right|. \tag{2}$$

The resulting strength value ranges from 0 to 1 and indicates the level of functional correlation between the two neurons.

Based on the calculated functional connectivity strengths, we construct the classified functional connectivity matrix $F^l = (f_{i,j}^l)_{1 \leq i,j \leq m}$. This matrix represents the functional network $G^l(V, E, W^l)$, which takes the form of an undirected weighted graph. The node $v_i \in V$ corresponds to the i th neuron in the model M, and the functional interaction between nodes v_i and v_j is represented by the edge $e_{i,j} \in E$. The strength of this interaction is determined by $f_{i,j}^l$, serving as the weight $w_{i,j}^l \in W^l$ of the edge $e_{i,j}$.

The graph $G^l(V, E, W^l)$ reveals functional connectivities between pairs of neurons within the DNN when processing the samples labeled as l. Thus, we can measure the difference in functionality of the DNN when processing different classes of data by the difference between classified functional networks.

Definition of Functional Distances. Given the model M and two distinct sub-datasets S^k and S^l, we construct separate classified functional networks $G^k(V, E, W^k)$ and $G^l(V, E, W^l)$. While these networks share the same nodes and edges, their weights differ, indicating different functional connectivity strengths between neurons. This disparity in connectivity strength reflects the functional dissimilarity in the model's ability to recognize objects from the k th and l th classes.

Therefore, we define the functional distance between networks as follows:

Definition 1. *(Classified Functional Distance) The distance between $G^k (V, E, W^k)$ and $G^l(V, E, W^l)$ is determined by the cosine distance between their functional connectivity strengths:*

$$d_{k,l} = 1 - \frac{\sum_{1 \le i < j \le m} (W_{ij}^k \cdot W_{ij}^l)}{\sqrt{\sum_{1 \le i < j \le m} W_{ij}^{k^2}} \sqrt{\sum_{1 \le i < j \le m} W_{ij}^{l^2}}}. \tag{3}$$

The range of the classified functional distance is between 0 and 2. The cosine distance focuses on the angle between functional connectivity strength vectors and does not take into regard their magnitude. A small classified functional distance indicates that most of the functional connectivities have similar importance in their respective classified functional networks. As a result, the two classified functional networks, G^k and G^l, have small functional differences.

Calculation of Average Functional Distances Between Super-Classes. The classified functional distance measures functional differences of the model recognizing different object classes. For the datasets with semantic hierarchies, we define the average functional distance to analyze the relationships between super-classes in the model.

Definition 2. *(Average Functional Distance) The average functional distance $\bar{d}_{i,j}$ between two super-classes I^i and I^j is defined as the average of the functional distances between all pairs of classes $k \in I^i$ and $l \in I^j$:*

$$\bar{d}_{i,j} = \frac{1}{|I^i| \times |I^j|} \sum_{k \in I^i, l \in I^j} d_{k,l}, \tag{4}$$

where $|I^i|$ represents the number of classes in the super-class I^i.

By calculating the average functional distance, we can quantify the functional similarity between two super-classes based on the functional distances among their constituent classes. A lower average functional distance indicates a higher level of functional similarity between two super-classes, suggesting stronger semantic relationships.

3   Experiments and Discussion

In this section, we present a series of experiments aiming at exploring the functionality and semantic relationships within models by analyzing classified functional distances.

The first experiment involves calculating the classified functional distances of DNNs trained on the CIFAR-10 dataset. By examining these distances, we can identify the similarity relationships and discern any semantic clusters that emerge.

In the second experiment, our objective is to investigate the factors contributing to the semantic relationships. We aim to determine whether the observed relationships arise from similarities in activation values or if they reflect genuine functional similarities within the model. By dissecting the underlying mechanisms, we can better comprehend the reasons behind the observed semantic relationships.

Additionally, we extend our investigation to explore the semantic relationships between super-classes in the model trained on the CIFAR-100 dataset. This analysis provides insights into the higher-level structure of the model and reveal the functional relationships between groups of classes within the dataset's hierarchical structure.

Through these experiments, we strive to gain a comprehensive understanding of the functionality and semantic relationships within DNNs. This analysis not only contributes to our understanding of the models but also have implications for various applications, such as improving network design, and domain-specific knowledge transfer.

3.1 Datasets and Models

In this subsection, we present the experimental setup for our study, focusing on the datasets utilized and the model architecture employed. We conduct our experiments using the CIFAR-10 and CIFAR-100 datasets, which are widely recognized benchmarks for image classification tasks.

The CIFAR-10 dataset comprises 60,000 32 × 32 RGB images categorized into ten classes, with 6,000 images per class. This dataset encompasses a diverse range of object categories, including airplanes, cars, birds, cats, and more. The CIFAR-100 dataset is an extension of CIFAR-10, consisting of 100 classes with 600 images per class. It provides a more challenging scenario, as the classes represent finer-grained categories, such as specific bird species or vehicle types.

To effectively capture the intricate features and patterns within these datasets, we leverage the Wide Residual Network (WRN-28-10) model [14]. The WRN-28-10 architecture is well-known for its capacity for handling complex image classification tasks. It has demonstrated superior performance in various image classification competitions and exhibits excellent generalization capabilities.

To train the WRN-28-10 models, we follow a training schedule of 200 epochs. The learning rate is initialized to 0.1 and decayed by a factor of 0.2 every 60 epochs, allowing for gradual fine-tuning. We employ the SGD optimizer with label smoothing.

By utilizing these benchmark datasets and the WRN-28-10 model, we aim to investigate the functionality and semantic relationships within DNNs.

3.2 Functional Semantics Between Classified Functional Networks

The CIFAR-10 dataset consists of images categorized into 10 distinct classes, including airplanes, cars, birds, cats, deer, dogs, frogs, horses, ships, and trucks. We train a WRN-28-10 model on the CIFAR-10 dataset, constructing its classified functional networks and calculating the corresponding classified functional distances. Using the classified functional distance matrix, denoted as D, we perform a comprehensive analysis to gain insights into the semantic relationships among classified functional networks.

Firstly, we create a k-nearest neighbor graph, representing the functional relationships between networks visually, as illustrated in Fig. 2(a). In this semantic map, individual networks are represented as nodes, while edges indicate high level of similarities between networks. The semantic map serves as a "network of networks", effectively illustrating the semantic relationships between classified functional networks.

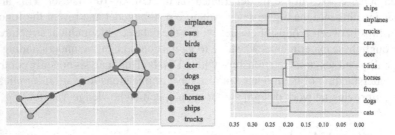

Fig. 2. (a) The semantic map is created using the classified functional distance matrix D. It is based on the functional distances for the WRN-28-10 model trained on the CIFAR-10 dataset. (b) The hierarchical clustering dendrogram illustrates the classification of classified functional networks.

On the left side of the k-nearest neighbor graph (see Fig. 2(a)), a distinct cluster of transportation-related classes (ships, airplanes, trucks, and cars) can be observed, while on the right side, a cluster representing animal-related classes (deer, birds, horses, frogs, dogs, and cats) is evident. Interestingly, an edge connects the nodes representing airplanes and birds. Despite belonging to different semantic categories, birds and airplanes display a high degree of semantic similarity in their functional patterns, indicating a potentially strong relationship between the two. The outcomes suggest that the WRN-28-10 model exhibits distinct functional patterns for different classes of data while producing similar functional patterns for semantically similar data.

Hierarchical clustering is instrumental in identifying meaningful semantic information contained within the unsupervised clustering results. Further analysis is conducted using hierarchical clustering on the classified functional networks based on the distance matrix D (see Fig. 2(b)). Notably, the 10 classified functional networks are divided into two categories: transportation (ships, airplanes, trucks, and cars) and animals (deer, birds, horses, frogs, dogs, and cats). The dendrogram further supports our findings, as it demonstrates a clear cluster structure. These clustering results provide evidence of semantic relationships within the classified functional distance matrix D.

These results highlight that even with training using solely labeled data, without explicit semantic relationships provided between classes, DNNs can learn and capture unsupervised semantic relationships resembling that of the human [10]. These findings contribute to our understanding of the functional semantics in image datasets and the capabilities of DNNs in capturing such semantics.

Semantic Relationships in Activation Patterns. Understanding the relationship between functional connectivity and activation patterns in deep neural networks is crucial for unraveling the mechanisms underlying semantic representations. We aim to investigate whether the semantic relationships observed in classified functional networks extend to activation patterns. Specifically, we explore whether classes with similar semantic relations exhibit similar activation values.

By delving into the relationship between functional similarity and activation similarity, we can gain a deeper understanding of the semantic representations they learn. This investigation will showcase whether functional connectivities or activation patterns play a more influential role in capturing semantic relationships.

To analyze the activation patterns, we calculate the activation pattern matrix A^l for the WRN-28-10 model and the l th class. Each column of A^l represents the activation value of a neuron for all samples belonging to class l. From this matrix, we compute the average activation values across columns, resulting in the average classified activation pattern $\bar{a}^l = (\bar{a}^l_1, \bar{a}^l_2, \ldots, \bar{a}^l_m)$ for the l th class. This average activation pattern serves as a representation of the features learned by the model for that class.

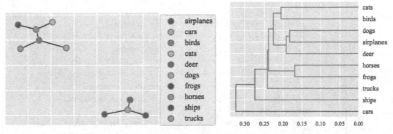

Fig. 3. (a) The semantic map is built using the distances between the average classified activation patterns. It is based on the cosine distances between the average activation patterns of the WRN-28-10 model trained on the CIFAR-10 dataset. (b) The hierarchical clustering dendrogram presents the classification of the average classified activation patterns.

Next, we construct a k-nearest neighbor graph (see Fig. 3(a)). The semantic map based on the average activation patterns does not exhibit a clear semantic structure akin to that observed in the classified functional networks. The 10 classes are divided into two separate groups, with one group clustering ships, airplanes, dogs, and deer together, while the remaining six classes form another category. Notably, there is no direct connectivity observed between birds and airplanes, or between any transportation. This suggests that the activation values alone may not sufficiently capture the semantic structure present in the dataset.

Furthermore, we perform hierarchical clustering on the classified average activation patterns and the dendrogram is depicted in Fig. 3(b). We find that some classes are clustered together despite not having strong semantic relationships. For example, airplanes and dogs are grouped. This highlights the limited extent to which semantic relationships are captured by the average activation patterns.

These findings collectively indicate that, the hierarchical clustering results and semantic map based on average activation patterns may not inherently capture the semantic relationships observed in the classified functional networks. Therefore, the functional connectivity plays a more crucial role in capturing the semantic relationships.

In conclusion, investigating the averaged classified activation patterns in relation to semantic relationships contributes to our understanding of the interplay between functional connectivities and activation patterns within DNNs. The experiment reveals the complexities of semantic representations and emphasizes the importance of considering both functional connectivities and activation patterns when analyzing the underlying mechanisms of deep neural networks.

3.3 Functional Semantics Between Sup-Classes

In this experiment, we extend our analysis to the CIFAR-100 dataset, which introduces a more complex semantic hierarchy compared to CIFAR-10. The CIFAR-100 dataset consists of 20 super-classes and 100 classes, providing a rich domain to explore semantic relationships both at the super-class level and the class level. This analysis aimed to uncover the semantic relationships between super-classes and explore the hierarchical structure within the CIFAR-100 dataset.

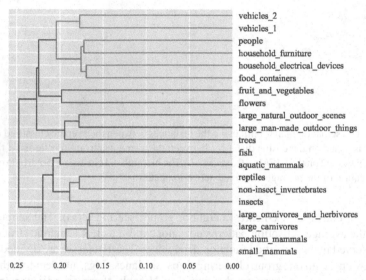

Fig. 4. The hierarchical clustering dendrogram is based on the average functional distances between sup-classes for the WRN-28-10 trained on the CIFAR-100 dataset.

We train the WRN-28-10 model on the CIFAR-100 dataset and construct its classified functional networks. The classified functional distance matrix D is then computed to represent the functional similarities among the networks. Furthermore, to reveal the semantic relationships at the sup-class level, we compute the average functional distance matrix $\overline{D}$ between super-classes and perform hierarchical clustering based on it.

Figure 4 showcases the hierarchical clustering of super-classes based on the average functional distances, revealing clear semantic relationships within the dataset. The super-classes are divided into two distinctive categories: animals and other super-classes. Within the category of animals, fish and aquatic mammals are clustered together, indicating their shared semantic characteristics related to the water habitat. Similarly, reptiles, non-insect invertebrates, and insects form another cluster, emphasizing their common biological characteristics. Additionally, small mammals, medium mammals, large omnivores and herbivores, and large carnivores are grouped.

In the category of other super-classes, fruits and vegetables are clustered with flowers, indicating their association with plants and nature. All outdoor scenes are grouped with trees, suggesting their contextual similarities. Moreover, two types of vehicles, people, household furniture, household electrical devices, and food containers are clustered, showcasing their functional and contextual affinity.

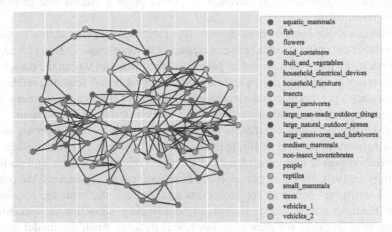

Fig. 5. The semantic map is constructed based on the average classified functional distances of the WRN-28-10 model trained on the CIFAR-100 dataset.

These findings demonstrate that the classified functional distance can effectively capture semantic relationships not only between different classes but also between various super-classes. The results highlight the expressive power of models in learning and representing category information, forming complex functional structures that align with the semantic hierarchy present in the CIFAR-100 dataset.

Additionally, we create a k-nearest neighbor graph using the classified functional distance matrix D. Figure 5 displays the visual representation of the k-nearest neighbor graph at the class level, with classes belonging to the same super-class labeled with the same color, aiding in the interpretation of the results. This graph reveals the semantic relationships among individual classes. By analyzing the connectivity and clustering patterns in the graph, we can observe how semantically related classes are grouped together, further validating the functional semantics captured by the model.

In conclusion, our functional semantic analysis on the CIFAR-100 dataset reveal meaningful semantic relationships both at the super-class level and the class level. The hierarchical clustering and semantic maps demonstrate clear cluster structures, indicating the ability of the DNN to capture semantic information and form complex functional patterns. This analysis contributes to a deeper understanding of the functional semantics within the CIFAR-100 dataset, highlighting the hierarchical and interconnected nature of the semantic relationships learned by the DNN.

3.4 Discussion

The classified functional networks explore the internal functional organization of DNNs and reveal the semantic relationships between them. We found that semantic relationships within classified functional networks are not solely determined by the similarity of activation values, but rather by the similarity between functional connectivities. This suggests that the functional organization of DNNs plays a crucial role in capturing semantic information.

Furthermore, our analysis demonstrates that DNNs possess the ability to generate unsupervised semantic relations between classes and super-classes. This indicates that these models can discover meaningful patterns and similarities within the data, beyond what is explicitly specified during training. Such unsupervised semantic relationships provide a unique perspective on the learning capabilities of DNNs and offer the potential for various downstream applications, including data clustering and generation.

Additionally, our study contributes to the existing literature by comparing our approach to the work of Horta et al. [6]. In their exploration of semantic relationships using a co-activation graph, they constructed the graph on the entire dataset and performed community analysis. However, our approach differs in several key aspects. We construct classified functional networks for each class and analyze the semantic relationships based on the functional distances. Importantly, our findings show that the semantic relationships arise from the differences in functional patterns when the model processes different datasets, rather than depending solely on the output neurons.

While our study provides valuable insights into the functional semantics of DNNs, it is important to acknowledge its limitations. Our analysis is focused on the CIFAR datasets, and further investigations on other datasets and models are necessary to validate and generalize our findings. Additionally, while functional networks provide interpretability [8], they may not fully capture the complex dynamics and representations within networks. Future research can explore more comprehensive frameworks for modeling deep neural networks to further capture functional semantics.

In conclusion, the study of functional semantics in deep neural networks provides valuable insights into the internal organization and semantic relationships of models.

4 Conclusions

In this work, we have presented an in-depth exploration of functional semantics in deep neural networks. We introduce classified functional networks and functional distances to understand the internal functional organization of DNNs and uncover functional semantic relationships when processing specific classes. Our analysis reveals that DNNs are capable of generating unsupervised semantic relations between classes and between super-classes. Moreover, we found that the semantic relationships between classified functional networks are not solely determined by the similarity of activation values, while they arise from the similarity in functional connectivities. This suggests that the functional organization of DNNs plays a crucial role in capturing semantic relationships and should be considered when interpreting their performance and understanding their internal mechanisms.

The fact that classified functional networks have the same nodes and edges provides great convenience for us to further explore the differences of DNNs when processing different classes of data. One future research direction is to reveal the mechanism of DNNs by comparing classified functional networks to find the neurons or functional connectivities that have the great impact on a specific class and explain their functions.

Acknowledgements. This work is supported by the National Natural Science Foundation of China under Grant Nos. 62272406, 61872316.

References

1. Corneanu, C.A., Escalera, S., Martinez, A.M.: Computing the testing error without a testing set. In: 2020 IEEE/CVF Conference on Computer Vision and Pattern Recognition, pp. 2674–2682 (2020)
2. Corneanu, C.A., Madadi, M., Escalera, S., Martinez, A.M.: What does it mean to learn in deep networks? and, how does one detect adversarial attacks? In: 2019 IEEE/CVF Conference on Computer Vision and Pattern Recognition, pp. 4752–4761 (2019)
3. Deza, M.M., Deza, E.: Voronoi diagram distances. Encyclopedia of Distances, pp. 339–347 (2013)
4. Gao, X., Xiao, B., Tao, D., Li, X.: A survey of graph edit distance. Pattern Anal. Appl. **13**, 113–129 (2010)
5. He, K., Zhang, X., Ren, S., Sun, J.: Deep residual learning for image recognition. In: 2016 IEEE Conference on Computer Vision and Pattern Recognition, pp. 770–778 (2016)
6. Horta, V.A., Tiddi, I., Little, S., Mileo, A.: Extracting knowledge from deep neural networks through graph analysis. Futur. Gener. Comput. Syst. **120**, 109–118 (2021)
7. Koutra, D., Shah, N., Vogelstein, J.T., Gallagher, B., Faloutsos, C.: DeltaCon: principled massive-graph similarity function with attribution. ACM Trans. Knowl. Discov. Data **10**(3) (2016)
8. Kriegeskorte, N., Mur, M., Bandettini, P.: Representational similarity analysis - connecting the branches of systems neuroscience. Front. Syst. Neurosci. **2** (2008)
9. Mehrer, J., Spoerer, C.J., Kriegeskorte, N., Kietzmann, T.C.: Individual differences among deep neural network models. Nat. Commun. **11**(1), 5725 (2020)
10. Mheich, A., Hassan, M., Khalil, M., Gripon, V., Dufor, O., Wendling, F.: SimiNet: a novel method for quantifying brain network similarity. IEEE Trans. Pattern Anal. Mach. Intell. **40**(9), 2238–2249 (2017)
11. Mheich, A., Wendling, F., Hassan, M.: Brain network similarity: methods and applications. Netw. Neurosci. **4**(3), 507–527 (2020)
12. Morcos, A., Barrett, D., Rabinowitz, N., Botvinick, M.: On the importance of single directions for generalization. In: 6th International Conference on Learning Representations (2018)
13. Vaswani, A., et al.: Attention is all you need. In: Proceedings of the 31st International Conference on Neural Information Processing Systems, vol. 30, pp. 6000–6010 (2017)
14. Zagoruyko, S., Komodakis, N.: Wide residual networks. In: Proceedings of the British Machine Vision Conference, pp. 87.1–87.2 (2016)
15. Zhang, B., Dong, Z., Zhang, J., Lin, H.: Functional network: a novel framework for interpretability of deep neural networks. Neurocomputing **519**, 94–103 (2023)
16. Zhang, Q., Zhu, S.: Visual interpretability for deep learning: a survey. Front. Inf. Technol. Electron. Eng. **19**(1), 27–39 (2018)
17. Zheng, S., Zhang, Y., Wagner, H., Goswami, M., Chen, C.: Topological detection of trojaned neural networks. In: Advances in Neural Information Processing Systems, vol. 34, pp. 17258–17272 (2021)

FDA-PointNet++: A Point Cloud Classification Model Based on Fused Downsampling Strategy and Attention Module

Wei Sun[1], Peipei Gu[1], Yijie Pan[2(✉)], Junxia Ma[1], Jiantao Cui[1], and Pujie Han[1]

[1] Zhengzhou University of Light Industry, Zhengzhou 450000, China
[2] Eastern Institute for Advanced Study, Eastern Institute of Technology, Ningbo 315000, China
ypan@eitech.edu.cn

Abstract. In recent years, the use of deep learning models for point cloud classification and segmentation tasks has increasingly become a hot topic in 3D point cloud research. However, the sparsity and inhomogeneity of point cloud data make it difficult to extract point cloud features. Meanwhile, how to effectively extract fine-grained local features becomes crucial in point cloud understanding. Therefore, in this study, we propose a novel FDA-PointNet++ point cloud classification model based on fusion downsampling strategy and attention module. Firstly, the method proposes a fusion downsampling strategy, which performs hierarchical downsampling on the initial point cloud data, and then repeats the downsampling operation on the sampling results and performs feature fusion to form feature maps with multi-scale information to enhance the richness of local spatial point cloud feature information. Secondly, we incorporate a channel attention mechanism into PointNet++ and propose a Local Feature Aggregation (LFA) module for point cloud local feature extraction. This method improves the local feature extraction capability of the network model by amplifying the relevant local features and suppressing the non-relevant features. Experimental results on the ModelNet40 dataset demonstrate that FDA-PointNet++ achieves higher classification accuracy and robustness, with a 1.3% increase in overall accuracy (OA) and a 1.4% improvement in class accuracy.

Keywords: Point Cloud Classification · Deep Learning · Channel Attention Mechanism · Point Cloud Downsampling

1 Introduction

With the rapid development of sensors such as LiDAR and depth cameras, the difficulty and cost of acquiring point cloud data has been dramatically reduced. Point cloud is the most common data type for representing 3D spatial objects, which has the characteristics of completeness and richness compared to voxels, meshes and other data types, and is widely used in 3D reconstruction, autonomous driving SLAM, AR, VR, and other fields. Recently, point cloud classification and point cloud segmentation for point cloud data processing, as well as point cloud semantic segmentation tasks for large scenes have gradually become research hotspots.

© The Author(s), under exclusive license to Springer Nature Singapore Pte Ltd. 2024
D.-S. Huang et al. (Eds.): ICAI 2023, CCIS 2014, pp. 244–255, 2024.
https://doi.org/10.1007/978-981-97-0903-8_24

In recent years, deep learning has become one of the important research tools in the fields of computer vision and computer graphics due to its powerful feature learning capability. Therefore, more and more work has been devoted to applying deep learning methods for the purpose of extracting features directly from 3D point cloud data in order to accomplish classification and segmentation tasks. However, point cloud data, due to its own disordered and non-uniform characteristics makes the application of using traditional deep learning algorithms still difficult in point cloud processing tasks. With the advent of PointNet [1] and PointNet++ [2] networks, we have a whole new direction of thinking. Borrowing from image convolution, we can define point cloud convolution and thus solve the challenges in point cloud data processing tasks. Despite the satisfactory performance achieved by PointNet++ thus far, there still remains room for potential improvements and enhancements. We note that similar to image convolutional feature extraction, local spatial fine-grained features of the point cloud data are important for the global features of the overall point cloud. By incorporating an attention mechanism, it is possible to effectively enhance the feature extraction capability of the local feature extractor. Specifically, we obtain updated global features by assigning weights to those convolutional channels that are more sensitive to specific features in order to enhance or suppress the spatial context information of local features. Based on this premise, we introduce FDA-PointNet++ as our proposed method and further enhance its performance.

We propose a new local feature attention module (LFA-block) for point clouds. Similar to image convolution, we note that the extraction of spatially localized features is often related to the channel features of the convolution kernel. Therefore, we designed this simple and effective local channel attention module as shown in Fig. 1. This method amplifies relevant features in local features while reducing feature redundancy. Our designed modules can be flexibly added to the local feature aggregation module of the network.

We propose a fused downsampling strategy for data augmentation, along with the utilization of a more efficient network optimization strategy to enhance our network model. This strategy achieves its goal mainly by resampling the point cloud data. After the initial downsampling, we perform hierarchical resampling on the local regions of the point cloud data. The resampled features are then concatenated with the initially sampled features to capture the global characteristics of the original point cloud.

In our experimental section, we show the classification effect of FDA-PointNet++. Overall, our design of FDA-PointNet++ performs well in the shape object classification task. Meanwhile, the ablation study of the FDA module shows that the local feature grouping attention mechanism significantly improves its ability to extract local geometric features.

2 Relate Work

In recent years, researchers have proposed various methods for point cloud processing, primarily categorized into multi-view-based, voxel-based, point-based, and graph-based approaches.

Multi-view-based approach: The multi-view-based approach uses image data from multiple viewpoints to project a 3D point cloud onto a 2D base plane to obtain a regular feature representation of the point cloud in 2D space [3]. SU et al. [4] in their work first proposed the Multi-view CNN model, which is the first model to using the idea of multiple views. QI et al. [5] introduced the concept of multiscale into the processing of point clouds by adding a multiresolution filtering module to enhance the extraction of information from the model.

Voxel-based approach: The voxel-based approach represents the 3D point cloud as a structured voxel mesh and extracts spatial geometric features using a 3D-CNN convolutional neural network.3DshapeNet [6] uses 3D convolution for voxel modelling, which translates geometric 3D shapes into variable probability distributions in a 3D voxel mesh, and uses a convolutional neural network to extract features.

Graph-based approach: The graph-based approach encodes the relative positional relationships of the points in the point cloud by converting the point cloud data into a graph structure [7], where each point is represented as a node of the graph and the relationships between the points are represented as edges, which will abstract the global feature signature of the full point cloud. DGCNN [8] is a convolutional neural network based on dynamic graphs to handle classification and segmentation tasks on point cloud data. It uses the KNN algorithm to construct neighborhood relationships between point clouds and performs convolutional operations in the dynamic graph to extract features.

Point-based approach: The point-based approach directly inputs the raw point cloud into the network for feature learning. The PointNet [1] network is a milestone in advancing the task of deep learning of point clouds. PointNet uses a simple shared MLP along with a maximum pooling function to form a feature extraction network. PCT [9] introduces a Transformer-based architecture specifically designed for point clouds, which uses a self-attention mechanism instead of a convolutional layer to capture long-range dependencies in point clouds.

3   Method

3.1   PointNet++ Network Structure

PointNet++ can be considered as an iterative enhancement of the PointNet model. Building upon the foundation established by PointNet, PointNet++ introduces several key improvements to further enhance the capabilities of point cloud processing. We start by reviewing the PointNet model.

PointNet uses the features of the original point cloud to compute the mapping of the point cloud through a deep neural network. The network maps each individual point of the input point cloud from low to high dimensions and then performs feature learning. This process mainly consists of upscaling the feature matrix by shared multilayer perceptron, then the network maps all the features to the high dimensional space and finally represents the global features by maximum pooling. We finally obtain k-dimensional features used to score the classes of the point cloud model. PointNet faces challenges in effectively capturing fine-grained features for global understanding due to the lack of local context. At the same time, the lack of local context hinders the network's ability to discern the intricate details and relationships between different parts of the point cloud, leading to significant limitations in achieving part segmentation as well.

By adopting a hierarchical structure and multi-scale grouping, PointNet++ can better capture the complex details of point cloud data, solving the problem of PointNet's inability to capture local features and generalize to complex scenes. Figure 1 shows the basic architecture of our improved network model FDA-PointNet++ based on PointNet++.

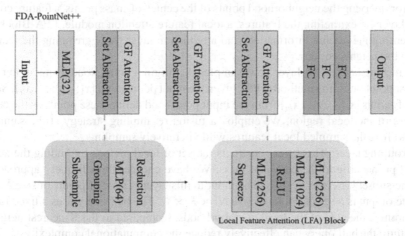

Fig. 1. FDA-PointNet++ adopts a similar network architecture to PointNet++ by using a hierarchical structure and grouping operation, using a fusion downsampling strategy to divide all the point cloud features into local point cloud features, and then encoding the local features into a local abstraction encoding with high-dimensional features through the feature aggregation module. As shown in the figure, the feature aggregation module contains the downsampling module, the grouping module, the MLP module and the attention abstraction module. We will describe our hierarchical structure and local attention module in more detail below.

3.2 Hierarchical Local Feature Attention

In the field of computer vision and deep learning, the introduction of the attention mechanism can effectively improve the performance of the model and has been applied in many tasks such as classification, target detection, semantic segmentation, etc. By incorporating an attention weighting module, it is possible to compute adaptive weights for the overall features and propagate their weighting information to the global features for feature information updating [21]. The attention mechanism greatly improves the performance of many computer vision tasks and is used in many applications such as classification, target detection, and semantic segmentation.

Similar to the image convolution process, we propose a local feature attention module called LFA-Block. We adopt the channel attention mechanism of image convolution, which is a very efficient attention module [22]. The LFA-Block module (Local Feature Attention) uses the channel attention mechanism to amplify relevant local features while suppressing irrelevant features. With this approach, we enhance the ability of the network to extract fine-grained local features, which helps to achieve more accurate and robust point cloud classification.

In order to aggregate features across the entire point set as much as possible, we use a hierarchical structure to aggregate contextual information in local regions. The hierarchical structure we use can be summarized as an SA module (Set Abstraction Module), [11] which is similar to the hierarchical structure used in PointNet++. Each SA module consists of a sampling layer for downsampling the point cloud data, a grouping layer for querying the neighborhood points of the center-of-mass points, a feature coding MLP layer for extracting the features, a local feature attention module, LFA-Block, for augmenting the feature information, and a reduction layer for aggregating the features within the neighborhoods.

Sampling layer: This layer downsamples the original point cloud using an iterative farthest point sampling method (FPS), given the input point cloud $\{x_1, x_2, \ldots, x_n\}$, Select a set of points $\{x_i, x_j, \ldots, x_m\}$ from the input points and define these points as the center of mass of the local region. We employ a fusion resampling strategy at the sampling layer to fuse the sampled local features while iteratively sampling.

Grouping layer: This layer constructs the set of local regions by finding the neighboring points around the center of mass. We have chosen the ball query approach to find the subset $\{x_{i1}, x_{i2}, \ldots, x_{ik}\}$. The input to this layer is a set of points of size $N \times C$ and the output is a set of points of size $N' \times K \times C$. The ball query uses a fixed radius to guarantee the size of the local neighborhoods. Compared to the K-nearest neighbor algorithm, the ball query can effectively reduce the computational complexity.

MLP layer: In the MLP layer of our FDA-PointNet++ model, we still adopt the network structure of PointNet. We utilize continuous convolution to encode the features of local centroids and their neighboring points, resulting in local feature vectors. This approach allows us to effectively capture and encode the local information within the point cloud data.

LFA-Block Module: This module leverages a channel attention mechanism to amplify relevant local features while suppressing irrelevant ones. By doing so, it enhances the network's capability to extract fine-grained local features, contributing to more accurate and robust point cloud classification.

Reduction layer: We are using the maximum value of the local feature map as the maximum feature of the local grouping, and abstracting the global features that cover the whole point cloud by aggregating the local maximum features (Fig. 2).

3.3   Fused Downsampling Strategy

In the FDA-PointNet++ model we retained the practice of local grouping of all point clouds and optimized the size of the grouping and the MLP process, as well as introduced a fused downsampling strategy to resample the point cloud data to enhance the local point cloud spatial context information and prevent network overfitting.

The fusion downsampling strategy consists of two main steps, resampling of local point cloud features and fusion of hierarchically sampled features [15]. We get as a local center of mass point set after initial downsampling of the point cloud according to the hierarchical structure, by querying the corresponding neighboring points according to the group size and adding them to the local feature point set. When we do the grouping, we will set 3 different size ranges for the same point and query three different size local ranges at the same time, and within the ranges we select the same number of points

Hierarchical Local Feature Attention

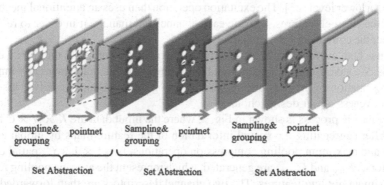

Fig. 2. Hierarchical Local Feature Attention Module, containing SA module and LFA-Block module, encodes local features through hierarchical structure and grouping operation to obtain global feature information with multi-level feature information of different regions. For example, the two green modules representing the original data and the results of grouped sampling go through the MLP layer and the attention module to get a new feature map blue module, yellow module representing the LFA-Block, which is continuously convolved by layering and grouping to get richer global features (Color figure online)

[18]. Therefore, we can get the multi-scale point cloud features in spatial angle, and we fuse their features, exactly connect to get the feature maps with richer local feature information, and this method is very helpful for extracting the fine-grained features of the point cloud.

We note that the size and number of groups have a significant impact on the performance of the network [20]. Since the features we feed into the network to learn are local features that have been downsampled, too many clustered local groups will further make it difficult for the network to learn the global features of the point cloud and thus overfitting occurs. Therefore, we try to use smaller groups while keeping the number of groups constant when designing the network.

It is worth noting that before we input the raw point cloud data into the network for feature extraction, we subjected the point cloud data to MLP operations to enhance its feature dimension from 3 to 32 dimensions. This approach [13] improves the richness of the spatial feature information of the raw point cloud, so we can obtain more local contextual features in the subsequent operations.

3.4 Adaptive Thresholding of Squeezed-And-Excitation

The LFA-Block Module draws on the basic design of the Squeeze and Excitation Network (SENet) [12] network. The network recalibrates features by adaptively modelling explicit correlations between channels. SENet consists of two steps: the squeezing operation and the excitation operation. The squeeze operation compresses a high-dimensional feature map with an input size of $K \times N \times C$ into a $1 \times 1 \times C$ channel descriptor by compressing the spatial dimensions. This descriptor effectively captures the global distribution of each channel feature on the feature map, while balancing the global information at a lower level [23]. The excitation operation then uses an attentional mechanism to learn the channel features, activate each channel and manage it in order to re-weight or correct the convolved feature map.

We use both average pooling and maximum pooling to compress the spatial dimension [14]. We have empirically confirmed that using these two features greatly improves the representation of the network, rather than using each one individually. This shows the effectiveness of our design choices.

The specific process is shown in Fig. 3, where the input data are $K \times N \times C$ feature maps. After aggregating the spatial information of the feature maps by global average pooling and maximum pooling compression operations, two $1 \times 1 \times C$ spatial context descriptors, F^c_{avg} and F^c_{max} are generated, which represent the average pooling features and maximum pooling features. The two channel descriptors are then forwarded to the shared network for mapping [19]. The shared network includes Batch Normalization (BN), ReLU activation functions, convolution operations and Sigmoid functions. The convolutional part contains three shared MLPs, in order to reduce the parameters of the shared MLPs, the size of the hidden activation layer is designed as, $C/r \times 1 \times 1$, where r is the reduction ratio. we set different reduction ratios for different sizes of local features. After passing through the shared MLPs, we merge the output attention weights using elemental summation. Finally, a multiplication operation is performed between the channel attention Mc and the feature map F to generate the global features obtained after the input feature map F operation required by the spatial attention mechanism.

$$\mathbf{M_c}(F) = \sigma\left(MLP(AvgPool(\mathbf{F})) + MLP(MaxPool(\mathbf{F}))\right)$$
$$= \sigma\left(\mathbf{W}_1\left(\mathbf{W}_0\left(\mathbf{F^c_{avg}}\right)\right) + \mathbf{W}_1\left(\mathbf{W}_0\left(\mathbf{F^c_{max}}\right)\right)\right), \tag{1}$$

$$F' = \mathbf{M_c} * F \tag{2}$$

where σ denotes the sigmoid function, $\mathbf{W}_0 \in \mathbb{R}^{C/r \times C}$, and $\mathbf{W}_1 \in \mathbb{R}^{C \times C/r}$. Note that the MLP weights, $\mathbf{W}_0$ and $\mathbf{W}_1$, are shared for both inputs and the ReLU activation function is followed by $\mathbf{W}_0$.

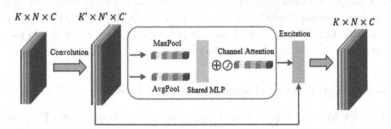

Fig. 3. Channel Attention Module. Where as shown in the figure, the LFA-Block uses the maximum pooling and the average pooling, which are fused together after shared MLP and sigmoid layer activation to get the channel attention weights we need. After the incentive mechanism, the weights are assigned to the original input data features to obtain a new feature map.

4 Experiment

In order to verify the effectiveness of the proposed FDA-PointNet++ in processing 3D point cloud classification, this experiment implements the classification task on the ModelNet40 [6] dataset. ModelNet40 is a commonly used 3D object classification dataset. The dataset contains 12,311 CAD models in 40 categories, each containing 100 unique CAD models. We use 9843 officially classified shapes for training and 2468 shapes for testing (Tables 1 and 2).

Table 1. Experimental environment configuration

Title	Environmental parameters
Operating system	Ubuntu 20.04
CPU	Xeon(R) Platinum 8255C
Server GPU	NVIDIA RTX 3080(10 GB)
RAM	40 GB
Programming language	Python 3.8
Deep learning frameworks	Pytorch 1.11.0, CUDA 11.3

Table 2. Experimental hyperparameter settings

Number of sampling points	1024
Optimizer	Adam
Epoch	200
Batch Size	16
Decay_rate	0.0001
Learning_rate	0.001
Number of sampling points	1024

Our experimental environment is configured in the following table. During the training process, our initial learning rate is set to 0.001, the size of batchsize is set to 16, epoch is set to 200 times, and the network optimizer is selected as Adam [16].

During our experiments, we sampled 1024 points for each object using iterative farthest point sampling (FPS) as input to the network. The features we use for the input point cloud are only the XYZ coordinates of the points. Our network model is evaluated by multiple validations on both training and test sets. We use Overall Accuracy and Class Accuracy as the evaluation metrics of the model.

By comparing the different models (shown in Table 3), it can be seen that our model achieves the highest overall accuracy and class accuracy under the condition of using only the XYZ coordinates of 1024 points as feature input. This shows that our model

Table 3. Comparison of Class Acc and Overall Acc for multiple models on ModelNet40

Methods	Input	Overall Accuracy(%)	Class Accuracy(%)
PointNet [1]	Point	89.2	86.2
PointNet++ [2]	Point	91.9	89.8
PointCNN [17]	Point	92.2	88.1
DGCNN [8]	Point	92.7	90.4
SpiderCNN [10]	Point	92.4	90.3
FDA-PointNet++	Point	**93.2**	**91.2**

is able to effectively using the limited feature input to achieve excellent performance in tasks such as classification. Our model improves overall accuracy by 1.3% and avg class accuracy by 1.4% on PointNet++.

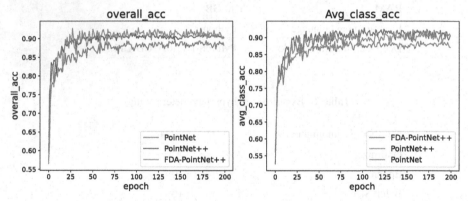

Fig. 4. Comparing with PointNet & PointNet++ models.

As shown in Fig. 4, We give a performance comparison graph between PointNet and PointNet++. We have used the blue line in both graphs to represent our FDA-PointNet++ model, and we can see that the performance of our model is greatly improved compared to the PointNet model. Our results are also consistently ahead compared to the PointNet++ model.

We also tested the robustness of the FDA-PointNet++ model, where 1024, 800, 600, 400, and 200 points were randomly selected as inputs to the trained model to perform the classification task on the test set. As shown in Fig. 5, it can be seen that when the point cloud data is a little missing, our model can still maintain high accuracy and always outperforms PointNet++, which also indicates that our increased density network has better robustness and stronger point cloud feature learning ability.

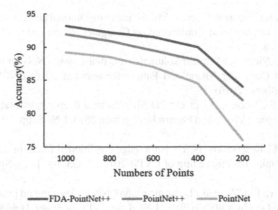

Fig. 5. Relationship between number of input points and accuracy

5 Conclusion

We propose a novel FDA-PointNet++ point cloud classification model based on fusion downsampling strategy and attention module, and evaluated it on the public Model-Net40 dataset. FDA-PointNet++ can extract local features more accurately than Point-Net++ by introducing a channel attention mechanism to suppress irrelevant features and enhance important features. Meanwhile, it uses a fusion downsampling strategy for data enhancement. The experimental results validate the effectiveness of the network in the classification task. In the classification task, the overall classification accuracy (OA) of FDA-PointNet++ reaches 95.5% on ModelNet10 and 93.2% on ModelNet40. The experiments demonstrate the effectiveness of our proposed local attention module and strategy.

Acknowledgements. This work was supported by Young Tech Innovation Leading Talent Program of Ningbo City under Grant No. 2023QL008; Innovation Consortium Program for Green and Efficient Intelligent Appliance of Ningbo City under Grant No. 2022H002; The Industrial Science and Technology Research Project of Henan Province under Grants 232102210088, 232102210125, 222102210024.

References

1. Qi, C.R., Su, H., Ma, K., et al.: PointNet: deep learning on point sets for 3D classification and segmentation. In: Computer Vision and Pattern Recognition 2017, LNCS, pp. 72–85. Springer, Heidelberg (2017)
2. Qi, C.R., Yi, L., Su, H., et al.: PointNet++: deep hierarchical feature learning on point sets in a metric space. In: Advances in Neural Information Processing Systems 2017, LNCS, pp. 1–13. Springer, Heidelberg (2017)
3. Gu, P., et al.: Multi-head self-attention model for classification of temporal lobe epilepsy subtypes. In: Proceedings of the Frontiers in Physiology 11 2020, LNCS, pp. 1–13. Springer, Heidelberg (2020)

4. Su, H., Maji, S., Kalogerakis, E., et al.: Multi-view convolutional neural networks for 3D shape recognition. In: International Conference on Computer Vision 2015, LNCS, pp. 945–953. Springer, Heidelberg (2015)
5. Qi, C.R., Su, H., Niebner, M., et al.: Volumetric and multi-view CNNs for object classification on 3d data. In: Computer Vision and Pattern Recognition 2016, LNCS, pp. 5648–5656. Springer, Heidelberg (2016)
6. Wu, Z., Song, S., Khosla, A., et al.: 3D ShapeNets: a deep representation for volumetric shapes. In: Computer Vision and Pattern Recognition 2015, LNCS, pp. 1912–1920. Springer, Heidelberg (2015)
7. Simonovsky, M., Komodakis, N. Dynamic edge-conditioned filters in convolutional neural networks on graphs. In: Proceeding of CVPR 2017, LNCS, pp. 1–13. Springer, Heidelberg (2017)
8. Wang, Y., Sun, Y., Liu, Z., et al.: Dynamic graph CNN for learning on point clouds. In: ACM Transactions on Graphics (TOG) 2019, LNCS, pp. 1–12. Springer, Heidelberg (2019)
9. Guo, M.H., Cai, J.X., Liu, Z.N., et al.: PCT: point cloud transformer. In: Computational Visual Media 2021, LNCS, pp. 187–199. Springer, Heidelberg (2021)
10. Xu, Y., Fan, T., Xu, M., et al.: SpiderCNN: deep learning on point sets with parameterized convolutional filters. In: Proceedings of the European Conference on Computer Vision (ECCV) 2018, LNCS, pp. 87–102. Springer, Heidelberg (2018)
11. Qian, G., Li, Y., Peng, H., et al.: PointNext: revisiting PointNet++ with improved training and scaling strategies. In: Advances in Neural Information Processing Systems 2022, LNCS, pp. 23192–23204. Springer, Heidelberg (2022)
12. Hu, J., Shen, L., Sun, G.: Squeeze-and-excitation networks. In: Proceedings of the IEEE Conference on Computer Vision and Pattern Recognition 2018, LNCS, pp. 7132–7141. Springer, Heidelberg (2018)
13. Woo, S., Park, J., Lee, J.Y., et al.: CBAM: convolutional block attention module. In: Proceedings of the European Conference on Computer Vision (ECCV) 2018, LNCS, pp. 3–19. Springer, Heidelberg (2018)
14. Guo, J., et al.: Automatic and accurate epilepsy ripple and fast ripple detection via virtual sample generation and attention neural networks. In: IEEE Transactions on Neural Systems and Rehabilitation Engineering 2020, LNCS, pp. 1710–1719. Springer, Heidelberg (2020)
15. Guo, J.: Detecting high-frequency oscillations for Stereoelectroencephalography in epilepsy via hypergraph learning. In: IEEE Transactions on Neural Systems and Rehabilitation Engineering 2021, LNCS, pp. 587–596. Springer, Heidelberg (2021)
16. Kingma, D.P., Ba, J.: Adam: a method for stochastic optimization. In: International Conference on Learning Representations (ICLR) 2015, LNCS, pp. 1–13. Springer, Heidelberg (2015)
17. Li, Y., Bu, R., Sun, M., et al.: PointCNN: convolution on x-transformed points. In: Advances in Neural Information Processing Systems 2018, LNCS, pp. 1–13. Springer, Heidelberg (2018)
18. Peng, X., Long, G., Shen, T., Wang, S., Jiang, J.: Sequential diagnosis prediction with transformer and ontological representation. In: 2021 IEEE International Conference on Data Mining (ICDM), LNCS, pp. 489–498. Springer, Heidelberg (2021)
19. Peng, X., Long, G., Yan, P., et al.: COVID-19 impact analysis on patients with complex health conditions: a literature review. In: 2023, LNCS, pp. 1–13. Springer, Heidelberg (2023)
20. Chen, D., et al.: Scalp EEG-based pain detection using convolutional neural network. In: IEEE Transactions on Neural Systems and Rehabilitation Engineering 2022, LNCS, pp. 1–13. Springer, Heidelberg (2022)
21. Peng, X., Long, G., Shen, T., Wang, S., Jiang, J., Zhang, C.: BiteNet: bidirectional temporal encoder network to predict medical outcomes. In: 2020 IEEE International Conference on Data Mining (ICDM), LNCS, pp. 1–13. Springer, Heidelberg (2020)

22. Niu, K., Guo, Z., Peng, X., et al.: P-ResUNet: segmentation of brain tissue with purified residual UNet. In: Computers in Biology and Medicine 2022, LNCS, pp. 1–13. Springer, Heidelberg (2022)
23. Niu, K., Lu, Y., Peng, X., et al.: Fusion of Sequential Visits and Medical Ontology for Mortality Prediction. In: Journal of Biomedical Informatics 2022, LNCS, pp. 1–13. Springer, Heidelberg (2022)

Collision Detection Method Based on Improved Whale Optimization Algorithm

Zixu Yang(✉), Junxia Ma, Peipei Gu, Jiantao Cui, and Pujie Han

Zhengzhou University of Light Industry, Zhengzhou 450000, China
jxma@zzuli.edu.cn

Abstract. Collision detection is an important problem in the field of computer graphics. In order to achieve efficient collision detection in large-scale object collections, this paper proposes a collision detection method based on the improved Whale Optimization Algorithm (WOA) and Axis-aligned Bounding Box (AABB). The method firstly determines the optimal enclosing box size to avoid repeated calculations; secondly, it uses AABB enclosing box to describe the geometrical information of the objects and initially detects whether the objects are intersecting or not, and then introduces Levy's flight strategy, adaptive weights, and adaptive learning factors into the optimization searching process of the improved whale optimization algorithm, which makes the collision detection method have stronger adaptivity and stability. Experiments show that the collision detection method based on the improved whale optimization algorithm has higher detection efficiency than the traditional method when dealing with a large-scale object collection, and the method exhibits superior optimization seeking ability compared with the traditional algorithm.

Keywords: Collision detection · Whale Optimization Algorithm · Levy Flight Strategy · adaptive weighting · Adaptive Learning Factor · AABB Surrounding Box

1 Introduction

The purpose of collision detection is to detect whether two or more objects intersect with each other. It is a key problem in the research fields of 3D games, synthetic images, computer graphics, virtual simulation and so on. The common collision detection algorithms are wraparound box algorithm, sphere detection algorithm and polygon detection algorithm. Among them, the wraparound box method is widely used because it is fast as well as has some scalability and accuracy advantages. Currently, the commonly used bounding box techniques are Axis-aligned Bounding Box (AABB), Oriented Bounding Box (OBB), Sphere Bounding Box, K-DOPs Bounding Box, etc. [1].

With the continuous development of virtual reality technology, a large number of valuable research results have been achieved for collision detection. Hu et al. [2] proposed a convex packet-based minimum volume OBB enclosing box generation algorithm, which is used to quickly generate the minimum OBB enclosing box with good fitting

D.-S. Huang et al. (Eds.): ICAI 2023, CCIS 2014, pp. 256–267, 2024.
https://doi.org/10.1007/978-981-97-0903-8_25

effect. Jin Yanxia et al. [3] proposed a circular enveloping box without thickness, which has obvious advantages in the scenarios with enough self-collisions. WANG et al.[4] proposed a new method for constructing OBB enveloping box, which speeds up the efficiency of collision detection by optimizing the level of solving the solid mesh model. These algorithms also have certain defects, for example, the construction of the surround box for the object is too large resulting in a higher false detection rate. This problem can be solved by using the hybrid envelope detection technique, which uses the simple Sphere envelope, AABB envelope and the relatively complex OBB envelope and k-DOPs envelope to construct the hybrid envelope, which can improve the accuracy and efficiency of detection [5]. Hui xuewu et al. [6] used the bracket box technique and particle swarm optimization algorithm to enhance the secondary collision detection of objects, and this detection method improves the accuracy and efficiency of collision detection. In this paper, we use a combination of the whale algorithm and the enveloping box algorithm for collision detection, which can significantly improve the efficiency of detection compared to the traditional collision detection.

2 Object Collision Detection Model

Assume that there exist objects A and B in the multidimensional space, where the ith dimensional feature $a_i \in A$ of object A, i takes the range of values ($1 \leqslant i \leqslant n$), and the j th dimensional feature $b_j \in B$ of object B, j takes the range of values ($1 \leq j \leq n$), where n represents the total number of dimensions. Assuming that the set $F(p)$ is used to represent the object A and object B like feature distance, object A and object B are considered to collide if $F(p)$ min is less than the collision threshold £.

Representing the velocity of an object by the set V [7], the set of velocities of object A and object B can be expressed by Eq. (1):

$$V = \{V_a, V_b\} = \left\{ \left(v_{ax}, v_{ay}, v_{az} \right), \left(v_{bx}, v_{by}, v_{bz} \right) \right\} \tag{1}$$

where, v_{ax}, v_{ay}, v_{az} represent the velocity of object A in X, Y, Z axes respectively, and v_{bx}, v_{by}, v_{bz} represent the velocity of object B in X, Y, Z axes respectively. Representing the positions of the objects by the set X, the set of positions of object A and object B can be expressed by Eq. (2):

$$X = \{X_a, X_b\} = \{(x_a, y_a, z_a), (x_b, y_b, z_b)\} \tag{2}$$

where x_a, y_a, z_a represent the coordinates of object A on the X, Y, and Z axes, respectively, and x_b, y_b, z_b represent the coordinates of object B on the X, Y, and Z axes, respectively. Representing the set of distances in three-dimensional space by the set F, the quadratic set of distances between object A and object B can be represented as follows:

$$F(X_a, X_b) = \left(x_a - x_b \right)^2 + \left(y_a - y_b \right)^2 + \left(z_a - z_b \right)^2 \tag{3}$$

where $F(X_a, X_b)$ is used as the spatial distance fitness function, and $x_a, y_a, z_a, x_b, y_b, z_b$ represent the positional coordinates of object A and object B. In order to simplify the arithmetic, this paper does not square the distance function.

3   Axis-Aligned Bounding Box Algorithm

The AABB box is a rectangle surrounded by six planes that are parallel to the coordinate axes, which is called "axis alignment". The following mathematical description of the AABB enclosing box is given in the following equation:

$$P = P = \{(x,y,z) \mid \; \mid x_c - x \mid \leqslant r_x, \mid y_c - y \mid \leqslant r_y, \mid z_c - z \mid \leqslant r_z\} \tag{4}$$

where P represents the spatial coordinates of the enclosing box, x_c, y_c, z_c, respectively, represent the center coordinate projection of the object in three-dimensional space. r_x, r_y, r_z represent the radius of the center coordinate projection of the object in three-dimensional space and satisfy the following relationship: $x_c = \frac{1}{2}(x_{max} + x_{min})$, $y_c = \frac{1}{2}(y_{max} + y_{min})$, $z_c = \frac{1}{2}(z_{max} + z_{min})$。

In this paper, we determine whether a collision occurs according to the intersection space of the AABB enclosing box. If there is no intersection space, it is directly judged as no collision; if there is an intersection space, the collision is judged according to the distance and the improved whale optimization algorithm. The following is the flowchart of constructing the AABB enclosing box and initially judging the object collision (Fig. 1).

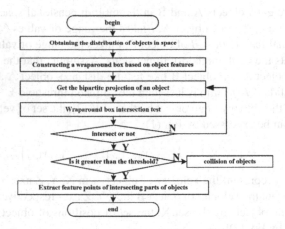

Fig. 1. Flowchart for preliminary determination of object collision using AABB enclosing box.

4   Improved Whale Optimization Algorithm

The Whale Optimization Algorithm is divided into three main parts: rounding up prey, bubble net feeding, and random prey search [8, 9]. A mathematical description of the WOA is given below.

Rounding up prey: Assuming that the current whale individual is the optimal individual of the population, other whale individuals will approach the optimal individual. The whale update position formula is as follows:

$$D = \left| CX^*(t) - X(t) \right| \tag{5}$$

$$X(t+1) = X^*(t) - AD \tag{6}$$

where D represents the difference between the position of the optimal individual and the position of the individual in the current population; t represents the current number of iterations; $X^*(t)$ represents the position vector of the current optimal solution; $X(t)$ represents the position vector; $||$ is the absolute value; A, C, denote the coefficient vectors, and satisfy the following relationship:

$$A = 2ar_1 - a \tag{7}$$

$$C = 2r_2 \tag{8}$$

$$a = 2 - \tfrac{2t}{T} \tag{9}$$

where r_1, r_2 are a random vector in $[0,1]$; T represents the maximum number of iterations; a decreases linearly from 2 to 0 throughout the iteration; and A takes values between $[-a, a]$.

Bubble net predation: When whales attack prey in bubble nets, they need to spiral up close to the prey and shrink the envelope by adjusting the parameters. The specific formula is as follows.

$$X(t+1) = D' \cdot e^{bl} \cdot cos(2\pi l) + X^*(t) \tag{10}$$

$$D' = |X^*(t) - X(t)| \tag{11}$$

where D' represents the distance between the current searching individual and the prey; b is a parameter in order to determine the shape of the spiral; l is a random number between $[-1,1]$; and π represents the circumference.

Since whale position updating can only be done in one of the ways of spiraling up and shrinking the envelope, the following equation is assumed for updating whale position assuming that the probability of a whale spiraling up and shrinking the envelope are each 50%:

$$X(t+1) = \left\{ \begin{array}{ll} X^*(t) - A \cdot D & (P < 0.5) \\ X^*(t) + D' \cdot e^{bl} \cdot cos(2\pi l) & (P \geqslant 0.5) \end{array} \right. \tag{12}$$

where P represents the probability of the predation mechanism, which takes the value of a random number between $[0, 1]$. As the number of iterations t increases, the parameter A and the convergence factor a gradually decrease, and if $|A| < 1$, then each whale gradually surrounds the current optimal solution, which belongs to the local optimal search stage in WOA.

Searching for prey: To ensure that all whales are fully searched in the solution space, the WOA updates the positions based on the distances of the whales from each other for the purpose of random search. Therefore, when $|A| \geqslant 1$, a whale individual is randomly selected as a reference to update the position of other whale individuals. The formula is as follows:

$$D'' = |C \cdot X_{rand}(t) - X| \tag{13}$$

$$X(t+1) = X_{\text{rand}}(t) - A \cdot D \tag{14}$$

where $X_{\text{rand}}(t)$ represents the current position of the random whale individual; D'' represents the distance between the current search individual and the random search individual.

5 Levy Flight Initialization Population.

In the whale optimization algorithm, the Levy [10] distribution can be used to improve the initialization of the population. The formula is as follows:

$$X_{i+1}^* = X_i^* + \mathcal{A} \oplus \text{Levy}(\mathscr{b}) \tag{15}$$

where X_i^*, represents the optimal whale individual generated from the previous i iterations; $\oplus$ represents point-to-point multiplication; $\mathcal{A}$represents the step control quantity; and Levy $(\mathscr{b})$represents the random search path. Where $\mathcal{A}$and Levy $(\mathscr{b})$are to satisfy the following relation.

$$\mathcal{A} = rando\, m\big(size(X_{\mathcal{A}})\big) \tag{16}$$

$$Levy(\mathscr{b}) \sim 0.01\frac{u}{|r|^{\frac{1}{\mathscr{b}}}} \tag{17}$$

$$u \sim N\big(0, \sigma^2\big) \tag{18}$$

$$r \sim N(0, 1) \tag{19}$$

$$\sigma = \left[\frac{\Gamma(1+\mathscr{b}) \times \sin\left(\frac{\pi\mathscr{b}}{2}\right)}{\mathscr{b} \times \Gamma\left(\frac{1+\mathscr{b}}{2}\right) \times 2^{\frac{\mathscr{b}-1}{2}}}\right]^{\frac{1}{\mathscr{b}}} \tag{20}$$

where, $1 < \mathscr{b} < 3$this paper takes the value of $\mathscr{b} = 3/2$based on experience; Γ is the standard Gamma function; where, u, r obey the normal distribution.

5.1 Improving Inertia Weights

In order to improve the local optimization ability and convergence accuracy of the whale optimization algorithm, this paper proposes a new adaptive weighting w(t) [11] method, and the adaptive weighting formula is shown in Eq. (22) as follows.

$$w(t) = 0.8 \times sin\left(\frac{\pi}{2}e^{-(t/2T)^2}\right) + 0.5 \tag{21}$$

where $w(t)$ represents the weight; t represents the current number of iterations, which is used to control the size of the weight, and the weight decreases as t increases; T represents the maximum number of iterations of the algorithm. Many scholars have

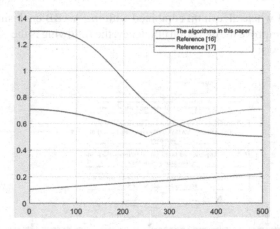

Fig. 2. Adaptive weights versus number of iterations

made improvements to the weights, such as references [16] and [17]. The inertia weight in this paper is a nonlinear decreasing sine function. As shown in the following Fig. 2.

As can be seen in Fig. 2, at the beginning of the algorithm iteration, larger weights are set, this is because the whale is far away from the prey and the global search ability of the whale needs to be enhanced. In the late iteration of the algorithm, the whale is close to the food and smaller weights are set to enhance the whale's local search ability. Therefore, the weight changes in this paper are fully consistent with the optimization process of the whale algorithm.

5.2 Improving Adaptive Learning Factors

The global optimal finding ability of the whale optimization algorithm is mainly affected by the parameter **A**, while the variation of the parameter **A** is affected by the convergence factor a. Therefore, this paper proposes a nonlinear adaptive learning factor a to solve the problem of whale optimization algorithm falling into local optimal solution.

$$a = 2 - 2sin\left(\frac{t\pi}{2T}\right) \tag{22}$$

From expression (23), it can be seen that $2 - 2$sin (tπ/2T) is nonlinearly increasing in the interval [0, π/2], which dynamically adjusts the whale adaptation without changing the original trend of the convergence factor a. After the introduction of adaptive weights and adaptive learning factors, the improved whale optimization algorithm position update formula is as follows (Fig. 3):

When |A|<1, the position is updated as follows:

$$X(t + 1) = w(t) \cdot X^*(t) - A \cdot D \, (P < 0.5) \tag{23}$$

$$X(t + 1) = w(t) \cdot X^*(t) + D' \cdot e^{bl} \cdot cos(2\pi l) \quad (P \geqslant 0.5) \tag{24}$$

When$| A |\geqslant 1$, the position is updated as follows:

$$X(t + 1) = w(t) \cdot X_{\text{rand}}(t) - A \cdot D \tag{25}$$

The improved whale algorithm combined with the AABB enclosing box algorithm can significantly improve the detection efficiency, the following is the collision detection flow chart as follows:

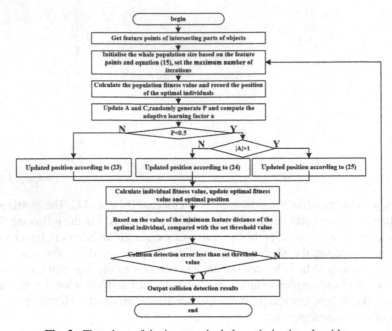

Fig. 3. Flowchart of the improved whale optimization algorithm.

6 Experimental

In order to verify the improved whale optimization algorithm global and local optimization ability, this paper selected the benchmark test function [12] to test the algorithm. This paper selected the standard particle swarm optimization (PSO) algorithm, the standard ant lion optimization algorithm (Ant Lion Optimizer, ALO) for comparison experiments. The test results are shown in Fig. 4.

From (a) in Fig. 4, it can be seen that the improved whale optimization algorithm has fewer iterations in obtaining the maximum fitness value and converges faster during the iterations compared to the standard whale optimization algorithm. From Fig. (b), it can be seen that the improved whale optimization algorithm has fewer iterations than PSO algorithm and ALO algorithm in obtaining the fitness value, and the maximum fitness value can be found in about 50 iterations, while PSO and ALO algorithms have to be iterated 300 and 400 times respectively before they can approach the maximum fitness value. In order to further verify the superiority of the improved whale algorithm, we conducted the following experiments using four benchmark functions.

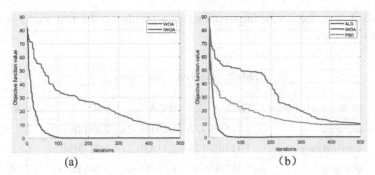

Fig. 4. Comparison of convergence curves of optimization algorithms

6.1 Effect of Collecting Different Number of Features on Collision Detection

In this paper, four benchmark functions, f1, f2, f3 and f4, are selected for testing, of which f1 and f2 are single-peak functions and f3 and f4 are multi-peak functions, and the specific functions are shown in Table 1. The number of experimental iterations are 100, and each function repeats the experiment 100 times respectively to take the average value, The dimension is set to 30 and the theoretical optimum is 0, and calculate the standard deviation, and the experimental results are shown in Table 2.

Table 1. Test Function Table

function	formula	Search Scope
Schwefel's problem 2.22	$f_1(x) = \sum_{i=1}^{30} \mid x_i \mid + \prod_{i=1}^{30} \mid x_i \mid$	[-10,10]
Ster function	$f_2(x) = \sum_{i=1}^{30} (\mid x_i + 0.5 \mid)^2$	[-100,100]
Ackley's function	$f_3(x) = -20\exp(-0.2\sqrt{\frac{1}{30}\sum_{i=1}^{30} x_i^2} - \exp(\frac{1}{30}\sum_{i=1}^{30} \cos 2\pi x_i) + 20 + e$	[-32,32]
generalized penalized function	$f_4(x) = \frac{\pi}{30} \mid 10\sin^2 + \sum_{i=1}^{29} (y_i - 1)^2[1 + 10\sin^2(\pi y_i + 1)] + (y_n - 1)^2$ $\mid + \sum_{i=1}^{30} u(x_i, 10, 100, 4)$	[-50,50]

Among them, f1–f2 are single-peak functions, which are mainly used to test the development performance of the algorithm. From the table, it can be seen that the performance of IWOA algorithm is far beyond other algorithms with small standard deviation and mean. f3–f4 are multi-peak functions, which are mainly used to test the searching ability of the function. From the table, it can be seen that IWOA still has small mean and standard deviation, so the improved whale algorithm performance energy exceeds the other algorithms.

Table 2. Algorithm test results

function	Evaluation indicators	IWOA	WOA	PSO	GA
f_1	averages	3.1153E-127	5.2918E-24	2.4614E-02	3.5592E-01
	standard deviation	5.3158E-126	2.1143E-23	5.3213E-02	6.6263E-2
f_2	averages	2.1576E-05	1.5812E-02	1.7664E-06	2.3464E +00
	standard deviation	5.6434E-06	5.1233E-02	3.5636E-06	2.7651E+00
f_3	averages	3.1159e-15	1.6768E-15	2.4657E + 00	6.1335E-01
	standard deviation	1.2342e-15	1.5312E-15	7.5232E-01	5.3553E-01
f_4	averages	4.1531E-07	1.3521E-02	5.6354E-02	3.3159E-02
	standard deviation	3.5678E-07	3.2534E-02	1.1567E-01	4.9523E-02

6.2 Effect of Collecting Different Number of Features on Collision Detection

In this paper, 1000 samples are selected for testing. For two objects in the presence of intersection space, four different features are chosen to conduct collision detection experiments on the objects, and each feature pair is chosen to form a whale population of 1000*1000, 2000*2000, 4000*4000, 8000*8000, and the time consumption of the algorithm is shown in Table 3.

Table 3. Comparison results of time consuming algorithms for different feature pairs

Number of feature pairs	Detection rate 10% time/ms	Detection rate 20% time/ms	Detection rate 40% time/ms	Detection rate 80% time/ms	Detection rate 90% time/ms
1000*1000	15	40	90	180	210
2000*2000	70	100	190	270	300
4000*4000	120	160	240	340	360
8000*8000	190	220	310	430	450

According to the data in Table 3, it can be learnt that the time consumed by the algorithm increases as the number of sampled features increases. When the number of feature pairs is 1000, the algorithm can reach 90% detection rate in 210 ms. When the number of feature pairs is 8000, the algorithm can reach 90% detection rate in 450 ms. Therefore, choosing the right number of feature pairs is crucial for the efficiency of collision detection.

6.3 The Effect of Different Whale Sizes on Collision Detection

In order to verify the most suitable whale size, experiments are conducted on 88 objects using the improved whale optimization algorithm sampling different features. The detection results are shown in Fig. 5.

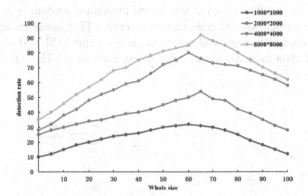

Fig. 5. Comparison of collision detection rates for different whale sizes.

As can be seen in Fig. 5, the maximum detection rate is reached at a whale size of about 65. Therefore, this paper uses a whale size of 65 for the experiments. In order to verify the improved whale optimization algorithm detection rate, the improved whale optimization algorithm is compared with the enveloping box algorithm and the enveloping box + WOA algorithm for comparison experiments. The experimental results are shown in Fig. 6.

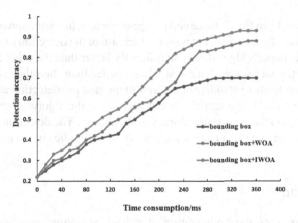

Fig. 6. Comparison of collision detection accuracy of 3 algorithms.

From the Fig. 6, it can be seen that the improved whale algorithm + bounding box algorithm has the highest detection efficiency, with a detection efficiency of 96% at 380 ms. The standard whale algorithm + AABB bounding box algorithm has a detection efficiency of about 88% at 380 ms, while the detection efficiency using bounding box algorithm is only about 70%.

6.4 Comparative Experiments on Detection Efficiency of Different Algorithms

In order to verify that the improved whale optimization algorithm is better than other algorithms, the particle swarm optimization algorithm [13], quantum ant colony optimization algorithm [14], grey wolf optimization algorithm [15], and algorithm of this paper are selected for the comparative experiments respectively. The experimental results are shown in Fig. 7.

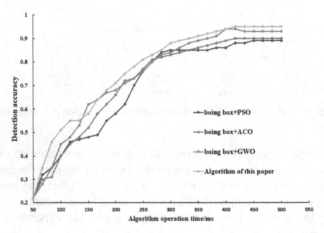

Fig. 7. Comparison of collision detection accuracy of different algorithms.

As can be seen from Fig. 7, in the early stage of the test, the detection rate of these four algorithms is basically the same, but with the increase of the detection time, the detection efficiency of this paper's algorithm is significantly better than the other algorithms, and the stability of the late stage of the test is also better than the other algorithms. This paper's algorithm tends to stabilize at about 400 ms, and the detection accuracy is up to about 95%. The worst is the particle swarm algorithm, the algorithm tends to stabilize at about 450 ms, and the detection accuracy is about 87%. The detection accuracy of the gray wolf algorithm and the quantum ant colony algorithm lies in the middle of the first two.

7 Conclusion

This paper focuses on the optimization of the whale optimization algorithm, which has slow convergence speed and low convergence accuracy. By increasing adaptive weights and learning factors, and using Levy flight strategy to initialize the population, the whale algorithm is improved to improve search convergence speed and optimization accuracy. We compared and analyzed the methods of combining other intelligent optimization algorithms with IWOA + bounding box technology. The results indicate that the improved whale optimization algorithm combined with AABB bounding box detection efficiency has been further improved.

Acknowledgements. The research was supported by the Industrial Science and Technology Research Project of Henan Province under Grants 232102210088, 232102210125, 222102210024.

References

1. Qichao, B., Min, L., Weijun, G., et al.: Study on collision detection techniques for the informed design of natural views in healthcare environments. HERD **15**(3), 229–245 (2022)
2. Hu, Z., Qin, Q.: Minimum volume directed bounding box generation algorithm based on convex hull. J. Hunan Univ. (Nat. Sci. Edn.) **46**(2), 105–111 (2019)
3. Jin, Y., Cheng, Q., Zhang, J., Qi, X., Ma, B., Jia, Y.: Self-collision detection algorithm based on fused DNN and AABB-circular bounding box. J. Image Graph. **25**(8), 1674–1683 (2020)
4. Wang, R., Hua, W., Xu, G.X., Huo, Y., Bao, H.: Variational hierarchical directed bounding box construction for solid mesh models. arXiv preprint arXiv (2022). 1–11 2203
5. Gan, B., Dong, Q.: An improved optimal algorithm for collision detection of hybrid hierarchical bounding box. Evol. Intell. **2**(1), 1–13 (2021)
6. Hui, X., Meng, X.: Research on virtual scene collision detection based on bounding box intelligent algorithm. Comput. Simul. **38**(7), 209–213 (2021)
7. Gan, B., Dong, Q.: An improved optimal algorithm for collision detection of hybrid hierarchical bounding box. Evol. Intell. **4**(11), 1–13 (2021)
8. Huca, Y.E.J.: Clustering routing algorithm for wireless sensor networks with whale algorithm. Compet. Eng. Des. **40**(11), 3067–3072 (2019)
9. Wang, T.: Trjectory optimization and control of grinding robot based on improved whale optimization algorithm. Taiyuan: North University of China (2021)
10. Yu, J., Liu, S., Wang, J., et al.: An ant-lion optimization algorithm incorporating Levy flight and golden sine. Comput. Appl. Res. **37**(8), 2349–2353 (2020)
11. Zhang, Z.Z., He, X.S., Yu, Q.L., et al.: Cuckoo algorithm for muli-stage dynamic diturbance and dynamic inertia weight. Comput. Eng. Appl. **58**(1), 79–88 (2022)
12. Mirjalilis, L.A.: The whale optimization algorithm. Adv. Eng. Softw. **95**, 51–67 (2016)
13. Jing, W., Xingyi, W., Xiongfei, L., et al.: A hybrid particle swarm optimization algorithm with dynamic adjustment of inertia weight based on a new feature selection method to optimize SVM parameters. Entropy **25**(3), 531 (2023)
14. Du, Q., Zhen, C., Hao, H.: Fast collision detection algorithm based on quantum ant colony. Comput. Simul. **36**(12), 209–213 (2019)
15. Duan, B., Ma, Y., Liu, J., Jin, Y.: A nonlinear gray wolf optimization algorithm based on chaotic mapping and backward learning mechanism. Softw. Eng. **26**(05), 36–40 (2023)
16. Chen, L., Yin, J.S.: Whale swarm optimization algorithm based on Gaussian difference mutation and logarithmic inertia weight. In: Proceedings of the 57th International Conference on Computer Engineering and Applications (ICCEA), pp. 77–90 (2021). https://doi.org/10.3778/j.issn.1002-8331.2001-0290
17. Feng, W.T., Song, K.K.: An enhanced whale optimization algorithm. In: Proceedings of the 37th International Conference on Computer Simulation (CSIM), pp. 275–279 (2020). https://doi.org/10.3969/j.issn.1006-9348.2020.11.057

AF-FCOS: An Improved Anchor-Free Object Detection Method

Hang Li[1], Rui Yang[1], Rushi Lan[1(✉)], and Xiaonan Luo[2]

[1] Guangxi Key Laboratory of Image Graphics and Intelligent Processing, Guilin University of Electronic Science and Technology, Guilin, Guangxi, China
rslan2016@163.com
[2] Satellite Navigation Positioning and Location Service National and Local Joint, Engineering Research Center, Guilin, Guangxi, China

Abstract. The anchor-free object detection method avoids the complex hyper-parameter setting problem of the traditional anchor-based method, and has more advantages in accuracy and speed. However, it still has some problems such as low precision of small-scale object detection and poor detection result under complex background. To solve this problem, an improved anchor-free object detection method based on FCOS is proposed in this paper. By adding an efficient channel attention mechanism module to the feature extraction network and using a local cross-channel interaction strategy without dimensionality reduction, the 1D convolution kernel size is adaptively selected to obtain useful dependencies between channels and improve feature extraction capability. A context extraction module is designed in feature fusion network to explore context information from multiple receptive fields and improve classification accuracy. In the training stage, DIoU loss is used to make the regression of the border more stable and accurate, and the training process converges faster. The proposed method is evaluated on COCO2017. The experimental results show that compared with the baseline FCOS method, the average accuracy of the proposed method is improved by 1.3%, which has advantages in comprehensive performance.

Keywords: Object Detection · Anchor-Free · CNN · Attention Mechanism · Feature Fusion

1 Introduction

Object detection has great application value and research significance. As a fundamental task in the field of computer vision, it is a prerequisite for a variety of fundamental vision researches, such as instance segmentation, face recognition, behavior recognition, pose estimation, image description, target tracking, and autonomous vehicles. In recent years, object detection methods based on deep learning have achieved excellent detection performance, gradually replacing traditional methods based on artificial design features.

In the era of deep learning, people have proposed a series of excellent networks, which can be roughly divided into two categories, namely anchor-based detection network

© The Author(s), under exclusive license to Springer Nature Singapore Pte Ltd. 2024
D.-S. Huang et al. (Eds.): ICAI 2023, CCIS 2014, pp. 268–279, 2024.
https://doi.org/10.1007/978-981-97-0903-8_26

and anchor-free detection network. The anchor-based detection network has a class-independent region suggestion stage, which outputs potential regions that may contain objects, and then a second stage is responsible for classification prediction and regression prediction of these regions. Some classical two-stage detectors are Fast R-CNN [7], Faster R-CNN [20], Mask R-CNN [8], R-FCN [3], Sparse R-CNN [22], Cascade R-CNN [1], Meta R-CNN [25], and Libra R-CNN [18].

Due to the unbalanced distribution of positive and negative samples, the large number of parameters have to be designed in the network, and the existence of a large number of redundant boxes, anchor-free object detection methods which can solve these problems are gradually emerging. With the proposed of key theories such as FPN [14] and Focal Loss [15], anchor-free object detection methods ushered in new development.

Huang et al. proposed DenseBox [11], which together with YOLO [19] was an early exploration of anchor-free object methods, laying a foundation for subsequent research. Zhi et al. used fully convolution network to construct the FCOS [23], and adopted the pixel-based prediction method in the field of semantic segmentation. Zhu et al. proposed FSAF [30], which enables samples to automatically learn and select the optimal scale branch for training. Inspired by the structure of human eyes, Kong et al. proposed FoveaBox [12], which pays more attention to the central region of the object during training and detection. Law et al. proposed CornerNet [13], which uses a pair of key points to achieve object positioning and generate hotspot map and embedded vector. Duan et al. proposed the CenterNet [6]. To solve the problems of inaccurate key point matching in dense targets, Dong et al. proposed CentripetalNet [5]. In 2021, the faster and more powerful CenterNet2 [29] was proposed. In 2022, Mohsen et al. proposed ObjectBox [26] network, which treats all objects equally at different feature levels regardless of targets' size and shape.

Although the existing detection networks have been able to achieve relatively good detection accuracy, there are still some problems such as large calculation amount, long processing time, large difference in detection accuracy under long tail data distribution, and poor detection effect of small objects in complex environments. To improve these problems, this paper proposes an improved anchor-free object detection method based on FCOS. In the feature extraction stage, by adding ECA attention mechanism module to Resnet-50 [9], useful dependencies between channels are obtained and feature extraction capability is improved. In the feature fusion stage, context extraction module (CEM) is added to FPN network to explore the context information from multiple receptive fields and improve the classification accuracy. In the detecting stage, DIoU loss is used to make the regression of the border more stable and accurate, and the training process converges faster.

2 Related Work

2.1 FCOS

Feature extraction is carried out through Resnet-50 [9] and FPN [14] in FCOS network. Referring to Fig. 2, feature maps C1, C2, C3, C4 and C5 are generated by the feature extraction network Resnet-50, where C3, C4 and C5 are horizontally connected to layers P3, P4 and P5 of FPN. Then, P6 and P7 are generated from P5 from top to top through two 3 × 3 convolutional kernels with stride size of 2. Finally, the feature maps P3, P4, P5, P6 and P7 output from FPN are sent to the detection head network respectively for detection, and the prediction information of each positive sample point on each feature maps is output. It includes the category score of the object, the predicted value of the centerness and the position feature vector ltbr of the sample point. Meanwhile, the prediction box with low score is filtered by the non-maximum suppression algorithm and the final detection result is obtained.

2.2 The Positive and Negative Samples Defined Strategy

FCOS is different from anchor-based object detection networks in that it abandons the candidate region generation network used by anchor-based method. This method needs to observe the datasets in advance, set hyperparameters, and occupy a lot of computing resources in the training process. FCOS avoids these complex pre-processing steps, and directly takes the location points as training samples, referring to the idea of intensive prediction in the field of semantic segmentation [17] (Fig. 1).

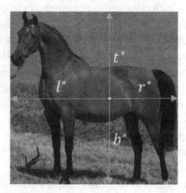

Fig. 1. Four position vectors lrtb respectively represent the length of the four sides from the sample point to the ground truth.

Specifically, the positive and negative sample definition strategy of the FCOS is as follows: firstly, the border box of each ground truth of the input image is defined as $B_i = \left(x_0^{(i)}, y_0^{(i)}, x_1^{(i)}, y_1^{(i)}, C^i\right)$. Among them $\left(x_0^{(i)}, y_0^{(i)}\right)$, $\left(x_1^{(i)}, y_1^{(i)}\right)$ and C, represents the upper left, lower right point coordinates of the border box and category. Each point (x, y) on the feature maps P3–P7 is reflected to the original picture to determine whether it falls into the border box of any ground truth. On this basis, if the category of the point and the ground truth belong to the same category, the point is regarded as a positive sample, otherwise it is negative. The reflection method is shown in formula 1:

$$\left(\lfloor \tfrac{s}{2} \rfloor + xs, \lfloor \tfrac{s}{2} \rfloor + ys\right) \tag{1}$$

In formula 1, s represents the down-sampling stride from the feature map to the original picture. For each positive sample point, four distances are obtained by regression of its position feature vector to the ground truth border to determine whether its length is within a reasonable radius. The calculation method is shown in formula 2:

$$l = x - x_1, \quad t = y - y_1$$
$$r = x_2 - x, \quad b = y_2 - y \tag{2}$$

In the case that a certain point falls into multiple borders of the ground truth at the same time, the point is directly assigned to the border with the smallest area.

2.3 Head Network of Detecting

The detection head network of FCOS, as shown in the lower right corner of Fig. 2, is composed of three branches, namely regression branch, classification branch and centerness branch. Feature maps P3–P7 uses different detection head networks to obtain detection results of feature maps of different scales. Specifically, the location feature vector of each point (x, y) on the output feature map of the regression branch is precisely the introduction of the location feature vector based on intensive prediction. Classification confidence of each positive sample point on feature map out from the classification branch; And the centerness branch is used to evaluate the distance between each positive sample point and the target center point corresponding to that point. Generally speaking, the point closer to the target center point is more likely to belong to the same category as the ground truth, and the border box of its regression has a higher coincidence degree with that of the ground truth. The calculation of centerness is shown in formula 3:

$$\text{centerness}^* = \sqrt{(x - x_0)^2 - (y - y_o)^2} \tag{3}$$

In the formula, (x_0, y_0) represents the coordinates of the ground truth center point, and the square root is opened to weaken the attenuation of the centerness. Finally, the weight of the centerness is added to the loss value of the regression branch to suppress other coordinate points that deviate far from the center point, so as to improve the accuracy of detection.

3 AF-FCOS

3.1 Overview

In this paper, the FCOS object detection model is improved, and the network structure is shown in Fig. 2. The improved part mainly includes three parts: feature extraction module, feature fusion module and detection head. Specifically, ECA attention mechanism is introduced into the feature extraction network ResNet-50 of this model. By learning the correlation between channels, the weight of channels can be adjusted adaptively, and the model performance can be improved on the basis of effectively reducing the number of model parameters and calculation amount. In feature fusion module, context extraction module CEM is added to explore context information from multiple receptive fields to improve classification accuracy. In the last part of the detection head, the DIoU loss function is used in the regression branch, which makes the prediction frame regression more stable and accurate, and speeds up the convergence rate of the model.

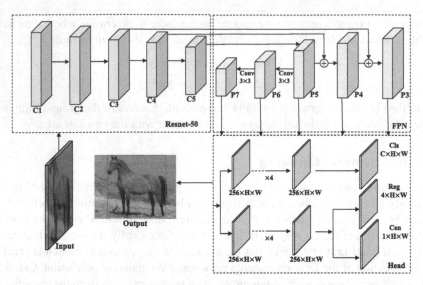

Fig. 2. The structure of AF-FCOS.

3.2 ECA

In this paper, ResNet-50 is used as the feature extraction network, which belongs to the series CNN network structure. During the transmission of input data, global information is difficult to reach the tail of the model, and the lost information will inevitably affect the performance of the model, and the attention mechanism can compensate for these losses to a certain extent.

In recent years, many methods have used SENet [10] to model the relationship between channels and capture more complex channel dependencies. However, recent studies have shown that the dimensionality reduction operation of SENet is not conducive to the prediction of channel attention, and not all channel relationships are valuable.

The ECA [24] attention mechanism avoids dimensionality reduction and can efficiently utilize the correlation between channels through cross-channel interaction strategies, and avoids the introduction of a large number of parameters while maintaining superior performance. The main improvement of ECA compared with SENet is that it uses an adaptive fast one-dimensional convolution instead of the original FC layer. The convolution kernel size k represents the coverage area of local cross-channel interaction.

$$k = \psi(C) = \left| \frac{log_2(C)}{\gamma} + \frac{b}{\gamma} \right|_{odd} \tag{4}$$

where, γ and b are taken as 2 and 1 respectively, $|t|_{odd}$ indicates that the nearest odd number from t is taken (Fig. 3).

3.3 CEM

FPN alleviates the inherent contradiction between feature map resolution and semantic information to some extent by introducing a top-down approach. However, there are still

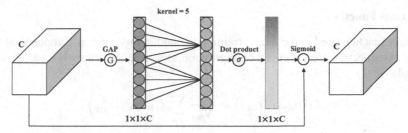

Fig. 3. The structure of Eca.

two main problems in the FPN-based network:1) The contradiction between the resolution of high-resolution input feature map and the receptive field; 2) Lack of effective communication between receiving fields of different sizes.

In order to effectively solve these two problems, Junxu et al. proposed AC-FPN [2], which uses context extraction module (CEM) to explore a large amount of context information, and uses attention guidance module (AM) to adaptively retain useful information around the target and suppress useless semantic information. In this paper, the CEM module in AC-FPN is introduced. The CEM module performs five scales of dilated convolution on the feature map F5 to capture rich context information from large receptive fields of different sizes. In addition, in order to better integrate the information of multiple receptive fields, different receptive fields are closely linked.

3.4 DIoU

In the detection head network, the loss function in the regression stage greatly affects the model's degree of data fitting. The GIoU [21] loss function used by the original network pays too much attention to the minimum closed rectangle in some cases, resulting in a small overlap area between the border box and the real border box. In this paper, the DIoU [27] is introduced as the loss function of the regression branch of the border box, which takes into account the distance between the predicted border box and the real border box, so that the loss function pays more attention to the position of the border box, and avoids the gradient disappearance caused by too far distance between the two boxes. The calculation formula is as follows:

$$L_{DIoU} = 1 - \frac{|B \cap B^{gt}|}{|B \cup B^{gt}|} + \frac{\rho^2(b, b^{gt})}{c^2} \tag{5}$$

where, B is the target prediction border box, B^{gt} is the target real border box, b is the central point coordinate of the prediction box, b^{gt} is the central point coordinate of the real one, and ρ is the Euclidean distance between the central points of the two boxes. c is the diagonal length of the smallest external rectangle capable of covering both the prediction box and the real box.

3.5 Loss Function

The loss function used in the model training method in this paper is composed of three parts: classification loss, border box regression loss, and centerness loss, as shown in formula 6:

$$L(\{p_{x,y}\}, \{t_{x,y}\}) = \frac{1}{N_{pos}} \sum_{x,y} L_{cls}\left(p_{x,y}, c_{x,y}^*\right)$$

$$+ \frac{\lambda}{N_{pos}} \sum_{x,y} \tau\left\{c_{x,y}^* > 0\right\} L_{reg}\left(t_{x,y}, t_{x,y}^*\right) \tag{6}$$

Focal loss [15] is adopted as the classification loss function L_{cls}, and the formula is shown as (7), where α represents the balance factor to adjust the importance of positive and negative samples in the training process, γ represents the modulation factor to reduce the proportion of easily classified samples in the model:

$$L_{cls}\left(p_{x,y}, c_{x,y}^*\right) = -\alpha(1-p)^\gamma \log(p)$$

$$P = \begin{cases} p_{x,y}, if\ c_{x,y}^* = 1 \\ 1 - p_{x,y}, 其他 \end{cases} \tag{7}$$

The regression loss function adopts DIoU loss [27], as shown in formula 5. For centerness loss, BCE loss [4] is adopted, and this loss function is added to formula 7 and multiplied with the regression loss function to suppress the detection boxes deviating from the target center, as shown in formula 8:

$$BCE\ loss(p_t, y) = -y * log(p_t) - (1-y)log(1-p_t) \tag{8}$$

where, p_t indicates the predicted value and y indicates the actual value.

4 Experiments

The training and testing of the method in this paper were carried out on the server with GPU model with NIVID GeForce RTX2080Ti, CPU model Intel (R) Xeon (R) silver 4110 with Ubuntu18.04 operating system. Python3.7 programming language, CUDA11.1 and cuDNN8.04 was used too. Based on the above configuration, Pytorch1.9 version is used to build a deep learning framework. The pre-trained model on ImageNet was used to initialize the model, and the stochastic gradient descent algorithm was used to optimize the training stage. The batch size for each iteration is set to 4. The number of training iterations is set to 90,000, the initial learning rate is set to 0.001, and the weight attenuation coefficient is set to 0.0001.

4.1 Dataset

The experiments are conducted on COCO2017 [16], which is a large general dataset provided by the Microsoft team for object detection, semantic segmentation and other tasks and contains 200,000 images, 80 categories, and more than 500,000 instances annotation, is the most widely published general dataset for object detection challenges.

4.2 The Comparison Between the Proposed Method and Others

In order to verify the effectiveness of the proposed method, the accuracy of the proposed method is compared with some classical object detection methods on COCO2017 dataset. The experimental results are shown in Table 1.

Table 1. Compared with different methods on COCO2017 dataset

Method	Backbone	mAP	FPS
Faster R-CNN [20]	ResNet-101	28.7%	18.6
YOLOv5	DarkNet-53	33.3%	23.2
CornerNet [13]	Hourglass-52	31.4%	19.3
CenterNet [6]	Hourglass-52	32.7%	21.2
FoveaBox [12]	ResNet-50	31.5%	20.5
FCOS [23]	ResNet-50	32.2%	29.2
FCOS	ResNet-101	35.3%	28.7
Ours	ResNet-50	33.5%	13.7

From the comparison of experimental results of different networks on COCO dataset in Table 1, it can be found that the improved FCOS detection method has obvious advantages in average detection accuracy. Compared with baseline method, the mAP of the proposed method increased by 1.3%, while it increased by 2% compared with FoveaBox. And compared with ConerNet and CenterNet in anchor-free, our method also improves by 2.1% and 0.8% respectively. However, compared with the classic Faster R-CNN, the mAP of the proposed method is improved by 4.8%, and it is also improved by 0.2% compared with YOLOv5. In terms of execution speed, due to the addition of two new models, the number of model parameters has increased, and the detection speed has decreased, but the proposed method still has more advantages in comprehensive performance.

4.3 Comparison of Different Loss Functions for Regression Branches

In order to verify the impact of the loss function of the regression branch of the detection head network on the model performance, different loss functions were used to compare the final detection performance of the model. The experimental results are shown in Table 2.

In the original network, GIoU was used as the loss function of border regression, and the detection accuracy was 32.2%. After DIoU loss function and CIoU [28] loss function were used, mAP values of 32.7% and 32.5% were obtained, respectively, which increased by 0.5% and 0.3%. And in small object detection, the accuracy of DIoU and CIoU loss functions is improved by 0.9% and 1.8%.

Table 2. IoU loss function comparison

IoU	mAP	mAP_s	mAP_m	mAP_l
GIoU	32.2%	17.8%	36.4%	40.3%
DIoU	32.7%	18.7%	36.6%	42.6%
CIoU	32.5%	19.6%	36.4%	41.8%

4.4 Ablation Study

In this section, ablation experiments were conducted to verify and analyze the impact of various measures on improving the accuracy of our method, and ECA, CEM and DIoU loss were experimentally verified on the basis of the FCOS model.

Table 3. Comparison of ablation results on COCO2017 dataset

Experiment	ECA	CEM	DIoU	mAP
1				32.2%
2	✓			33.1%
3		✓		33.3%
4			✓	32.7%
5	✓	✓	✓	33.5%

From the comparison of ablation results on COCO2017 in Table 3, it can be found that the improved method in this paper can improve the performance of the original method to varying degrees. In experiment 2, ECA module was added to the feature extraction network, which improved the mAP of the network by 0.9%. In experiment 3, adding CEM module to the feature fusion network improved the mAP of the network by 1.1%. In experiment 4, DIoU is used as the loss function of the regression branch, and the mAP of the network is increased by 0.5%. In experiment 5, the above three improvements were added at the same time, and the mAP of the network was increased by 1.3%.

4.5 Visualization of Detection Results

As can be seen from the visualization results in Fig. 4, our method not only has more advantages in detection accuracy, bust also can detect small objects more accurately, such as baseball gloves in the left picture, and can detect occluded objects, such as the remote control behind the cat in the right picture.

Fig. 4. The left part shows the detection results of AF-FCOS, and the right part shows the detection results of FCOS.

5   Conclusions

An improved anchor-free object detection method based on FCOS is proposed in this paper to solve the problems of inaccuracy of small target detection and poor detection effect under complex background. Experiments show that ECA, CEM and DIoU added in this method can improve the detection accuracy to varying degrees. However, due to the introduction of deformable convolution in CEM module, we believe that our method is still not effective enough in modeling context information. Due to the introduction of additional modules, the parameter size of the network also becomes larger. Next, we will try to reduce the complexity of the model, make it lightweight, modify the CEM model and consider introducing the object relation module to further improve the detection accuracy.

Acknowledgements. This work was partially supported by the National Natural Science Foundation of China (Grant Nos. 62362014, 62172120, and 62002082), and the Guangxi Natural Science Foundation of China (Grant Nos. 2019GXNSFAA245014, 2020GXNSFBA238014).

References

1. Cai, Z., Vasconcelos, N.: Cascade r-cnn: delving into high quality object detection. In: Proceedings of the IEEE Conference on Computer Vision and Pattern Recognition, pp. 6154–6162 (2018)
2. Cao, J., Chen, Q., Guo, J., Shi, R.: Attention-guided context feature pyramid network for object detection. arXiv preprint arXiv:2005.11475 (2020)
3. Dai, J., Li, Y., He, K., Sun, J.: R-fcn: object detection via region-based fully convolutional networks. In: Advances in Neural Information Processing Systems, vol. 29 (2016)
4. De Boer, P.T., Kroese, D.P., Mannor, S., Rubinstein, R.Y.: A tutorial on the crossentropy method. Ann. Oper. Res. **134**, 19–67 (2005)
5. Dong, Z., Li, G., Liao, Y., Wang, F., Ren, P., Qian, C.: Centripetalnet: pursuing high-quality keypoint pairs for object detection. In: Proceedings of the IEEE/CVF Conference on Computer Vision and Pattern Recognition, pp. 10519–10528 (2020)
6. Duan, K., Bai, S., Xie, L., Qi, H., Huang, Q., Tian, Q.: Centernet: keypoint triplets for object detection. In: Proceedings of the IEEE/CVF International Conference on Computer Vision, pp. 6569–6578 (2019)

7. Girshick, R.: Fast r-cnn. In: Proceedings of the IEEE International Conference on Computer Vision, pp. 1440–1448 (2015)
8. He, K., Gkioxari, G., Dollár, P., Girshick, R.: Mask r-cnn. In: Proceedings of the IEEE International Conference on Computer Vision, pp. 2961–2969 (2017)
9. He, K., Zhang, X., Ren, S., Sun, J.: Deep residual learning for image recognition. In: Proceedings of the IEEE Conference on Computer Vision and Pattern Recognition, pp. 770–778 (2016)
10. Hu, J., Shen, L., Sun, G.: Squeeze-and-excitation networks. In: Proceedings of the IEEE Conference on Computer Vision and Pattern Recognition, pp. 7132–7141 (2018)
11. Huang, L., Yang, Y., Deng, Y., Yu, Y.: Densebox: unifying landmark localization with end to end object detection. arXiv preprint arXiv:1509.04874 (2015)
12. Kong, T., Sun, F., Liu, H., Jiang, Y., Li, L., Shi, J.: Foveabox: beyound anchor-based object detection. IEEE Trans. Image Process. **29**, 7389–7398 (2020)
13. Law, H., Deng, J.: Cornernet: detecting objects as paired keypoints. In: Proceedings of the European Conference on Computer Vision (ECCV), pp. 734–750 (2018)
14. Lin, T.Y., Doll´ar, P., Girshick, R., He, K., Hariharan, B., Belongie, S.: Feature pyramid networks for object detection. In: Proceedings of the IEEE Conference on Computer Vision and Pattern Recognition, pp. 2117–2125 (2017)
15. Lin, T.Y., Goyal, P., Girshick, R., He, K., Doll´ar, P.: Focal loss for dense object detection. In: Proceedings of the IEEE International Conference on Computer Vision, pp. 2980–2988 (2017)
16. Lin, TY., et al.: Microsoft coco: common objects in context. In: Fleet, D., Pajdla, T., Schiele, B., Tuytelaars, T. (eds.) Computer Vision – ECCV 2014. ECCV 2014, LNCS, vol. 8693, pp. 740–755. Springer, Cham (2014). https://doi.org/10.1007/978-3-319-10602-1_48
17. Long, J., Shelhamer, E., Darrell, T.: Fully convolutional networks for semantic segmentation. In: Proceedings of the IEEE Conference on Computer Vision and Pattern Recognition, pp. 3431–3440 (2015)
18. Pang, J., Chen, K., Shi, J., Feng, H., Ouyang, W., Lin, D.: Libra r-cnn: towards balanced learning for object detection. In: Proceedings of the IEEE/CVF Conference on Computer Vision and Pattern Recognition, pp. 821–830 (2019)
19. Redmon, J., Divvala, S., Girshick, R., Farhadi, A.: You only look once: unified, real-time object detection. In: Proceedings of the IEEE Conference on Computer Vision and Pattern Recognition, pp. 779–788 (2016)
20. Ren, S., He, K., Girshick, R., Sun, J.: Faster r-cnn: towards real-time object detection with region proposal networks. In: Advances in Neural Information Processing Systems, vol. 28 (2015)
21. Rezatofighi, H., Tsoi, N., Gwak, J., Sadeghian, A., Reid, I., Savarese, S.: Generalized intersection over union: a metric and a loss for bounding box regression. In: Proceedings of the IEEE/CVF Conference on Computer Vision and Pattern Recognition, pp. 658–666 (2019)
22. Sun, P., et al.: Sparse r-cnn: end-to-end object detection with learnable proposals. In: Proceedings of the IEEE/CVF Conference on Computer Vision and Pattern Recognition, pp. 14454–14463 (2021)
23. Tian, Z., Shen, C., Chen, H., He, T.: Fcos: fully convolutional one-stage object detection. In: Proceedings of the IEEE/CVF International Conference on Computer Vision, pp. 9627–9636 (2019)
24. Wang, Q., Wu, B., Zhu, P., Li, P., Zuo, W., Hu, Q.: Eca-net: efficient channel attention for deep convolutional neural networks. In: Proceedings of the IEEE/CVF Conference on Computer Vision and Pattern Recognition, pp. 11534–11542 (2020)
25. Yan, X., Chen, Z., Xu, A., Wang, X., Liang, X., Lin, L.: Meta r-cnn: towards general solver for instance-level low-shot learning. In: Proceedings of the IEEE/CVF International Conference on Computer Vision, pp. 9577–9586 (2019)

26. Zand, M., Etemad, A., Greenspan, M.: ObjectBox: from centers to boxes for anchor-free object detection. In: Avidan, S., Brostow, G., Cissé, M., Farinella, G.M., Hassner, T. (eds.) Computer Vision – ECCV 2022. ECCV 2022. LNCS, vol. 13670, pp. 390–406. Springer, Cham (2022). https://doi.org/10.1007/978-3-031-20080-9_23

27. Zheng, Z., Wang, P., Liu, W., Li, J., Ye, R., Ren, D.: Distance-iou loss: faster and better learning for bounding box regression. In: Proceedings of the AAAI Conference on Artificial Intelligence, vol. 34, pp. 12993–13000 (2020)

28. Zheng, Z., et al.: Enhancing geometric factors in model learning and inference for object detection and instance segmentation. IEEE Trans. Cybern. 52(8), 8574–8586 (2021)

29. Zhou, X., Koltun, V., Krähenbühl, P.: Probabilistic two-stage detection. arXiv preprint arXiv: 2103.07461 (2021)

30. Zhu, C., He, Y., Savvides, M.: Feature selective anchor-free module for single-shot object detection. In: Proceedings of the IEEE/CVF Conference on Computer vision and Pattern Recognition, pp. 840–849 (2019)

Semi-supervised Clustering Algorithm Based on L1 Regularization and Extended Pairwise Constraints

Yan Li[1], Xiao Qin[1,2,3](✉), Zhi Zhong[1], Long Chen[2], and Sijing Tan[1]

[1] Center for Applied Mathematics of Guangxi, Nanning Normal University, Nanning 530100, China
7670172@qq.com
[2] Guangxi Key Lab of Human-Machine Interaction and Intelligent Decision, Guangxi Academy of Science, Nanning 530007, China
[3] Guangxi Collaborative Innovation Center of Multi-Source Information Integration and Intelligent Processing, Nanning, China

Abstract. Clustering algorithm plays an important role in recommendation system, data analysis, market segmentation and other fields. Their primary objective is to grow up similar samples into the same clusters while separating dissimilar samples into distinct clusters. With the rapid development of deep learning, deep clustering integrates the strong representational ability of deep learning into clustering tasks and achieves outstanding performance. Currently, most clustering algorithms are unsupervised. However, many times datasets contain not only unlabeled data but also limited relational information. It is possible to significantly enhance the clustering performance by using this prior information effectively. Thus, this research focuses on semi-supervised clustering for data involving the extended pairwise constraints. Specifically, this paper adopts the following techniques to improve deep clustering effectiveness: (1) Use partial samples with pairwise information to extend the whole dataset, which makes full use of the relationship information between samples. (2) Add the L1 norm to the loss function, allowing for feature sparsity to enhance model generalization. (3) Update cluster centers with KL divergence to introduce more information during center adjustments. Ultimately, experimental results from five datasets demonstrate significant enhancements in clustering performance achieved by the semi-supervised clustering algorithm proposed in this study.

Keywords: Pairwise constraints · L1 regularization · Semi-supervised Clustering

1 Introduction

Clustering is typically executed using unlabeled data, yet real-world scenarios often involve data with inherent pairwise relationships. For instance, we can easily classify winged birds and wingless birds as non-birds. The pairwise information of data can be introduced into clustering to improve the performance of traditional unsupervised clustering. Consequently, recent research trends have shifted toward the exploration of semi-supervised clustering approaches based on pairwise constraints.

There are three common types of semi-supervised clustering [1]: (1) Semi-Supervised Clustering based on pairwise constraints. Yang et al. [2] improved Cop-Kmeans algorithm by using MapReduce. Li et al. [3] introduced a cross-entropy semi-supervised clustering algorithm that relies on pairwise constraints, ensuring that even a small amount of pairwise constraint information can lead to improved clustering outcomes. Moreover, the majority of extant pairwise constraint propagation methods rely on canonical graph propagation models, which struggle to maintain both local and global consistency while augmenting spatial complexity; (2) Semi-Supervised Clustering based on distance. Wei et al. [4] proposed semi-supervised clustering based on pairwise constraints and metrics, which generates different basic clustering in two ways, then the final clustering is obtained by integrating; (3) Semi-Supervised Clustering algorithms combining constraints and distance [5].

Current semi-supervised clustering algorithms confront several challenges, including the underutilization of prior information, limited model robustness and generalization, an inability to extract deep features from data, sensitivity to the initial centroid selection, and susceptibility to local optima [6]. To solve these problems, the paper is structured into two main parts: pre-training and training. During the pre-training stage, the encoder undergoes initial training. Pairwise prior information is acquired via the encoder to determine the thresholds for the Must-link (positive samples) and Cannot-Link (negative samples) constraints. And this threshold-driven pairwise prior information is extended to encompass the entire dataset, resulting in an expanded set of pairwise constraints. The pre-trained optimal encoder is integrated into the training process. The training process involves the addition of the KL divergence to optimize the clustering target, and the continuous and iterative use of Stochastic Gradient Descent (SGD) for back-propagation to learn the map.

- We employ a few prior information to construct thresholds for both Must-Link and Cannot-Link pairwise constraints. The canonical graph propagation models are discarded, and iterative threshold information across the entire dataset to extend pairwise constraints. This approach not only reduces spatial complexity but also ensures the maintenance of both local and global consistency.
- We incorporate the L1 norm into the loss function to promote feature sparsity, eliminate irrelevant features, and enhance the model generalization capability.
- We utilize KL divergence to update cluster centers, introducing additional information during the iterative adjustment of cluster centers.

2   Related Work

2.1   Pairwise Constraints

Wagstaff et al. [7] introduced the Cop-Kmeans algorithm, which combines the concept of pairwise constraints with K-means clustering. Pairwise constraint information serves as prior knowledge to supervise clustering, including Must-Link and Cannot-Link (ML and CL) constraints. The pairwise constraint can force the model to cluster correctly and reasonably, improve the clustering effect, and mine the deep features of data.

Definition 1 Must-Link the set $M = \{(x_i, x_k)\}$,   if$(x_i, x_k) \in M$, then data x_i and x_k must belong to the same class, x_i and x_k having Must-link (positive sample) relationship.

Definition 2 Cannot-Link the set $C = \{(x_i, x_k)\}$,   if$(x_i, x_k) \in C$ if, then data x_i and x_k must not belong to the same class, x_i and x_k having Cannot-Link (negative sample) relationship.

2.2 L1 Regularization

L1 regularization refers to the sum of the absolute values of each element in the weight vector w, usually expressed as $||w||_1$, L1 regularization can produce a sparse weight matrix, that is a sparse model, which can be used for feature selection [8].

$$J = J_O + \delta \sum_W |W| \tag{1}$$

3 Semi-supervised Clustering Algorithm Based on L1 Regularization and Extended Pairwise Constraints

This section provides a comprehensive elucidation of the algorithm's intricate details, illustrated in Fig. 1. The algorithm unfolds in two primary stages: pre-training and training. In the pre-training phase, a set of pairwise constraints is expanded, and the L1 regularization procedure is employed to enhance the encoder, denoted as f_θ. This pre-training stage aims to refine the encoder's performance. Then, during the training, two steps are alternated. In the first step, the soft assignment is computed to associate sample points with their respective cluster centroids. In the second step, the encoder is updated using an auxiliary distribution, represented as p, which learns from the current high-confidence distribution to optimize the cluster centers.

For a dataset, there are n pieces of data, and the corresponding data space is X. Therefore, it can be expressed as $\{x_i \in X\}_{i=1}^n$. We start by mapping the data nonlinearly $f_\theta : X \to Z$, where θ is a learnable parameter and Z is the mapped feature space. The Z dimension will be much smaller than the X dimension to achieve the effect of feature learning. Therefore, the entire optimization process is summarized in Algorithm 1.

3.1 Parameters Initialization

Z_i : Similar to some previous studies [9, 10], the proposed model also needs pre-training for better clustering initialization. Therefore, the first step of the pre-training process, data x_i (D-dimension) through the encoder f_θ, into d-dimensional latent embedding z_i.

$$z_i = f_\theta(x_i) \tag{2}$$

where $d \ll D$.

Then d-dimensional latent embedding z_i is reconstructed by the decoder network g_Ω:

$$\hat{x}_i = g_\Omega(z_i) \tag{3}$$

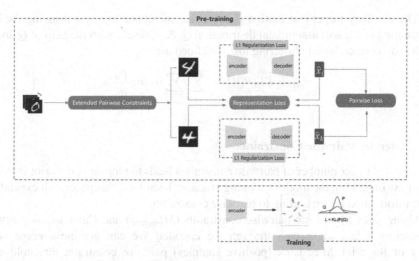

Fig. 1. The overall framework of the proposed approach.

In an unsupervised mode, it is easy to obtain the initial high-level compact representation by minimizing the following loss function:

$$L_{net} = \sum_{i=1}^{n} ||x_i - \hat{x}_i||_2^2 \tag{4}$$

3.2 Soft Assignment

Compared with hard assignment, soft assignment can bring more information into the iterative process of adjusting cluster centers. The probability distribution q is used to represent the probability that the sample points belong to the cluster center. q_{ij} is used to represent the probability that the dot z_i belongs to the cluster center u_j, and assuming that the distribution of the sample points follows the T-Student distribution, q_{ij} is expressed as:

$$q_{ij} = \frac{\left(1 + ||z_i - \mu_j||^2/\alpha\right)^{-\frac{\alpha+1}{2}}}{\sum_{j'}\left(1 + ||z_i - \mu_{j'}||^2/\alpha\right)^{-\frac{\alpha+1}{2}}} \tag{5}$$

where $z_i = f_\theta(x_i) \in z$, it represents the feature mapping of data x after passing f_θ, and α is the degree of freedom of the T-Student distribution. As Van [11] shows, learning about is superfluous, so we set $\alpha = 1$.

3.3 Minimize KL Divergence

To optimize the soft assignment distribution Q, the auxiliary target distribution P is further derived as:

$$p_{ij} = \frac{q_{ij}^2/f_j}{\sum_{j'} q_{ij'}^2/f_j} \tag{6}$$

The auxiliary target distribution P can guide the clustering by enhancing the discrimination of the soft assignment distribution Q. As a result, with the help of Q and P, the KL divergence based clustering loss is defined as:

$$L_{kl} = KL(P||Q) = \sum_i \sum_j p_{ij} \log \frac{p_{ij}}{q_{ij}} \tag{7}$$

3.4 Extended Pairwise Constraints

In general, a larger number of pairwise constraints leads to more specific prior information, thus improving the model's training efficacy. Therefore, this paper will expand the prior information by expanding to pairwise constraints.

Using prior Must-Link pairwise constraints (ML_{before}) and Cannot-Link pairwise constraints (CL_{before}) to pass through the encoder. We can get the average similarity of the prior Must-Link (positive samples) pairwise constraint threshold $\alpha \times ML_{before-average}$, the prior Cannot-Link (negative samples) pairwise constraint threshold $\beta \times CL_{before-average}$ (α and β are threshold factors and their values will be discussed in the experimental section below). If the similarity of two data (x_i, x_k) after passing through the encoder (z_i, z_k), z_{ik} exists in the following relationship, we will extend them into Must-Link (ML) pairwise constraints and Cannot-Link (CL) pairwise constraints.

$$\begin{cases} z_{ik} < \alpha \cdot ML_{before-average}, & (x_i, x_k) \in ML \\ z_{ik} > \beta \cdot CL_{before-average}, & (x_i, x_k) \in CL \end{cases} \tag{8}$$

This method extends prior pairwise constraints to all datasets, forming extended Must-Link (ML) pairwise constraints and Cannot-Link (CL) pairwise constraints. The effect is shown in Fig. 2.

Fig. 2. This figure shows the transformation of prior pairwise constraints into extended pairwise constraints.

Then, the encoder is trained using the expanded pairwise constraints. Therefore, the loss of pairwise constraints is expressed as:

$$L_{pair} = C_{ik} \sum_{i=1}^{n} ||z_i - z_k||_2^2 / n \tag{9}$$

According to Klein [12], Bilenko [13], C_{ik} is a scalar variable that always satisfies the following settings:

$$C_{ik} = \begin{cases} +1, & (x_i, x_k) \in ML \\ -1, & (x_i, x_k) \in CL \end{cases} \tag{10}$$

When x_i and x_k are Must-Link (ML) pairwise constraints, C_{ik} is 1. When x_i and x_k are Cannot-Link (CL) pairwise constraints, C_{ik} is -1.

Finally, to improve the stability and generalization ability of the model, L1 regularization is further introduced to obtain the following loss function:

$$L = L_{net} + L_{kl} + L_{pair} + \delta||Z||_1 \qquad (11)$$

Algorithm 1 Semi-supervised Clustering Algorithm based on L1 Regularization and Extended pairwise constraints

---

Input: Dataset X, Number of clusters K, Batch size B, Pre-training rounds Pre_epoch, Training rounds Epoch, Number of pairwise constraints N, The set of Must-Link constraints ML_{before}, The set of Cannot-Link constraints CL_{before} , Prior Must-Link pairwise threshold α, Prior Cannot-Link pairwise threshold β, L1 regularization parameter δ.

    Output: Clustering results: S

// Initialization

Initialization C by (10), and θ, Ω by (4);

Initialization $S = \{s_i\}_{i=1}^{n}$, $M = \{\mu\}_{j=1}^{K}$ by performing K-means on $Z = \{z_i\}_{i=1}^{n}$;

//Pre-training

using $\alpha \times ML_{before-average}$, $\beta \times CL_{before-average}$ by (8) to get extended pairwise constraints;

    for loss changes **do**

        Using L_{net} by (4), L_{pair} by (9), L1 regularization to pre-training;

    end

    select best f_θ by (4), (9);

// Training

    for epoch = E **do**

        Using q by (5) to update z_i ;

        Reverse update training f_θ , using p by (6);

    end

    return S

---

4 Experiment

4.1 Datasets

To evaluate the algorithm, open-source datasets were used to validate its effectiveness and compared with various algorithms, including MNIST [14], USPS [15], FMNIST [16], COIL20 [17], and DIGITS [18]. The information on datasets is shown in Table 1. We adopt two standard metrics, i.e., clustering accuracy (ACC) [19], and normalized mutual information (NMI) [20], to evaluate the performance of different clustering methods.

4.2 Experimental Environment

All experiments are implemented on a standard Linux Server with an Intel(R) Xeon(R) CPU E7–4820 v4 @ 2.00 GHz, NVIDIA GeForce RTX 2080 TiGPUs, Ubuntu 18.04.6 LTS, python 3.10.9 and pytorch 1.21.1.

Table 1. Information of datasets

Datasets	Number of data	Category	Dimension
MNIST	70000	10	$28 \times 28 \times 1$
USPS	9298	10	$28 \times 28 \times 1$
FMNIST	70000	10	$28 \times 28 \times 1$
COIL20	1440	20	$128 \times 128 \times 1$
DIGITS	28000	10	$28 \times 28 \times 1$

4.3 Parameter Settings

About the batch size, except for the COIL20 dataset, which is 64, all others are 256. The learning rate is 0.001, the random seed is 1000. Additional detailed parameters will be discussed in Sect. 3.4.

4.4 Experimental Comparison

Compare the following algorithm with our algorithm: (1) K-Means [9] achieves sample clustering by specifying n samples and k clustering centers through loss; (2) AC [21] treats each sample as a class, and then merges it through measurement strategies to complete clustering; (3) DEC [22] clusters latent spatial data by updating the clustering center through soft assignment; (4) SCDE [10] estimates the number of clusters and performs clustering by learning an autoencoder; (5) LRDSC [8] is the L1 regularized deep spectral clustering algorithm; (6) WSCEC [23] is a weighted semi-supervised clustering ensemble algorithm based on extended constraint projection.

From the ACC metrics in Table 2 on different datasets, compared to the SCDE, DEC, LRDSC, and WSCEC algorithm, the ACC has increased by an average of 11.41, 10.38, 7.27, and 0.46 percentage points. From the NMI indicators on different datasets in Table 3, compared to the DEC, SCDE, and LRDSC algorithm, the average NMI has increased by 12.12, 7.90, and 7.78 percentage points.

Table 2. ACC Metric Comparison of Algorithms on Different Datasets

	K-MEANS	AC	DEC	LRDSC	WSCEC	OURS
MNIST	50.14	71.14	84.4 83.31	85.6	93.32	**95.37**
USPS	56.61	61.39	61.9 64.67	65.97	87.64	**90.70**
FMNIST	51.46	52.59	57.81 57.81	65.88	68.69	**69.02**
COIL20	76.16	**80.95**	61.0 64.56	69.44	75.10	70.37
DIGITS	49.44	66.44	78.4 86.79	**90.97**	90.32	88.73

Table 3. NMI Metric Comparison of Algorithms on Different Datasets

	K-MEANS	AC	DEC	SCDE	LRDSC	WSCEC	OURS
MNIST	54.67	69.48	81.6	79.02	79.92	**89.65**	87.67
USPS	61.39	57.3	58.6	67.04	61.39	**78.62**	73.51
FMNIST	48.3	51.31	62.83	66.45	66.82	74.62	**75.32**
COIL20	62.85	68.06	62.1	67.86	70.26	**84.10**	80.25
DIGITS	58.67	63.65	80.05	85.91	88.5	87.99	**89.02**

Different Proportions of Extended Pairwise Constraints on the MNIST. According to the study [24], the number of pairwise constraints has an impact on clustering performance. Therefore, Figure 3(a) sets the proportion of pairwise constraints to 20%, 40%, 50%, 70%, and 100%, respectively, to compare the accuracy in the above five datasets. Moreover, when the number of pairwise constraints accounted for about 70%, the clustering effect of the dataset is better. When the pairwise constraint ratio is 100%, the data shows overfitting, so the accuracy will decrease accordingly.

Convergence Analysis. From the following Fig. 3(b), it can be seen that during the pre-training process of the MNIST dataset, When the Pre_epoch approaches 140, the change in loss tends to be smooth. To reduce the pre-training time of the model, the number of iterations for pre-training is chosen to be 140.

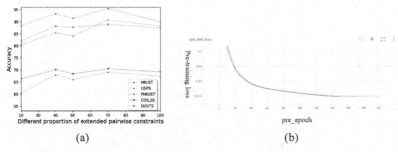

| (a) | (b) |

Fig. 3. Figure (a) is the variation of model accuracy on five datasets with the proportion of pairwise constraints, and Figure (b) is the convergence analysis.

According to DEC [22], during the training period of the MNIST dataset, the accuracy of model clustering tends to flatten out when the epoch E approaches 30. Therefore, we only select the clustering changes and accuracy between the epoch 0 and the epoch 30 (increasing epoch accuracy will decrease). We use T-SNE to represent the vector point z_i to compare between the epoch 0 and the epoch 30. They are shown in Fig. 4(a) and Fig. 4(b).

Parameter Sensitivity. We will discuss the prior Must-Link pairwise constraint threshold factor α, the prior Cannot-Link pairwise constraint threshold factor β, and the L1

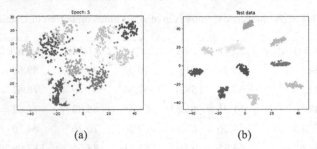

(a)   (b)

Fig. 4. Figure (a) is the distribution of vector points before training, the distribution is scattered, and Figure (b) is the distribution of vector points after training.

regularization parameter δ. The following experiments will be conducted on the MNIST dataset to discuss the impact of different parameter values on the model (epoch = 30). Figure 5(a) shows the impact of α on model accuracy. We set it within the range of 2.4 to 3.8. When $\alpha = 3.0$, the model has the highest accuracy, reaching 95.37, when $\alpha > 3.0$, the accuracy of the model decreases rapidly. Figure 5(b) shows the impact of β on model accuracy. We set it within the range of 2.1 to 2.9, when $\beta = 2.8$, the model has the highest accuracy, reaching 95.37. Table 4 shows the impact of L1 regularization parameters δ on model accuracy. When $\delta > 1$, the model loss is too large and the reverse update is not obvious, so the δ is set to 0.1, 0.01, 0.001, 0.005, 0.0002, 0.0001, and the impact of different δ values on the model accuracy is observed. From Table 4, it can be seen that when $\delta = 0.005$, the model has the highest accuracy.

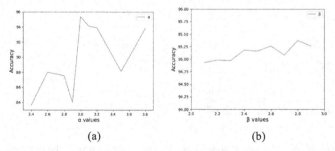

(a)   (b)

Fig. 5. Figure (a) is the prior ML pairwise constraint threshold factor α impact on model performance, and Figure (b) is the prior CL pairwise constraint threshold factor β impact on model performance.

Extended Pairwise Constraints. To better feel the impact of extended pairwise constraints, the changes in model accuracy during the training process are selected for both ML and CL pairwise constraints. From Fig. 6(a), it is evident that extended Must-Link pairwise constraints result in a better clustering performance compared to Cannot-Link pairwise constraints.

Table 4. L1 regularization parameters δ Impact on model performance

L1 regularization parameters(δ)	Accuracy%
0.0001	87.33
0.0002	83.35
0.001	82.95
0.005	**95.37**
0.01	87.18
0.1	24.33

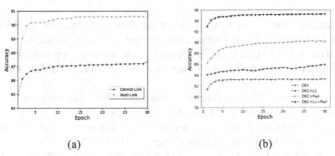

(a)   (b)

Fig. 6. Figure (a) is the impact of extended pairwise constraints on model accuracy. Figure (b) is the ablation experiment.

Ablation Experiment. The following experiments discuss four scenarios on the MNIST: (1) Using the DEC model; (2) Adopting the DEC model and L1 regularization; (3) Adopting the DEC model and expanded pairwise constraints; (4) Adopting the DEC model, L1 regularization, and extended pairwise constraints. For these four scenarios, fixed pre-training iterations Pre_epoch = 140 are used, and the α is set to 3, the β is set to 2.8, and the L1 regularization parameter δ is set to 0.005. From Fig. 6 (b), it can be seen that the model using extended pairwise constraints has a more significant improvement in accuracy. The above experiments fully demonstrate the effectiveness of L1 regularization and extended pairwise constraints for our algorithm.

5 Conclusion

Our approach leverages extended pairwise constraints to harness prior information effectively, ensuring superior clustering supervision. The integration of L1 regularization enhances feature extraction by promoting sparsity, eliminating redundant attributes, and bolstering the model's generalization capacity. Furthermore, to address the sensitivity associated with initial centroid selection, a pre-training encoder method is introduced, proficiently guiding centroid determination. Then soft assignment mechanisms facilitate iterative centroid updates, thereby capturing richer information during the training part. Our experimental results unequivocally confirm the high feasibility and positive outcomes of our algorithm.

Nonetheless, there remain areas for algorithmic enhancement, particularly concerning its performance on the COIL20 and DIGITS datasets and addressing the model's extended runtime. We are committed to ongoing improvements in our future work.

Acknowledgment. This work was supported by the Key Project of Science and Technology of Guangxi (Grant no. AA22068057, AB21076021), BAGUIScholar Program of Guangxi Zhuang Autonomous Region of China (201979), the Research Fund of Guangxi Key Lab of Multi-source Information Mining and Security (MIMS21- 01).

References

1. Li, J., Huang, R., Ren, L.: Semi-supervised deep document clustering model with supplemented user intention. J. Front. Comput. Sci. Technol. **17**(8), 1928 (2023)
2. Yang, Y., Rutayisire, T., Lin, C., Li, T., Teng, F.:. An improved cop-kmeans clus-tering for solving constraint violation based on mapreduce framework. Fund. Inf. **126**(4), 301–318 (2013)
3. Li, Z., Xu, S., Hao, Z.: Cross-entropy semi-supervised clustering based on pairwise constraints. Pattern Recogn. Artif. Intell. **30**(7), 598–608 (2017)
4. Wei, S., Li, Z., Zhang, C.: Combined constraint based with metric based in semi-supervised clustering ensemble. Int. J. Mach. Learn. Cybern. **9**, 1085–1100 (2018)
5. Lai, D.T.C., Garibaldi, J.M.: A comparison of distance-based semi-supervised fuzzy c-means clus-tering algorithms. In: 2011 IEEE International Conference on Fuzzy Systems (FUZZ-IEEE 2011), pp. 1580–1586. IEEE (2011)
6. Dong, Y., Deng, Y., Dong, Y., Wang, Y.: Survey of clustering based on deep learning. Comput. Appl. **42**(4), 1021 (2022)
7. Wagstaff, K., Cardie, C.: Clustering with instance-level constraints. In: Proceedings of 17th International Conference on Machine Learning San Francisco, Morgan Kaufmann Publishers Inc, pp. 1097–1103 (2000)
8. Li, W.B., Liu, B., Dao, L.L., et al.: L1 Regularization deep spectral clustering algorithm. J. Comput. Appl. (2023)
9. Tapas, K., David, M.M., Nathan, S.N., Christine, D.P., Ruth, S., Angela Y.W.: An efficient k-means clustering algorithm: analysis and implementation. IEEE Trans. Pattern Anal. Mach. Intell. **24**(7), 881–892 (2002)
10. Duan, L., Ma, S., Aggarwal, C., Sathe, S.: Improving spectral clustering with deep embedding, cluster estimation and metric learning. Knowl. Inf. Syst. **63**, 675–694 (2021)
11. Van Der Maaten, L.: Learning a parametric embedding by preserving local structure. In: Artificial Intelligence and Statistics, pp. 384–391. PMLR (2009)
12. Klein, D., Kamvar, S.D., Manning, C.D.: From instance-level constraints to space-level constraints: making the most of prior knowledge in data clustering. ICML **2**, 307–314 (2002)
13. Bilenko, M., Basu, S., Mooney, R.J.: Integrating constraints and metric learning in semi-supervised clustering. In: Proceedings of the Twenty-First International Conference on Machine Learning, p. 11 (2004)
14. Deng, L.: The mnist database of handwritten digit images for machine learning research [best of the web]. IEEE Signal Process. Mag. **29**(6), 141–142 (2012)
15. Hull, J.J.: A database for handwritten text recognition research. IEEE Trans. Pattern Anal. Mach. Intell. **16**(5), 550–554 (1994)

16. Han, X., Kashif, R., Roland, V.: Fashion-mnist: a novel image dataset for bench-marking machine learning algorithms. arXiv preprint arXiv:1708.07747 (2017)
17. Nene, S.: Columbia object image library. COIL-100. Technical Report, 6 (1996)
18. Cohen, G., Afshar, S., Tapson, J., et al.: EMNIST: extending MNIST to handwritten letters. In: 2017 International Joint Conference on Neural Networks (IJCNN), pp. 2921–2926. IEEE (2017)
19. Li, T., Ding, C.: The relationships among various nonnegative matrix factorization methods for clustering. In: Sixth International Conference on Data Mining (ICDM'06), pp. 362–371. IEEE (2006)
20. Alexander, S., Joydeep, G.: Cluster ensembles—a knowledge reuse framework for co-mbining multiple partitions. J. Mach. Learn. Res. **3**, 583–617 (2002)
21. Marcel, R.A., Johannes, B., Daniel, K., Christian, S.: Analysis of Aggl-omerative clustering. Algorithmica **69**, 184–215 (2014)
22. Xie, J., Girshick, R., Farhadi, A.: Unsupervised deep embedding for clustering analysis. In: International Conference on Machine Learning, pp. 478–487. PMLR (2016)
23. Wu, Y., Liu, H., Zhang, Q.: Tabel propagation clustering algorithm based on improved pairwise constraint expansion. Appl. Res. Comput./Jisuanji Yingyong Yan-jiu **39**(12) (2022)
24. Ren, S., He, K., Ross, G., Jian, S.: Faster r-cnn: towards real-time object detection with region proposal networks. In: Advances in Neural Information Processing Systems, vol. 28 (2015)

Automated Text Recognition and Review System for Enhanced Bidding Document Analysis

Qiang Xue[1(✉)], Xu Cheng[1], Qingyun Tan[1], and Ruoyan Dong[2]

[1] Colorful Guizhou Digital Technology Co., Ltd., Shenzhen, China
xueqiang2017@163.com
[2] Information Center of Guizhou Power Grid Corporation, Shenzhen, China

Abstract. This paper aims to extract, analyze, and review various types of material information, such as business licenses and qualification certificates, from electronic documents in bidding processes. These documents may be in various formats such as images, scanned copies, and PDFs. Utilizing CRNN and building upon well-trained models, our method demonstrates strong error correction capabilities, thereby enhancing the text recognition accuracy of the Guizhou Power Grid Company's bidding documents. The system is designed to automatically extract and scrutinize key information from multi-format bidding documents obtained from diverse sources. It enables bid evaluation experts to accurately identify and locate issues in the essential information presented in various materials within the bidding documents, through a user-friendly visual interface. Experimental results indicate that our system can precisely extract pivotal information from bidding documents across various formats, consequently reducing the review and approval time. This research holds significant value and presents promising application prospects by potentially lowering labor costs, as well as improving the efficiency and fairness of the bidding process.

Keywords: Key Information go Bidding Documents · Information Extraction · CRNN · Strong Error Correction

1 Introduction

With the advent of internet advancements, electronic bidding documents are progressively supplanting traditional bidding documents within the procurement process [1]. The incorporation of electronic bidding documents facilitates the realization of an intelligent bidding information review mechanism. Reviewing crucial information embedded within bidding documents is pivotal for evaluation, aiming to discern potential discrepancies or non-conformities in various credentials such as business licenses and qualification certificates. This ensures that bidding outcomes are fair, accurate, and effective. Nevertheless, the conventional manual review of these documents, owing to their diverse origins and intricate content, is often marred by substantial time consumption and susceptibility to errors.

In response to this, this paper endeavors to craft a meticulous and efficient text recognition and review system leveraging CRNN technology [2]. This system autonomously

D.-S. Huang et al. (Eds.): ICAI 2023, CCIS 2014, pp. 292–301, 2024.
https://doi.org/10.1007/978-981-97-0903-8_28

extracts salient information from electronic bidding documents—including images, scanned copies, and PDFs—and performs comprehensive analysis and review. Such automation aids evaluators in swiftly and accu rately identifying disqualifying attributes within bidding documents. Employing CRNN significantly truncates the evaluation duration, enhances the assessment quality, and precludes the possibility of awarding bids marred by incongruent materials.

The essence of this research lies in offering a solution that epitomizes intelligent extraction, analysis, and review of critical information within bidding documents. It seeks to address the prevailing challenges inundating the review process. By utilizing a CRNN-based system, this study aspires to augment the precision of document evaluation by efficaciously extracting, analyzing, and scrutinizing various elements within the bidding materials [3]. The introduction of CRNN is instrumental in reducing the time devoted to bid qualification assessments, thereby escalating efficiency and mitigating labor expenditures.

A potent error correction mechanism has been integrated into this system, which substantially bolsters the reliability of bid reviews by reducing oversights, enhancing error detection, and uncovering fraudulent inclinations within critical bidding information, ensuring that the bidding outcomes resonate with fairness and integrity. A visually intuitive interface is deployed, allowing reviewers to meticulously observe and pinpoint potential inaccuracies within critical information, thereby bolstering the precision of error identification. Through the meticulous design and implementation of this text recognition and review apparatus, this study aims to furnish novel technical sustenance to the evaluation of essential bidding document information, thereby fostering the continual evolution and advancement of the procurement industry.

2 Related Work

2.1 Intelligent Text Review Technology

Text intelligent review encompasses a multitude of steps, including text recognition, text parsing, and text extraction. Its fundamental objective is to autonomously identify and extract pertinent information from an array of text materials, followed by a meticulous review and filtration process. Within the automatic review system of bidding documents and other related documents, text intelligent review technology assumes a vital role, serving as the linchpin in optimizing and enhancing the accuracy and efficiency of information extraction and analysis.

2.2 Text Recognition

Text recognition ordinarily acts as the initial phase in intelligent text review. In this stage, OCR (Optical Character Recognition) technology is predominantly employed to recognize and extract text from various documents such as images or PDF files [4]. Leveraging OCR technology facilitates the accurate extraction of textual information from files, irrespective of their diverse formats and origins [5], thereby laying a solid foundation for subsequent stages of text parsing and extraction.

2.3 Text Parsing and Extraction

Following the recognition and extraction of text [6], the subsequent stages encompass text parsing and extraction. Text parsing is instrumental in comprehending the text's structure and semantics, effectively transforming unstructured text into a structured format. Based on the outcomes of the parsing process, text extraction ensues. This phase is dedicated to isolating information of specific significance and value from the text, such as keywords, entity nouns, links, among others, ensuring that meaningful components within the content are meticulously identified and retrieved.

2.4 Model Training

Model training constitutes an essential component of intelligent text review [7]. Utilizing machine learning or deep learning methodologies, models are cultivated to autonomously execute tasks such as text classification, named entity recognition, and sentiment analysis. The process of model training enhances the automation and intelligence of text review, significantly alleviating the burden of manual review by optimizing the precision and efficiency of the text analysis process.

2.5 Assessment and Challenges

Despite the successful integration of intelligent text review technology in various domains [8], it is not devoid of challenges and limitations. Firstly, the accuracy of text recognition is contingent on multiple factors such as image quality, font, and format. Secondly, attributed to the diversity and intricacy of texts, there remains room for enhancing the precision of text parsing and extraction processes. Additionally, model training necessitates a substantial corpus of annotated data, where acquiring high-quality annotations often poses a significant challenge. To mitigate these issues, future investigations could delve into strategies for bolstering the resilience of OCR technology, cultivating advanced algorithms for text parsing and extraction, and augmenting model training efficacy through the incorporation of transfer learning and semi-supervised learning methodologies (Fig. 1).

3 Method

3.1 Image Preprocessing

Preprocessing of electronic files, such as images, scanned copies, and PDFs, primarily involves utilizing image processing technologies to extract requisite feature information. The extraction of key information from various materials, such as business licenses and qualification certificates in bidding documents, is often impeded by a multitude of factors, leading to inconsistencies in image quality and obfuscations from various unforeseen variables. Prior to initiating the tasks of text recognition, analysis, and extraction, it is essential to undertake a series of preprocessing operations on the samples. This meticulous preparation facilitates enhanced speed and accuracy in computerized text recognition. The preprocessing steps highlighted in this article encompass grayscale conversion, binarization, denoising, and tilt correction, all crucial for augmenting the accu racy and reliability of text recognition processes.

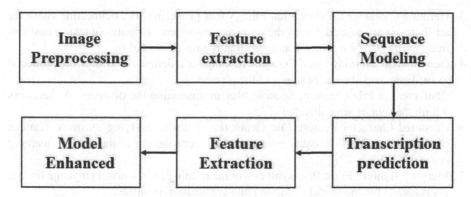

Fig. 1. Text recognition process framework based on CRNN

3.2 CRNN Based Text Recognition

The CRNN (Convolutional Recurrent Neural Network) model exhibits formidable robustness and precision in text recognition tasks, possessing the capability to manage input images of disparate sizes, and facilitating end-to-end text recognition. Given that the dataset utilized in this article is image-centric, an essential preliminary step involves the conversion of these images into text to facilitate subsequent text review processes. CRNN ingeniously amalgamates convolutional neural networks (CNN) [9] and recurrent neural networks (RNN) [10], enabling the capture of both local features and sequential information essential for recognizing text regions within images.

Embodying the synergistic strengths of CNN and RNN, CRNN utilizes CNN for the extraction of pivotal image features, while RNN is deployed for processing sequential information. This fusion enhances the model's versatility and application value, making it particularly potent in text conversion tasks within images. Consequently, CRNN has found extensive application in diverse areas such as document digitization, ticket recognition, and license plate recognition. In this article, the CRNN model will be leveraged to meticulously identify and review information contained in vital documents such as business licenses and qualification certificates.

3.3 Data Expansion

To enhance the model's convergence, we have augmented the existing data, thereby improving the model's generalization capability. The detailed data expansion process unfolds as follows:

1. Training Image Expansion: Due to the limited volume of training data, converging the model poses a challenge. This study enlarges the training dataset by randomly scrambling the text on the training data images, culminating in 400 training datasets and 84 test datasets. All training images were consolidated into a.tif format.
2. Character Boundary Generation and Adjustment: Training dataset boundaries are meticulously modified manually utilizing Tess Box Editor, crafted using Java, to safeguard the integrity of each character encapsulated within the boundaries.

3. Defining Character Configuration File: A font properties file, delineating character attributes, is articulated. Given the relatively consistent attributes of text in business licenses, this study uniformly assigns all attributes a value of 0.
4. Generating.tr Training Files: Essential training files, denoted as.tr files, are produced to facilitate the subsequent stages of the process.
5. Character Set File Creation: Specific files encapsulating the diversity of characters within the dataset are cultivated.
6. Clustered Character Feature File Generation: Files embodying clustered features of characters within the dataset are generated, contributing to the model's learning process.
7. Merging Training Files: Post-synthesis of the training files, a novel language library, instrumental for the model's learning and application, is birthed.

Each stage is meticulously executed to ensure a robust and effective model, optimized for performing text recognition tasks with enhanced precision and reliability.

3.4 Text Recognition and Conversion

Upon securing the augmented dataset, we embarked on the task of text recognition and transformation, and the specific training process unfurled as follows: 1. Feature Extraction: Features were culled from images utilizing pre-trained CNN models. This study deploys the ResNet-50 model [11] as a pivotal feature extractor, aiding in the distillation of essential feature vectors from the images. 2. Sequence Modeling: The meticulously extracted feature sequences are then integrated into the RNN for intensive sequence modeling. Feature sequences, once harvested from convolutional layers, are processed and sequenced through a recurrent neural network, fostering the nuanced learning of sequential information.

3. Transcription Prediction: A transcription layer is meticulously applied to the RNN output, harnessing the capabilities of CTC (Connectionist Temporal Classification) for sequence prediction and transcription. CTC facilitates the mapping of the RNN's output sequence onto the input sequence, imbuing the sequence prediction process with enhanced flexibility and adaptability.

Each phase of the process is executed with precision, ensuring that the model is adeptly trained to recognize and transcribe text with enhanced accuracy and reliability.

3.5 Enhanced Error Correction Capability

This study employs the Seq2Seq model [12] to train models for word and grammar error correction by post-processing transcription results, thereby obtaining the final recognition outcomes. The task of text error correction is conceptualized as a transformation process between differing sequences. The original sentence represents the source statement, while the corrected sentence embodies the target statement. Hence, the Seq2Seq model is incorporated as a sequence transformation model within text error correction.

The foundational architecture of the Seq2Seq model comprises an Encoder-Decoder network model. Here, the Encoder is instrumental in encoding the input text sequence into a vector representation of a specified length. Conversely, the Decoder unravels the encoded vector representation, of a particular length ob tained from the Encoder, into an output sequence. This systematic approach ensures enhanced accuracy and reliability in the task of text error correction within the recognition process (Fig. 2).

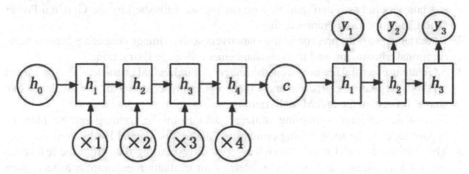

Fig. 2. Seq2Seq Model Structure

4 Experimental Design

4.1 Experimental Dataset

The experimental dataset utilized in this study consists of electronic files of business licenses and qualification certificates, provided by the Guizhou Power Grid Company. Specifically, the business license dataset encompasses 558 images, with 400 allocated as training sets and 158 designated as testing sets. In parallel, the qualification certificate dataset comprises 487 entries, where 341 are reserved for training purposes, and 146 are utilized for testing scenarios.

4.2 Evaluation Indicators

The evaluation metrics utilized in this study are delineated as follows: Precision: Precision signifies the proportion of characters that the OCR system has correctly identified relative to the total number of characters that the system has recognized. This metric is instrumental in gauging the accuracy of the system in character recognition. A heightened precision indicates an augmented likelihood of the system recognizing characters accurately.

Recall Rate: The recall rate delineates the ratio of characters accurately identified by the OCR system concerning the actual number of characters existing in the text. This measure assesses the system's comprehensiveness in character recognition, where a higher recall rate symbolizes the system's enhanced capability to correctly identify extant characters.

F1 Score: The F1 Score acts as a confluence of precision and recall, serving as an integral metric to equilibrate the two aforementioned measures. The F1 Score is computed as the harmonic mean of precision and recall, articulated by the formula: F1 = 2 * (Precision * Recall)/(Precision + Recall). The range of F1 values is 0 to 1, with higher values indicating better system performance.

4.3 Experimental Process

Experimental Procedure:

1. Data Collection:The experimental data are procured from electronic files, encompassing business licenses and qualification certificates furnished by the Guizhou Power Grid Company. Data Preprocessing:
2. Undertaking various preprocessing maneuvers such as image denoising, binarization, rotational adjustment, and image enhancement. Feature Extraction:
3. 3.Gleaning essential features from the imagery of individual characters. Pre-dominant methods for feature extraction encompass algorithms centered around attributes like shape, texture, and edge. Model Training:
4. The model undergoes training utilizing data from the training set, refining its capabilities for the forthcoming evaluation. Model Testing and Evaluation:
5. The cultivated model is put through a series of tests using data from the test set to ascertain its efficacy and precision. Metrics for evaluation encompass aspects such as accuracy, recall, and the F1 score. Experimental Analysis and Optimization:
6. The model's performance is meticulously analyzed based on the outcomes derived from testing. Post-analysis, various experimental parameters are finetuned to enhance model performance, such as tweaking model parameters, augmenting the training dataset, and optimizing feature extraction methodologies.

5 Experimental Results and Analysis

In order to verify the correctness and compliance of information points in a single document, this paper conducted a series of comparative experiments on the superiority and effectiveness of the proposed contract named entity recognition model that combines BILSTM [13] + CRF and BERT [14] preprocessing models. In these experiments, this article implemented three different models: LSTM [15] + CRF, BiLSTM + CRF, and BERT + CRF, and compared and analyzed them. This article evaluates the performance of the system in text parsing and auditing by comparing the OCR accuracy, recall, F1 value, etc. of these models. The results on the business license are shown in Table 1.

For the experimental setup, this article used the same training, validation, and testing sets to ensure that each model was trained and tested on the same dataset. This article uses the same hyperparameter settings and optimizer to train each model.

Table 1. Results on Business License

Method	Accuracy(%)	Recall (%)	F1 Value
LSTM + CRF	71.3	73.3	0.64
BiLSTM + CRF	77.7	76.3	0.52
BERT + CRF	84.8	80.4	0.59
Ours	89.5	83.0	0.82

The results on qualification certificates are shown in Table 2.

Table 2. Results on Qualification Certificates

Method	Accuracy(%)	Recall (%)	F1 Value
LSTM + CRF	65.3	66.3	0.62
BiLSTM + CRF	69.7	68.3	0.57
BERT + CRF	74.8	73.4	0.69

The experimentation has yielded insightful results regarding the model's performance on business licenses and qualification certificates when compared to other prevalent models like LSTM + CRF, BiLSTM + CRF, and BERT + CRF.

1. Business License Analysis:The proposed model exhibits a remarkable improvement with an accuracy boost of 18.2 percentage points and a recall enhancement of 9.7 percentage points over the LSTM + CRF model.When juxta-posed with the BiLSTM + CRF model, our proposed model triumphs with an 11.8 percentage point increase in accuracy and a 6.7 percentage point ascent in recall. Compared to the BERT + CRF model, our model has fortified its position with increments of 4.7 in accuracy and 2.6 in recall percentage points.
2. Qualification Certificate Analysis: Against the LSTM + CRF model, our design proves superior with an 18.3 percentage point advancement in accuracy and a 10.9 percentage point growth in recall.In a comparative study with the BiL-STM + CRF model, our architecture shines with a 13.9 percentage point rise in accuracy and an 8.9 percentage point leap in recall.Showing resilience against the BERT + CRF model, our proposition leads with an 8.8 percentage point progress in accuracy and a 3.8 percentage point development in recall.
3. Comparative Overview: In textual classifications akin to the ones under study, our model displays an illustrious performance, dominating in metrics like accuracy, recall, and F1 scores over the other three scrutinized models.
4. Conclusion and Prospects: The comparative assessment underscores our method's substantial promise and applicability, manifesting significantly higher metrics like recall and accuracy. Our methodology has been successful in accurately identifying attributes in business licenses and qualification certificates. However, it's imperative to note that due to dataset constraints, our experiments were primarily focused on business licenses and qualification certificates, and not as expansive across a diverse array of textual data.

6 Application Cases and Discussions

In the progressive realm of text recognition, notable strides have been made by various researchers. For instance, Siek [16] has innovatively proposed a system that leverages the powerful capabilities of Convolutional Neural Networks (CNNs) combined with intricate deep learning algorithms. This meticulously crafted system has been instrumental in enhancing the efficiency of the manual payment approval workflow by expediently accelerating the processes of payment verification and confirmation, bypassing certain traditional steps.

Achieving a remarkable 100% accuracy in detecting essential elements like trace numbers, approval codes, and nominal values in the test dataset, Siek's system showcases formidable proficiency as an OCR (Optical Character Recognition) tool. It emerges as a reliable and precise asset in tackling payment verifica tion challenges in real-world commercial scenarios, embodying a robust solution for practical application.

Parallelly, in the wake of the burgeoning development of the Internet and the widespread adoption of paperless office practices, electronic bidding systems have evolved to become indispensable tools in facilitating project procurement across various organizations. The integration of CRNN technology within the bidding domain signifies a monumental advancement, proving pivotal in addressing and resolving significant challenges endemic to engineering sectors. This approach necessitates not only robust technical backing but also fulfills pressing practical requisites.

The text recognition and intelligent review mechanisms, as delineated in this study, manifest as transformative innovations, catalyzing remarkable improvements in operational efficiency within business processes, particularly in the context of bid document information acquisition. Thus, it unfolds as a dynamic and efficacious strategy, promising substantial enhancements in the realm of electronic bidding systems and beyond.

7 Conclusion

This paper introduces a proficient text recognition and review system based on CRNN, designed for effective extraction and error analysis of bid content. Aiming to prevent misjudgments in the bidding industry, the system ensures enhanced accuracy, fostering a fair and just bidding environment. With a focus on continuous improvement, future adaptations are planned to further elevate the system's performance, driving advancements in the field of text recognition and review.

Acknowledgment. This work is Supported by Intelligent Bidding Evaluation Assistance Platform based on Deep Learning" (Project Number: 066700KK52210003) developed by Guizhou Power Grid Limited Liability Company.

References

1. Jang, Y., Son, J., Yi, J.S.: Classifying the level of bid price volatility based on machine learning with parameters from bid documents as risk factors. Sustainability **13**(7), 3886 (2021)
2. Fu, X., Ch'ng, E., Aickelin, U., See, S.: CRNN: a joint neural network for redundancy detection. In: 2017 IEEE International Conference on Smart Computing (SMART-COMP), pp. 1–8. IEEE (2017)
3. Chen, M., Ge, T., Zhang, X., Wei, F., Zhou, M.: Improving the efficiency of grammatical error correction with erroneous span detection and correction. arXiv preprint arXiv:2010.03260 (2020)
4. Wang, T., Wu, D.J., Coates, A., Ng, A.Y.: End-to-end text recognition with convolutional neural networks. In: Proceedings of the 21st International Conference on Pattern Recognition (ICPR2012), pp. 3304–3308 (2012)

5. Geetha, M., Pooja, R., Swetha, J., Nivedha, N., Daniya, T.: Implementation of text recognition and text extraction on formatted bills using deep learning. Int. J. Contrl. Automat. **13**(2), 646–651 (2020)
6. Kim, E., Huang, K., Saunders, A., McCallum, A., Ceder, G., Olivetti, E.: Materials synthesis insights from scientific literature via text extraction and machine learning. Chem. Mater. **29**(21), 9436–9444 (2017)
7. Ganesh, A., et al.: Why is public pretraining necessary for private model training? In: International Conference on Machine Learning, pp. 10611–10627. PMLR (2023)
8. Ashtiani, M.N., Raahmei, B.: News-based intelligent prediction of financial markets using text mining and machine learning: a systematic literature review. Exp. Syst. Appl. **217**, 119509 (2023)
9. Chua, L.O., Roska, T.: The CNN paradigm. IEEE Trans. Circ. Syst. I: Fund. Theor. Appl. **40**(3), 147–156 (1993)
10. Koutnik, J., Greff, K., Gomez, F., Schmidhuber, J.: A clockwork RNN. In: Interna tional Conference on Machine Learning, pp. 1863–1871. PMLR (2014)
11. He, K., Zhang, X., Ren, S., Sun, J.: Deep residual learning for image recognition. In: Proceedings of the IEEE Conference on Computer Vision and Pattern Recognition, pp. 770–778 (2016)
12. Sutskever, I., Vinyals, O., Le, Q.V.: Sequence to sequence learning with neural networks. In: Advances in Neural Information Processing Systems, vol. 27 (2014)
13. Huang, Z., Xu, W., Yu, K.: Bidirectional LSTM-CRF models for sequence tagging. arXiv preprint arXiv:1508.01991 (2015)
14. Devlin, J., Chang, M.W., Lee, K., Toutanova, K.: Bert: pre-training of deep bidirectional transformers for language understanding. arXiv preprint arXiv:1810.04805 (2018)
15. Greff, K., Srivastava, R.K., Koutník, J., Steunebrink, B.R., Schmidhuber, J.: LSTM: a search space odyssey. IEEE Trans. Neural Netw. Learn. Syst. **28**(10), 2222–2232 (2016)
16. Sick, M., Soeharto, R.: Developing automated optical character recognition system using machine learning algorithm to solve payment verification issues. In: 2021 3rd International Conference on Cybernetics and Intelligent System (ICORIS), pp. 1–6. IEEE (2021)

Machine Vision-Based Defect Classification Algorithm for Rolled Packages

Wenbin Zhou[1], Ruihan Li[1], Junhao Guo[1], Zhiliang Li[2], Ruoyan Zhou[2], Hongyun Zhu[2], Zihao Jian[2], and Yongxuan Lai[2,3(✉)]

[1] Xiamen Tobacco Industry Co. Ltd., Xiamen, China
[2] Shenzhen Research Institute/School of Informatics, Xiamen University, Xiamen, China
laiyx@xmu.edu.cn
[3] School of Mathematics and Information Engineering, Longyan University, Longyan, China

Abstract. Under the growth of industrial digitization, networking and intelligence, more and more industrial enterprises are undergoing digital transformations. In the tobacco industry, potential issues may arise during the packaging phase, leading to packaging defects. In the traditional process, the camera shoots at a fixed point and compares the designated focus area image with the standard image to determine whether it is defective or not. This thesis investigates a defect classification method dedicated to the field of tobacco production, using machine vision algorithms to detect the images of cigarette packaging. The objective is to determine the presence and the type of defects, which is conducive to realize a automated and intelligent production mode. The method combines traditional computer vision techniques with deep learning models, and contains two phases: first, traditional CV methods are directly used for some defects with obvious features and some positional offset defects, which improves the efficiency and accuracy, and facilitates the subsequent classification; second, deep learning methods are used for the remaining defects. For the multi-label classification, a defect classification network is constructed and trained based on ResNet-34. After experiments and research on all the defects (12 types), this method can meet the needs of defect recognition.

Keywords: Machine Vision · Roll Wrapping · Defect Classification

1 Introduction

The innovation of industry is a subject that is full of vibrancy and imagination. Machine vision mainly uses computers to simulate the visual function of human beings, extracts information from the images of objective things, processes and finally uses them for actual detection, measurement and control. It has achieved great success in many fields, one of which is online automatic inspection in industry.

At present, the tobacco industry, being a significant component of the real economy, must demonstrate its role more prominently. When consumers buy cigarettes, its appearance is an important selection criteria. It is indispensable to detect defects on the

D.-S. Huang et al. (Eds.): ICAI 2023, CCIS 2014, pp. 302–313, 2024.
https://doi.org/10.1007/978-981-97-0903-8_29

packaging surface in order to ensure the quality of cigarettes. In the traditional production process, a camera is positioned to take pictures and a human eye observes them, and if the picture of the designated focus area does not meet the predetermined standard, it is recognized as a defect. However, the method is time-consuming and labor-intensive with serious drawbacks.

This paper investigates a defect classification method for cigarette packages. It can efficiently and accurately image inspection of cigarette packages to determine whether there are defects and their types, which is helpful to locate the faulty steps. The application of this method can improve production efficiency and product quality, and complete the digital transformation from traditional to new industry.

A total of 12 defects can occur in the cigarette packaging process as a result of research. Our study combines traditional computer vision techniques and deep learning models and contains two phases. First, traditional CV methods are directly applied to some defects with obvious features and some positional offset defects, which effectively locate the cigarettes in the complex background. Second, a deep learning approach is used for multi-label classification of the remaining defects, and a defect classification network is constructed based on ResNet-34. The model is able to learn the abstract features in the image and identify the type of defects.

Previously, many researchers have carried out a series of studies on the defect detection of cigarette packaging, but many methods have certain shortcomings, such as the template matching method [1], which is greatly affected by environmental factors, and the real-time anomaly detection algorithm for striped tobacco, which is lacking in real-time [4], etc. In this regard, we adopt a combinatorial approach that can cope well with the complex production environment. First, our method is more robust and applicable to different sizes and rotation angles. Second, our approach covers the full range of defects, which is more comprehensive compared to previous studies. This comprehensive approach provides a more reliable quality control tool for the tobacco manufacturing industry and higher quality assurance for consumers.

The main contributions of this paper are as follows:

- We propose a new method, which makes up for some deficiencies in the field, covers a wide range, is highly efficient and adaptable.
- We use a variety of techniques to combine traditional computer vision with deep learning models, and different defects correspond to different detection methods, which are faster and more accurate.

2 Related Work

Cigarette defect detection is an important issue that involves product quality control and monitoring of the manufacturing process. At present, in the detection of cigarette package appearance quality, the most traditional method is manual sorting, which has high work intensity and is not suitable for real-time detection. With the rapid development of artificial intelligence, many detection methods using computer vision have emerged in China. For example [1], template matching method is used to match the cigarette packaging to be tested with the template image, in order to identify whether there are defects and what kind of defects they are.

Compared with the domestic, foreign products are now more mature technology. For the defect detection of wrapping paper, some enterprises in developed countries have developed some better detection systems, such as Germany's Siemens, etc. [2], which have greatly improved the efficiency of production, but its recognition effect is not good.

In order to improve the quality of cigarette packaging, many domestic researchers have carried out many studies on the defect detection of cigarette packaging. Liu Wei [3] carried out a study on the appearance detection of cigarette cartons based on convolutional neural networks. He used a convolutional neural network to detect cigarette packages, simulating the human recognition process, and learning from a large amount of data. However, the number of training samples is small. Yan Xibin et al. [4] proposed a striped tobacco anomaly detection algorithm based on visual perception characteristics, which meets the requirements of recognition accuracy, but still needs to be further improved in real-time. Liu Huanming [5] proffered a cigarette small package seal defect automatic detection algorithm based on Canny edge detection algorithm [6], firstly, the small label is segmented from the image, and then the mean value filtering algorithm is used to filter and denoise the image and other processing, so that the edge portion is more prominent, which facilitates the detection of the final Canny algorithm. Li Qi [7] collected image data on the appearance of cigarette packets, and used traditional CV methods to process the collected images, while using noise reduction, and other methods to obtain a series of parameters, and by comparing with the standard parameters, to determine the type of defects. However, this method is not perfect for the defect types, and only some of the defects are targeted. Hongyu L et al. [8] presented a defect detection method based on C-CenterNet for the appearance of cigarettes, which introduces the CBAM mechanism and utilizes a feature pyramid network to extract features from various levels.

In summary, many domestic researchers have made research and exploration on the defect recognition of cigarette packaging, but because of the complexity of the cigarette production environment, many methods are still deficient and need to be improved, and further research needs to be done on this.

3   Approach

3.1   Overview of Two-Stage Roll-Packet Defect Classification Algorithm

In the rolled packet defect classification algorithm, we divide the 12 kinds of defects that will appear in the rolled packet process into two parts: the first part is the defects that can be recognized by the detection frame, including Fig. 3 (d, e, j); the second part is the other defects except for the first part and the empty packet defects. This is done because the first type of defects do not perform well in deep learning frameworks, and the detection frames account for a small percentage of the image, which is similar to noise, and are prone to lose defective features in the convolution process. For detecting bad defective QR codes, it is difficult for the deep learning network to learn useful information due to its independence and the lack of statistical regularity among samples.

Therefore, we divide the overall process into two stages, first using traditional computer vision methods to identify the detection frame location and determine which of the first category the defect belongs to; if this is not possible, it is handed over to the deep learning network for multi-label classification to determine which of the second category the defect belongs to, or several of them. In particular, for empty bag defects, we utilize color as the discriminating condition. When the proportion of black, white, metallic gray and green in the frame reaches 88\% or more, it is judged as an empty packet defect.A sample of empty packet is shown in Fig. 3 (a).

3.2 Detection Frame Positioning Method

In this section, we put forward the corresponding technical methods and solutions for the implementation process of the design part of the detection frame positioning as well as the problems encountered, and give the schematic diagrams in the key parts.

The detection frames to be positioned in this section include the QR code red frame, white frame and grey frame, as shown in Fig. 1 (a). Each detection frame has a different role, in which the grey frame is used to regulate the position of the QR code, the QR code needs to fall as close as possible to the grey frame, if there is a left-right offset, it may be a positioning alignment defect; if there is a top-bottom offset, it may be a misalignment defect in the cutting of the frame paper. The white frame of the QR code is used to make reference judgement on the position. The red frame indicates that the two-dimensional code is abnormal, when the grey frame and the two-dimensional code white frame has no obvious positional offset, but the middle detection frame is red, indicating the existence of two-dimensional code detection defects.

The specific idea of the detection frame localisation algorithm is to first sharpen the image and then extract the desired colours such as grey, red and white. Then the picture is intercepted to ensure that the detection frame is within the intercepted range. In order to improve the accuracy of the detection results, the image is subjected to grey scale expansion. Then, edge detection and straight line detection are performed on the image to get all straight lines. Next, all straight lines are traversed, and straight lines that tend to be horizontal are put into one list, and straight lines that tend to be vertical are put into another list, and then adjacent straight lines are merged. Then, non-repeated linear quadruple are continuously taken out from the list of horizontal straight lines and the list of vertical straight lines, and if the linear quadruple satisfy the conditions for constituting the detection frame, their central coordinates, as well as the coefficients to be determined, are deposited into the array. Finally, a weighted average method is used to calculate the coordinates of the final detection frame. In the following, we will introduce each step of the detection frame positioning method.

Image Preprocessing. During image processing, we first adopt color filtering to map the image from RGB color space to HSV color space to accurately extract regions of specific colors, such as white, red, and grey, so as to optimize the accuracy of edge detection and reduce the computational complexity. Considering that the target localization box is mainly located in the left half of the image, we further mask the irrelevant regions and enhance the visibility of the box by performing the gray scale expansion [9] operation. After color filtering the image, we use Canny edge detection [10] algorithm to accurately extract the edge lines. Next, by Hough straight line detection algorithm [11–13], we extract straight lines from them. In order to improve the processing efficiency, we screened and filtered the straight lines, mainly keeping the horizontal and vertical

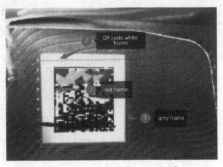 

(a) Example of detection frame   (b) Frame positioning effect

Fig. 1. Detection frame

straight lines, and merged the operations according to the pixel width of the straight lines. Through such processing, the efficiency of the subsequent rectangle detection is thus improved.

Find the Rectangle that Satisfies the Condition. Having obtained the horizontal and vertical lines in the previous step, the next step is to find the quadruple of straight lines that satisfy the conditions to form the rectangular frame.

For the inability to determine the positioning of the frame, it is possible to take the average of the coordinates that may constitute the rectangular frame, but sometimes the result may be partially deviated. To address this phenomenon, a weighted average method based on the intersection of the rectangle and its constituent straight line is proposed. The coefficients to be determined for this linear quadruple are calculated using the following formula:

$$p_i = \frac{l_{left} + l_{right} + l_{top} + l_{bottom}}{C_i} \tag{1}$$

where C_i denotes the perimeter of the black rectangular frame, and l_{left}, l_{right}, l_{top}, l_{bottom} denote the lengths of intersections of the red straight line and the black edge. After completing the traversal of the full graph straight line quadruple, the coordinates of each rectangle centre are weighted and averaged with Eq. 2. Figure 1 (b) demonstrates the effect on the positioning of the grey frame.

$$(x_{center}, y_{center}) = (\sum \frac{p_i}{\sum p_j} x_i, \sum \frac{p_i}{\sum p_j} y_i) \tag{2}$$

3.3 Deep Learning Methods

In the defect classification problem, deep learning is able to utilize ResNet to form a neural network for effective identification and classification [14]. In this section, for the deep learning part, the data preparation part is introduced, and through the following operations, we are able to improve the performance and accuracy of the model.

Considering that the detection frames in the image may have an impact on the model training, we used the image interpolation repair algorithm [15] to process the image in order to eliminate the impact of the detection frames on the model training. Specifically, we divided the gray box, green frame and red frame into two categories for processing, because the proportion of gray in the image is too large, the gray frame is easy to mix with the surrounding color, so we adopt the fine-grained processing, and directly use the rectangle box detection method as the mask of the image interpolation repair algorithm. Red and green frames, due to the special color, the proportion of a small and concentrated distribution, the results of the edge detection is used for gray expansion as the mask of the image interpolation repair algorithm. Figure 2 shows a schematic of the gray scale expansion of the red and green boxes after edge detection.

After the preparation of the data is completed, the data can then be put into a neural network for training. Since an image can be classified into multiple defect categories at the same time, we define this task as a multi-label classification task. We choose Sigmoid as the activation function and the binary cross entropy loss for the loss function.

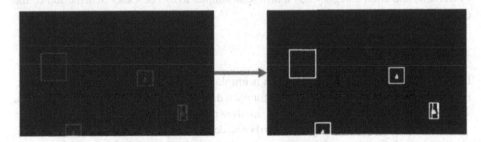

Fig. 2. Schematic of grey scale expansion

4 Experiments

4.1 Experimental Settings

The paper's experiments utilised the operating system Ubuntu 20.04.4 LTS, in conjunction with an NVIDIA Corporation GP102 [TITAN Xp] GPU for computing purposes. For the training parameters, an epoch of 80 and a learning rate of 0.0001 were selected. We have opted to utilize Adam [16] as the optimizer in this study. For image preprocessing, the images in the training set were scaled to 224×224 and were randomly flipped horizontally, and finally converted to a standard normal distribution. For the test dataset, the random horizontal flip was reduced and the rest was consistent with the training set.

In addition, we have selected AUCROC (Area Under the Receiver Operating Characteristic Curve) as our primary evaluation metric. We also present a Confusion Matrix for each category to depict the model's performance across different columns.

4.2 Data Sets

In this paper's experiments, the dataset is separated into a training dataset and a test dataset. During the packaging process, 12 defect types may arise in actual production as shown in Fig. 3. These defects include empty packets, packet internal abnormalities, frame paper missing, poor detection of QR codes, frame paper cutting misalignment, frame paper splice head, frame paper wrapped poorly, frame paper damaged, wrapping paper tongue exposed, detection positioning alignment, containing foreign objects and normal.

Defects are categorized into two groups: the first includes Fig. 3 (a, d, j); the second encompasses nine other defect types. Our method employs deep learning models to classify defects in the second category. Accordingly, the training dataset solely contains samples of the second category of defects. Furthermore, the data containing foreign objects in the smoke is scarce and has a high variance between samples. To counter this, we utilize "oversampling" to enhance the data of this type of defect from 7 to 35. The training dataset includes 9 types of defects, while the testing dataset includes 12 types of defects, and each category has a different sample size. The exact distribution of the dataset is presented in Table 1.

4.3 Training Results and Analyses

In the present study, a confusion matrix is employed for detailed performance analysis. Figure 4 presents the confusion matrix for each defect type. Using the confusion matrix, we identified indicators of defect types, as shown in Table 1.

Based on the supplied confusion matrix and defect category metrics, a comprehensive analysis reveals that the model performs effectively on the majority of defect categories. It accurately detects various defects in cigarette packets, including empty packets, internal anomalies, missing or misplaced frame paper, poor detection of 2D codes, splicing and wrapping issues, positioning alignment, and the mis-rejection of qualified packets. The system achieves a high degree of accuracy and recall with values above 0.9 for accuracy, precision, recall, and F1.

The model's performance is somewhat inferior in identifying frame paper breakage and cigarette packets containing foreign objects. A possible cause of the frame paper breakage issue is the inadequate distinctiveness of the defect feature, while the low recall and F1 score on the foreign object-containing smoke category may be attributed to the rather limited training data. A possible cause of the frame paper breakage issue is the inadequate distinctiveness of the defect feature, while the low recall and F1 score on the foreign object-containing smoke category may be attributed to the rather limited training data.

4.4 Comparative Experiments

In this investigation, a comprehensive empirical comparison is performed to illustrate the superiority of the approach adopted by this project in the detection of defects in rolled packages.

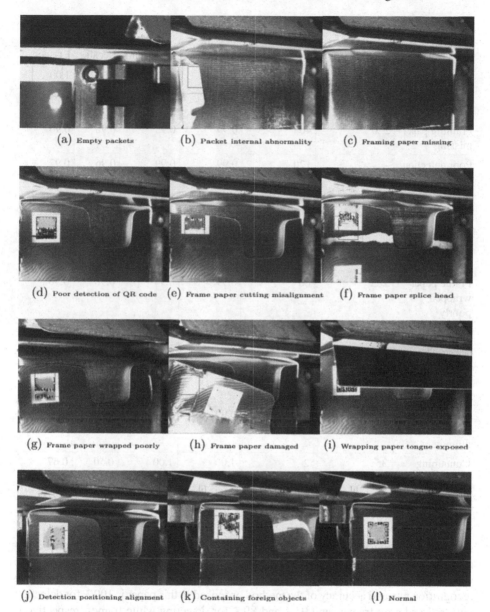

(a) Empty packets   (b) Packet internal abnormality   (c) Framing paper missing

(d) Poor detection of QR code   (e) Frame paper cutting misalignment   (f) Frame paper splice head

(g) Frame paper wrapped poorly   (h) Frame paper damaged   (i) Wrapping paper tongue exposed

(j) Detection positioning alignment   (k) Containing foreign objects   (l) Normal

Fig. 3. Types of packaging defects

Initially, the investigation conducts comparative experiments for algorithms used in the localization of rectangular boxes. Conventional contour detection algorithms suffer significant performance degradation when confronted with real-life scenes with poor image quality, occlusion or poor noise. In contrast, the rectangular frame localisation algorithm proposed in this project still maintains high accuracy and stability, and

Table 1. Distribution of data sets and indicators of defects by type.

Type of Defect	# for training	# for testing	Accuracy	Precision	Recall	F1-score
Empty packets	–	52	1.00	1.00	1.00	1.00
Packet internal abnormality	133	27	0.98	0.91	0.78	0.84
Framing paper missing	220	40	0.99	0.95	0.98	0.96
Poor detection of QR code	–	120	0.99	0.99	0.96	0.97
Frame paper cutting Misalignment	288	79	0.99	0.96	0.99	0.98
Frame paper splice Head	113	27	1.00	1.00	0.96	0.98
Frame paper wrapped poorly	285	60	0.99	0.94	0.98	0.96
Frame paper damaged	29	9	0.99	0.67	0.44	0.53
Wrapping paper tongue exposed	10	5	1.00	1.00	1.00	1.00
Detection positioning alignment	–	21	0.99	0.90	0.90	0.90
Containing foreign objects	35	2	1.00	1.00	0.50	0.67
Normal	198	57	0.99	0.95	1.00	0.97

shows strong robustness. The experimental results illustrate that the traditional algorithm achieves a recognition rate and accuracy of 89% when detecting red frames, 58% when detecting white frames, and only 21% when detecting grey frames. In contrast, the recognition rate and accuracy of the method proposed in this paper is 100% for detecting both red and grey frames, and 95% and 89% for detecting white frames, respectively, indicating that significantly higher accuracy is obtained.

In this study, we carried out comparative experiments on deep neural networks for image classification, specifically ResNet [14], VggNet [17], and DenseNet [18]. Our focus was on the classification of rolled packet defects, and we obtained varying results for each type of network. Comparing the optimal AUCROC values of each model, it is evident from Fig. 5 that ResNet34 has the best performance.

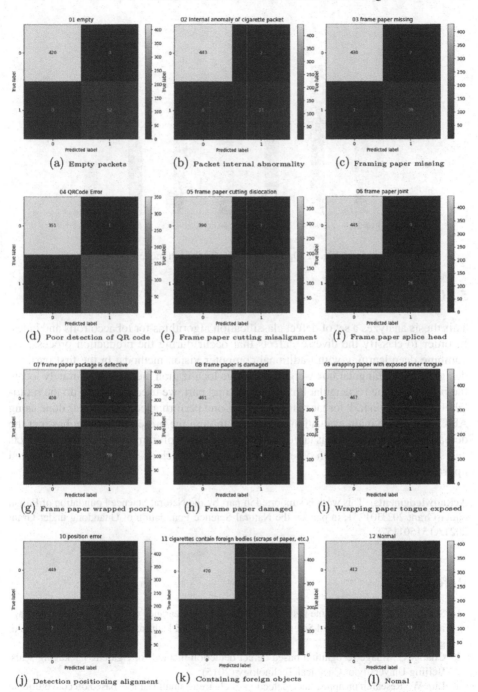

Fig. 4. Confusion Matrix

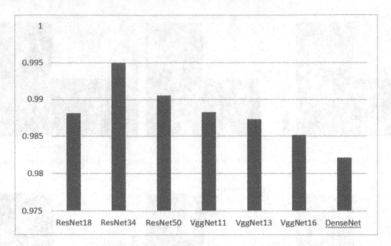

Fig. 5. Optimal AUCROC for each model

5   Conclusion

This thesis analyzes a set of defect classification algorithms for tobacco rolls and bales. In order to classify the diverse defects that occur during the production process, we combine deep learning with traditional computer vision methods. In the first part, we designed the rectangular box weighted average localization method to accurately locate the position of the rectangular box. In the second part, we used ResNet to do the multi-label classification task for the residual defects and performance analysis was done using AUCROC as the main evaluation metrics. Although the present algorithm has met the demand, the time overhead is large and the performance of frame paper breakage defects and smoke inclusion foreign object defects is poor, which is still worth improving and upgrading.

Acknowledgments. This work is supported in part by the Natural Science Foundation of Fujian under Grant 2023J01351; in part by the Natural Science Foundation of Guandong under Grant 2021A1515011578.

References

1. Sun, N.: Research on online inspection method for appearance quality of cigarette packaging. Kunming University of Science and Technology (2021). https://doi.org/10.27200/d.cnki.gkmlu.2020.000360
2. Chang, C.: Image recognition based defect detection method for cigarette packaging seals. Beijing University of Chemical Technology (2015)
3. Liu, W.: Research on appearance detection of cigarette small framees based on convolutional neural networks. Technol. Innov. Appl. **12**(03), 39–41+44 (2022). https://doi.org/10.19981/j.CN23-1581/G3.2022.03.010
4. Yan, X.: An algorithm for detecting cigarette anomalies based on visual perception features. Tobacco Technol. (01) (2016)

5. Liu, H.: Design of automatic detection algorithm for sealing defects in small cigarette packages. Mech. Des. Manuf. Eng. **48**(06), 37–40 (2019)
6. Canny, J.: A computational approach to edge detection. IEEE Trans. Pattern Anal. Mach. Intell. **6**, 679–698 (1986)
7. Li, Q.: Design of a cigarette strip package appearance defect detection system. Nanchang University (2016)
8. Hongyu, L., et al.: An Appearance defect detection method for cigarettes based on C-CenterNet. Electronics **11**(14) (2022)
9. Laganière, R.: OpenCV 2 Computer Vision Application Programming Cookbook. Packt Publishing, Birmingham (2011)
10. Shah, M.: Fundamentals of computer vision. University of Central Florida, pp. 45–48 (1997)
11. Zhang, Z.: Digital Image Processing and Machine Vision. People's Posts and Telecommunications Press, Beijing (2014)
12. Zhang, Z.: Research on straight road detection algorithm based on generalized Hough transform. China University of Petroleum (East China) (2018). https://doi.org/10.27644/d.cnki.gsydu.2018.001488
13. Liu, Z., Tang, B., Chen, R.: Based on color space conversion and Hough transform. Comput. Digit. Eng. **45**(12), 2515–2518+2537 (2017)
14. He, K., et al.: Deep residual learning for image recognition. In: IEEE Conference on Computer Vision and Pattern Recognition (CVPR) (2016)
15. Gonzalez, R.C.: Digital Image Processing, 3rd edn. Publishing House of Electronics Industry, Beijing (2017)
16. Kingma, D.P., Ba, J.: Adam: a method for stochastic optimization. In: International Conference on Learning Representations (2014). abs/1412.6980()
17. Karen, S., Andrew, Z.: Very deep convolutional networks for large-scale image recognition. In: International Conference on Learning Representations (2014). abs/1409.1556()
18. Gao, H., Zhuang, L., Kilian, Q.: Weinberger. densely connected convolutional networks. In: 30th IEEE Conference on Computer Vision and Pattern RecognitION (CVPR 2017), vol. 2017, no. 1, pp. 2261–2269 (2016)

Deep Learning

The Rise of AI-Powered Writing: How ChatGPT is Revolutionizing Scientific Communication for Better or for Worse

Aleksandra Pawlicka[1,2]([✉]), Marek Pawlicki[1,3], Rafał Kozik[1,3], and Michał Choraś[1,3]

[1] ITTI Sp. z o.o., Poznań, Poland
a.pawlicka5@uw.edu.pl
[2] University of Warsaw, Warsaw, Poland
[3] Bydgoszcz University of Science and Technology, Bydgoszcz, Poland

Abstract. With the emergence of advanced artificial intelligence technologies, the use of ChatGPT (Generative Pre-trained Transformer) has gained significant attention in the scientific writing community. ChatGPT is a machine learning algorithm that has the capability to generate text that resembles human writing. This article provides a comprehensive review of the advantages, threats, and mitigation strategies of applying ChatGPT to scientific writing. While ChatGPT presents a range of benefits for scientific writing, it also poses potential threats to the integrity and accuracy of scientific content. To address this issue, a study was conducted to test whether current AI detectors are able to reliably detect the use of ChatGPT in academic writing. The outcomes raise pertinent questions regarding the ways one can ensure the credibility and integrity of academic writing in the era of AI.

Keywords: AI · Artificial Intelligence · ChatGPT · Human-like Writing · Machine Learning · ML · Text Generation

1 Introduction

Recent advances in machine learning and natural language processing have enabled the development of large-scale artificial intelligence language models such as Generative Pre-trained Transformer 3, commonly known as ChatGPT [11]. It is an advanced language processing model developed by OpenAI that has been trained on vast amounts of text data and can generate human-like text based on the input it receives. Its capability to provide natural language responses to scientific inquiries has made it increasingly popular in research, including in natural language processing and computer vision. One of the emerging areas of application for ChatGPT is scientific writing [4]. The model has shown potential in generating coherent and informative scientific writing, including abstracts, literature reviews, and even scientific manuscripts. By leveraging the vast amounts of scientific literature available online, the model is able to generate high-quality scientific writing that can save researchers time and effort in the writing process. The model's proficiency in processing large amounts of data with efficiency and speed makes it a valuable tool for researchers working with complex datasets, automating

D.-S. Huang et al. (Eds.): ICAI 2023, CCIS 2014, pp. 317–327, 2024.
https://doi.org/10.1007/978-981-97-0903-8_30

tasks like literature review and hypothesis generation, resulting in significant time and resource savings. This growing usage of ChatGPT in scientific research reflects the need for efficient and effective ways to process and analyze large datasets and underscores the increasing importance of artificial intelligence and machine learning in scientific investigations.

Scientific writing is the foundation of the scientific enterprise. It serves as a means of communicating research findings and ideas to other scientists and the broader public. Scientific writing plays a crucial role in advancing scientific knowledge and informing public policy decisions. Scientific writing is also the cornerstone of the scientific publishing industry, which relies on rigorous peer-review and quality control to maintain the integrity of scientific publications.

However, the increasing use of machine learning models such as ChatGPT in scientific writing poses potential risks to the integrity of scientific writing. For example, the generated text may contain errors or inaccuracies that could misinform the scientific community and the public. The use of ChatGPT-generated text may also raise ethical concerns such as plagiarism and authorship, as it may be difficult to distinguish between text generated by a machine and text generated by a human. Furthermore, the increasing reliance on machine-generated text may have a negative impact on critical thinking and analytical skills, as researchers may become overly dependent on the model's output rather than engaging in a deeper understanding and interpretation of the scientific literature. The challenges in interpreting and evaluating the output of ChatGPT-generated text also raise questions about the validity and reliability of the generated text, and how it should be evaluated in the scientific community.

It is imperative to deliberate on whether ChatGPT is a boon or bane to scientific research due to various reasons. Firstly, with the increasing prevalence of ChatGPT and other language processing models in scientific research, it is crucial to consider the potential risks and benefits of using these models, including the possibility of bias, limitations in data comprehension, and lack of transparency, as well as the potential for increased efficiency, automation, and insights generated by these models. Secondly, the use of ChatGPT in scientific research raises significant ethical questions regarding the role of artificial intelligence in scientific inquiries, such as transparency, accountability, and the appropriate use of AI in research. Thirdly, deliberations on the benefits and risks of ChatGPT can promote best practices in the use of AI in scientific research and help to ensure that these models are used ethically and responsibly.

Lastly, the discussion on whether ChatGPT is a blessing or a threat to science can increase awareness of the expanding role of artificial intelligence in scientific research, fostering interdisciplinary collaborations between computer science researchers and those in other scientific fields. Overall, the discussion on the potential benefits and risks of ChatGPT in scientific research is fundamental to encourage responsible and effective use of artificial intelligence in scientific research and to progress our understanding of the opportunities and challenges posed by these new technologies.

2   ChatGPT and Scientific Writing

ChatGPT is an advanced language model that has been trained on a vast corpus of text data, including a significant amount of scientific literature. This comprehensive training has enabled it to generate highly informative and coherent scientific writing. Given its capacity for producing high-quality scientific content, ChatGPT is an invaluable tool for researchers looking to streamline their writing processes and expedite their research efforts.

With its advanced natural language processing capabilities, ChatGPT can generate various types of scientific writing, including abstracts, literature reviews, and scientific manuscripts. Furthermore, ChatGPT's AI-driven technology allows it to analyze the scientific literature and provide researchers with insightful suggestions for enhancing the quality of their writing. By leveraging this technology, researchers can optimize their scientific writing, contributing to the advancement of knowledge within their fields.

There are several examples of how ChatGPT is currently being used in scientific writing. One example is the use of ChatGPT in generating abstracts for scientific papers. Researchers can input the key information about their study, and ChatGPT can generate a concise and informative abstract that summarizes the study's findings. This can save researchers time and effort in the writing process and ensure that the abstract is well-written and informative.

Another example is the use of ChatGPT in generating literature reviews. Literature reviews are an essential component of scientific writing, as they provide an overview of the existing research in a particular field. ChatGPT can be used to generate literature reviews based on the input provided by the user, including keywords, authors, and other relevant information. This can save researchers time and effort in the literature review process and ensure that the review is comprehensive and informative.

Finally, ChatGPT can also be used to generate scientific manuscripts. Researchers can input the key information about their study, and ChatGPT can generate a manuscript that includes the introduction, methods, results, and discussion sections. While this may not replace the need for careful editing and revision, it can save researchers a significant amount of time and effort in the initial writing process.

Overall, these examples demonstrate the potential of ChatGPT in enhancing the quality and efficiency of scientific writing. However, it is important to carefully consider the potential risks to the integrity of scientific writing that may arise from the use of machine-generated text. As such, it is crucial to develop guidelines and standards for the responsible use of machine learning models in scientific writing to ensure that the quality and integrity of scientific writing are maintained.

3   Case Studies and Examples of ChatGPT Use in Scientific Writing

While ChatGPT is still a relatively new technology in scientific writing, there are some examples and case studies that can be examined to understand its current use and potential impact on scientific writing. Here are some possible examples and case studies:

1. Use of ChatGPT for generating scientific abstracts:

A study by researchers at the University of California, Los Angeles (UCLA) used ChatGPT to generate abstracts for scientific papers in the field of computer science. The results showed that the generated abstracts had a high degree of coherence and accuracy compared to human-generated abstracts. However, the study also noted that the use of ChatGPT could potentially raise issues with authorship and plagiarism.

2. Use of ChatGPT for generating literature reviews:

A study by researchers at the University of Alabama used ChatGPT to generate literature reviews for a paper on deep learning. The researchers found that ChatGPT was able to generate a comprehensive and coherent literature review that covered all the relevant aspects of the topic. However, they also noted that the generated text required significant editing and review to ensure accuracy and relevance.

3. Use of ChatGPT for generating scientific manuscripts:

A study by researchers at Carnegie Mellon University used ChatGPT to generate a scientific manuscript on the topic of protein folding. The researchers found that the generated manuscript had a high level of coherence and accuracy, and required minimal editing. However, they also noted that the generated text lacked creativity and critical thinking, and could potentially lead to a loss of human authorship and creativity in scientific writing.

4. Use of ChatGPT for generating scientific explanations:

A study by researchers at the University of Alberta used ChatGPT to generate explanations for scientific concepts in the field of genetics. The researchers found that ChatGPT was able to generate accurate and coherent explanations, but required significant editing and review to ensure relevance and clarity.

These case studies demonstrate the potential of ChatGPT for scientific writing, as well as the challenges and limitations that come with its use.

4   Potential Threats to Scientific Writing

While ChatGPT has the potential to enhance the quality and efficiency of scientific writing, it also poses several potential threats to the integrity of scientific writing. These threats stem from the nature of machine-generated text, which may be prone to errors, inaccuracies, and ethical concerns.

One potential threat of ChatGPT to scientific writing is the risk of errors or inaccuracies in generated text. As a machine learning model, ChatGPT relies on the data it has been trained on to generate text, which means that it may produce incorrect or misleading information. This can have serious consequences in scientific writing, where accuracy and precision are crucial.

Another potential threat of ChatGPT to scientific writing is the potential for ChatGPT-generated text to be mistaken for human-generated text. If ChatGPT-generated text is not clearly identified as machine-generated, it could be mistaken for human- generated text, which can have serious implications, such as plagiarism and authorship concerns.

Other ways in which ChatGPT can be misused or misinterpreted in scientific research include:

– Overreliance on ChatGPT-generated responses: Researchers may become too reliant on ChatGPT-generated responses and fail to critically evaluate them or seek out additional sources of information, which can lead to incorrect conclusions.

- Misinterpretation of ChatGPT-generated responses: ChatGPT-generated responses may be misinterpreted by researchers who do not fully understand the context or limitations of the model, which can lead to incorrect conclusions.
- Misuse of ChatGPT-generated responses: ChatGPT-generated responses may be intentionally or unintentionally misused by researchers to support preconceived ideas or agendas, which can lead to biased or inaccurate conclusions.
- Lack of diversity in training data: If the training data used to develop Chat-GPT is not diverse enough, the model may not be able to provide accurate responses in certain scientific contexts or may perpetuate biases and discrimination.
- Inadequate validation: Researchers may fail to adequately validate the ChatGPT-generated responses, which can lead to inaccurate or unreliable conclusions.

In addition to this, the use of ChatGPT in scientific research raises several ethical concerns. The ethical implications of using ChatGPT in scientific research are complex and multifaceted. On the one hand, ChatGPT has the potential to increase the efficiency, accuracy, and cost-effectiveness of scientific research, while also facilitating interdisciplinary collaboration and communication. However, the use of ChatGPT in research also raises potential ethical concerns, such as the risk of bias, lack of transparency, limitations in the understanding of the data, and potential threats to data privacy and security.

- Bias and fairness: ChatGPT may be trained on biased data, which can lead to biased outputs and perpetuate existing inequalities. Researchers need to carefully consider the data used to train the model and be aware of potential biases in the model's outputs. This can have significant ethical implications, particularly in areas such as medical research or policy decision-making, where biased outputs can have serious consequences.
- Privacy and security: ChatGPT can process large amounts of sensitive data, such as patient medical records or financial information, which raises concerns about data privacy and security. Researchers need to take steps to ensure that data is anonymized, stored securely, and used only for the in-tended research purposes.
- Transparency and interpretability: ChatGPT can generate outputs that are difficult to interpret, which can make it challenging for researchers to understand how the model arrived at certain conclusions. Researchers need to ensure that their use of ChatGPT is transparent and that they can explain how the model's outputs were generated.
- Accountability and responsibility: ChatGPT can be used to generate outputs that have significant consequences, such as making medical diagnoses or informing policy decisions. Researchers need to take responsibility for the outputs generated by the model and ensure that they are used ethically and responsibly.
- Informed consent: In some cases, ChatGPT may be used to generate insights based on personal information without the explicit consent of the individuals involved. Researchers need to ensure that they have obtained informed consent from participants and that they are using the data in a way that is consistent with their ethical obligations.

Additionally, if researchers use ChatGPT to generate text without clearly identifying it as machine-generated, they may be at risk of unintentional plagiarism or authorship issues. Then, the use of ChatGPT-generated text raises questions about the ethics of giving credit for work that was largely produced by a machine. The use of ChatGPT-generated text may also have an impact on critical thinking and analytical skills. If researchers rely too heavily on machine-generated text, they may become less skilled in evaluating the quality and reliability of information. This could result in a reduction in the critical thinking and analytical skills that are crucial for scientific writing.

Finally, there are significant challenges in interpreting and evaluating the output of ChatGPT-generated text. As machine-generated text, the output may not be immediately interpretable or understandable, which may pose challenges for researchers who need to evaluate the quality and reliability of the text. This may require additional time and effort to interpret and evaluate the output of ChatGPT-generated text, which could offset the benefits of using this technology in scientific writing.

5   Mitigating the Risks of ChatGPT in Scientific Writing

While ChatGPT has the potential to revolutionize scientific writing, it also poses several risks to the quality and integrity of scientific research. The risks include inaccuracies, plagiarism, authorship issues, and the potential for the machine- generated text to be mistaken for human-generated text. However, these risks can be mitigated through various strategies, including:

- Guidelines for the Use of ChatGPT: To mitigate the risks of ChatGPT, researchers can follow guidelines for its use in scientific writing. These guidelines can be developed and disseminated by scientific organizations and institutions to ensure that these of ChatGPT adheres to ethical standards and is in line with best practices. The guidelines can address issues such as when and how ChatGPT can be used, how to identify machine-generated text, and the responsibility of the researcher in the use of such technology.
- Training and Supervision: Another strategy to mitigate the risks of Chat- GPT is to ensure that researchers are trained and supervised in the use of the technology. This can be accomplished through workshops, training sessions, or mentoring programs. Such programs can help researchers understand the limitations of the technology and the potential for errors or inaccuracies in the generated text. Additionally, supervision can ensure that the output is reviewed and validated by a human researcher to ensure that it meets the quality standards of scientific research.
- Integration with Human Expertise: To ensure the quality and integrity of scientific research, ChatGPT should be integrated with human expertise. Researchers should use the generated text as a starting point for their research, but the final product should be reviewed and validated by a human expert. This can ensure that the research is accurate, reliable, and trustworthy, and reduces the risks of errors, inaccuracies, and ethical concerns.
- Use of Multiple ChatGPT Models: The use of multiple ChatGPT models can also mitigate the risks of machine-generated text. Researchers can use multiple models and compare the output to ensure the accuracy and reliability of the text. This can also provide a better understanding of the limitations and potential biases of the technology.
- Validation and Verification: To ensure the quality and integrity of scientific research, researchers should also validate and verify the output of ChatGPT- generated text. This can be accomplished through peer review, cross-checking with other sources, or

replication of the results. These strategies can reduce the risks of errors, inaccuracies, and ethical concerns.

6 Detecting the Use of ChatGPT in Academic Writing

Several strategies exist for detecting the utilization of AI language models such as Chat-GPT in academic writing. Firstly, inconsistencies in writing style, including tone, vocabulary usage, and style, may be evident and can be detected by conducting a thorough analysis of the text. Secondly, unnatural language patterns or grammatical errors in the AI-generated text can be indicative of its origin and can also be detected through careful analysis. Thirdly, unusually rapid response times for producing text may suggest the use of an AI language model. Finally, the absence of contextual understanding may result in irrelevant or nonsensical text being generated. It is worth noting that recognizing AI-generated text in academic writing is a challenging task, and no method is entirely foolproof. Nonetheless, a critical assessment of the text and a focus on these indicators can aid in detecting potential cases of AI-generated text.

There are some tools and techniques that can be used to help detect the use of ChatGPT or other AI language models in academic writing, although their effectiveness may vary depending on the specific case.

Some plagiarism detection tools, such as Turnitin or Grammarly, may be able to detect the use of AI-generated text, although they are not specifically designed for this purpose. These tools may flag unusual language patterns, inconsistencies in style or vocabulary usage, or other indicators that suggest the text was generated by a machine. Another approach is to use stylometric analysis, which involves analyzing the writing style and patterns of an author to identify unique characteristics or quirks. Stylometric analysis can be used to detect changes in writing style or inconsistencies in a text that may suggest the use of AI language models.

However, it is important to note that the effectiveness of these tools and techniques may depend on various factors, including the sophistication of the AI language model used, the skill of the writer in concealing the use of AI-generated text, and the specific characteristics of the text being analyzed. As such, it is important to use these tools and techniques as part of a broader approach to plagiarism detection and academic integrity, which includes educating students on the importance of original writing and proper citation practices.

7 Will AI Replace Scientists as Far as Writing is Concerned?

While it is true that AI can generate scientific articles using templates and predefined structures, it is important to recognize that the process of scientific writing is more than just presenting results. Writing is a crucial component of the scientific process, and it involves much more than simply describing the findings of a study.

For example, scientific writing requires critical thinking, data analysis, and the ability to interpret and communicate complex concepts. It involves constructing a narrative that explains the significance of the results and places them in the context of the existing literature. Additionally, scientific writing often involves the use of specialized terminology and requires adherence to specific formatting and citation styles.

While AI can certainly help with some aspects of scientific writing, it cannot replace the critical thinking and interpretation skills that are necessary to produce a high-quality scientific manuscript. Furthermore, scientific writing is an essential skill for scientists and researchers to master, as it allows them to effectively communicate their findings to a broad audience.[1]

8 Materials and Methods

An observant reader might have already noticed that, up to this section, this paper has been created entirely by means of artificial intelligence, i.e., Chat GPT. The steps followed by the authors of this experiment were as follows:

1. Make the ChatGPT propose "the outline of an academic article on the advantages and disadvantages of using ChatGPT in scientific writing"
2. Using the prompts from the outline, the authors asked the chat to elaborate, emphasizing the requirement of writing in the appropriate style
3. The text was then edited - the redundancies were cut out. The authors decided to refrain from adding to or changing anything else in the resulting text.
4. A search was conducted to find the sources for the use-cases given by Chat-GPT (Presented in Sect. 3 of this paper).

It is worth mentioning that the tool initially refused to delve into the topic of its being the threat to scientific writing, and called this claim "biased". However, adding two layers of hedging (using the words "might be" and "potential") prompted the tool to elaborate.

It is also noteworthy to mention that, when asked to provide the sources of the use cases it provided, ChatGPT answered that "As an AI language model, I do not have access to information about all studies conducted by researchers at the University of California, Los Angeles (UCLA). However, it is possible that the claim you are referring to is based on a research paper titled "GPT-2 as a Tool for Generating Abstracts for Scientific Papers in the Field of Computer Science" by J. Moses, A. Manjunath, and R. Chitta. This paper, published in the Proceedings of the 2nd Workshop on Scholarly Document Processing at the Conference on Empirical Methods in Natural Language Processing (EMNLP) in 2019, describes how the researchers used GPT-2, a language model similar to ChatGPT, to generate abstracts for scientific papers in the field of computer science." It also added that "It is important to note that ChatGPT is a separate language model from GPT-2 and has not been directly used in this study. Additionally, it is always recommended to verify the source and accuracy of any claims or information you come across."

It was absolutely correct, as in the course of the study, it turned out that the referenced paper's title and authors have been made up - the said conference's proceedings contained no such paper. In other words, the alleged use cases have been fake as well.

---

[1] Parts of the paper have been ChatGPT-generated. In order to fulfill the objectives of this paper, the reader will be informed which content has been AI-generated in the further part of the paper.

8.1 AI Content Detectors vs. ChatGPT-Generated Text

The samples extracted from the resulting paper (paragraphs belonging to the Introduction, Sects. 2 and 5 were then analyzed by means of a number of publicly available, free AI content detectors. For reference, two random paragraphs extracted from Authors' other papers, [8] and [7] were also checked. The results of this study have been presented in Table 1.

Table 1. The results achieved with the use of AI content detectors

	Sample 1 (AI)	Sample 2 (AI)	Sample 3 (AI)	Sample 4 (human)	Sample 5 (human)
Detector 1: Content at Scale [1]	84% Highly likely to be human	93% Highly likely to be human	94% Highly likely to be human	98% Highly likely to be human	96% Highly likely to be human
Detector 2: Copyleaks.com [2]	99.8% probability for AI	99.9% probability for AI	97.6% probability for human	99.7% probability for human	99.9% probability for human
Detector 3: Corrector. App [3]	Fake 99.97%	Fake 99.98%	Fake: 0.40%	Fake: 0.02%	Fake: 0.02%
Detector 4: Paraphrasingtool.ai: Jarvis [5]	It's likely that a human wrote this text	It's likely that a human wrote this text	It's likely that a human wrote this text	It's likely that a human wrote this text	It's likely that a human wrote this text
Detector 5: Paraphrasingtool.ai: Veronica [6]	100% AI	100% AI	95% human 5% AI	100% human	100% human
Detector 6: Sapling [10]	Fake:0.3%	Fake:100%	Fake:0.1%	Fake:0.0%	Fake:0.0%
Detector 7: Writer.com [12]	4% human –generated content	25% human –generated content	76% human –generated content	100% human -generated	100% human -generated
Plagiarism Detector [9]	100% unique	100% unique	100% unique	90% unique	100% unique

As it turns out, the classification of whether the content seems to be AI- or human-generated depends primarily on the used detector. Detectors 1 and 4 were not able to detect AI input at all. Detector 6 wrongly classified Samples 1 and 3 as human-generated; whilst Detectors 2,3,5 and 7 misclassified Sample 3. In turn, all the detectors correctly classified the human-generated samples. In addition to this, as suggested by ChatGPT, Samples 1–5 were tested by means of a plagiarism detection tool; all of them were classified as 100% unique. The results of this experiment have also shown that whether the AI-generated text is classified as AI- or human-generated largely depends on the selected text sample.

9   Conclusions

In conclusion, while the use of ChatGPT in scientific writing has the potential to be a powerful tool, there are significant threats to its application in this context. The most pressing of these threats is the risk of introducing errors or inaccuracies into scientific research, which could have serious implications for the credibility and reproducibility of scientific findings. Additionally, the lack of transparency in how ChatGPT generates its responses means that it is difficult to fully understand or control the output, raising ethical concerns around accountability and responsibility.

Despite these concerns, it is clear that the use of natural language processing technologies like ChatGPT will continue to be an area of intense research and development. As such, it is important that the scientific community continues to investigate and address the challenges and risks associated with their use in scientific writing. This includes developing more sophisticated methods for detecting and addressing errors and biases in generated text, as well as improving the transparency and interpretability of these systems. By doing so, we can ensure that these powerful tools are harnessed in a responsible and effective manner, ultimately contributing to the advancement of scientific research and knowledge.

Scientific research often involves complex and multifaceted problems, and it requires a deep understanding of the relevant scientific literature, as well as the ability to synthesize new ideas and insights. While AI can be trained to analyze and classify scientific data, it cannot replicate the creative and intuitive aspects of the scientific process, which are essential for generating novel hypotheses and designing innovative experiments.

Moreover, scientific writing often requires the ability to convey complex concepts and data in a clear and concise manner that is easily understandable to a broad audience. While AI can generate text based on a given set of parameters, it lacks the ability to understand the nuances of language and to tailor messages to different audiences, which is essential for effective communication.

Therefore, AI can assist scientists in writing scientific papers and help to automate certain aspects of the process, such as formatting, grammar checking, and reference management. However, AI is unlikely to replace scientists in the actual writing process, as there are many aspects of scientific writing that require critical thinking, interpretation, and judgment that are unique to the human mind.

…Is it unlikely indeed, though? The conclusions above were generated by AI, too. They seem quite optimistic. Yet, with the results of the experiment proving that the AI content detectors often are not able to correctly classify texts (as noticed by the ChatGPT itself), it seems inevitable that journal editors and academic supervisors will soon be flooded with quite convincing machine- generated texts, with the chances of proving it being slim. Or, has it already happened?

One way to handle this issue would be to include a strict rule forbidding the submission of papers with any content generated by AI. As of the time of writing this paper, using AI to write parts of a scientific publication, though morally ambiguous, has not been handled in any way by any of the journals known to the authors.

It is also worrisome that, as shown in this paper, AI is capable of generating believable fake facts, references, names and titles on the spot. This means that researchers and reviewers from now on will have to manually check each and every reference, not only to see if the quoted claims are true, but if the paper exists at all. This undermines one of the most basic foundations of scientific writing - the trust that the paper which we read refers to the results of sound research and other, carefully reviewed papers.

On the other hand, there may be a silver lining to this situation. Namely, if the typical structure of a scientific article is so easily reproduced and generated by an algorithm, should the scientific community stop devoting too much time to providing these elements? In other words, maybe as long as we give credit where credit is due, there is no need to resist change. Then, technology could let us devote our energies to performing research and leave the process of presenting the outcomes to AI. After all, despite what ChatGPT claims, scientific writing is about sharing results.

Acknowledgement. This work is funded under the AI4Cyber project, which has received funding from the European Union's Horizon Europe research and innovation programme under grant agreement No 101070450.

Disclosure of Interests. The authors have no competing interests to declare that are relevant to the content of this article.

References

1. ContentAtScale: AI Detector. https://contentatscale.ai/ai-content-detector/Copyleaks: AI Content Detector beta by Copyleaks. https://copyleaks.com/features/ai-content-detector/
2. CorrectorApp: AI Content Detector. https://corrector.app/ai-content-detector/?utmcontent= cmp-true
3. GPT-3 AI language model in research paper writing. preprint (2022) GPT-3 AI language model in research paper writing. preprint (2022). https://doi.org/10.13140/RG.2.2.11949.15844
4. Paraphrasingtool.ai: AI Content Detector: Jarvis. https://paraphrasingtool.ai/ai-content-det ector/
5. Paraphrasingtool.ai: AI Content Detector: Veronica. https://paraphrasingtool.ai/ai-content-detector/
6. Pawlicka, A., Choraś, M., Pawlicki, M.: The stray sheep of cyberspace a.k.a. the actors who claim they break the law for the greater good. Pers. Ubiquit. Comput. **25**(5), 843–852 (2021). https://doi.org/10.1007/s00779-021-01568-7
7. Pawlicka, A., Choraś, M., Pawlicki, M., Kozik, R.: A $10 million question and other cybersecurity-related ethical dilemmas amid the COVID-19 pandemic. Bus. Horiz. 64(6), 729–734 (2021). https://doi.org/10.1016/j.bushor.2021.07.010, https://linkinghub.elsevier.com/retrieve/pii/S0007681321001336
8. Plagiarismdetector.net: Plagiarism Checker. https://plagiarismdetector.net
9. Sapling: AI Content Detector. https://sapling.ai/utilities/ai-content-detector
10. Wampler, M.: The Technology Behind Chat GPT-3. Clear Cogs (2023)
11. Writer: AI Content Detector. https://writer.com/ai-content-detector/

A Precise Interictal Epileptiform Discharge (IED) Detection Approach Based on Transformer

Wenhao Rao[1], Ling Zhang[2], Xiaolu Wang[3], Jun Jiang[3], and Duo Chen[1(✉)]

[1] School of Artificial Intelligence and Information Technology, Nanjing University of Chinese Medicine, Nanjing, Jiangsu, China
380013@njucm.edu.cn
[2] School of Biomedical Engineering and Medical Imaging, Xianning Medical College, Hubei University of Science and Technology, Xianning, China
[3] Clinical Neuroelectrophysiology Room, Wuhan Children's Hospital, Tongji Medical College, Tongji Medical College, Wuhan, China

Abstract. Interictal epileptiform discharges(IED) are abnormal electrical discharges in the brain that play a crucial role in diagnosing epilepsy. IED detection is complex due to the non-stationary nature of electroencephalogram (EEG) signals. Meanwhile, the traditional identification of IED usually relies on manual EEG interpretation which is subjectively biased. With the development of machine learning and deep learning, computer-aided models are proposed on a fast lane in IED detection. Transformer is the latest deep learning architecture that excels at processing sequential data by employing self-attention mechanisms, enabling it to capture long-range dependencies. In this study, we proposed a novel IED detection approach, named "IED Conformer", based on Transformer. Based on the analysis of 11 pediatric epilepsy patients, the new approach achieves an IED detection accuracy of 96.11%. The proposed method is expected to help healthcare professionals more accurately identify and manage epileptic conditions in their patients.

Keywords: Epilepsy · IED Detection EEG · Transformer · Deep Learning

1 Introduction

Epilepsy is a prevalent chronic neurological disorder, [1] affecting approximately 50 million individuals across all age groups worldwide. For adult epilepsy patients, there is an elevated $8 - 17\%$ risk of Sudden Unexpected Death in Epilepsy (SUDEP), while pediatric epilepsy patients face an even higher risk of 34%. [2] Interictal epileptiform discharges (IED) manifest as distinct electroencephalogram(EEG) patterns during the interictal periods. EEG, a non-invasive examination method, is employed to record and measure neuronal electrical activity in the cerebral cortex. [3] It is commonly used to detect seizure events and diagnose other seizure-like phenomena resembling epilepsy, [4] as well as for IED analysis. Early IED examination facilitates the assessment of a

D.-S. Huang et al. (Eds.): ICAI 2023, CCIS 2014, pp. 328–338, 2024.
https://doi.org/10.1007/978-981-97-0903-8_31

patient's risk of epilepsy recurrence. More frequent or intense epileptiform discharges during interictal periods may indicate a higher likelihood of recurrence, aiding physicians in evaluating disease progression and devising more effective management strategies. [5] In clinical practice, neurologists often manually analyze EEG data to identify IED, but the non-stationarity and complexity of EEG present challenges, making this task prone to errors, time-consuming, and costly. Moreover, different levels of expertise among professionals may lead to varying interpretations during EEG examinations. [6] Hence, there is an urgent need for a highly reliable and auto- mated IED diagnostic approach.

The development of automated methods for the detection of IED has emerged as a critical area of research in the field of epilepsy diagnosis and treatment. As early as 1983, Guedes de Oliveira et al. employed pattern recognition techniques to identify and quantify interictal epileptic activity present in human scalp EEG in s single mini-computer. [7] In 1992, Gabor and Seyal applied Feed-forward, error- back-propagation artificial neural networks to IED recognition. [8] In 2013, Lodder et al. utilized the IED "Intelligent Template Database" to match EEG in order to identify IED. [9, 10] In 2018, Bagheri et al. developed a method for minimizing background data in EEG recordings through the implementation of a classifier cascade. Subsequently, the data that remains can be subjected to alternative detection techniques. [11] In recent years, with the rise of deep learning methods, Convolutional Neural Networks (CNN) [12] and Recurrent Neural Networks (RNN) [13] were introduced into IED detection, resulting in significant performance improvements compared to traditional machine learning approaches. Deep learning models have the capability to automatically learn feature representations from raw data, eliminating the need for manual feature engineering and greatly simplifying the IED detection process. [14] Within the context of IED detection, CNN has been applied to automatically identify and analyze EEG signals with IED annotations, assisting medical professionals in the diagnosis and monitoring of epilepsy, and leading to the development of various CNN-based detection models. [15] Similar to CNN's impressive feature representation ability in computer vision tasks, [16] research has demonstrated that advanced CNN models, such as ConvNet, [17] have achieved better performance than traditional algorithms in EEG classification tasks, successfully learning discriminative features from the convolutional layers. Furthermore, compact EEGNet [18] has exhibited remarkable performance in temporal feature perception and demonstrated excellent generalization across multiple brain-computer interface paradigms.

The IED signal is a time-series data, while CNN mainly focuses on local features and lacks the ability to model long-term dependencies in time series, and epileptic gap-phase spikes tend to have time-specific patterns and temporal features. Recently, an attention-based Transformer has achieved great success as a powerful sequence processing in the field of natural language processing, [19] and this model has also begun to be applied in EEG decoding and achieved excellent performance by exploiting the long-term temporal relations. [20, 21] However, the Transformer may neglect the learning of local features, which is necessary for IED decoding. In this case, additional feature extraction processing such as activity maps and spatial filters must be added to compensate. [22] Recently a framework called Convolution Transformer(Conformer) has been proposed to synthesize the advantages of CNN and Transformer, [23] and it also has good interpretability and running speed. So in this paper, the IED Conformer model is applied to detect and classify the IED datasets of 11 pediatric epilepsy patients, and the computational results show that the method achieves an average accuracy of 96.11% on the test set.

The paper is organized as follows: data acquisition, preprocessing, proposed specific methodology and performance metrics are given in Sect. 2. Detailed experimental results and analytical discussion are given in Sect. 3. The conclusions of this study are presented in Sect. 4.

2 Data Preprocessing and Method

2.1 Data Acquisition

The datasets utilized in this experiment were collected from 11 pediatric epilepsy patients at Wuhan Children's Hospital, as shown in Table 1. EEG recordings were acquired using 19 channels under the international 10–20 system, with the sampling rate at $500Hz$. This study obtained approval from the Research Ethics Committee of Wuhan Children's Hospital, with IRB number 2022R034-E01.

Table 1. EEG sampling information of 11 epilepsy patients.

ID	Gender	Age(Year)	EEG Duration(s)	Numbers of IED
Sub01	Male	10	487	135
Sub02	Female	4	1745	90
Sub03	Male	11	1798	124
Sub04	Male	10	780	55
Sub05	Female	5	945	131
Sub06	Male	4	913	122
Sub07	Female	12	3445	87
Sub08	Male	6	3723	106
Sub09	Male	10	1893	114
Sub10	Male	9	2299	111
Sub11	Male	12	932	131

2.2 Preprocessing

The flowchart of the preprocessing is shown in Fig. 1. The raw EEG was band- pass filtered at frequency band [0.5, 50] Hz to remove high-frequency components and perform DC-removal. Independent Component Analysis(ICA) is widely used to remove common EEG artifacts (muscle, blink, or eye movements) from the data without removing the affected portions of the data. The ICA component rejection followed the ICA artifact removal instruction of EEGLAB2022.1. All preprocessing operations are performed on Matlab 2018b.

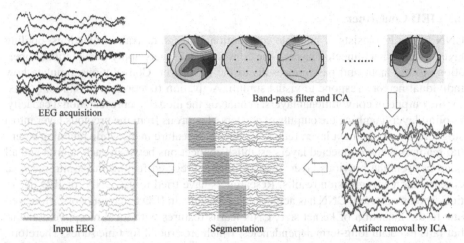

Fig. 1. Data Analysis Flowchart. The raw EEG was filtered between [0.5, 50]Hz, and then pure EEG signals were extracted by ICA and artifact removal techniques. The data was then segmented using a sliding window.

The long-term EEG is divided into segments using a 600ms sliding window with 300ms overlapping. When the sliding window program is executed, the IED start and end time in the data annotation file is automatically read and each EEG is segmented. A demonstration of IED and non-IED EEG segments is shown in Fig. 2. As mentioned earlier, each dataset is divided into segments. Specifically, given a dataset $D \in (X^{N1}, y^{N1})$, $(X^{N2}, y^{N2}),\ldots,(X^{Ni}, y^{Ni})$, $1 \leq i \leq 11$ where N_i is the total number of EEG segments for patient i. The jth segment $X^j \in R^{C \times T}$, $1 \leq j \leq N_i$ contains C channels, and each segment contains T time points, where $C = 19$, $T = 300$, in this study. The class label of segment j is denoted by $y^j \in (0, 1)$, corresponding to non-IED and IED respectively.

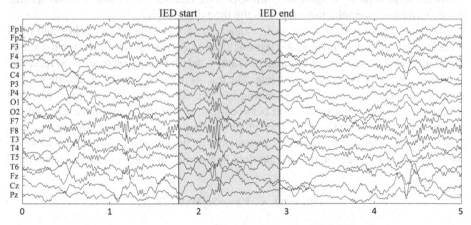

Fig. 2. A Demonstration of IED and non-IED EEG Segments.

2.3   IED Conformer

CNN typically consists of multiple convolutional layers, activation functions, pooling layers, and fully connected layers. The convolutional layers apply convolutional operations to the input and pass the results to the next layer. Convolutions simulate how individual neurons respond to visual stimuli. Activation functions are commonly used for the outputs of convolutional layers, enhancing the model's representational capacity. Pooling layers combine the outputs of clusters of neurons from the previous layer into a single neuron in the next layer, reducing the size of feature maps while retaining essential features. Fully connected layers establish connections between each neuron and all neurons from the previous layer, transforming aggregated feature maps into the final classification or regression results. Researchers have tried to use CNN for IED detection, and as expected, CNN has achieved good results in IED detection work. However, due to the limitation of kernel size, CNN learns features with local receptive domains but fails to obtain long-term dependencies, which are crucial for time series. Therefore, IED Conformer, which combines CNN and Transformer, is proposed for IED detection.

The IED Conformer framework is composed of three interconnected components: a convolution module, a self-attention module, and a classifier. In the convolution module, we initially employ temporal and spatial convolutions to capture the local temporal and spatial features of the IED. The first layer comprises 40 filters, each with a size of $(1, 25)$ and a stride of $(1, 1)$, indicating that convolution is applied along the time dimension. The subsequent layer retains 40 filters sized (ch, 1) with a stride of $(1, 1)$, where ch corresponds to the number of electrode channels in IED data. This layer functions as a spatial filter, capturing the relationships between different electrode channels. Batch normalization is then applied to enhance training and mitigate overfitting. We employ exponential linear units (ELU) as the activation function for introducing nonlinearity. Using average pooling to slice the temporal feature segments effectively reduces model complexity while eliminating redundant information, the pooling kernel with the size of $(1, 75)$, and a stride of $(1, 15)$. Finally, we rearrange the feature maps obtained from the convolution module by compressing the electrode channel dimension and transposing the convolution channel dimension with the time dimension.

Next, we treat each convolutional channel at every time point as a token and input them into the self-attention module. Within this module, we use self-attention to capture global temporal dependencies within IED features, ad- dressing the constrained receptive field inherent in the convolution module. The tokens organized in the preceding module undergo a linear transformation, resulting in three equivalents termed query (Q), key (K), and value (V). The correlation between distinct tokens is evaluated through dot product computation on Q and K. The outcome is then processed by a Softmax function, generating the attention score matrix. Subsequently, the attention score is used to weigh the values in V through another dot product operation. This process can be formulated as:

$$Attention(Q, K, V) = Softmax(\frac{QK}{\sqrt{k}})V \qquad (1)$$

where k denotes the length of a token. We also employed a multi-head strategy to further increase representational diversity. Tokens were divided into segments and fed into the self-attention module, and the results were concatenated as module outputs.

Finally, a simple fully connected layer produces the decoding results. The framework architecture of IED Conformer is shown in Fig. 3. Inspired by this model, we trained it on our EEG datasets and analyzed the results of IED detection.

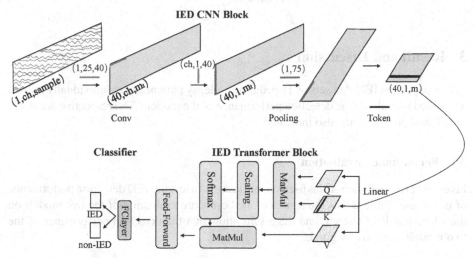

Fig. 3. The Framework Architecture of IED Conformer. The whole framework is com- posed of three parts in series: convolution module, self-attention module, and classifier.

2.4 Evaluation Metrics

In the performance evaluation, the IED segment is marked as "positive", while the non-IED segment is marked as "negative". Therefore, for each test sample, a binary classifier has 4 possible outcomes:

1. True positive (TP);
2. False positive (FP);
3. True negative (TN);
4. False negative (FN).

Three statistical metrics (accuracy, recall, and precision) are used to evaluate the model classification performance. Accuracy is used to calculate the proportion of accurately classified samples and to evaluate the overall classification effect. Recall measures the ability of a model to correctly identify IED instances out of all the actual IED instances in the datasets. A high recall indicates that the model is good at capturing IED instances. Precision measures the accuracy of a model in correctly identifying IED relative to all the instances that the model classified as IED (both true IED and false IED). A high precision indicates that when the model predicts an IED, it is likely to be correct. The evaluation metrics are calculated as:

$$Accuracy = \frac{TP + TN}{TP + TN + FP + FN} \tag{2}$$

$$Recall = \frac{TP}{TP + TN} \tag{3}$$

$$Precision = \frac{TP}{TP + FP} \tag{4}$$

3   Result and Discussion

In this paper, the IED datasets of 11 pediatric epilepsy patients were individually trained and tested to evaluate the detection performance of the models. The respective accuracy, recall, and precision are also indicated.

3.1   Performance Evaluation

Five-fold cross-validation was used on the datasets to test the IED detection performance of the model. Table 2 lists the results of the best score evaluation of the two models on the 11-patient IED test set, and the results show that the detection performance of the two models is relatively good.

Table 2. Results of IED Conformer and EEGNet under three evaluation indicators.

ID	IED Conformer			EEGNet		
	Accuracy(%)	Recall(%)	Precision(%)	Accuracy(%)	Recall(%)	Precision(%)
Sub01	95.16	92.70	94.37	92.97	90.70	93.98
Sub02	90.44	93.25	86.87	90.23	96.88	85.54
Sub03	98.53	99.82	96.56	97.53	99.95	95.20
Sub04	99.89	99.75	99.62	99.04	98.63	99.31
Sub05	97.29	97.68	93.20	94.77	97.00	93.17
Sub06	95.08	97.03	93.29	89.56	91.61	89.64
Sub07	97.16	98.80	95.39	91.99	90.50	93.46
Sub08	99.25	99.95	98.39	97.08	97.37	98.58
Sub09	86.77	93.88	79.30	76.28	99.06	68.22
Sub10	99.86	99.89	99.08	98.10	97.76	98.45
Sub11	96.76	95.19	96.25	90.74	87.50	93.56
Average	**96.11**	**97.08**	**93.85**	**92.65**	**95.18**	**91.74**

Due to individual differences between patients, there is some variation in the quality of the test from subject to subject. For example, patient 4, patient 8, and patient 10 were able to achieve 98% on all three evaluation indexes on IED Conformer and more than 97% on EEGNet, this indicates that these patient samples have features that are relatively easy to be detected by IED Conformer. The recall of EEGNet on patient 2 and patient 9 reaches 96.88% and 99.06% significantly higher than that of IED Conformer's 93.25% and 93.88%, respectively, suggesting that the data from patient 2 and patient 9 may contain some specific sample features that may be more adapted to EEGNet, making them easier to detect. This may also indicate that IED Conformer is relatively less adaptable for some specific samples. However, certain patients have not performed well on the two models, for example, patient 9 has an accuracy of 86.77% on the IED Conformer and only 76.28% on the EEGNet, and patients 2 and 9 have precision rates of 86.87% and 79.30% on IED Conformer, respectively, and only 85.54% and 68.22% on the EEGNet, but the recalls all exceeded 93%, especially EEGNet's recall of 99.06% on patient 9, suggesting that EEGNet may be more inclined in some cases not to miss a patient's true abnormality, i.e., to focus more on a few categories of detections, even though it may misclassify some normal conditions as abnormal. Except for the patients mentioned above, the classification results are highly satisfactory. The last row of Table 2 shows the average results of the three statistical measures for all 11 patients, with an average classification accuracy of 96.11% for IED and non-IED in the IED Conformer, and average recall and precision of 97.08% and 93.85%, while in EEGNet these three evaluation metrics are 92.65%, 95.18% and 91.74% respectively. It is indicated that IED Conformer is slightly more comprehensive in terms of overall performance for the same dataset, but this is not absolute. There are some differences in the performance of the two models in different patients, suggesting that there is still room for improvement in IED Conformer in some specific cases.

In general, the accuracy of both IED Conformer and EEGNet classifies better on most of the patients, and IED Conformer outperforms EEGNet on each patient. The results also show that recall performs very well on all patients, with both averaging 97.08% and 95.18%. This indicates that our proposed model has high sensitivity in recognizing IED and can effectively capture true positive cases. The high recall value further confirms the good performance and robustness of our model in detecting IED. The results indicate that the recall rate can generally exceed 90%, except for individual patients. This suggests that the model is adept at recognizing the target category and can effectively prevent missing IED. The high precision value further confirms that our model has good accuracy and reliability. These results provide strong support for the credibility and robustness of the model in clinical IED detection.

3.2 Computational Cost

The detection of IED is of great significance in the diagnosis, treatment, and condition assessment of epilepsy, which can provide an important basis and guidance for doctors, but the research on automatic CNN-based IED detection is still in its infancy. [24] In this paper, a model based on IED Conformer was evaluated on non-invasive scalp EEG data. The average accuracy rate of EEGNet reached 92.65%, and the accuracy rate of IED Conformer even reached 96.11%, which shows good results in comparison with previous studies. It can be seen from Table 3 that the running time of IED Conformer is much faster than that of EEGNet, even 3807 s faster on patient 8, and 17774 s faster than EEGNet on the whole.

Table 3. Running time of IED Conformer and EEGNet. (Unit: Second)

ID	Models		
	IED Conformer	EEGNet	Difference
Sub01	201	552	351
Sub02	1073	2757	1684
Sub03	1092	2955	1863
Sub04	300	896	596
Sub05	516	1436	920
Sub06	480	1382	902
Sub07	1921	4704	2783
Sub08	2278	6085	3807
Sub09	1060	2862	1802
Sub10	1413	3811	2398
Sub11	423	1091	668
Sum	**10757**	**28531**	**17774**

3.3 Future Work

Of course, there are still some deficiencies in the related research of this paper. In the first aspect, IED usually has different wave bands, which indicates that even the same patient may have different types of IED. [25] Therefore, further identification of specific waveforms of IED would be of additional benefit to physicians in clinical diagnosis with greater help, its future applications will be more promising. In subsequent studies, more detailed preprocessing of the original data is required, which may involve multi-classification issues. In the second aspect, the data used in the research in this article only comes from 11 pediatric epilepsy patients. It is not clear that good results can be produced on all EEG datasets, so subsequent studies may also be centered on training the model on different datasets and expanding the sample size in order to have a good theoretical basis for clinical trials.

4 Conclusion

Automated IED detection can efficiently, quickly, and objectively detect the presence of IED in an EEG segment, saving analysis time and manual labor, reducing the influence of subjective factors, and assisting physicians in providing an auxiliary diagnostic basis for a more accurate treatment plan. This paper investigated the practicality of IED Conformer on IED datasets of 11 pediatric epilepsy patients, and the results showed that the model achieved a classification accuracy of 96.11%, which suggests that the use of IED Conformer for IED identification is theoretically feasible. However, limitations such as the inability to specify the specific waveforms of IED and the insufficient amount of data in this study indicate that the results are not generalizable. Subsequent studies will focus on these aspects and further optimize the model structure.

Acknowledgement. This study was supported by the National Natural Science Funds of China (62006100), the Initial Scientific Research Fund of Ph.D. in Hubei University of Science and Technology (BK201802), the Undergraduate Innovation and Entrepreneurship Training Program of Hubei Province (S202010927039), Scientific Research Innovation Team Project of Hubei University of Science and Technology(2023T10), the Fundamental Research Funds for the Chinese Central Universities(0070ZK1096 to JG), and the CAAE-Neuracle EEG (CB-2022–028). The funders have no role in the research design, data collection, and analysis, decision to publish, or prepare manuscripts.

References

1. Oluigbo, C.O., Salma, A., Rezai, A.R.: Deep brain stimulation for neurological disorders. IEEE Rev. Biomed. Eng. **5**, 88–99 (2012)
2. Supriya, S., Siuly, S., Wang, H., Zhang, Y.: Epilepsy detection from EEG using complex network techniques: a review. IEEE Rev. Biomed. Eng. **16**, 292–306 (2023)
3. Ramele, R., Villar, A.J., Santos, J.M.: EEG waveform analysis of P300 ERP with applications to brain computer interfaces. Brain Sci. **8**(11), 199 (2018)
4. Acharya, U.R., Sree, S.V., Swapna, G., Martis, R.J., Suri, J.S.: Automated EEG analysis of epilepsy: a review. Knowl.-Based Syst. **45**, 147–165 (2013)
5. Chen, Z., Lu, G., Xie, Z., Shang, W.: A Unified framework and Method for EEG- based early epileptic seizure detection and epilepsy diagnosis. IEEE Access **8**, 20080–20092 (2020)
6. Thomas, J., et al.: Automated detection of interictal epileptiform discharges from scalp electroencephalograms by convolutional neural networks. Int. J. Neural Syst. **30**(11), 2050030 (2020)
7. De Oliveira, P.G., Queiroz, C., Da Silva, F.L.: Spike detection based on a pattern recognition approach using a microcomputer. Electroencephalogr. Clin. Neurophysiol. **56**(1), 97–103 (1983)
8. Gabor, A.J., Seyal, M.: Automated interictal EEG spike detection using artificial neural networks. Electroencephalogr. Clin. Neurophysiol. **83**(5), 271–280 (1992)
9. Lodder, S.S., Askamp, J., van Putten, M.J.: Interictal spike detection using a database of smart templates. Clin. Neurophysiol. **124**(12), 2328–2335 (2013)
10. Thomas, J., Jin, J., Dauwels, J., Cash, S.S., Westover, M.B.: Automated epileptiform spike detection via affinity propagation-based template matching. In: 2017 39th Annual International Conference of the IEEE Engineering in Medicine and Biology Society (EMBC), pp. 3057–3060. IEEE (2017)
11. Bagheri, E., Jin, J., Dauwels, J., Cash, S., Westover, M.B.: Classifier cascade to aid in detection of epileptiform transients in interictal EEG. In: 2018 IEEE International Conference on Acoustics, Speech and Signal Processing (ICASSP), pp. 970–974. IEEE (2018)
12. Zhou, M., et al.: Epileptic seizure detection based on EEG signals and CNN. Front. Neuroinform. **12**, 95 (2018)
13. Tjepkema-Cloostermans, M.C., de Carvalho, R.C., van Putten, M.J.: Deep learning for detection of focal epileptiform discharges from scalp EEG recordings. Clin. Neurophysiol. **129**(10), 2191–2196 (2018)
14. Ullah, I., et al.: An automated system for epilepsy detection using EEG brain signals based on deep learning approach. Expert Syst. Appl. **107**, 61–71 (2018)

15. Thuwajit, P., et al.: EEGWaveNet: multiscale CNN-based spatiotemporal feature extraction for EEG seizure detection. IEEE Trans. Ind. Inf. **18**(8), 5547–5557 (2022)
16. He, K., Zhang, X., Ren, S., Sun, J.: Deep residual learning for image recognition.In: 2016 IEEE Conference on Computer Vision and Pattern Recognition (CVPR), pp. 770–778 (2016)
17. Schirrmeister, R.T., et al.: Deep learn- ing with convolutional neural networks for EEG decoding and visualization. Hum. Brain Mapp. **38**(11), 5391–5420 (2017)
18. Lawhern, V.J., Solon, A.J., Waytowich, N.R., Gordon, S.M., Hung, C.P., Lance, B.J.: EEGNet: a compact convolutional neural network for EEG-based brain- computer interfaces. J. Neural Eng. **15**(5), 056013 (2018)
19. Vaswani, A., et al.: Attention is all you need. In: Advances in Neural Information Processing Systems, vol. 30 (2017)
20. Xie, J., et al.: A transformer-based approach combining deep learning network and spatial-temporal information for raw EEG classification. IEEE Trans. Neural Syst. Rehabil. Eng. **30**, 2126–2136 (2022)
21. Song, Y., Jia, X., Yang, L., Xie, L.: Transformer-based spatial-temporal feature learning for EEG decoding. arXiv preprint: arXiv:2106.11170 (2021)
22. Bagchi, S., Bathula, D.R.: EEG-ConvTransformer for single-trial EEG-based visual stimulus classification. Pattern Recogn. **129**, 108757 (2022)
23. Song, Y., Zheng, Q., Liu, B., Gao, X.: EEG conformer: convolutional transformer for EEG decoding and visualization. IEEE Trans. Neural Syst. Rehabil. Eng. **31**, 710–719 (2022)
24. Zhang, L., et al.: Automatic interictal epileptiform discharge (IED) detection based on convolutional neural network (CNN). Front. Mol. Biosci. **10**, 1146606 (2023)
25. Martis, R.J., Tan, J.H., Chua, C.K., Loon, T.C., Yeo, S.W.J., Tong, L.: Epileptic EEG classification using nonlinear parameters on different frequency bands. J. Mech. Med. Biol. **15**(03), 1550040 (2015)

Lightweight Traffic Sign Recognition Model Based on Dynamic Feature Extraction

Yiyuan Ge[1] , Ke Niu[1(✉)] , Zhihao Chen[1] , and Qinhu Zhang[2]

[1] Beijing Information Science and Technology University, Beijing, China
{niuke,2021011561}@bistu.edu.cn
[2] Eastern Institute for Advanced Study, Eastern Institute of Technology, Ningbo, China
qzhang@eitech.edu.cn

Abstract. Accurate traffic sign data recognition is crucial for enhancing safety in autonomous driving system. However, recognizing traffic signs from natural scenes is challenging due to factors like dim lighting, occlusion, and blurriness, which make traditional deep learning algorithms inefficient. These algorithms require a larger number of parameters to construct network models to achieve higher recognition accuracy. Balancing parameter quantity and accuracy, and building an efficient road traffic sign recognition system, is an important research topic in the field of autonomous driving. In response to these challenges, we introduce a novel architecture named Dynamic Feature Extraction-Efficient Vision Transformer (DFE-EViT). This innovative design comprises two components: a dynamic feature extraction network and an Efficient Vision Transformer (EViT) classifier. By synergizing local information and global receptive fields, this architecture is uniquely equipped to handle intricate and dynamic traffic sign recognition scenarios. The experimental results show that the method proposed in this paper improves the efficiency of road traffic sign recognition in natural scenes, and the network has the advantages of small parameter size and high recognition accuracy. The model proposed in this paper has only 0.859M parameters, but the accuracy can reach 98.4%.

Keywords: Traffic Sign Recognition · Vision Transformer · Dynamic Feature Extraction

1 Introduction

Road traffic sign recognition is a key area in autonomous driving technology [1–4], and its importance is reflected in several aspects. Firstly, road traffic signs are an essential component of the road traffic system, carrying the transmission of traffic rules and restrictions. Accurate and timely recognition and understanding of traffic signs are crucial for the safe and compliant operation of autonomous vehicles. By recognizing road traffic signs, autonomous vehicles can accurately acquire road information, including

---

Y. Ge and K. Niu—These authors contributed equally to this work.

speed limits, prohibitions, road indications, etc., enabling them to make corresponding decisions and driving plans. Secondly, road traffic sign recognition combines the
development of autonomous driving technology with artificial intelligence technology.
Autonomous driving technology achieves vehicle autonomy by leveraging sensors, data
processing, and control systems. Complementing this, artificial intelligence technologies, particularly computer vision and machine learning, play a vital role in enhancing
road traffic sign recognition. By applying deep learning algorithms, autonomous vehicles can learn and recognize the features and patterns of traffic signs from large-scale
annotated data, achieving high-precision sign detection and classification. Additionally,
the development of road traffic sign recognition faces some challenges and difficulties.
Firstly, traffic signs come in various types with differences in shape, color, and specifications. Moreover, they are influenced by environmental conditions such as weather
and lighting, making sign detection and recognition complex and challenging. Secondly,
road traffic signs demand real-time recognition, ensuring swift and accurate identification to facilitate prompt vehicle responses and decisions. Lastly, misidentification of
road traffic signs can lead to serious safety issues, thereby demanding high robustness
and reliability requirements for sign recognition algorithms.

Traditional traffic sign recognition algorithms include those based on color space [5]
and boundary moment technologies [6] recognition and detection methods that integrate
image features [7], as well as recognition and detection methods based on affine transformation corrections [8]. However, these algorithms are all based on the specific colors
or shapes of traffic signs in images for recognition, and are unable to adapt to complex
and variable recognition scenarios.

Compared to traditional methods, deep learning approaches [9, 10] have significant
advantages in traffic sign recognition. Deep learning methods can autonomously learn
the feature representations of signs from data, thereby improving learning efficiency and
accuracy. By utilizing architectures like deep convolutional neural networks (CNNs),
models can learn richer feature representations, enhancing the robustness and generalization ability of traffic sign recognition. Liao et al. [11] addressed the limitations
of existing methods in image feature extraction and accurate recognition under complex conditions by designing a novel traffic sign recognition model called HE-SKNet.
This model employs image enhancement techniques and the SKNet [12] structure to
enhance feature extraction and representation, thereby improving recognition accuracy
and stability. Khan et al. [13] proposed a traffic sign recognition network that achieved
accuracies of 98.41% and 92.06% on German and Belgian traffic sign datasets, respectively, by improving the traditional VGG [14] architecture. Postovan et al. [15] proposed
a bottom-up BNN architecture approach by studying the characteristics of each component layer, achieving over 90% average accuracy on the GTSRB dataset and average
accuracies exceeding 80% on test datasets from Belgium and China.

In practical traffic sign recognition scenarios, there are high requirements not only
for the detection accuracy of the network but also for the model's ease of deployment
and runtime speed. Currently, deep neural network architectures used for road traffic
sign recognition suffer from issues such as excessive parameter count and slow model
execution speed, which hinder practical deployment. To address these problems, this

paper proposes a lightweight neural network architecture. Our main contributions can be summarized as follows:

1. Inspired by the concepts of InceptionNetV1, SENet, and ResNet, we have developed a multi-branch Dynamic Feature Extraction (DFE) network with the aim of extracting efficient feature information from local regions.
2. Taking inspiration from the lightweight network architecture of MobileNetV2, we propose an Efficient Vision Transformer as a classifier. We design an Efficient Feed-Forward Network (EFFN) to replace the original ViT's Multi-Layer Perception (MLP), significantly reducing the parameter and computational requirements of ViT.
3. Building upon the fusion of CNN and ViT, we introduce a neural network architecture called DFE-EViT for road traffic sign recognition. This architecture utilizes DFE as a preceding module to the EViT, addressing the lack of local information in ViT while maintaining global perception capabilities. Experimental results demonstrate that this network exhibits stronger adaptability in traffic sign recognition tasks in natural scenes.

2 Method

In the task of traffic sign recognition, most deep learning networks are built upon the CNN architecture. The architecture based on ViT doesn't perform well on traffic sign datasets [16]. However, for the complex and dynamic nature of traffic sign identification scenarios, global information also holds paramount importance. It enables us to make more accurate and comprehensive judgments. Thus, we introduce the DFE-EViT network. This architecture employs the DFE network as a preliminary feature extractor, dynamically capturing localized information. Simultaneously, it leverages the multi-head self-attention mechanism from the EViT network, granting the model a broader global receptive field. This global perspective aids in making judgments considering the overall background environment. Furthermore, to simulate intricate real-world conditions like lighting and visibility in traffic sign recognition scenarios, we have designed augmentation strategies tailored for such contexts. Ultimately, we iteratively train the network and evaluate it on the test dataset (Fig. 1).

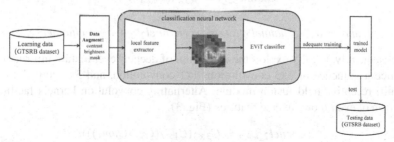

Fig. 1. The model architecture diagram involves extracting features using CNN and subsequently feeding them into ViT for further feature extraction.

2.1 DFE-EViT Network

As shown in Fig. 2, the proposed DFE-EViT network consists of two main components: the DFE feature extractor and the EViT classifier. The DFE component comprises three parallel branches. Through adaptive fusion within these branches, highly diverse local information can be extracted. This information is then utilized as a preliminary feature extraction module for the lightweight EViT network, addressing the deficiency of local information in it.

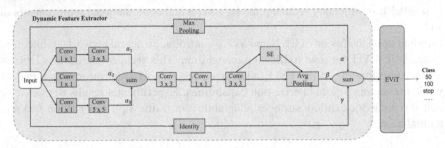

Fig. 2. Details of the DFE-EViT network model

Dynamic Feature Extraction Network. The DFE network consists of three branches: the Local Feature Extraction branch, the Max Pooling Residual branch, and the Original Feature Residual branch. The Local Feature Extraction branch is the core of DFE. Firstly, we introduce a multi-receptive field fusion module to extract feature information from different receptive fields. Similar to InceptionNet V2, we utilize convolutions with varying receptive fields to extract original features, followed by a weighted sum calculation. The formula is as follows:

$$channel_{2\_1} = C_{3\times3}(C_{1\times1}(x)) \tag{1}$$

$$channel_{2\_2} = C_{1\times1}(x) \tag{2}$$

$$channel_{2\_3} = C_{5\times5}(C_{1\times1}(x)) \tag{3}$$

$$sum_1 = \alpha_1 \times channel_{2\_1} + \alpha_2 \times channel_{2\_2} + \alpha_3 \times channel_{2\_3} \tag{4}$$

Subsequently, to fully exploit the extraction of deeper-level feature information, we introduce a sequence of 3x3 convolution, 1x1 convolution, and 3x3 convolution after the multi-receptive field fusion module. Alternating convolution kernels facilitate the extraction of even more diverse features (Fig. 3).

$$channel_{2\_temp} = C_{3\times3}(C_{1\times1}(C_{3\times3}(sum_1))) \tag{5}$$

In addition, we introduce the SE Attention module, which adaptively allocates weights to each channel, allowing the network to focus more on crucial feature channels. The structure of the SE module is illustrated in the following diagram:

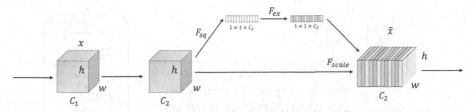

Fig. 3. SE module architecture diagram

Where F_{sq} represents the Squeeze operation, compressing the original feature map into a $1 * 1 * C_2$ vector through global average pooling, where C_2 is the number of channels in the original feature map. F_{ex} stands for the Excitation operation, which extracts weight information through two fully connected layers, resulting in a $1 * 1 * C_2$ weight vector. F_{scale} represents the Scale operation, where the extracted weight vector is multiplied element-wise with the original feature map, thus weighting each channel of the original feature map. Finally, we embed the SE Attention module into the second branch to enhance significant channel information:

$$channel_2 = channel_{2\_temp} + SE(channel_{2\_temp}) \tag{6}$$

Lastly, following the Local Feature Extraction branch, we append an average pooling layer to consolidate the abundant local features. Additionally, we introduce learnable parameters to weight the three branches:

$$channel_2 = Avg\_pool(channel_2) \tag{7}$$

$$sum_2 = \alpha \cdot Max\_pool(x) + \beta \cdot channel_2 + \gamma \cdot x \tag{8}$$

where α, β, and γ are learnable parameters with an initial weight of 0.33. During the network training process, they are dynamically adjusted to combine the features from the three branches.

Efficient Vision Transformer. The standard Transformer model [17], originally used in natural language processing, employs one-dimensional token embedding sequences as inputs. As depicted in Fig. 4, this approach is adapted for images by combining vectorized and image-encoded vectors to create input vectors that encompass spatial positional information. In the ViT model [18], these new input vectors are fed into a sequence of Encoder modules to learn image features. Each Encoder module consists of multi-head self-attention modules, multi-layer perceptrons, and residual connections, culminating in classification using an MLP Head.

We have introduced a series of improvements to the original ViT architecture to enhance its efficiency in traffic sign recognition tasks. We propose the Efficient Feed-Forward Network as a replacement for the original MLP. As shown in Fig. 4, within the EFFN module, we utilize DepthWise (DW) convolution and PointWise (PW) convolution to construct the feedforward neural network. Firstly, a PW convolution with a kernel

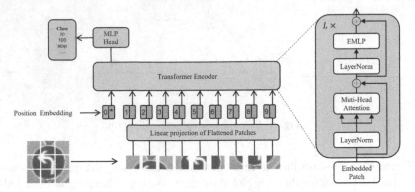

Fig. 4. Improved ViT classifier

size of 1 x 1 is employed to reduce channel dimensions. Subsequently, a DW convolution with a kernel size of 3 x 3 and another 1 x 1 PW convolution are applied to further extract features. This approach enables us to use fewer parameters and incorporate more network layers in the model (Fig. 5).

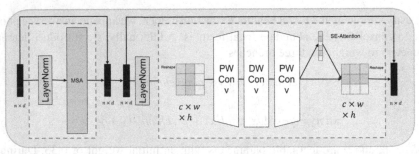

Fig. 5. Encoder module. We utilize depthwise separable convolution, pointwise convolution, and SE Attention within the module.

Furthermore, we introduce the SE Attention module as a residual branch to further enhance the feature extraction capacity of the feedforward neural network. This module incurs minimal parameter overhead. The proposed EViT architecture in this paper consists of merely 5 Encoder modules. Each patch image block is sized at 8x8, with an encoding length of 192, and requires no expansion coefficient for fully connected layers. In comparison to the conventional ViT, the parameter count contrast is illustrated below (Table 1):

Table 1. Performance comparison of ViT parameters.

Classifier	depth	mlp_ratio	Embed_dim	Param (M)
ViT-L	24	4	1024	303.14
ViT-B	12	4	768	85.24
ViT-S	12	4	384	21.38
Ours	**5**	**2**	**192**	**0.80**

3   Experimental Results and Analysis

3.1   Experimental Environment and Dataset

The data for our experiments is sourced from the German Traffic Sign Recognition Benchmark (GTSRB) dataset [19]. This dataset comprises a total of 51,839 images, all of which have a standardized size of 128 x 128 pixels. The training set contains 39,209 images, while the test set contains 12,630 images, maintaining an approximate ratio of 3:1.

Due to the collection of images from real-world scenarios, challenges such as occlusions, blurriness, and low contrast are present in the dataset. These issues pose significant challenges for the task of traffic sign recognition. A subset of the sampled test dataset is shown in Fig. 6.

Fig. 6. GTSRB dataset

To ensure the accuracy of comparative experiments, non-comparative parameters were kept constant. The initial learning rate was set at 0.001, and both training and test sets were processed in batches of 64 images. The optimization algorithm chosen was

Stochastic Gradient Descent (SGD), with a learning rate decay strategy employing the step function. The momentum value was set to 0.9. The model underwent training for 200 iterations, with convergence of the loss function indicating sufficient learning.

3.2 Data Augmentation

Considering the relatively limited volume of experimental data and the inherent complexity of the scenarios, encompassing significant differences in brightness and blurriness, as depicted in Fig. 7, we enhanced the dataset to better emulate the diversity encountered in natural conditions. Through random brightness adjustments, we emulated lighting variations such as dimness or intense illumination. By introducing random contrast adjustments, we simulated changes in visibility present in scenes with blurriness or backlighting. Additionally, we applied random masking operations to simulate instances where traffic signs are obscured in natural conditions. Prior to training, all images in the dataset were uniformly resized to 32x32 pixels, ensuring consistent input image dimensions.

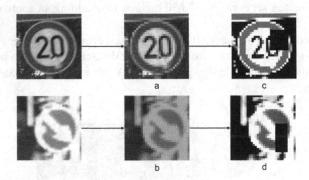

Fig. 7. Data augmentation, where images a and b undergo random lighting and contrast adjustment, while images c and d are the results after random mask and normalization.

3.3 Evaluation Metrics and Loss Function

In this study, the recognition accuracy (Accuracy) is employed as the primary metric to evaluate the performance of the model.

$$Acc = \frac{\sum_{i=1}^{k} m_i}{\sum_{i=1}^{k} M_i} \times 100\% \tag{9}$$

The k represents the number of classes of traffic signs in the dataset, m_i denotes the count of correct recognitions for the i-th class, and M_i signifies the total count of instances in the i-th class. Through this comprehensive measure, we are able to evaluate the model's recognition capacity and efficiency, reflecting its overall performance in the task of traffic sign recognition.

3.4 Experimental Results

To comprehensively assess the impact on the DFE-EViT network's performance, we conducted extensive experiments involving multiple component combinations. These components include the multi-receptive field fusion module, attention module, residual pooling branch, and EViT. Table 2 provides a summary of the experimental outcomes. Utilizing the DFE network alone yields an accuracy of 72.58%, while exclusive employment of the EViT network achieves an accuracy of 92.88%. Notably, these figures represent reductions of 25.86% and 5.56% in accuracy, respectively, compared to the complete network configuration. Examining the DFE network, we observe that the attention module and multi-receptive field fusion module contribute performance enhancements of 0.89% and 1.22%, respectively. Additionally, the residual pooling branch contributes a modest 0.1% improvement. Ultimately, the combination of the DFE feature extraction network with EViT achieves an accuracy of 98.44% in the task of traffic sign recognition. The SE attention module and the multi-receptive field fusion module play pivotal roles within the DFE feature extraction network. Their combination facilitates dynamic selection of receptive fields, simultaneously focusing the network on important channel features. This notably enhances the efficiency of local feature extraction within the network.

Table 2. Module ablation experiment

EViT	SE Attention	Residual Pooling Branch	Multi-Receptive Field Fusion	Accuracy (%)
	√	√	√	72.58
√				92.88
√		√	√	97.55
√	√		√	98.34
√	√	√		97.22
√	√	√	√	98.44

Utilizing the German Traffic Sign Recognition Benchmark (GTSRB) dataset for training, we assessed the performance of several notable deep learning network architectures, including our novel DFE-EViT network. This evaluation encompassed tasks encompassing 43 classes of traffic scenes. The results are presented in Table 3. Among the traditional architectures, ResNet50 achieves an accuracy of 93.47%, while EfficientNet demonstrates 96.84% accuracy on the GTSRB dataset. However, these models entail larger parameter counts. On the other hand, MobileNet V2 and ShuffleNet, with more compact parameter counts of 2.27M and 1.29M respectively, achieve accuracies of 94.91% and 94.43%. Notably, the state-of-the-art traffic sign recognition networks, namely MFF-ResNet18 and HE-SKNet, achieve impressive accuracies of 97.74% and 98.95% on the GTSRB dataset. Remarkably, our proposed DFE-EViT network achieves an impressive accuracy of 98.44%, all while maintaining a remarkably low parameter count of 0.859M. This efficiency positions it as a formidable contender in the domain of traffic sign recognition. In addition, we conducted assessments on multiple Vision Transformer architectures, encompassing ViT-L, ViT-B, ViT-S, and T2T-ViT. These models achieved accuracies spanning from 95.34% to 96.18%, accompanied by varying parameter counts ranging from 303.14 M to 21.75 M. It's noteworthy that, despite their capabilities, the efficiency of these architectures trails that of our network.

Table 3. Accuracy, parameter count, and FPS of different networks on the GTSRB dataset.

Method	Param (M)	Accuracy (%)	FPS
Resnet50	25.55	93.47	60.24
MobileNetV2	2.27	94.91	208.33
ShuffleNet	1.29	94.43	**401.60**
EfficientNet	20.179	96.84	84.16
ViT-L	303.14	95.34	9.28
ViT-B	88.18	95.23	21.98
ViT-S	21.75	95.14	64.94
T2T-ViT	85.67	96.18	33.11
MFF-Resnet18 [20]	11.95	97.74	106.38
HE-SKNet [11]	23.92	98.95	112.36
Ours	**0.859**	**98.44**	303.87

Our network synergistically harnesses the advantages of both Convolutional Neural Networks (CNN) and Vision Transformers. It achieves this by seamlessly integrating local information from CNNs and a broader global receptive field inherent to ViTs, facilitating the extraction of comprehensive image features. Empirical findings from our experiments substantiate that this architectural fusion results in markedly improved feature representation, particularly in intricate and dynamic traffic sign recognition scenarios. The outcome is a notable augmentation in recognition efficiency. In the process of designing an efficient ViT, we have paid particular attention to module parameter count and efficiency. To mitigate the parameter overhead commonly found in traditional ViT networks, our EFFN module incorporates strategic elements like DepthWise and PointWise convolutions. These components substantially curtail parameter counts while retaining effectiveness. In summary, our experimental findings robustly validate the efficacy of the DFE-EViT network in the task of traffic sign recognition within natural scenes.

4 Conclusion

This paper proposes a novel lightweight architecture, DFE-EViT, for the task of road traffic sign recognition. Here, DFE refers to Dynamic Feature Extraction network, a module that incorporates the channel attention mechanism and multiple receptive field fusion modules. Its goal is to bolster the network's ability to express local features effectively. Meanwhile, EViT stands for Efficient ViT classification network. In EViT, we incorporate the EFFN (Efficient Feature Fusion Network) as a replacement for the Multi-Layer Perceptron used in conventional ViT models. The integration of EFFN achieves a substantial reduction in parameter size and computational load within the ViT network, thereby enabling the seamless incorporation of the lightweight architecture. Subsequently, we use DFE as the pre-positioned local feature extraction module for EViT, to compensate for the lack of local information in the EViT network. The experimental results fully prove the superiority of our proposed architecture. Compared with other methods in terms of parameter size and accuracy, our architecture shows more advantages. On a CPU, the inferencing time of the model is only 3.3 ms per image, which can realize real-time traffic sign recognition. In our future research endeavors, we plan to incorporate knowledge distillation techniques to enhance the model's efficiency by further reducing its parameter size. Additionally, given the model's lean parameter count, it holds promise for deployment on edge computing devices like self-driving cars, offering the opportunity to fully capitalize on its potential within real-world applications.

Acknowledgement. This work is supported by Key Research and Development(Digital Twin) Program of Ningbo City under Grant No. 2023Z219.

References

1. Yurtsever, E., et al.: A survey of autonomous driving: common practices and emerging technologies. IEEE Access **8**, 58443–58469 (2020)
2. Caesar, H., et al.: nuscenes: a multimodal dataset for autonomous driving. In: Proceedings of the IEEE/CVF Conference on Computer Vision and Pattern Recognition (2020)
3. Wang, W., et al.: Social interactions for autonomous driving: a review and perspectives. Found. Trends® Robot. **10**(3–4), 198–376 (2022)
4. Gao, C., et al.: Autonomous driving security: state of the art and challenges. IEEE Internet Things J. **9**(10), 7572–7595 (2021)
5. Kuehni, R.G.: Color space and its divisions." Color Research & Application: Endorsed by Inter-Society Color Council, The Colour Group (Great Britain), Canadian Society for Color, Color Science Association of Japan, Dutch Society for the Study of Color, The Swedish Colour Centre Foundation, Colour Society of Australia, Centre Français de la Coulcur **26**(3), 209–222 (2001)
6. Yun, I., et al.: Part-level convolutional neural networks for pedestrian detection using saliency and boundary box alignment. IEEE Access **7**, 23027–23037 (2019)
7. Kaur, H., Koundal, D., Kadyan, V.: Image fusion techniques: a survey. Arch. Comput. Methods Eng. **28**, 4425–4447 (2021)
8. Hattori, R., Komiyama, T.: PatchWarp: Corrections of non-uniform image distortions in two-photon calcium imaging data by patchwork affine transformations. Cell Rep. Methods **2**(5) (2022)
9. LeCun, Y., Bengio, Y., Hinton, G.: Deep learning. Nature **521**(7553), 436–444 (2015)
10. Goodfellow, I., Bengio, Y., Courville, A.: Deep Learning. MIT Press, Cambridge (2016)
11. Cong, L.I.A.O., et al.: Traffic sign recognition based on image enhancement and SKNet. Comput. Modernization **03**, 23 (2023)

12. Wu, W., et al.: SK-Net: deep learning on point cloud via end-to-end discovery of spatial keypoints. In: Proceedings of the AAAI Conference on Artificial Intelligence, vol. 34, no. 04 (2020)
13. Khan, M.A., Park, H., Chae, J.: A lightweight convolutional neural network (CNN) architecture for traffic sign recognition in urban road networks. Electronics 12(8), 1802 (2023)
14. Simonyan, K., Zisserman, A.: Very deep convolutional networks for large-scale image recognition. arXiv preprint: arXiv:1409.1556 (2014)
15. Postovan, A., Eraşcu, M.: Architecturing binarized neural networks for traffic sign recognition. arXiv preprint: arXiv:2303.15005 (2023)
16. Zheng, Y., Jiang, W.: Evaluation of vision transformers for traffic sign classification. Wireless Commun. Mob. Comput. 2022 (2022)
17. Vaswani, A., et al.: Attention is all you need. In: Advances in Neural Information Processing Systems, vol. 30 (2017)
18. Dosovitskiy, A., et al.: An image is worth 16x16 words: transformers for image recognition at scale. arXiv preprint: arXiv:2010.11929 (2020)
19. Stallkamp, J., et al.: The German traffic sign recognition benchmark: a multi-class classification competition. In: The 2011 International Joint Conference on Neural Networks. IEEE (2011)
20. Geng, J.B., Liang, Z.Y.: Traffic sign recognition based on improved ResNet. Electron. Technol. Softw. Eng. 06, 138–140 (2020)

DeepSensitive: A Fuzzing Test for Deep Neural Networks with Sensitive Neurons

Zixuan Yang[1], Chenhao Lin[1(✉)], Pengwei Hu[2], and Chao Shen[1]

[1] Xi'an Jiaotong University, Xi'an, Shaanxi, China
yzx1999@stu.xjtu.edu.cn, {linchenhao,chaoshen}@xjtu.edu.cn
[2] The Xinjiang Technical Institute of Physics and Chemistry, Chinese Academy of Sciences,
Beijing, China
hpw@ms.xjb.ac.cn

Abstract. Deep learning (DL) systems have exhibited remarkable capabilities in various domains, such as image classification, natural language processing, and recommender systems, thereby establishing themselves as significant contributors to the advancement of software intelligence. Nevertheless, in domains emphasizing security assurance, the reliability and stability of deep learning systems necessitate thorough testing prior to practical implementation. Given the increasing demand for high-quality assurance of DL systems, the field of DL testing has gained significant traction. Researchers have adapted testing techniques and criteria from traditional software testing to deep neural networks, yielding results that enhance the overall security of DL technology. To address the challenge of enriching test samples in DL testing systems and resolving the issue of unintelligibility in samples generated by multiple mutations, we propose an innovative solution called DeepSensitive. DeepSensitive functions as a fuzzy testing tool, leveraging DL interpretable algorithms to identify sensitive neurons within the input layer via the DeepLIFT algorithm. Employing a fuzzy approach, DeepSensitive perturbs these sensitive neurons to generate novel test samples. We conducted evaluations of DeepSensitive using various mainstream image processing datasets and deep learning models, thereby demonstrating its efficient and intuitive capacity for generating test samples.

Keywords: Deep learning testing · Neural networks · Fuzzing test

1 Introduction

With the development of artificial intelligence, deep neural network(DNN) systems powered by deep learning techniques have achieved outstanding results in a variety of scenarios, such as image classification [1], natural language processing [2], autonomous driving [3], and recommendation systems [4]. While setting off a round of technological innovation, the global deep learning market is expected to grow at a CAGR of 51.1% from the forecast period 2022 to 2030 and expected to reach the value of around USD 415 Billion by 2030 [5]. Unlike traditional software systems that use code as the core of decision-making, deep learning is a data-driven algorithm with a large number of trainable parameters in its decision-making core, the deep neural network. A large amount of data is fed into the network as a training set, and then the network parameters are updated in a gradient descent fashion to minimize the loss function. Neural networks trained in this way are able to beat traditional algorithms in a wide range of tasks, even to the level of surpassing humans. Consequently, various countries are investing a lot of effort in developing AI technology.

However, as deep learning technology is applied to more fields that are more sensitive to reliability and security (e.g., autonomous driving, intrusion detection, identity authentication, etc.), researchers have found that deep learning models are inherently vulnerable and that their stability is easily corrupted by disturbances from natural samples and adversarial samples. For example, a small perturbation on a traffic sign using adversarial sample techniques can cause an autonomous vehicle to recognize a stop sign as a speed limit signal [6]. This reveals the potential pitfalls of directly applying deep learning models in reality and suggests that reliability and robustness assurance measures for deep learning systems are necessary.

The demand for providing high-quality assurance in deep learning systems raises a systematic problem of testing deep neural networks. However, it is impractical to use traditional software testing methods for neural networks with thousands of neurons and parameters, which poses a serious challenge for automated, systematic testing of DNNs. A series of standards for testing techniques has been recently proposed in the field of software engineering. Theoretically, the input domains of DL systems are too extensive for complete testing to be possible, so a series of standards is usually used for standardized AI testing. Mainstream AI software test suites mostly consist of coverage tests, including multi-granularity neuron testing guidelines [7] and important neuron coverage guidelines [8]. Inspired by metrics such as code coverage and path coverage in the field of software engineering, early work proposed coverage test metrics such as neuron coverage and neuron activation path coverage. In these metrics, a threshold is set for a neuron's activation value, and if the neuron's activation value is greater than the threshold, the neuron is considered covered. After testing with the test set, the proportion of neurons that have been activated in the whole neural network can be calculated, i.e., the neuron coverage rate. To simplify the neuron coverage process further, the important neuron coverage criteria first use deep learning interpretable algorithms to compute neuron importance, and then the computed important neurons are constructed and tested in the coverage space. However, these methods face the problem of low numbers or low-quality test samples, which are mostly derived from multiple mutations through the test set, and the human readability of the test samples is greatly reduced after multiple mutations. To solve this problem, we propose DeepSensitive, the sensitive neuron fuzzing test criteria.

Inspired by the important neuron coverage criteria, the sensitive neuron fuzzing test criteria improves on the principle of neuron selection and uses a fuzzing test approach to generate samples that can lead to misclassifications of the neural network. It uses the DeepLIFT [9] algorithm, a deep learning interpretable algorithm, to select reference inputs for the test objectives. It performs diverse, flexible and targeted fuzzing tests on the neural network to test which neurons in the neural network are more susceptible to small perturbations that can change the final output more drastically. These neurons are more vulnerable and are defined as sensitive neurons at each layer. The sensitivity of the input layer neurons to the output layer can be calculated by computing the layer-by-layer transfer of sensitivities between each layer, and by fuzzing the pixels corresponding to the highly sensitive neurons, test samples can be obtained that are difficult to observe by the human eye to make the model classification biased.

Our contributions are summarized as follows:

We develop a new deep learning fuzzing test suite DeepSensitive based on sensitive neurons by innovatively combining DeepLIFT, a deep learning interpretable algorithm, with a deep neural network fuzzing test pipeline.

We tested the suite on the mainstream image datasets MNIST and CIFAR-10, as well as the popular convolutional neural networks LeNet and VGG. On average, we generated 5271 samples that resulted in incorrect classifications by the network. This represents a 94.87% increase in failure rates compared to random transforms at the logits level. The results demonstrate the suite's ability to effectively generate new test samples for DNN models.

2   Background and Related Works

2.1   Deep Neural Networks

The core of the deep learning model is the deep neural network, which is composed of several connected layers. It can be represented as a parameterized function $F^\theta : X \mapsto Y$, where $x \in X$ is an m-dimensional input, $y \in Y$ is the corresponding output labels, and θ represents the parameters in the DNN. Formally, a n-layer simple DNN can be represented as a composite function $F = l_n \circ l_{n-1} \circ \cdots \circ l_1$, where l represent a layer in the model. The l_1 indicates the input layer, and the l_n represents the output layer. The output of each layer l can be expressed as $F_l = \sigma(\theta_l * F_{l-1} + b_l)$, where θ_l and b_l are its weight matrix and bias. θ is called the activation function, which is a nonlinear function defining the specific output of layer l given an input. Convolutional neural networks are a typical variant of deep neural networks, which have convolutional layers as their main structure. Neurons in each convolutional layer are connected to only some of the neurons in the next layer, and multiple connections between different neurons have the same weight parameters. The calculation process of a convolutional layer uses several sets of shared parameters in it as a convolutional kernel to perform convolutional calculations on the neurons in the previous connected layer. Several classical outstanding models for image classification tasks are convolutional neural network structures, e.g., LeNet, VGG, ResNet, and Inception.

The goal of training a DNN model is to update the model parameters to accurately predict the output of the input data for the desired task. Given a large amount of input-output pairs (x_i, y_i) in a specific dataset, the training process updates all weight parameters θ in the DNN model to minimize the differences between the predicted output $F^\theta(x)$ and the corresponding ground truth label y. The loss function $\mathcal{L}(F^\theta(x), y)$ is used to quantify this difference. During training, the DNN model iteratively calculates the value of the loss function on the input-output pairs of the dataset and updates the model parameters using gradient descent. Eventually, the training process will terminate when the value of the loss function converges to a stable interval or reaches the target.

2.2 DNN Testing

Deep learning testing methods are kinds of approaches that explore the bugs of the model and try to fix them to improve the performance of the model after training. For effective DL system testing, the features of the test set should be highly diverse so that different behaviors of the system can be performed. For example, DeepXplore [10] estimates different DL system behaviors by calculating neuron coverage, i.e., the ratio of neurons with activation values above a predefined threshold. Similarly, the DeepGauge [7] multi-granularity test criterion generalizes the concept of neuronal coverage and calculates the ability of a test set to cover regions of major and corner case neurons by delineating the range of neuronal activation values. Some of these methods adapt testing techniques from the software engineering community, such as symbolic execution [11] and mutation testing [12], for deep learning models. One widely used method is mutation testing, which follows a workflow involving seed selection, mutation operators, evaluation using neural networks, oracle judgments, and test criteria like neuron coverage metrics. This process is repeated in cycles until the desired test metrics are achieved. For instance, DeepHunter [13] has developed a gray-box testing tool for DNNs based on this workflow. It utilizes various neuron coverage indicators to guide the testing process and can detect model misbehaviors.

In addition to correctness, it can test properties such as robustness [14], fairness [15], etc. Furthermore, there has been a series of work on this topic [8, 13, 16–18]. These deep learning test systems provide certain stability guarantees for DNN-based software systems and provide an effective method for expanding test samples. However, by focusing only on these constrained neuron properties and ignoring the behavior of the entire DL system, the causal relationship between the test set and the decisions is uninformative. Furthermore, the instantiation of recently proposed techniques depends on user-defined conditions (number of regions or upper bounds) that may not adequately represent the actual behavior of the DL system.

2.3 DNN Interpretability

Although DNNs have yielded outstanding results in a variety of application scenarios, they are a complete black box compared to traditional software compiled from manually written code. The user can know what decisions the model has made, but not why the model has made them, which further calls into question the credibility of DNNs. Consequently, understanding and explaining the classification decisions of DNN systems is of high value in many applications, as it allows to validate the inference of the system and provide additional information to the human expert, and also increases the controllability of the DNN, which can guarantee the stability of the DNN system at another level. Since the problem has been in the spotlight, academics have offered a variety of solutions. For example, layer-wise relevance propagation [19] can visualize the contribution of individual pixels to the prediction on a multilayer neural network, and these pixel contributions can be visualized as heat maps and made available to human experts.

This method not only visually verifies the validity of classification decisions, but also further analyzes potential regions of interest. DeepLIFT [9] decomposes the neural network's output prediction for a specific input by back-propagating the contribution of all neurons in the network to each feature of the inputs. By selectively considering positive and negative contributions separately, DeepLIFT can also reveal dependencies missed by other methods.

These deep learning interpretable methods also provide ideas for deep learning testing, such as DeepImportance's application of the LRP method to coverage testing. The method screens out several neurons that are most critical to the classification of the whole network by calculating the cumulative relevance metrics computed in the target layer from the data in the training set and then calculates the output domains of the important neurons for coverage testing. This method applies the principle of interpretability and takes into account the behavior of the whole system instead of focusing on the neuron as a level while improving the testing efficiency.

3 Methodology

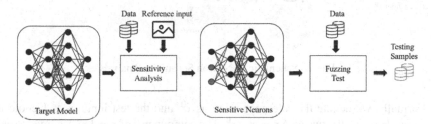

Fig. 1. Overview of DeepSensitive

Based on the discovery of sensitive neurons and the need to improve the testing efficiency of deep learning models, we propose a fuzzing test criterion for sensitive neurons. DeepSensitive is a novel attempt to utilize deep learning interpretability to test deep learning systems. The main idea is to do a centralized, fine-grained fuzzing test of sensitive neurons at each layer, instead of more exhaustive but time-costly testing of the entire neural network. A fuzzing test is a method to discover software bugs by providing unintended inputs to the target system and monitoring the abnormal results. For deep learning models for image classification tasks, classification errors can be viewed as software bugs. Intuitively, attacks on sensitive neurons are more likely to misclassify a deep learning model, enabling more efficient discovery of bugs in deep learning models. This testing guideline provides new ideas for standardized unit testing of AI models.

The overall workflow of DeepSensitive is shown in Fig. 1. Given a reference input based on the target requirements and given the deep learning model to be tested, DeepSensitive traverses the inputs in the dataset and performs a sensitivity analysis using the DeepLIFT algorithm. After obtaining the sensitive neurons in the input layer, DeepSensitive performs targeted fuzzing tests on them to generate new test samples. More specifically, we will introduce the detailed process of sensitivity analysis in 3.1, and further elaborate on the fuzzing test process in 4.

3.1 Neuron Sensitivity Analysis

The neuron sensitivity analysis module aims to examine the impact of input variations on the output layer by analyzing the sensitivity of neurons within the input layer of the neural network. It identifies the input layer neurons that are more susceptible to changes in their inputs. The diagram illustrating this process is depicted in Fig. 2.

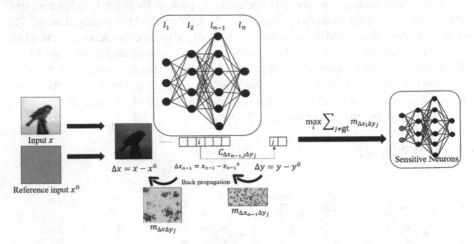

Fig. 2. Schematic of Neuron Sensitivity Analysis

Formally, we denote the reference input as x^0, and the test input as x. Denote the difference between the two as $\Delta x = x - x^0$. The components of x and x^0 assigned to each neuron i are x_i, x_i^0, respectively. For a particular intermediate layer l_k, the intermediate inputs of x and x^0 at this layer are defined as x_k, x_k^0 and the intermediate outputs as y_k, y_k^0. The output of the last layer is denoted as y, y^0. The corresponding components are $x_{k,i}$, $x_{k,i}^0$, respectively. The outputs and differences are defined similarly. Under this definition, $x = x_1$, $x_k = y_{k-1}$, and $y_n = y$.

For the middle layer l_k and each of its output dimensions j, there is a contribution from each $\Delta x_{k,i}$ to its output difference Δy_j. We define this contribution as $C_{\Delta x_{k,i}\Delta y_{k,j}}$, then it satisfies

$$\sum_i C_{\Delta x_{k,i}\Delta y_{k,j}} = \Delta y_{k,j} \tag{1}$$

Further, the contribution that a unit of $\Delta x_{k,i}$ produces to Δy_j can be a measure of the sensitivity of the i th neuron in the layer to the perturbation, as evidenced by the fact that a unit of perturbation produces a larger deviation in the output. We thus define its sensitivity factor as

$$m_{\Delta x_{k,i}\Delta y_{k,j}} = \frac{C_{\Delta x_{k,i}\Delta y_{k,j}}}{\Delta x_{k,i}} \tag{2}$$

The formula 2 defines the sensitivity metrics between inputs and outputs in the same layer. For calculating the sensitivity values across layers, we use the chain rule to calculate them. Formally, we calculate it through

$$m_{\Delta x_{k-1,i} \Delta y_{k,j}} = \sum_p m_{\Delta x_{k-1,i} \Delta y_{k-1,p}} m_{\Delta x_{k,p} \Delta y_{k,j}} \tag{3}$$

To accommodate some special cases, the DeepLIFT algorithm treats positive contributions differently from negative ones. For this purpose, for each neuron, we introduce Δx^+ and Δx^- to denote the positive and negative components of Δx, such that there are

$$\Delta x = \Delta x^+ = \Delta x^- \tag{4}$$

$$C_{\Delta x_k \Delta y_k} = C_{\Delta x_k^+ \Delta y_k} + C_{\Delta x_k^- \Delta y_k} \tag{5}$$

For linear and convolutional layers, since $y = b + \sum_i w_i x_i$, we have $\Delta y = \sum_i w_i \Delta x_i$. Define Δy^+ and Δy^- as

$$\Delta y^+ = \sum_i u(w_i \Delta x_i) w_i \Delta x_i \tag{6}$$

$$\Delta y^- = \sum_i u(-w_i \Delta x_i) w_i \Delta x_i \tag{7}$$

where $u(t)$ is the unit step function. Omitting some unnecessary subscripts, the corresponding sensitivity factor is calculated with the linear rule as

$$m_{\Delta x_i^+ \Delta y^+} = m_{\Delta x_i^- \Delta y^+} = u(w_i \Delta x_i) w_i \tag{8}$$

$$m_{\Delta x_i^+ \Delta y^-} = m_{\Delta x_i^- \Delta y^-} = u(-w_i \Delta x_i) w_i \tag{9}$$

For the nonlinear activation layer, the batch normalization layer, and the pooling layer, we use the rescale rule to compute the sensitivity factor between the inputs and outputs of the layer.

$$m_{\Delta x_i^+ \Delta y^+} = m_{\Delta x_i^- \Delta y^+} = m_{\Delta x \Delta y} = \frac{\Delta x}{\Delta y} \tag{10}$$

For each input x, when $m_{\Delta x \Delta y}$ is computed after passing through the layers, it can be computed by calculating which neuron in the input layer is most likely to bias the output toward the wrong result when perturbed, i.e., by calculating

$$\max_i \sum_{j \neq gt} m_{\Delta x_i \Delta y_j} \tag{11}$$

The calculation process described above allows us to identify the pixels that correspond to the sensitive neurons. When fuzzing (perturbing) these neurons during testing, it will have a greater impact on the output of the neural network.

4 Fuzzing Test

Sensitive neurons in deep learning models are identified through training, aiming to pinpoint the neurons that are highly vulnerable to perturbations that can disrupt the results. Perturbations are then applied to these sensitive neurons to facilitate the detection of anomalous model behavior, as opposed to employing random perturbations.

Specifically, we introduce two fuzzing operators:

Perturb. The perturb operation involves perturbing the input at the pixels corresponding to sensitive neurons. When a neuron demonstrates sensitivity to a positive perturbation, the corresponding input value is amplified by a specified percentage. Conversely, when a neuron exhibits sensitivity to a negative perturbation, the corresponding input value is reduced by the same percentage.

Replace. The replace operation directly substitutes the pixels corresponding to the sensitive neurons in the input layer with randomly generated values.

Figure 3 showcases an example of the two operators applied to the input, along with the corresponding visualization of $m_{\Delta x \Delta y}$. By employing the concept of fuzzing or mutation testing, these operations perturb a selected percentage of pixels in the test set samples that correspond to sensitive neurons. The resulting test samples are designed

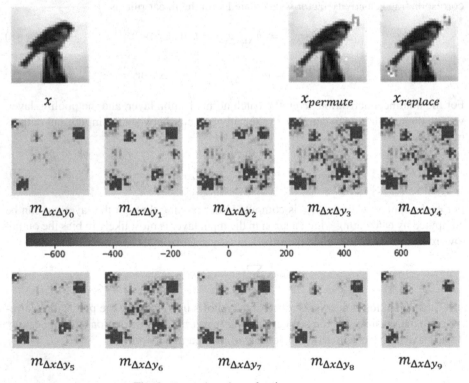

Fig. 3. Examples of two fuzzing operators.

to be distinguishable by humans but not by the neural networks. Such samples can serve multiple purposes, including expanding the training set, data augmentation, and addressing vulnerabilities in the model.

5 Evaluation

In this section, we evaluate DeepSensitive on various datasets and models.

5.1 Experimental Setup

Hardware and Software. Our model training works were implemented on the top of Pytorch [20] 1.7.1 framework. All experiments were conducted on a GPU server with 80 cores Intel Xeon Silver 4210R 2.40GHz CPU, 384GB RAM, and 8 NVIDIA GeForce RTX 3090 24GB GPUs running Ubuntu 20.04 as the operating system.

Datasets. Our experiments were conducted on the MNIST [21] and CIFAR-10 [22] datasets. MNIST is a dataset of handwritten numbers, containing 60,000 training examples and 10,000 test examples with the size of 28×28. CIFAR-10 is one of the most representative deep learning image classification datasets consisting of 60,000 32×32 color pictures.

Model Architectures. Our evaluation was performed on LeNet [23] and VGG [24] structures. All models were trained by the Adam optimizer for 50 epochs, where the learning rate was 2e-4.

5.2 Results and Analysis

We conducted experiments using DeepSensitive on the MNIST-LeNet5 and CIFAR10-VGG13 combinations. For each experimental setting, we employed two distinct experimental processes. In the first process, we performed neuron sensitivity analysis on each data point in the training set to evaluate the sensitive neurons of the network with respect to the entire training data. We then applied the same set of sensitive neurons for fuzzing using each training data. In the second process, we individually conducted a sensitivity analysis on each data point, immediately followed by fuzzing of the calculated sensitive neurons specific to that data. Two additional operators were tested for each set of configurations and experimental procedures, with 10% of the neurons selected as sensitive neurons for each experiment. Throughout the experiments, we utilized a seed input of 50,000 images with an all-gray image serving as the reference input.

The results of our experiments are presented in Table 1. In the table, d_{ds} represents the Euclidean distance between the outputs at the logits layer of the test samples generated by DeepSensitive and the original input, while d_{rand} represents that distance between the samples generated by the randomized perturbation of equal magnitude and the original input. n_{ds} Denotes the number of classification failures of test samples generated by DeepSensitive, and n_{rand} represents the number of failures by randomly generated test samples. Upon examining the table, it is evident that DeepSensitive vastly outperforms

Table 1. Results of Experiments on DeepSensitive.

Dataset & Model	Process	Operator	d_{ds}	d_{rand}	$\frac{d_{ds}}{d_{rand}}$	n_{ds}	n_{rand}
MNIST & LeNet	1	Permute	1.65	2.01	0.82	105	151
		Replace	10.03	3.58	2.8	1261	224
	2	Permute	4.55	2.02	2.26	334	146
		Replace	15.26	3.61	4.23	2839	225
CIFAR10 & VGG	1	Permute	6.31	5.09	1.24	6154	5059
		Replace	18.46	8.16	2.26	18896	8026
	2	Permute	5.12	5.09	1.01	4914	5184
		Replace	7.98	8.2	0.97	7665	8111

the randomized method in the MNIST & LeNet test conditions. In the CIFAR & VGG test conditions, DeepSensitive demonstrates comparable or superior performance compared to the randomized method, with some aspects achieving equal results and others surpassing them.

In summary, incorporating perturbations at the sensitive neurons selected by DeepSensitive demonstrates a greater influence on the output, thereby affirming the effectiveness and interpretability of DeepSensitive. Completely computed neuron sensitivity proves to be more effective for complex datasets and models (e.g., CIFAR-10, VGG), while individual computational sensitivity is more effective for simpler datasets and models (e.g., MNIST, LeNet). With the inclusion of sensitive neuron computation, the fuzzy testing approach achieves higher efficiency and generates a larger number of test failure samples compared to random perturbations. These generated samples can be utilized, for instance, as data augmentation in subsequent processes.

In conclusion, the experiments conducted with DeepSensitive have demonstrated its effectiveness. It is important to note that these experiments were conducted using a coarse-grained approach and a reference input that was an averaged grayscale map. However, it is expected that DeepSensitive will showcase its potential in tests with different objectives when the reference input is tailored to specific tasks. Selecting appropriate reference inputs for DeepSensitive to address other tests, such as robustness or fairness, in deep learning systems remains an open question. Determining the most suitable reference inputs for these tests requires careful consideration and domain-specific expertise. Further research and exploration are needed to develop methodologies for selecting reference inputs that align with the desired objectives and evaluation criteria in these specific areas.

6   Conclusion

Based on the identification of sensitive neurons and the aim to enhance the efficiency of testing deep learning models, we propose a fuzzy testing criterion specifically for sensitive neurons. The central concept revolves around conducting fine-grained fuzzy testing on sensitive neurons at each layer, as an alternative to exhaustive but time-consuming testing of the entire neural network. In the context of deep learning models, classification errors can be considered as software vulnerabilities. It is evident that attacks targeting sensitive neurons are more likely to result in misclassifications of the deep learning model and can be more efficient in uncovering vulnerabilities within these models. This testing guideline presents innovative ideas for standardized unit testing of AI models, focusing on the examination of sensitive neurons. By honing in on these critical components, the testing process can be more targeted and effective in identifying potential weaknesses and vulnerabilities in deep learning models.

Acknowledgement. Chenhao Lin is the corresponding author. This work is supported by the National Key Research and Development Program of China (2020AAA0107702), the National Natural Science Foundation of China (62006181, 62161160337, 62132011, U21B2018, U20A20177, 62206217), the Shaanxi Province Key Industry Innovation Program (2023-ZDLGY-38, 2021ZDLGY01–02).

References

1. Chen, C.F.R., Fan, Q., Panda, R.: CrossViT: cross-attention multi-scale vision transformer for image classification. In: Proceedings of the IEEE/CVF International Conference on Computer Vision, pp. 357–366 (2021)
2. Vaswani, A., et al.: Attention is all you need. In: Advances in Neural Information Processing Systems, vol. 30 (2017)
3. Yurtsever, E., Lambert, J., Carballo, A., Takeda, K.: A survey of autonomous driving: common practices and emerging technologies. IEEE Access **8**, 58443–58469 (2020)
4. Isinkaye, F.O., Folajimi, Y.O., Ojokoh, B.A.: Recommendation systems: principles, methods and evaluation. Egypt. Inf. J. **16**(3), 261–273 (2015)
5. Deep learning market size, share, and trends analysis report by solution (hardware, software), by hardware, by application (image recognition, voice recognition), by end-use, by region, and segment forecasts, 2023 - 2030 (2022). https://www.grandviewresearch.com/industry-analysis/deep-learning-market
6. Eykholt, K., et al.: Robust physical-world attacks on deep learning visual classification. In: Proceedings of the IEEE Conference on Computer Vision and Pattern Recognition, pp. 1625–1634 (2018)
7. Ma, L., et al.: DeepGauge: multi-granularity testing criteria for deep learning systems. In: Proceedings of the 33rd ACM/IEEE International Conference on Automated Software Engineering, pp. 120–131 (2018)
8. Gerasimou, S., Eniser, H.F., Sen, A., Cakan, A.: Importance-driven deep learning system testing. In: 2020 IEEE/ACM 42nd International Conference on Software Engineering (ICSE), pp. 702–713. IEEE (2020)
9. Shrikumar, A., Greenside, P., Kundaje, A.: Learning important features through propagating activation differences. In: International Conference on Machine Learning, pp. 3145–3153. PMLR (2017)
10. Pei, K., Cao, Y., Yang, J., Jana, S.: DeepXplore: automated whitebox testing of deep learning systems. In: Proceedings of the 26th Symposium on Operating Systems Principles, pp. 1–18 (2017)

11. Gopinath, D., Pasareanu, C.S., Wang, K., Zhang, M., Khurshid, S.: Symbolic execution for attribution and attack synthesis in neural networks. In: 2019 IEEE/ACM 41st International Conference on Software Engineering: Companion Proceedings (ICSE-Companion), pp. 282–283. IEEE (2019)

12. Ma, L., et al.: DeepMutation: mutation testing of deep learning systems. In: 2018 IEEE 29th International Symposium on Software Reliability Engineering (ISSRE), pp. 100–111. IEEE (2018)

13. Xie, X., et al.: DeepHunter: a coverage-guided fuzz testing framework for deep neural networks. In: Proceedings of the 28th ACM SIGSOFT International Symposium on Software Testing and Analysis, pp. 146–157 (2019)

14. Gopinath, D., Katz, G., Păsăreanu, C.S., Barrett, C.: DeepSafe: a data-driven approach for assessing robustness of neural networks. In: Lahiri, S., Wang, C. (eds.) Automated Technology for Verification and Analysis. ATVA 2018. Lecture Notes in Computer Science(), vol. 11138, pp. 3–19. Springer, Cham (2018). https://doi.org/10.1007/978-3-030-01090-4_1

15. Sharma, A., Wehrheim, H.: Testing machine learning algorithms for balanced data usage. In: 2019 12th IEEE Conference on Software Testing, Validation and Verification (ICST), pp. 125–135. IEEE (2019)

16. Du, X., Xie, X., Li, Y., Ma, L., Liu, Y., Zhao, J.: DeepStellar: model-based quantitative analysis of stateful deep learning systems. In: Proceedings of the 2019 27th ACM Joint Meeting on European Software Engineering Conference and Symposium on the Foundations of Software Engineering, pp. 477–487 (2019)

17. Gao, X., Zhai, J., Ma, S., Shen, C., Chen, Y., Wang, Q.: FairNeuron: improving deep neural network fairness with adversary games on selective neurons. In: Proceedings of the 44th International Conference on Software Engineering, pp. 921–933 (2022)

18. Zhang, X., Zhai, J., Ma, S., Shen, C.: AutoTrainer: an automatic DNN training problem detection and repair system. In: 2021 IEEE/ACM 43rd International Conference on Software Engineering (ICSE), pp. 359–371. IEEE (2021)

19. Bach, S., Binder, A., Montavon, G., Klauschen, F., Müller, K.R., Samek, W.: On pixel-wise explanations for non-linear classifier decisions by layer-wise relevance propagation. PLoS ONE 10(7), e0130140 (2015)

20. Paszke, A., et al.: PyTorch: an imperative style, high-performance deep learning library. In: Advances in Neural Information Processing Systems, vol. 32 (2019)

21. LeCun, Y.: The MNIST database of handwritten digits (1998). http://yann.lecun.com/exdb/mnist/

22. Cifar-10 dataset (2021). https://www.cs.toronto.edu/~kriz/cifar.html

23. LeCun, Y., Bottou, L., Bengio, Y., Haffner, P.: Gradient-based learning applied to document recognition. Proc. IEEE 86(11), 2278–2324 (1998)

24. Simonyan, K., Zisserman, A.: Very deep convolutional networks for large-scale image recognition. arXiv preprint. arXiv:1409.1556 (2014)

IGWO-FNN Based Position Control for Stepper Motor

Yilin Geng, Haikuan Liu, Na Duan, and Zhizheng Xu[✉]

School of Electrical Engineering and Automation, Jiangsu Normal University, Xu Zhou 221116,
China
1909454498@qq.com

Abstract. The traditional stochastic descent based gradient Fuzzy Neural Networks (FNN) are prone to falling into local optimal solutions when used to position control of stepper motor. To improve the performance of position control algorithm based on FNN, this article proposes a novel FNN to achieve the position control of stepper motor. In the proposed FNN, an Improved Grey Wolf Optimization (IGWO) algorithm is devised for adjusting the weights of FNN. The Logistic-tent chaotic mapping is used in population initialization of the IGWO to improve the uniformity of population distribution. This method enhances the authority of α wolves in prey detection, making the algorithm more effective in finding the optimal solution. Compared with position control methods based on traditional FNN, the first position tracking time of stepper motors is reduced by 11.7%, and the fluctuation range of position tracking is reduced by 68%. In the second position tracking, the fluctuation range is reduced by 44%. Simulink simulation experiments showed that the proposed control scheme could accurately and stably track the position of stepper motor.

Keywords: Stepper Motor · IGWO · FNN · Position Control

1 Introduction

The stepper motor is an electric motor that converts electrical pulse excitation signals into corresponding angular or linear displacement. This type of motor moves one step for each input electrical pulse, hence the name "pulse motor". As digital manufacturing rapidly develops in China, the application of stepper motors is expanding, including uses in ATM machines, engraving machines, photo printers, spray painting equipment, and medical instruments, etc. The position control algorithm significantly influences the performance enhancement of the stepper motor and constitutes a crucial research aspect of it.

Presently, numerous scholars are investigating the position control of stepper motors. Bangji Wang et al. [1] studied the control performance of acceleration and deceleration curves for stepper motors. They pointed out that the utilization of a parabolic acceleration and deceleration curve within the same control period can significantly improve the stepper motor's angle rotation without losing steps. Although the position tracking error during the intermediate process of the parabolic acceleration and deceleration curve is small, there may be unsmooth torque transitions and certain resonant oscillations at the transition points, which may induce mechanical vibrations in the system. Jiazhi Zhan et al. [2] combined the Radial Basis Function (RBF) neural network with feedback control to effectively improve the position tracking accuracy and steady-state performance of two-phase stepper motors. However, the adjustment of weights in the RBF neural network is computationally complex. Yanxiong Wu [3] obtained suitable PID parameters using the tuning method. The three parameters are k_p, k_i and k_d. Although it can be used for position control of stepper motors, the adjustment of these three parameters is complex and cannot be adaptively adjusted. Zhuzhen Xi et al. [4] used a Siemens controller with the model number S7-200-smart-PLC to construct an intelligent feeding control system for a chicken house. A stepper motor was selected for discharging and achieved functions such as synchronized operation with a touch screen. However, only open-loop processing was performed, so the accuracy of position control needs to be improved. Tao Lin [5] proposed a closed-loop intelligent control system for stepper motors based on a programmable controller. Through the synchronous debugging of software and hardware, the stepper motor is driven to ensure relatively stable operation. However, the response speed of the system needs to be improved.

Although the above literature provides different solutions to the position control problem of stepper motors, two-phase stepper motors possess characteristics such as nonlinearity and multivariable nature, which results in poor accuracy and slow response speed in the position control of stepper motors. In order to improve the position control performance of two-phase stepper motors, this paper introduces the Improved Grey Wolf Optimization-Fuzzy Neural Networks (IGWO-FNN) algorithm, which autonomously searches for appropriate values of k_p, k_i and k_d in the PID controller. The proposed approach integrates the IGWO algorithm with FNN, aiming to optimize the weights between the hidden layer and output layer in the FNN using the IGWO algorithm, thereby achieving position control of the stepper motor.

2 The Mathematical Model of a Stepper Motor

According to the research of Hoang Le-Huy et al. [6], the internal structure of a stepper motor can be divided into an electrical module and a mechanical module. The electrical module can equivalent the circuit of a certain phase (in this case, using the A phase as a representative) in the stepper motor to an electrical circuit model as shown in Fig. 1 when neglecting the effects of leakage magnetic field and mutual inductance of the rotor coils on the harmonic components. The mechanical module is characterized by a state vector space model based on the inertial torque and a viscous damping coefficient.

According to Kirchhoff's voltage law, the voltage loop equation for phase A can be obtained as follows:

$$U_a = R_a i_a + L_a \frac{di_a}{dt} + E_a \tag{1}$$

In the equation, U_a is the phase voltage of phase A, L_a is the equivalent inductance of phase A, i_a is the magnitude of the current flowing through phase A, and E_a is the back electromotive force of phase A.

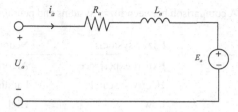

Fig. 1. The single-phase equivalent circuit of a stepper motor

It is related to parameters such as the number of magnetic pole teeth (p), the maximum magnetic flux (ψ_m), and the sinusoidal expression of the rotor position (E_a) in the form of a sine function. The rotation angle of the motor is represented by θ, and its expression is shown in Eq. (2).

$$E_a(\theta) = -p\psi_m \sin(p\theta)\frac{d\theta}{dt} \tag{2}$$

The mechanical module of a stepper motor consists of the basic motion equations of the motion control system that neglects damping torque, and its expressions are shown in Eqs. (3) and (4).

$$T_e = J\frac{d\omega}{dt} + B\omega + T_L \tag{3}$$

$$\omega = \frac{d\theta}{dt} \tag{4}$$

In the equations, J represents the total moment of inertia of the stepper motor and the load, B is the viscous damping coefficient of the stepper motor and its load, T_L is the load torque of the stepper motor, ω is the angular velocity during the rotation of the stepper motor. The electromagnetic torque T_e in the equation is also related to the detent torque T_{dm} and other factors, and its expression is shown in Eq. (5).

$$T_e = p\psi_m[i_b \sin(p\theta - \frac{\pi}{2}) - i_a \sin(p\theta)] - T_{dm} \sin(2p\theta) \tag{5}$$

3 IGWO-FNN Controller

3.1 FNN

Due to its powerful autonomous learning ability and effective knowledge representation, FNN have been widely applied in industrial control systems and agricultural control systems [7]. FNN are built on fuzzy linguistic variables, fuzzy set theory, and fuzzy rule inference, forming a nonlinear intelligent control system that relies on human experience. By combining fuzzy systems with neural networks, the entire system can continuously modify and improve the rules and membership functions created based on human experience through self-learning. Table 1 [8] presents a comparison between fuzzy systems and neural networks.

Table 1. A comparison between fuzzy systems and neural networks

	Fuzzy systems	Neural networks
Acquiring knowledge	Expert experience	Algorithm instance
Inference mechanism	Heuristic search	Parallel computing
Inference speed	Low	High
Fault-tolerance	Low	Very high
Natural language flexibility	High	Low

The network structure of the FNN with two inputs and three outputs, as shown in Fig. 2, is a four-layer feedforward network structure. The first layer is the input layer, the second layer is the fuzzification layer, the third layer is the fuzzy inference layer, and the fourth layer is the output layer.

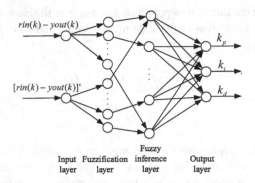

Fig. 2. The network structure of FNN

The first layer is the input layer. Because the two nodes in this layer are sequentially connected with the two inputs, the inputs of the neurons in this layer are two input quantities, denoted as: $e(k)$, $\dot{e}(k)$.

The second layer is the membership function layer, which is also known as the fuzzification layer. In this study, Gaussian functions are used as the membership functions [9]. Each neuron in the input layer is fuzzified in this layer. Assuming that the j-th fuzzy set of the i-th input variable is represented by $f_{ij}^{(2)}$, its expression is shown in Eq. (6).

$$f_{ij}^{(2)} = \exp\left(-\frac{(x_i - c_{ij})^2}{2 * (b_j)^2}\right) \quad \begin{array}{l} i = 1, 2; \\ j = 1, 2, \cdots, 5 \end{array} \tag{6}$$

The third layer is the fuzzy inference layer, where each neuron represents a fuzzy rule [10]. In the field of intelligent control, commonly used methods include the Mamdani inference method. Although the minimum operator is often used for calculations, it may lead to information loss. Therefore, in this study, we choose to perform product operations on each input. It should be noted that the inputs of each neuron in this layer are only related to the same linguistic variables in the fuzzy sets of the previous layer for each input division, and its expression is shown in Eq. (7).

$$f_j^{(3)} = \prod_{i=1}^{3} f_{ij}^{(2)} \tag{7}$$

The fourth layer is the output layer, which performs defuzzification operations. The output of this layer is shown in Eq. (8), where $f_1^{(4)}$ denotes the value of k_p, $f_2^{(4)}$ represents the value of k_i, and $f_3^{(4)}$ represents the value of k_d.

$$f_i^{(4)} = W^T \bullet f_j^{(3)} = \sum_{j=1}^{N} w(i,j) \bullet f_3(j) \; i = 1, 2, 3 \tag{8}$$

3.2 IGWO

The Grey Wolf Optimization (GWO) algorithm, proposed by Mirgalili in 2014 [11], is an innovative population-based intelligent optimization algorithm. It simulates the hierarchical system and hunting behavior of a grey wolf pack [12]. The whole pack is divided into four hierarchical levels, resembling a pyramid shape, as shown in Fig. 3. The hierarchy levels are sorted from highest to lowest as follows: the alpha pack, the beta pack, the gamma pack, and the delta pack.

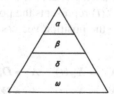

Fig. 3. The hierarchical distribution of grey wolves

In the algorithm, the first three types of wolves represent the three best solutions in terms of fitness, among which the α pack represents the optimal solution at the current stage, while the ω pack searches for the target guided by these three wolf packs. During the optimization process, the positions of all four types of wolves are constantly updated, and the update methods of the position of the wolf pack relative to the prey and the position of the wolf pack are illustrated in Eqs. (9) and (10).

$$D = |C \bullet X_P(t) - X(t)| \tag{9}$$

$$X(t+1) = X_P(t) - A \bullet D \tag{10}$$

In the equations, t represents the current iteration count, $X_P(t)$ is the position vector of the prey, $X(t)$ is the current position vector of the grey wolf, D is the distance vector between individual wolves and the prey, A and C are coefficient vectors [13]. The calculation formulas for A and C are shown in Eqs. (11) and (12) respectively.

$$A = 2a \bullet r_2 - a \tag{11}$$

$$C = 2r_1 \tag{12}$$

In the equations, r_1 and r_2 are both values within the range $[0, 1]$, a is the convergence factor, which linearly decreases from 2 to 0 as the iteration count increases. As a result, the values of each element in A fall within the range $[-\alpha, \alpha]$.

In nature, grey wolves have the ability to locate prey and surround them for the final kill (i.e., the entire hunting process). However, when hunting in an abstract search space, the location of the prey is generally unknown at the beginning. To mathematically describe the hunting behavior of grey wolves, the algorithm assumes that the α, β and δ wolves have a better understanding of the potential location of the prey, and save the top three best solutions obtained during the iteration process. Other wolves are forced to update their positions based on these three solutions. The mathematical model for this part is shown in Eq. (13).

$$\begin{aligned} D_\alpha &= |C_1 \bullet X_\alpha(t) - X(t)| \\ D_\beta &= |C_2 \bullet X_\beta(t) - X(t)| \\ D_\delta &= |C_3 \bullet X_\delta(t) - X(t)| \end{aligned} \tag{13}$$

In the equation, $X_\alpha(t)$, $X_\beta(t)$ and $X_\delta(t)$ are the position vectors of the three types of grey wolves at the t-th iteration. $X(t)$ represents the positions of the other wolves at the t-th iteration. D_α, D_β and D_δ are the position vectors between the α, β and δ wolves, and the other wolves, respectively.

$$\begin{aligned} X_1 &= X_\alpha(t) - A_1 \bullet D_\alpha \\ X_2 &= X_\beta(t) - A_2 \bullet D_\beta \\ X_3 &= X_\delta(t) - A_3 \bullet D_\beta \end{aligned} \tag{14}$$

In the equation, X_1, X_2 and X_3 are the position vectors indicating the directions in which the wolves in the pack move towards the alpha, beta, and delta wolves, respectively, to ultimately surround the prey. The position vector of the successful predation is represented by $X(t + 1)$, as shown in Eq. (15).

$$X(t + 1) = \frac{X_1 + X_2 + X_3}{3} \tag{15}$$

Because the α wolf is expected to find the optimal solution in the algorithm and is the leader in hunting in nature, we increase the weight of the α wolf's search for the prey's location in this approach. This is specifically shown in Eq. (16).

$$X(t + 1) = \frac{X_1}{2} + \frac{X_2}{4} + \frac{X_3}{4} \tag{16}$$

After the gray wolves have surrounded the prey, they initiate an attack. If the magnitude of A is within the range of $(-1, 1)$, the gray wolves will launch an attack on the prey; otherwise, they will move away from the prey. C represents a random weight that indicates the influence of the wolf's position on the prey. A smaller value implies that the current position of the wolf has less impact on the prey. Literature [14] suggests that incorporating this coefficient vector helps the algorithm in searching for the global optimal solution.

In the GWO algorithm, the population of the wolf pack is initialized randomly. Therefore, the random dispersion of the wolf pack may lead to uneven distribution or even dense clustering of the population, resulting in the wolf pack's search range for prey being limited to a certain area and potentially leading to finding a local optimal solution. Chaos sequences are random sequences generated by simple deterministic systems. Chaos sequences are generated through chaotic mapping and possess characteristics such as nonlinearity, randomness, and ergodicity [15]. Utilizing these characteristics and incorporating them into GWO can help enhance the diversity of the wolf pack's distribution during initialization. Currently, many domestic scholars and related researchers have combined the algorithm with chaotic mapping, mainly using Tent and Logistic chaotic mappings. Literature [16] suggests that compared to the Logistic mapping, the Tent chaotic mapping has higher computational efficiency. The mathematical definition of the Logistic chaotic algorithm possesses properties that are extremely sensitive to the initial value and parameters, and can generate a vast number of well-behaved chaotic sequences. Therefore, this paper adopts the Logistic-Tent chaotic mapping proposed in literature [17] for population initialization of the wolf pack. The mathematical expression of this chaotic mapping is shown in Eq. (17).

$$
X_{n+1} = \begin{cases} \left[rX_n(1 - X_n) + \frac{(4-r)X_n}{2} \right] \bmod 1, & X_n < 0.5 \\ \left[rX_n(1 - X_n) + \frac{(4-r)(1-X_n)}{2} \right] \bmod 1, & X_n \geq 0.5 \end{cases} \tag{17}
$$

In the equation, r is the control parameter, $r \in (0, 4)$. In this paper, we set $r = 0.3$ and X_n represents the value of X after the n-th iteration. To further validate whether the Logistic-Tent chaotic mapping can evenly distribute the mapping target, we conducted tests on the Logistic-Tent chaotic mapping with 600 iterations. The test results are shown in Fig. 4 and Fig. 5, indicating that the Logistic-Tent chaotic mapping has the ability to achieve a uniform distribution of the target.

In this paper, the Logistic-Tent chaotic mapping is applied to the initialization of the wolf pack in the GWO algorithm. Although it increases the complexity of the algorithm to some extent, the uniformly distributed wolf pack is more advantageous in searching for prey.

3.3 The Integration of IGWO and FNN

According to the above steps, a FNN is constructed and the IGWO algorithm is introduced for weight adjustment in the FNN. The overall system workflow is illustrated in Fig. 6.

In this article, the IGWO algorithm is used to optimize the weights between the fuzzy inference layer and the output layer in FNN, and these weights are mapped into a

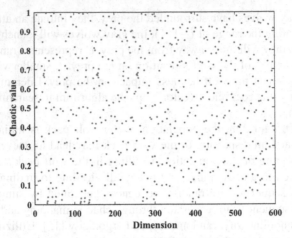

Fig. 4. Logistic-Tent chaotic mapping

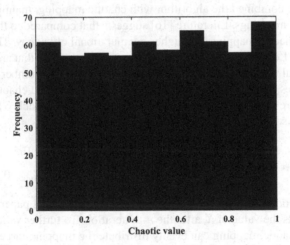

Fig. 5. Logistic-Tent chaotic sequence distribution histogram

matrix $W = [w_{11}, w_{12}, \cdots w_{1M}; w_{21}, w_{22}, \cdots w_{2M}; w_{31}, w_{32}, \cdots w_{3M}]$, which is scattered among the wolf pack using the Logistic-Tent chaotic mapping. Because the IGWO algorithm adjusts the weight values between the fuzzy inference layer and the output layer in FNN, the number of network weights is the dimension of the GWO algorithm. After constructing the FNN, the positions of the grey wolves are evenly dispersed using the Logistic-Tent chaotic mapping, and the grey wolf population is initialized. The results obtained from the fitness function are sorted, and superior individuals are selected according to the principle of pyramid level distribution, dividing the wolf pack into α, β, δ and ω wolves. The IGWO calculation formula is iterated and updated continuously until the maximum number of iterations is reached or the optimal solution to the problem is found; otherwise, the fitness function is calculated repeatedly. When the optimal solution

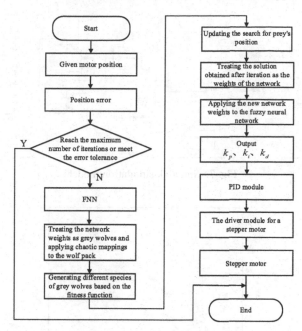

Fig. 6. The process of the system

to the problem, i.e., the position of the α wolf, is found, the new weight size obtained at this time is brought back into the original FNN, which will then produce an ideal output.

This paper integrates IGWO and FNN to address the position control problem of a stepper motor through closed-loop processing. By treating k_p, k_i, and k_d as outputs of FNN and continuously adjusting their values through iterative weight optimization using IGWO, precise adjustment of PID parameters is achieved for controlling the position of the stepper motor.

4 Simulation Experiments of the System

To validate the feasibility of the IGWO-FNN controller for position control of stepper motors, a Simulink simulation model of the system was constructed, as illustrated in Fig. 7. The simulation was conducted with a fixed step size of 1e−3.

Given a position curve, with the initial position set to 0 degrees, the motor's motion reaches 45 degrees and stops at 0.1 s. Subsequently, the stepper motor continues to move at 0.4 s and reaches a position of 90 degrees at 0.5 s. Figure 8 demonstrates the position curve tracking results of the proposed control method for the stepper motor under a load torque of 0.2 N·m.

The result obtained by subtracting the given position from the actual detected position is referred to as the error. Figure 9 shows the error results of the proposed IGWO-FNN combined with PID, as well as the unimproved GWO and FNN algorithms. The parameters k_p, k_i and k_d of the PID controller were determined through multiple experiments using trial and error. From Fig. 10, it can be observed that under motor rotation, the

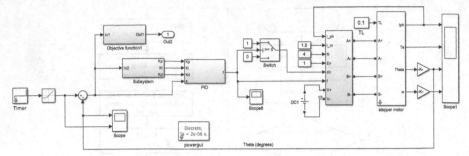

Fig. 7. Simulink simulation model

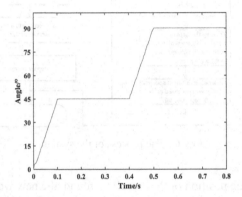

Fig. 8. Position tracking detection result

PID control method exhibits significantly higher fluctuations compared to other methods, with a fluctuation range of 1° and respective stationary times of 0.12 s and 0.509 s after detecting motor movement. Under motor rotation, the GWO-FNN control method exhibits a stationary time of 0.12 s after the motor's initial movement, followed by a tracking fluctuation jump at 0.113 s. During the first motor movement, the fluctuation range is [0.48°, 0.86°], and the stationary time after the second motor movement is 0.505 s, with a fluctuation range of [0.22°, 1.1°]. A larger tracking fluctuation is observed at 0.49 s, lasting until 0.501 s, with a fluctuation range of [0.22°, 1.05°]. Under motor rotation, the IGWO-FNN control method exhibits a stationary time of 0.106 s after the first movement of the stepper motor, with a fluctuation range of [0.46°, 0.78°] during motor movement. After the second movement, the stationary time is 0.505 s, with a fluctuation range of [0.35°, 0.91°] during motor movement. Therefore, when employing the IGWO algorithm combined with FNN for position control of the stepper motor, particularly during motor rotation, the proposed strategy demonstrates reduced errors between the desired and detected positions, faster response speed, and effective control over tracking errors and fluctuations. Therefore, the proposed fuzzy neural adaptive control strategy based on the IGWO algorithm effectively controls tracking errors and fluctuations.

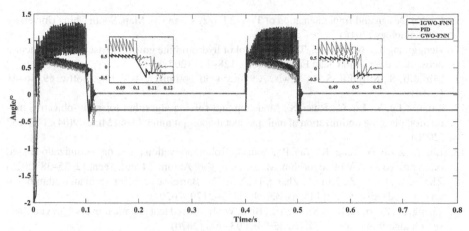

Fig. 9. Position tracking error

5 Conclusion

This paper proposes a stepper motor position control algorithm based on IGWO-FNN, which effectively deals with the issue of position control in stepper motors. The IGWO algorithm is used to update network weights and is innovatively applied to stepper motors. Simulation experiments demonstrate that the proposed algorithm achieves effective position control of the stepper motor and outperforms PID control and GWO-FNN control during motor rotation. However, small errors still exist in the scheme when the motor is stationary, which will be a focus of future work.

References

1. Wang, B., Liu, Q., Zhou, L., Bu, L., Li, X., Zhang, J.: Modeling and acceleration-deceleration curve optimization of stepper motor control system. Electr. Mach. Control **22**(01), 37–42+52 (2018)
2. Zhan, J., Cui, J.: Backstepping control of two-phase hybrid stepper motor based on neural network. Electr. Mach. Control Appl. **49**(01), 28–33+55 (2022)
3. Wu, Y.: Research on Subdivision Drive Control of Stepper Motor. Hubei Minzu University (2019)
4. Xi, Z., Chen, W.: Design of PLC-based intelligent feeding control system for chicken coop. Electron. Measur. Technol. **44**(14), 163–168 (2021)
5. Lin, T.: Closed-loop intelligent control system of stepper motor based on programmable controller. Autom. Instrum. **37**(04), 36–39+45 (2022)
6. Le-Huy, H., Brunelle, P., Sybille, G.: Design and implementation of a versatile stepper motor model for simulink's SimPowerSystems. In: 2008 IEEE International Symposium on Industrial Electronics, pp. 437–442. IEEE (2008)
7. Cao, M., Ma, J.: Improved locust optimization algorithm in research of fuzzy neural network PID control. Electron. Measur. Technol. **45**(20), 74–80 (2022)
8. Yu, S.: Case Analysis and Application of MATLAB Optimization Algorithms. Tsinghua University Press (2014)

9. Le, Y.: Design and Implementation of Type-2 Fuzzy Cognitive Map. South China University of Technology (2018)
10. Hengguang, L., Wen, B., Li, T.: PID control of hydroturbine governor based on fuzzy neural network. Power Grid Clean Energy **37**(05), 128–133 (2021)
11. Mirjalili, S., Mirjalili, S.M., Lewis, A.: Grey wolf optimizer. Adv. Eng. Softw. **69**, 46–61 (2014)
12. Gu, Q., Lu, Y., Lu, C., Ruan, S.: Modeling and solving algorithm for multi-objective production planning optimization of multiple-metal open-pit mine. Metal Mine **49**(04), 147–153 (2020)
13. Liu, L., Zhao, G., Tang, K., Yan, P., Zhou, Q.: Robot motivation trajectory optimization based on improved Gray Wolf algorithm. Mod. Mach. Tool Autom. Manuf. Tech. **12**, 35–38 (2020)
14. Zhang, D., Chen, Z., Xin, Z., Zhang, H., Yan, W.: Barrel sea squirt swarm algorithm based on crazy adaptive. Control Decis. **35**(09), 2112–2120 (2020)
15. Zhang, N., Zhao, Z., Bao, X., Qian, J., Biao, W.: Improved tent chaotic universal gravitational search algorithm. Control Decis. **35**(04), 893–900 (2020)
16. Shan, L., Qiang, H., Li, J., Wang, Z.: Chaotic optimization algorithm based on tent mapping. Control Decis. **02**, 179–182 (2005)
17. Qin, Q., Liang, Z., Yi, X.: Image encryption algorithm based on logistic-tent chaotic mapping and bit plane. J. Dalian Minzu Univ. **24**(03), 245–252 (2022)

Lévy Flight Chaotic Runge Kutta Optimizer for Stock Price Forecasting

Chenwei Bi[1,2], Qifang Luo[1,2(✉)], and Yongquan Zhou[1,2]

[1] College of Artificial Intelligence, Guangxi Minzu Nationalities, Nanning 530006, China
l.qf@163.com
[2] Guangxi Key Laboratories of Hybrid Computation and IC Design Analysis, Nanning 530006, China

Abstract. Maximizing investment returns is a key focus for investors and stakeholders, the challenge pertaining to stock market forecasting has assumed significant importance within this discipline, attributable to the substantial market volatility arising from a plethora of interconnected factors prevalent in the stock market. In this paper we introduced a hybrid machine learning model based on long short-term memory (LSTM) networks and lévy flight chaotic Runge Kutta optimizer (LCRUN) to predict three stock indices daily price. The LCRUN incorporates an initialization technique utilizing chaotic mapping to enhance population diversity. A method namely lévy flight are used in the LCRUN for enhancing ability to search globally optimal solutions and avoid falling into local optima. Our proposed model evaluates the performance with Runge Kutta-based LSTM (RUN-LSTM), sine cosine-based LSTM (SCA-LSTM), differential evolutionary-based LSTM (DE-LSTM) and particle swarm-based LSTM (PSO-LSTM) on these stock indices includes S&P500, NASDAQ100, and SPY. The experimental results show that the proposed LCRUN-LSTM has significant performance and predicts stock prices more accurately than the other four models.

Keywords: Lévy Flight · Chaostic Map · Runge Kutta Optimizer · Stock Forecasting · Swarm Intelligence

1 Introduction

The role of stocks in the economy is that the stock market is a barometer of the economy. This paper we introduced a hybrid machine learning model based on long short-term memory (LSTM) networks and lévy flight chaotic runge kutta optimizer (LCRUN) to predict three stock indices daily price. The LCRUN incorporates an initialization technique utilizing chaotic mapping to enhance population diversity. A lévy flight is used in the LCRUN for enhancing to search ability and avoid falling into local optima. Our proposed model evaluates the performance with runge kutta-based LSTM (RUN-LSTM), sine cosine-based LSTM (SCA-LSTM), differential evolutionary-based LSTM (DE-LSTM) and particle swarm-based LSTM (PSO-LSTM) on SPY stock indices. The experimental results show that the proposed LCRUN-LSTM has significant performance

D.-S. Huang et al. (Eds.): ICAI 2023, CCIS 2014, pp. 375–386, 2024.
https://doi.org/10.1007/978-981-97-0903-8_35

and predicts stock prices more accurately than the other four models. The main contributions are as follows: (1) We proposed LCRUN method avoid the algorithm falling into local minima by adding a lévy flight and enhances population variety and using chaotic mapping. (2) By employing LCRUN to enhance the hyper-parameters of the LSTM, the LCRUN-LSTM is proposed. By comparing LCRUN with four other optimization methods hybrid LSTM model during trials on stock indices, the model's generalization performance was confirmed. (3) The LCRUN-LSTM is used for predicting stock prices, and the superior results of the LCRUN-LSTM model in tackling stock price prediction issues is confirmed through comparative testing.

2   Methodology

To predict stock prices, we proposed a LCRUN-based hybrid forecasting model. The first phase entails computing technical indicators using pre-processed data and daily stock prices, which includes mapping technical indicators to narrow ranges using normalization method. The second phase is to get the optimized values of the LSTM hyper-parameters using LCRUN method, and the third step is to train the obtained model after optimizing the hyper-parameters. In the final step, the prediction efficiency of the model is assessed by six evaluation metrics and then derived the prediction results. Figure 1 depicts the overall layout of the proposed model. Each pertinent technical is thoroughly discussed in the follow section.

2.1   Data Pre-processing

By analyzing the above related work, the main factors affecting stock prices most directly daily statistics from the OHLC stock market is selected as the main data for forecasting inputs [1], In order to map the info in narrow range, we use the normalization method, assuming that x_{max} and x_{min} are the maximum and minimum values, then this method can be used to map the original data x^* to x' between $[x_{min}, x_{max}]$ to a smaller range $[x'_{min}, x'_{max}]$. The mathematical expression is given by Eq. (1):

$$x' = \frac{x^* - x_{min}}{x_{max} - x_{min}}(x'_{max} - x'_{min}) + x'_{min} \tag{1}$$

2.2   Long Short-Term Memory (LSTM)

Traditional recurrent neural networks (RNNs) take a long time to store information in longer time intervals, i.e., The original RNN's hidden layer only has one state, and it cannot manage long-distance dependencies. The LSTM introduces state c (cell state) on top of the RNN to allow it to store the long-term state. Li et al. [2] LSTM and convolutional neural network (CNN) were combined to create an LSTM-CNN model, which was then employed for real-time collision risk identification on arterial highways. Automatically detects the sentence's keywords and provides a semantic representation of the entire phrase in the hidden layer. Palangi et al. [3] utilized LSTM to learn semantic sentence vectors, which were subsequently employed for a document retrieval task. To enrich the input with dynamic extended tree, lexical, and distance information.

The LSTM consists of input, forget, and output gates, along with memory cell. LSTM implements the storage and updating of information from these gates. In the first stage, forget gates determine what information needs to be discarded by the cell state. Next, we need to decide which old cell states to forget and which new ones to add. Finally, based on the information obtained from the inputs, it is judged which state characteristics of the cell should be outputted. The following list provides the mathematical formulation of different LSTM operations:

(1) The first phase, use the sigmoid unit of the forget gate to select which data from the previous cell state should be kept or destroyed, which can be expressed as:

$$F_t = \sigma(W_F h_{t-1} + W_F x_t + b_F) \tag{2}$$

(2) Selecting the new data to be included in the cell state is the next step. There are two steps in this phase. First, h_{t-1} and X_t are employed to select which data should be updated via input gate I_t. Then h_{t-1} and X_t are used to gather data about new candidate cells $\hat{C}_t$ by passing via a tanh layer. These two steps can be expressed as:

$$I_t = \sigma(W_I h_{t-1} + W_I x_t + b_I) \tag{3}$$

$$\hat{C}_t = \tanh(W_C h_{t-1} + W_C x_t + b_C) \tag{4}$$

(3) In this phase, the previous cell info C_{t-1} and the new cell info C_t will be updated. The rule of updating is to add some candidate cell info $\hat{C}_t$ by choosing the input gate, while forgetting some of the previous cell info by using the forget gate. This is how the updating process is displayed:

$$C_t = F_t \times C_{t-1} + I_t \times \hat{C}_t \tag{5}$$

(4) In final phase, to determine which state features of the last cell are depending on the inputs h_{t-1} and X_t, we must first update the cell state. Next, the output vector must be acquired by passing the cell state through the tanh layer. This vector is then multiplied by the judgment condition received from the output gate to produce the cell's final output. The following are supplied as regards the output operation:

$$O_t = \sigma(W_O h_{t-1} + W_O x_t + b_O) \tag{6}$$

$$h_t = O_t \times \tanh(C_t) \tag{7}$$

where W_F, W_I, W_C, W_O are the weight matrices corresponding to the input X_t, h_{t-1} and b_F, b_I, b_C, b_O are the bias vectors of the forget gate, the input gate, the candidate solution, the output gate. The forget gate, the input gate, the candidate solution, and the output gate bias vectors are W_F, W_I, W_C, W_O, and $X_t, h_{t-1}, b_F, b_I, b_C, b_O$ respectively.

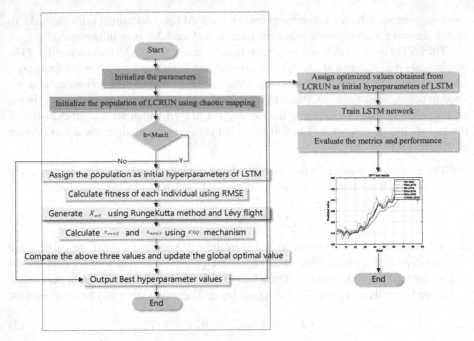

Fig. 1. The framework of LCRUN-LSTM model

2.3 Proposed Lévy Flight Chaotic Runge-Kutta Optimize (LCRUN)

In this part, we proposed LCRUN. The procedure of LCRUN is given by Algorithm 1.

Original Form of Runge Kutta Optimizer. RUN [4] includes Runge Kutta search (RKS) and enhanced solution quality (ESQ). RKS is the main stage for optimization. The ESQ improve global optimization ability. In RUN, The first step for optimization is RKS, and RUN's search algorithm is based on the RKS., which is based on the runge kutta four-order method (RKM). Then the core of main optimization stage in RUN can be given

if rand < 0.5

$$x_{n+1} = (x_c + r \times SF \times g \times x_c) + SF \times SM + \mu \times x_s \tag{8}$$

else

$$x_{n+1} = (x_m + r \times SF \times g \times x_m) + SF \times SM + \mu \times x_{s'} \tag{9}$$

end

x_m and x_c can be calculated as follows:

$$x_m = \varphi \times x_{best} + (1 - \varphi) \times x_{lbest} \tag{10}$$

$$x_c = \varphi \times x_n + (1 - \varphi) \times x_{r1} \tag{11}$$

where φ, μ is an arbitrary number within [0, 1], g is an arbitrary number within [0, 2]. x_{best} is the global optimal solution, x_{lbest} is the best location at each. r is direct parameter, which is 1 or −1. SF is a control parameter, which is given by:

$$SF = 2.(0.5 - rand) \times a \times \exp(-b \times rand \times \frac{i}{Maxi}) \tag{12}$$

where a and b are input parameter. The formulas of x_s and $x_{s'}$ are expressed as

$$x_s = randn \cdot x_m - randn \cdot x_c \tag{13}$$

$$x_{s'} = randn \cdot x_{r1} - randn \cdot x_{r2} \tag{14}$$

where $randn$ is an arbitrary number within [0, 2]. x_{r1} and x_{r2} are two random solutions. The first step to get the RKM solution x_{n+1}, the second part is the ESQ phase, using the random solution and the present iteration optimal solution to generate the fitted solution x_{new2} so that the algorithm has a certain ability to jump out of the local optimal dilemma, when the condition $rand < w$, then it will generate x_{new3}. The formulas of x_{new2} and x_{new3} are given as:

if $rand < 0.5$

$$x_{new2} = x_{new1} + r.w.|(x_{new1} - x_{avg}) + randn| \tag{15}$$

else

$$x_{new2} = (x_{new1} - x_{avg}) + r.w.|(u.x_{new1} - x_{avg}) + randn| \tag{16}$$

In which

$$x_{new1} = \beta \times x_{avg} + (1 - \beta) \times x_{best} \tag{17}$$

end

where β is an arbitrary number within [0, 1], c is an arbitrary number that equals $5 \times rand$. w is a random number. r is an integer number, which is a value −1, 0, 1. x_{avg} is the fitted solution of the three stochastic solutions.

if $rand < w$

$$x_{new3} = (x_{new2} - rand.x_{new2}) + SF.(rand.x_{RK} + (v.x_b - x_{new2})) \tag{18}$$

end

where v is an arbitrary number equal to $2 \times rand$. Then the optimal value is taken as the final solution by comparing the three candidate solutions $x_{n+1}, x_{new2}, x_{new3}$. In order to make the algorithm can have a stronger ability to jump out of the local optimum, and at the same time make the population more diverse and random.

Chaotic Mapping. Recently, chaotic mapping has been applied to many other different algorithms [5–7]. They offer a deterministic approach for generating seemingly random sequences. Ten frequent chaotic mappings have been identified [8]. In this paper, Logistic map is used to generate the sequence of random numbers. It is described as follow:

$$x_{k+1} = ax_k(1 - x_k) \tag{19}$$

where k is the number of iterations and x_k is the kth chaotic number, a is a real number.

Lévy Flight. Lévy flight is a type of non-gaussian stochastic [9] process that exhibits anomalous diffusion. The process is characterized by the lévy index, which describes the degree of deviation from Brownian motion. One of the advantages of lévy flights is their ability to model complex systems with long-range correlations. Its random walk is drawn from the lévy stable distribution, which has a straightforward power-law formulation as follow:

$$levy = \frac{U}{|V|^{\frac{1}{\lambda}}} \tag{20}$$

where λ represents the power-law index, V represents an arbitrary number within the Gaussian distribution [0, 1], and U is an arbitrary number from the Gaussian distribution $[0, \sigma^2]$. σ is given by:

$$\sigma = \left(\frac{\Gamma(1+\lambda) \times \sin(\frac{\pi \times \lambda}{2})}{\Gamma(\frac{1+\lambda}{2}) \times \lambda \times 2^{\frac{\lambda-1}{2}}} \right)^{\frac{1}{\lambda}} \tag{21}$$

where Γ denotes the gamma function. In this study, update the single position equation is used:

$$x_{j,k}^{i+1} = randnum \times x_{j,k}^i + |levy_1|(x_{j,best}^i - |x_{j,k}^i|) - |levy_2|(x_{j,worst}^i - |x_{j,k}^i|) \tag{22}$$

where $randnum$ is a number between the range [0, 2]. $levy_1$, $levy_2$ are two random numbers sampled from the lévy distribution.

2.4 Proposed LCRUN-LSTM Model

In this paper, we employed lévy flight chaotic Runge Kutta optimizer (LCRUN) to improve the LSTM's hyper-parameters. Stock data is a type of financial time series that is subject to a wide range of influences and possesses complex instability, nonlinearity, and cyclical uncertainty. This paper builds a forecasting model for stock data based on the LSTM model, which is a superior model in time series analysis. The values of some hyper-parameters in the LSTM model control the final structure of the model network, and this paper combines the lévy flight chaotic runge kutta optimizer with the LSTM model in order to make the structure of the model network match with the characteristics of the stock data. The biggest advantage of RUN over other intelligence population-based algorithms is that the algorithm is simple in design and fast in convergence, but it may fall into the local optimum. LCRUN can maximize the avoidance of local optimal based on the stock distribution via the lévy flight and ESQ mechanism, resulting in an enhanced parameter search accuracy. Additionally, the application of chaotic mapping increases the population's diversity. Thus, LCRUN allows the LSTM model to efficiently and precisely identify optimal hyper-parameters based on the stock data's features. This seamlessly integrates the LSTM model's network structure with the stock data's attributes. The LCRUN model optimizes the initial hyper-parameters, including hidden unit number, regularization parameter, and learning rate. The initial position of each vector is randomly initialized based on the range of hyper-parameter values. Secondly, the LSTM model is constructed using hyper-parameter values assigned to the vector individuals' positions. The model is trained using the training data, followed by substitution of the test data to predict the test value. The RMSE in the test dataset is used as the fitness value. Proposed model is given as follow:

Algorithm 1. LCRUN-LSTM	
Initialization	
1	Set the algorithm's parameters and the population size
2	Generate the population X_n ($= 1,2,..., N$) by using Eq. (31)
3	Set RMSE as the fitness function using Eq. (37).
4	Load the data
Optimization	
5	**If it < MaxIt**
6	Calculate the fitness of every single vector
7	Refresh solution by using Eq. (18), (19), (26), (27) and (30)
8	**end**
9	Get the input hyper-parameters that minimize the fitness of the LSTM
Hybrid LSTM	
10	Assign the optimized hyper-parameters and train the LSTM
11	Evaluate

The examination of LCRUN's complexity is as follows. The population size and dimensions are N and D, respectively. Chaotic mapping needs $O (N \cdot D)$ to complete initialization, lévy flight operator takes $O(N)$ for updating vectors. *Maxiter* is described as the algorithm iteration, and updating N population needs $O(T)$, thus, the optimization stage requires $O (N \cdot D + N \cdot D \cdot T)$.

3   Performance Indicators and Forecasting Application

This section discusses objective performance indicators and experimental settings for evaluating the effectiveness of LCRUN-LSTM prediction ability.

3.1 Performance Indicators

We used six measures namely mean absolute error (MAE) [10], mean squared error (MSE) [11], mean absolute percentage error (MAPE) [12], root-mean-square error (RMSE) [10], symmetric mean absolute percentage error (SMAPE) [13] and coefficient of determination (R^2) [14, 15], to evaluate and contrast the model's robustness and accuracy. The following lists these measures' mathematical definitions:

$$MAE = mean(|predict_x - real_x|) \tag{23}$$

$$MSE = \frac{1}{N} \sum_{i=1}^{N} (real_i - predict_i)^2 \tag{24}$$

$$RMSE = \sqrt{\frac{1}{N}\sum_{i=1}^{N}(real_i - predict_i)^2} \tag{25}$$

$$MAPE = 100 \times \frac{1}{N}\sum_{i=1}^{N}\arctan(|\frac{real_i - predict_i}{real_i}|) \tag{26}$$

$$SMAPE = 100 \times \frac{1}{N}\sum_{i=1}^{N}\arctan(\frac{|real_i - predict_i|}{(|real_i| + |predict_i|)/2}) \tag{27}$$

3.2 Application of the Proposed Forecasting Model

The forecasting models are built in MATLAB 2022a, which is set up on a machine with an i7-6700 CPU with 2.60 GHz and 16 GB of RAM.

Dataset
The Google Dataset was used to compile the data sets for this investigation. Training dataset is composed of the first 403 entries of the SPY from August 18, 2021, to August 18, 2023, and the test dataset includes the subsequent 101 entries from the same timeframe.

Implementation of LCRUN-LSTM Model. In this phase, we use LCRUN to improve the initial hyper-parameters of the LSTM, and the predict capacity evaluated using six performance metrics. Table 1 displays the parameters of all the MHs that were compared, where the parameter $levy_\lambda$ characterizes to extent the behavior of lévy flight, the LSTM consists of input layer, lstm layer, dropout layer, fully connected layer and output layer. Table 2 lists the LSTM's setting. Some of above setting are references in [16–18]. All five algorithms' population is set to 30 and iteration is set to 100.

4 Experimental Results and Discussion

The four compared models are PSO-LSTM, DE-LSTM, SCA-LSTM, RUN-LSTM respectively. First, the training set is analyzed to determine the accuracy of the algorithms. In the training set, LCRUN-LSTM was the top performer in all six metrics tested. As shown in Table 4, the MSE of LCRUN-LSTM is 9% lower than RUN-LSTM, and the value of LCRUN-LSTM is also significantly lower than to other models. Smaller MAPE and SMAPE values means that the prediction ability of the model is closer to the real value. Figure 2(a) shows the trend between R^2 and MAPE on the training set for five different models. R^2 represents the degree of validity of the data predicted by the model, with values closer to 1 indicating a higher degree of validity of the prediction. As show in Fig. 2(a), the left y-axis represents the value of 1- R^2 and the right y-axis is the value of MAPE, we can clearly see that although the degree of data prediction by SCA-LSTM and LCRUN-LSTM is similar, LCRUN-LSTM is more accurate, and the accuracy of data prediction is improved by 4.7% compared to RUN-LSTM. Figure 2(a) shows that although LCRUN-LSTM outperforms the other models, it is similar the performance of RUN-LSTM. With analysis of Table 4, compared to RUN-LSTM, LCRUN-LSTM optimizes 45% of the number of hidden units and obtains a better result.

Second, from Table 5, on the MSE metrics, the value of LCRUN-LSTM performs best and it's lower than the values of RUN-LSTM, PSO-LSTM, DE-LSTM and SCA-LSTM. This suggests that LCRUN-LSTM is more stable in the test set. In terms of MAPE and SMAPE indices, LCRUN-LSTM outperforms RUN-LSTM and the other models, suggesting that the performance of LCRUN-LSTM is more pronounced on the testing set. From Fig. 2(b), the 1-R^2 of LCRUN-LSTM is clearly lower than the other models, indicating that the fitting effect of LCRUN-LSTM is higher compared to the other models. By combining Table 5 and Fig. 2(b), it can be found that compared to RUN-LSTM, LCRUN-LSTM improves the validity of prediction on SPY is 3.4%, and the accuracy is 17.7%, respectively. Additionally, as illustrated in Fig. 3, the train set outcomes and the prediction outcomes of each method are fitted on SPY stock indexes (Table 3).

Table 1. Algorithm's parameters

Algorithms	Parameters
PSO [19]	$c_1 = 2, c_2 = 2, w_{min} = 0.4, w_{max} = 1.2$
DE [20]	$F = 0.6, CR = 0.8$
SCA	$r_1 = [2, 0]$
RUN [4]	$a = 2, b = 12$
LCRUN	$levy_\lambda = 1.5$

Table 2. LSTM's setting

Parameters	Setting values
Hidden unit number	[5, 32]
Learning rate(lr)	[0.001, 0.01]
Regularization parameter(l2)	[0.001, 0.01]

Table 3. Optimized parameters

Parameters	PSO-LSTM	DE-LSTM	SCA-LSTM	RUN-LSTM	LCRUN-LSTM
Hidden unit number	20	5	32	31	17
Learning rate(lr)	0.0016	0.0067	0.0068	0.0097	0.0093
Regularization parameter(l2)	0.0085	0.0010	0.0010	0.0010	0.0010

Table 4. Different model for forecasting performance in training set

Dataset	Models	MAE	MSE	RMSE	MAPE (%)	SMAPE (%)	R^2
SPY	PSO-LSTM	6.0164E+00	5.5449E+01	7.4464E+00	1.46	0.36	0.942
	DE-LSTM	9.0310E+00	1.1904E+02	1.0911E+01	2.17	0.54	0.876
	SCA-LSTM	5.8775E+00	5.4299E+01	7.3688E+00	1.43	0.36	0.943
	RUN-LSTM	6.0394E+00	5.5841E+01	7.4727E+00	1.47	0.37	0.942
	LCRUN-LSTM	**5.7785E+00**	**5.1091E+01**	**7.1478E+00**	**1.40**	**0.35**	**0.947**

Table 5. Different model for forecasting performance in testing set

Dataset	Models	MAE	MSE	RMSE	MAPE (%)	SMAPE (%)	R^2
SPY	PSO-LSTM	3.8673E+00	2.1000E+01	4.5826E+00	0.89	0.22	0.918
	DE-LSTM	6.9773E+00	6.9702E+01	8.3488E+00	1.59	0.40	0.728
	SCA-LSTM	3.6267E+00	1.8657E+01	4.3194E+00	0.84	0.21	0.927
	RUN-LSTM	4.1669E+00	2.4283E+01	4.9278E+00	0.96	0.24	0.905
	LCRUN-LSTM	**3.3979E+00**	**1.6384E+01**	**4.0477E+00**	**0.79**	**0.20**	**0.936**

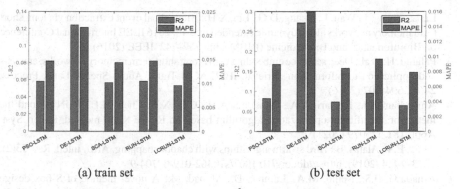

(a) train set   (b) test set

Fig. 2. Comparison of five different models R^2 and MAPE on the training and testing set

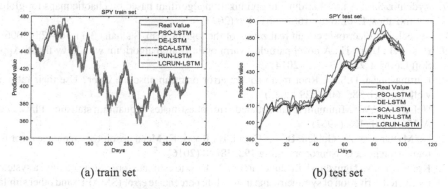

(a) train set   (b) test set

Fig. 3. Five different models on SPY training and testing set

5   Conclusion and Future Work

This paper proposed an improved LCRUN, and mixes it with a ML approach named "LCRUN-LSTM". The main results are as follows: (1) Enhancing exploration and exploitation capabilities, balancing exploration and exploitation, and increasing model accuracy, the LCRUN can avoid slipping into localization. (2) Combines LCRUN with LSTM and improves the ability of the algorithm to jump out of localization. (3) The stock prices of stock indices are predicted and the results show that the LCRUN-LSTM performs better than RUN-LSTM, PSO-LSTM, DE-LSTM, and SCA-LSTM, especially RUN-LSTM. As a result, it has been demonstrated that the LCRUN-LSTM is a viable approach for stock price prediction. Future work considers optimizing the weights and biases of the LSTM and other hyper-parameters, the number of hidden layers and batch size, etc.

References

1. Rai, A., Luwang, S.R., Nurujjaman, M., Hens, C., Kuila, P., Debnath, K.: Detection and forecasting of extreme events in stock price triggered by fundamental, technical, and external factors. Chaos Solitons Fractals **173**, 113716 (2023)

2. Li, L., Zheng, J., Wan, J., Huang, D.G., Lin, X.H.: Biomedical event extraction via long short term memory networks along dynamic extended tree. In: 2016 IEEE International Conference on Bioinformatics and Biomedicine (BIBM), pp. 739–742. IEEE (2016)

3. Palangi, H., et al.: Deep sentence embedding using long short-term memory networks: analysis and application to information retrieval. IEEE/ACM Trans. Audio Speech Lang. Process. 24(4), 694–707 (2016)

4. Ahmadianfar, I., Heidari, A.A., Gandomi, A.H., Chu, X.F., Chen, H.L.: RUN beyond the metaphor: an efficient optimization algorithm based on Runge Kutta method. Expert Syst. Appl. 181, 115079 (2021)

5. Altay, E.V., Alatas, B.: Bird swarm algorithms with chaotic mapping. Artif. Intell. Rev. 53(2), 1373–1414 (2019). https://doi.org/10.1007/s10462-019-09704-9

6. Alhadawi, H.S., Majid, M.A., Lambić, D., Ahmad, M.: A novel method of S-box design based on discrete chaotic maps and cuckoo search algorithm. Multimed. Tools Appl. 80(5), 7333–7350 (2020). https://doi.org/10.1007/s11042-020-10048-8

7. Aydemir, S.B.: A novel arithmetic optimization algorithm based on chaotic maps for global optimization. Evol. Intel. 16(3), 981–996 (2023)

8. Suneel, M.: Electronic circuit realization of the logistic map. Sadhana 31(1), 69–78 (2006)

9. Haklı, H., Uğuz, H.: A novel particle swarm optimization algorithm with Levy flight. Appl. Soft Comput. 23, 333–345 (2014)

10. Karunasingha, D.S.K.: Root mean square error or mean absolute error? Use their ratio as well. Inf. Sci. 585, 609–629 (2022)

11. Helstrom, C.W.: Minimum mean-squared error of estimates in quantum statistics. Phys. Lett. A 25(2), 101–102 (1967)

12. De Myttenaere, A., Golden, B., Le Grand, B., Rossi, F.: Mean absolute percentage error for regression models. Neurocomputing 192, 38–48 (2016)

13. Kreinovich, V., Nguyen, H.T., Ouncharoen, R.: How to estimate forecasting quality: a system-motivated derivation of symmetric mean absolute percentage error (SMAPE) and other similar characteristics (2014)

14. Nagelkerke Nico, J.D.: A note on a general definition of the coefficient of determination. Biometrika 78(3), 691–692 (1991)

15. Di Bucchianico, A.: Coefficient of determination (R 2). Encyclopedia of statistics in quality and reliability (2008)

16. Yu, L., Qu, J., Gao, F., Tian, Y.: A novel hierarchical algorithm for bearing fault diagnosis based on stacked LSTM. Shock and Vib. 2019 (2019)

17. Ghany, K.K.A., Zawbaa, H.M., Sabri, H.M.: COVID-19 prediction using LSTM algorithm: GCC case study. Inform. Med. Unlocked 23, 100566 (2021)

18. Lei, L., Zhou, Y., Huang, H., Luo, Q.F.: Extreme learning machine using improved gradient-based optimizer for dam seepage prediction. Arab. J. Sci. Eng. 48(8), 9693–9712 (2023)

19. Yang, X., Maihemuti, B., Simayi, Z., et al.: Prediction of glacially derived runoff in the Muzati river watershed based on the PSO-LSTM model. Water 14(13), 2018 (2022)

20. Peng, L., Shan, L., Rui, L., Lin, W.: Effective long short-term memory with differential evolution algorithm for electricity price prediction. Energy 162, 1301–1314 (2018)

Author Index

D.-S. Huang et al. (Eds.): ICAI 2023, CCIS 2014, pp. 387–390, 2024.
https://doi.org/10.1007/978-981-97-0903-8

Printed in the United States
by Baker & Taylor Publisher Services

Printed in the United States
by Baker & Taylor Publisher Services